BRUCE SPRINGSTEEN, CULTURAL STUDIES, AND THE RUNAWAY AMERICAN DREAM

For Barb Brunhuber

602042

Bruce Springsteen, Cultural Studies, and the Runaway American Dream

KENNETH WOMACK
Penn State University, USA

JERRY ZOLTEN
Penn State University, USA

MARK BERNHARD
University of Southern Indiana, USA

ASHGATE

Published by
Ashgate Publishing Limited
Wey Court East
Union Road
Farnham
Surrey, GU9 7PT
England

Ashgate Publishing Company
Suite 420
101 Cherry Street
Burlington
VT 05401-4405
USA

www.ashgate.com

British Library Cataloguing in Publication Data
Bruce Springsteen, cultural studies, and the runaway American dream. -- (Ashgate popular and folk music series)
    1. Springsteen, Bruce--Criticism and interpretation. 2. Rock music--Social aspects--United States. 3. Rock music--United States--History and criticism.
    I. Series II. Womack, Kenneth. III. Zolten, J. Jerome. IV. Bernhard, Mark.
    782.4'2166'092-dc22

Library of Congress Cataloging-in-Publication Data
Womack, Kenneth.
 Bruce Springsteen, cultural studies, and the runaway American dream / Kenneth Womack, Jerry Zolten and Mark Bernhard.
    p. cm. -- (Ashgate popular and folk music series)
    Includes bibliographical references and index.
    ISBN 978-1-4094-0497-2 (hardcover : alk. paper) -- ISBN 978-1-4094-3435-1 (ebook) 1. Springsteen, Bruce--Criticism and interpretation. 2. Rock music--United States--History and criticism. 3. Rock music--Social aspects--United States. I. Zolten, J. Jerome. II. Bernhard, Mark. III. Title.

ML420.S77W66 2011
782.42166092--dc22

2011014432

ISBN 9781409404972 (hbk)
ISBN 9781409434351 (ebk)

Printed and bound in Great Britain by the MPG Books Group, UK

Contents

Notes on Contributors

Spencer L. Allen holds a Ph.D. in Hebrew Bible/Old Testament from the University of Pennsylvania and a Master of Theological Studies in Scripture and Interpretation from Harvard Divinity School. He has done extensive work on both ancient and modern theology and is especially interested in contemporary interpretations of sacred texts and imagery. While at the University of Pennsylvania, he taught the course The Bible and Popular Music, which explored the use of biblical allusions and themes in rock, hip-hop, and country music. He is currently teaching in the Division of Biblical Studies at John Brown University in Siloam Springs, Arkansas.

Mark Bernhard is Associate Provost for Outreach and Engagement at the University of Southern Indiana. He holds a PhD in Workforce Planning and Development from Penn State University. He co-edited, with William J. Rothwell and James Alexander *Cases in Government Succession Planning: Action-Oriented Strategies for Public Sector Human Capital Management*, published by HRD Press in 2008.

Lauren Boehm earned her MA in English from Stanford University. She is currently applying to medical school.

Jefferson Cowie is an Associate Professor of History at Cornell University. His latest book, *Stayin' Alive: The 1970s and the Last Days of the Working Class*, published by The New Press in 2010, received the Francis Parkman Prize from the Society of American Historians and the Merle Curti Award from the Organization of American Historians, among several other awards. His essays and reviews have appeared in the *New York Times, American Prospect, Dissent, The New Republic*, and other popular outlets.

Donna Montanaro Dolphin is an Associate Professor in Media Studies and Television Production at Monmouth University, New Jersey. She has an MFA from the Mason Gross School of the Arts at Rutgers, the State University of New Jersey, an MA from Montclair State College, and a BA from Clark University.

Steven Fein is a Professor of Psychology at Williams College, in Williamstown, Massachusetts. He received his bachelor's degree from Princeton University and his PhD from the University of Michigan. His research focuses on stereotyping and prejudice, influences of the media, and self-esteem concerns in the context of academic and athletic performance. His first date with the woman he would marry was at a Springsteen concert. He has guest co-hosted several shows on "Live From E Street Nation" on Sirius-XM.

David N. Gellman is Associate Professor of History at DePauw University in Greencastle, Indiana. He is author of *Emancipating New York: The Politics of Slavery and Freedom, 1777-1827* and "Going Nowhere: Bruce, the Beatles, Neil Young, Talking Heads and Others," collected in *Bruce Springsteen and the American Soul: Essays on the Songs and Influence of a Cultural Icon*, edited by David Garrett Izzo.

Howard Kramer is the Curatorial Director of the Rock and Roll Hall of Fame and Museum in Cleveland, Ohio. Since joining the museum in 1996, Kramer has curated exhibits on Elvis Presley, The Supremes, Hank Williams, The Doors, Roy Orbison, Tom Petty and the Heartbreakers, The Beach Boys, and many others. His writings have appeared in *Rolling Stone*, the *Cleveland Plain Dealer*, and *Gadfly* magazine.

John Massaro is SUNY Distinguished Teaching Professor and Professor of Politics Emeritus at the State University of New York Potsdam. He has published articles in scholarly and other journals and is the author of Supremely Political: The Role of Ideology and Presidential Management in Unsuccessful Supreme Court Nominations (SUNY Press, 1990). His current research and writing interests stem from the two courses he continued to teach in his retirement before moving to Maine in 2009: "Walking Tall: Beauty, Meaning and Politics in the Lyrics of Bruce Springsteen" and "The Politics of Basketball World."

Edward U. Murphy teaches graduate courses in the Global Studies and Human Services programs at the College of Professional Studies at Northeastern University. He also consults with non-profit organizations on program evaluation, anti-poverty initiatives, and qualitative research. He holds a doctorate in Social Policy from the Heller School, Brandeis University. Bruce Springsteen has been a key source of inspiration for both his dissertation, published as *Men, Poverty, and Social Welfare Policy* (Brandeis University, 2003), and his current book project on the politics of compassion.

Matthew Orel is an Information Technology professional and a longtime fan of Bruce Springsteen and his music. His websites include a Springsteen discography and "The Songs of the Seeger Sessions" (bruce.orel.ws/seegersessions.html).

Samuele F.S. Pardini is Visiting Assistant Professor of American Studies and Italian Studies at Elon University. He is the editor of *The Devil Gets His Due. The Uncollected Essays of Leslie Fiedler* (Counterpoint 2008, paperback edition 2010). He is currently working on a book on African Americans, Italian Americans and modernity called *In the Name of the Mother*.

Elizabeth M. Seymour teaches anthropology, communications, history and women's studies at Penn State University's Altoona College. Her recent research focuses on identity and popular culture in the United States, Australia and the Middle East.

Jason P. Stonerook is in the Ph.D. program in government and politics at the University of Maryland College Park. He received his bachelor's degree from Luther College in Decorah, Iowa, in 2000 and earned a master's degree in political science in 2004 from Iowa State University in Ames. From 2004-2010 he was a political science instructor at Luther, teaching courses on American politics, American political thought, politics and the media, and the politics of rock and roll music. In 2008, he published *Rock 'N' Politics: A State of the Union Address*, which explores the connection between the spirit of politics and the spirit of rock and roll.

Heather Stur is Assistant Professor of History at the University of Southern Mississippi. Her first book, *Beyond Combat: Women and Gender in the Vietnam War Era*, was published by Cambridge University Press in September 2011. She is also the author of several articles, including "Borderless Troubadour: Bob Dylan's Influence on International Protest During the Cold War," in *Highway 61 Revisited: Bob Dylan's Road from Minnesota to the World* (University of Minnesota Press, 2009).

Scott Wagar is a Ph.D. candidate in English Composition and Rhetoric at Miami University, Oxford, OH. He received his M.A. from North Carolina State University. His interest in Bruce Springsteen's music began when "Thunder Road" played on his Walkman radio as he trudged across a windy parking lot to class at the State University of New York at Buffalo.

Kenneth Womack is Professor of English and Associate Dean for Academic Affairs at Penn State University's Altoona College. His book publications include: *Postwar Academic Fiction: Satire, Ethics, Community* (Palgrave, 2001); *Key Concepts in Literary Theory* (Columbia, 2001); *Mapping the Ethical Turn: A Reader in Ethics, Culture, and Literary Theory* (Virginia, 2001); *Reading the Beatles: Cultural Studies, Literary Criticism, and the Fab Four* (SUNY, 2006); *Postmodern Humanism in Contemporary Literature and Culture: Reconciling the Void* (Palgrave, 2006); *Long and Winding Roads: The Evolving Artistry of The Beatles* (Continuum, 2007); *The Cambridge Companion to The Beatles* (Cambridge, 2009); and a novel, *John Doe No. 2 and the Dreamland Motel* (Switchgrass, 2010).

Liza Zitelli is a doctoral candidate in English at Fordham University, where she is currently working on a dissertation that examines the role played by American literature in the cultural representation of cognitive disability. Her interests include gender studies, cultural studies, jokes and humor, and disability in American literature. She is a lifelong Bruce Springsteen fan.

Jerry Zolten is Associate Professor of Communication Arts and Sciences at Penn State University's Altoona College, where he teaches courses on Communications, American Studies, and Popular Music. He is the producer of CDs by the Fairfield Four and their bass singer Isaac Freeman, co-host with cartoonist Robert Crumb of *Chimpin' the Blues*, a public radio program on the history of early blues, and the author of *Great God A'Mighty! The Dixie Hummingbirds: Celebrating the Rise of Soul Gospel Music* (Oxford, 2002).

General Editor's Preface

The upheaval that occurred in musicology during the last two decades of the twentieth century has created a new urgency for the study of popular music alongside the development of new critical and theoretical models. A relativistic outlook has replaced the universal perspective of modernism (the international ambitions of the 12-note style); the grand narrative of the evolution and dissolution of tonality has been challenged, and emphasis has shifted to cultural context, reception and subject position. Together, these have conspired to eat away at the status of canonical composers and categories of high and low in music. A need has arisen, also, to recognize and address the emergence of crossovers, mixed and new genres, to engage in debates concerning the vexed problem of what constitutes authenticity in music and to offer a critique of musical practice as the product of free, individual expression.

Popular musicology is now a vital and exciting area of scholarship, and the *Ashgate Popular and Folk Music Series* presents some of the best research in the field. Authors are concerned with locating musical practices, values and meanings in cultural context, and draw upon methodologies and theories developed in cultural studies, semiotics, poststructuralism, psychology and sociology. The series focuses on popular musics of the twentieth and twenty-first centuries. It is designed to embrace the world's popular musics from Acid Jazz to Zydeco, whether high tech or low tech, commercial or non-commercial, contemporary or traditional.

Professor Derek B. Scott
Professor of Critical Musicology
University of Leeds

Foreword

Howard Kramer

Since Elvis Presley died over thirty years ago, the examinations of his art, career, and musical legacy have undergone several major shifts. Beginning with the shock of his death there was myopic nostalgia, reflection on the state of American popular culture and a callous disregard for Presley's human shortcomings, as if he weren't permitted any. In the following decade or so, Presley's life was seemingly a footnote to his posthumous popularity as exhibited in displays of adoration from his committed fan base and a crass commercialization of his name and image. Eventually, his recorded works, Presley's true measure, were given a proper treatment by his record company in the form of decade-themed boxed CD sets. The Sun sessions, a seismic shift in American music, were upgraded and repackaged twice. A definitive biography by Peter Guralnick set the story straight in an informative and unsensationalistic manner. Even his own company, Elvis Presley Enterprises, seemed to get a handle on who Elvis was and how to treat the legacy it so closely safeguarded. Elvis was durable enough to withstand all forms of licensing and tell-alls. Elvis even survived, as it were, the sale of EPE. I'm not saying the final word on Elvis Presley has been written or that there will be an end to tasteless exploitation, but time has allowed Presley to remain in focus and be seen with much greater objectivity than ever before.

When you're dealing with the subject of Bruce Springsteen, Elvis Presley is a good place to start. Springsteen might not exist as we know him if not for Presley. Springsteen was just shy of his seventh birthday when he saw Presley's first appearance on the *Ed Sullivan Show*, an admitted watershed moment for the young kid from New Jersey. Springsteen's embrace of rock and roll as defining purpose in life was all-encompassing. The pure energy of the music held hands with the myths that rock and roll conjured about itself and the people who made the music. Springsteen keenly used mythology and imagery for his own ongoing metamorphoses. Hell, you could sing half of Springsteen's catalog in an Elvis-styled voice and you'd swear that he wrote the songs with Elvis in mind. Try it. It's a fun game to play at parties. (Skip "Fire" and try "Atlantic City" or "Tougher than the Rest.")

There's a significant difference in the two artists as it relates to this particular type of publication. You see, Elvis had the luxury of having never heard, or even possibly encountered, an academic level of scrutiny. His death aside, he never sat for an interview and revealed the depth of his influences, the thrall that devotional music held on his life, what it was like to be dirt-poor or why he bought so many

Cadillacs. Springsteen, on the other hand, is alive and well. He has cloaked himself, and then revealed himself, at various times throughout his life. Numerous in-depth interviews show Springsteen discussing virtually all facets of his life, art, philosophy, geography—just about everything but the names of his pets. Then there's his life as performing artist, meticulously documented through the miracle of surreptitious recording. Every song intro, stage rap, tall tale, and performer's yarn from more than three decades of concerts are now distributed at lightning speed on the Internet. Combine that with a superior body of work and a voracious fan base, which seems to possess a disproportionate number of graduate degrees as compared to the general population, and, *voilà*, you get academic examination and theorizing. Springsteen, certainly, can pay no mind, and that's likely his reaction. Nonetheless, to quote one of his titles, it's the price you pay.

What is it that has carried Springsteen from Jersey Shore guitar hotshot and Class of '73/New Dylan to elder statesman of American popular song? Thinking back to his debut-era contemporaries—John Prine, Loudon Wainwright III and Steve Goodman—all were talented, if not gifted, song-crafters. All established an audience and, except for the late Mr Goodman, found the long arc of their careers to include renaissance and late-game triumphs. Springsteen took a significantly different path than his then-contemporaries. Sure, he's a singer-songwriter, but he was, and is, a rock and roll performer. Folk-rock confessional may have informed Springsteen, but it was a drop in the stream of influences that were constantly manifest and revealed—rock and roll as salvation, a generational voice, a declaration of independence, a bridge to the larger world, a great beat you could dance to, and the joy of life itself.

Additionally there was no small amount of ambition involved. The drive to achieve a real career in music, or, more to the point, the lack thereof, has left many a talented artists stuck at a sophomore record. As Springsteen's journey unfolded, the arithmetic of his singleness of purpose and enormous talent became clear. Despite some rocky times, he was going to be an artist of merit and a massive success, the rarest of combinations.

So the kid from Freehold hits big. What do you make of it? Part and parcel of being an artist is the reaction and impact that one's art has on the listener. It's the variable that is often the most difficult thing for an artist to reconcile and face. And sometimes they don't. Once the record is out there, and once it's internalized by the listener, there's an irrevocable transfer of ownership. In that process new meanings are imagined. Listeners project onto the song, the artist, the characters within the song, and even the dynamic of the lead break what they feel within and what it means in the context of their own lives and cultural reference points. The rabid Springsteen fans from Manasquan and Trondheim may sing the same song at the top of their respective lungs, but where is the common ground? Taking it a step further, when faced with music that challenges and moves you, what about the deeper meaning? Where is the Promised Land? What is a last-chance power drive?

As I read the chapters presented here, I felt a strange range of reactions. Part of it is based in my own deeply rooted cynicism. Over the course of my career,

I've seen the man and woman behind the curtain many times. Philosophically, I don't believe in placing artists on too high a pedestal. The fall is far no matter what. Trust the art, not the artist. And who am I to say what they mean in a song? There really isn't a high degree of hero worship displayed here, but there is a massive amount of admiration and respect. I vacillated between awe at the level of intellectual discourse, second-guessing the authors' theorems, and wondering if I missed something the first 500 times I listened to *Darkness on the Edge of Town* or *Tunnel of Love*.

It is an amazing testimony to the enduring nature of an artist's work when so many in the audience can feel and retain so much of what is given. Looking back at Presley and moving forward to Bob Dylan, another Springsteen touchstone, the case is made that rock and roll was elevated. The music that the music industry initially didn't care about was more than mere commerce. Dylan's command of language and poetic insight into the human condition came along at a point in history when his artistry was needed most. He fulfilled his promise and loomed huge over the landscape of his contemporaries. Springsteen did much the same and, contained within this collection, is sure proof.

The key elements presented here revolve around simple tenets: identity, humanity, responsibility, and faith. The identity of Springsteen as an artist, his methods of interpretation, how he contextualizes his characters and the lives they live in relation to the experiences of the world at large are all explored. Humanity is measured by the actions of the characters, what occurs to a person or character when faced with a crucial choice, how Springsteen presents the role of women, the value of individual lives and lives of his characters as we see them in ourselves. Anybody who has seen a Springsteen show since 1984 knows that responsibility is a mantra to him—responsibility to our communities, families, friends, strangers, and the political process to make sure voices are heard and holding responsible those who hold power. The concept of faith takes on an extraordinary range of examination, not the least of which is seen through the lens of Catholicism. As someone whose religious orientation comes from another part of the spectrum, I was amazed to see the resonance and fascination that religious imagery in Springsteen's songs has for some of the writers.

The bond of any relationship is based in trust. Great art speaks truth. Great art is also honest. There lies the crux of the relationship between artist and audience. Honesty is the single currency exchanged. That honesty is the underpinning of every essay and paper contained in this book. These writers are believers, but not true believers. They know the authenticity of Springsteen's work is deeply rooted. And it is that authenticity that permits them the platform to create their own honest dialogue about his art.

Acknowledgements

The editors would like to thank the many friends and colleagues who helped bring this anthology to fruition, including Lori J. Bechtel-Wherry, Laura Palmer, Beth Seymour, Bob Trumpbour, and Jeanine Womack. We are especially grateful to the exemplary team at Ashgate Publishing, especially Heidi Bishop, Linda Cayford, Sarah Charters, Rachel Lynch, and series editor Derek Scott. For their steadfast assistance in securing copyright permissions, we owe a debt of thanks to Mona Okada and Brittany Pollard. As always, we are thankful for the tireless efforts of our superb Penn State Altoona support staff, particularly Michele Kennedy, Brigid Sheedy, and Nancy Vogel.

Introduction

"Dream Baby Dream": Bruce Springsteen's American Serenade

Kenneth Womack and Jerry Zolten

There was a time when rock and roll was new, when the genre was not taken seriously in any quarter—not by parents, not by music critics, and certainly not by scholars. In a 1959 period piece, highly regarded jazz critic and historian Leonard Feather dismissed rock and roll as "coarse-grained" and "vulgar"—a genre that "said so much, so loudly, to so little artistic effect" and that, in the end, was a "passing fad" with "very few of the attributes of a valid art form" (66-67). Yet within a few years the winds would shift. A case in point is critic Robert Shelton's thoughtful 1961 *New York Times* review of a Bob Dylan performance that helped propel Dylan's career and signaled that pop music fare could and should be taken seriously.

By the mid-1960s magazines such as *Rolling Stone* and *Creem* offered critical reviews and revolutionary writing that kept pace with the velocity of expanding rock and roll. The best reporters and critics wrote with the same panache and anarchy that characterized the musicians about whom they wrote. Careers were born, some of the more outstanding being those of Ralph Gleason, Greil Marcus, Lester Bangs, Paul Williams, Nick Tosches, Robert Christgau, Dave Marsh, and Jon Landau. The latter two would have direct ties to Bruce Springsteen's career. Marsh emerged as Springsteen's principal chronicler, his most recent title being *Bruce Springsteen: Two Hearts* (2004). Landau, on the other hand, shifted from observer to participant, becoming Springsteen's manager, a position that he still holds.

Contemporarily, writing both critically and with a classroom bent about the broad spectrum of rock and roll has become convention as opposed to exception. Given rock and roll's more than sixty-year history, analytical retrospection is a natural inclination, and who could be more legitimate as a subject of inquiry than Bruce Springsteen, the consummate rock and roller famously characterized by Robert Christgau as "the first rock star in history ever to be propelled into prominence by print information." In that spirit, this volume offers a multi-dimensional inquiry into the arc of Springsteen's career, played out as much on page as on stage.

Indeed, there is little question about the incredible power of Springsteen's work as a particularly transformative art, as a lyrical and musical fusion that never shies away from sifting through the rubble of human conflict. As *Rolling Stone* magazine's Parke Puterbaugh observes, Springsteen "is a peerless songwriter and consummate artist whose every painstakingly crafted album serves as an impassioned and literate pulse taking of a generation's fortunes. He is a self-described prisoner of the music he loves, for whom every show is played as if it might be his last." In recent decades, Puterbaugh adds, "Springsteen's music developed a conscience that didn't ignore the darkening of the runaway American Dream as the country greedily blundered its way through the 1980s" and into the sociocultural detritus of a new century paralyzed by isolation and uncertainty.

This anthology provides readers with the first book-length critical study devoted to Springsteen's multifaceted work. In an effort to afford readers with a broad overview of his contributions to American culture, we have assembled a collection of essays that reflects the significant critical interest in understanding Springsteen's resounding impact on the ways in which we think and feel about politics, Americana, social justice, narrative, multiculturalism, and citizenship. Divided into four descriptive sections, *Bruce Springsteen, Cultural Studies, and the Runaway American Dream* traces the sociocultural impact of Springsteen's work in terms of its influential commentary about the American Dream. In Springsteen's textual world, the American Dream shares crucial interstices with religion, gender, class, and politics. In Part I, "'Land of Hope and Dreams': Springsteen's Working-Class Heroes and the Search for American Identity," David N. Gellman, Lauren Boehm, Jefferson Cowie, Donna M. Dolphin, and Elizabeth M. Seymour trace Springsteen's illustration of working-class life in terms of the songwriter's enduring search for American identity amidst a postmodern world in which local value systems, individualism, and patriotism have lost their sway. Drawing upon theories of nostalgia and social history, the essays in this section pit Springsteen's brash populism against the songwriter's own misgivings about the capacity of the American Dream to make a genuine difference amongst a nation drowning in the waters of its own materialism and greed.

Part II, "'There's a Sadness Hidden in that Pretty Face': Springsteen and Gender Identity," features chapters by Liza Zitelli, Samuele F.S. Pardini, and Heather Stur that investigate the ways in which Springsteen's female characters contend with a masculinized society that traffics in highly complex value systems wrought by religious hegemony and war. In Part IV, "'Lost in the Flood': Springsteen and Religion," Spencer L. Allen, Matthew Orel, and Scott Wagar examine Springsteen's spiritual explorations, especially in terms of his interest in revivifying Biblical stories and reflecting upon the mysteries of faith. In the collection's final section, "'It's Hard to Be a Saint in the City': Springsteen, Ethics, and Social Justice," Edward U. Murphy, Jason P. Stonerook, Steven Fein, and John Massaro discuss Springsteen's postulation of a sharply liberal, progressive politics both in his music and his public life on the global stage. They devote particular attention to Springsteen's ethical imperatives for developing senses of community and compassion in a political arena bifurcated by ideologies of blame and retribution.

By assembling a host of essays that engage in interdisciplinary commentary regarding one of Western culture's most enduring artistic and socially radicalizing phenomena, *Bruce Springsteen, Cultural Studies, and the Runaway American Dream* offers a cohesive, intellectual, and often entertaining introduction to the many ways in which Springsteen continues to impact on our lives by challenging our minds through his lyrics and music. Yet our critical enterprise in relation to Springsteen's career is also about his enduring attempt to ferret out the beauty of our existence even as we strive for the achievement of a greater interhuman good. As Springsteen recently observed during an October 2007 interview with Joe Levy, "It comes down to trying to make people happy, feel less lonely, but also being a conduit for a dialogue about the events of the day, the issues that impact people's lives, personal and social and political and religious. That's how I always saw the job of our band. That was my service. At this point, I'm in the middle of a very long conversation with my audience."

In many ways, this anthology is about bringing to life the very conversation that Springsteen describes. Drawing on the insights of literary theory, psychology, musicology, and social history, our contributors pit Springsteen's brash populism against the songwriter's own misgivings about the capacity of the American Dream to make a genuine difference amongst a nation drowning in the waters of its own materialism and greed. Yet they also demonstrate Springsteen's abiding efforts to posit presence over absence at nearly every juncture, and to elevate ideas of peace and hope in a world that is too often lost in the murky seas of its own self-delusion.

PART I
"Land of Hope and Dreams": Springsten's Working-Class Heroes and the Search for American Identity

Chapter 1

"Darkness on the Edge of Town": Springsteen, Richard Ford, and the American Dream

David N. Gellman

Introduction

A man makes his way northward on the New Jersey turnpike in his car; it is late at night and the lights of passing traffic blur into a tapestry of hypnotic motion: "Up ahead of me on the turnpike, blue lights flash far and near as I clear the toll plaza and start toward Cataret and the flaming refinery fields and cooling vats of Elizabeth" (Ford, *Independence Day* 175); the man contemplates relationships, complicated and unfulfilled. Later, on slightly less crowded roads, he finds himself checking into a hotel where a murder has just occurred. Another man, driving a stolen car, makes his way with his daughter and his girlfriend from Montana to Florida. Still another man, out of work, the day before the Fourth of July, contemplates why his wife, a waitress at a bar, has chosen to share his dead-end life; later, the couple wave sparklers in the backyard and dance in the rain. A boy, sixteen, discovers that a gulf between his own life and that of his parents has grown irreparably large—the boy learning that he can no longer count on or define himself according to his own father's pain. It is the end of childhood, time to think about leaving home, to cast the past aside, though the storyteller is clearly marked by the memory of that moment when independence came not as choice but as a literal and a psychological necessity.

This kaleidoscope of themes, plots, and images are familiar parts of the Springsteen repertoire. Yet, they are drawn not from Springsteen's work, but instead from a writer who is as accomplished in his field as Springsteen is in popular music. Richard Ford has published eight books of fiction. The most celebrated of these, *Independence Day*, received both the Pulitzer Prize and the PEN/Faulkner Award. A member of the American Academy of Arts and Letters, he has garnered teaching appointments at some of the nation's most prestigious universities. Ford, the traveling salesman's son from Jackson, Mississippi, much like the bus driver's son from Freehold, New Jersey, has lived out an artist's version of the American dream (Walker, *Richard Ford* xi-xiii; Glynda Duncan 3).

Ford, like Springsteen, has created rich fictional worlds, in a variety of idioms, some spare and unsparing, some richly populated with personality and images

(Walker, *Ford* 118). In both men's work the idiosyncrasies of human frailty and big dreams of mobility are played out across a variety of American landscapes. Springsteen and Ford, each in his own way, subvert and render ironic as much as they affirm the American dream of fame, fortune, and independence, offering a wide array of characters whose lives are lived in the shadow of that dream.

An exploration of what these artists share and what they do not share in terms of imagery, sensibility, and character enhances our understanding of their work, showing how Springsteen is in dialogue with other important contemporary artists working in non-musical genres. The "darkness" that threatens to keep the American Dream permanently veiled from its aspirants has vexed Springsteen's characters almost from the beginning in ways that seem to affirm, in his famous words from "No Surrender," that you can learn "more from a three-minute record than [you] ever learned in school." Ford, with the additional leeway afforded a novelist, explores the possibilities for rendering that darkness through a less time-constrained art form which allows him to expand the imagery and storylines of wanderers and dreamers in the promised land.

Taken together, their work constitutes an ongoing cultural conversation about generational conflict, class, law, and the symbols of American nationhood, in which Springsteen has become a major participant; so doing helps to highlight what is distinctive about Springsteen's voice in a shared conversation. This essay will focus in particular on Springsteen's and Ford's use of Western landscapes and Independence Day metaphors. Each artist frequently accesses these landscapes and metaphors through narratives of father-son conflict.[1] Such a comparison rescues Springsteen from the hagiography that critic A.O. Scott has noted marks much of even the most serious writing about him. Thus, we can more readily appreciate how Springsteen's is a collaborative project in illuminating, through flashes of artistry, the darkness that forms the backdrop for even the most celebratory American imagery. Rather than emphasize Springsteen's role as the torch-bearer for an "American Tradition" (Cullen; Garman, *A Race of Singers*), this approach highlights the imaginative projects Springsteen shares with one of his most accomplished literary contemporaries.[2]

Treating Springsteen as a literary artist is quite appropriate, even though such a move entails a certain amount of historical irony. In a classic 1970s stage

---

[1]   These themes hardly exhaust the ways in which these two artists can be brought into a lively dialogue. For example, the prominent Catholic cultural critic Andrew Greeley has made a powerful case for the Catholic, and specifically Easter, symbolism of Springsteen's *Tunnel of Love* album, while Ford commentators have noted that his first Frank Bascombe/ New Jersey novel, *The Sportswriter*, which takes place over an Easter weekend, evokes images of death and rebirth (Greeley 155-65; Cullen 157-89; Bonetti 30-31; Guagliardo, "Marginal" 16-17; Caldwell 47). An entirely separate essay might be devoted to comparing the ethnic and racial population of the two men's creative landscapes.

[2]   Bob Crane suggests Barbara Kingsolver, Tony Hillerman, and Jane Smiley as Springsteen's contemporary literary peers (339).

monologue delivered in the midst of the song "Growin' Up," Bruce Springsteen spoke humorously of his parents' career aspirations for their son—his father suggested lawyer, his mother author—but Bruce, launching back into the song commented "tonight, you'll both just have to settle for rock and roll" (*Live* disc 1, track 7). A quarter of a century later, the notion of Springsteen as lawyer still seems humorously far-fetched, but Springsteen-as-author has gained tremendous currency. Looking at the body of his work, critics and admirers have compared or linked him to many non-guitar-slinging artists, from poets Walt Whitman and William Carlos Williams to fiction-writers John Steinbeck, Flannery O'Connor, William Faulkner, and Walker Percy (Garman, *A Race of Singers*; Coles 12-19, 22-28; Cullen 48-49; Sheehy; Crane 339). Springsteen's own comments encourage this line of inquiry, as when he directs such interviewers as Will Percy and Nicholas Dawidoff to the sources of his own literary inspirations and the way in which he constructs stories. Moreover, in the introductory essays to his published anthology, *Songs*, Springsteen discusses how he intentionally and self-consciously sought to develop characters (25, 46, 68, 100, 190-91, 274; see also Frith 135). Springsteen placed these characters in a variety of American landscapes to explore intensely personal themes that also speak to the broader American and human condition of their times (Marsh, *Glory Days* 93-94). Bruce Springsteen is many things— performer, political activist, celebrity—and author.

Springsteen's influence on other authors—including Ford—as well as filmmakers, is a matter of record (Alterman, *It Ain't No Sin to Be Glad You're Alive* 176-77), but should be treated as more than just so many feathers in the Boss's cap. Ford has made no secret of his interest in Springsteen. In 1985 he published a thoughtful, largely laudatory appraisal of Bruce during the height of the Boss's *Born in the USA*-era popularity. More to the point, Ford himself has indicated that the title and the rudiments of the plot of his masterpiece, *Independence Day*, derive from the Springsteen song of the same name. As Ford told Elinor Ann Walker in 1997, Springsteen's "great song, 'Independence Day,' this great anthem to leaving home, was probably the first thing that moved me along the path to writing a novel called *Independence Day*. The title for my book comes as much from his song as all the other sources that name could come from." (Walker, "Interview" 131-32 and *Ford* 22, 133, 203).

The question of influence, however, is at best only a departure point. Springsteen may at certain moments have inspired Ford, but he bears a different relationship to Ford's prose than to Bobbie Ann Mason's evocative and, from a distance of twenty years, eerily prescient *In Country*. In Mason's 1985 novel, Springsteen and the album *Born in the USA* become virtual characters as the teenage protagonist Samantha explores the echoes of Vietnam, a foreign adventure with daunting domestic consequences. This essay is not about Springsteen as character, but rather about the character of a certain broad swathe of Springsteen's work, and is thus first and foremost about dialogue. Richard Ford's America and Bruce Springsteen's America occupy overlapping actual and interpretive spaces. Both artists investigate the implications for the collective and individual psyche of inhabiting America in the late twentieth century (Guagliardo, "Introduction" xiii and "Marginal" 5, 22). Intentionally or coincidentally, they are in dialogue by virtue of working the same landscape so thoughtfully and reconfiguring the same historical allusions. Psychiatrist-author Robert Coles, scholar Daniel Cavicchi, and Springsteen himself all have expressed the importance of dialogue and communication not only amongst Springsteen fans, but also between performer and audience (see esp. Cavicchi 88-95). In this essay, the dialogue is between authors and their culture, mediated not by fans, but fictional characters. Often those characters travel the open roads of America, hoping to construct new lives or reconstruct old ones—the past, personal and collective alternately informing or obstructing them from reaching their own imperfectly imagined destinations.

Land of Hope and Dreams or Darkness on the Edge of Town?

Ford, a native southerner, and Jersey's Springsteen have both turned to the American West in the quest for evocative landscapes that expand the scope of their work well beyond the narrowly biographical or the narrow confines of regionalism (Walker, *Ford* 13, 64-68; Walker, "Interview" 133-34; Hobson). Much of Ford's best work is set in Montana. He presents Montana as a lonely, quiet landscape where violence, theft, and betrayal are not cowboy tales, but rather the combined product of calculation, impulse, and a psychological distance between would-be intimates that is mirrored in the distances between sparsely populated towns on the vast American plains (Walker, *Ford* 122). The stories collected in Ford's *Rock Springs* explore the interior and exterior spaces of Western characters often hovering uncomfortably on the edges of towns like Rock Springs and Great Falls (Folks 143, 154). The narrators grapple with crimes, sometimes against property, sometimes against bodies, and sometimes against hearts and souls. The characters reflect with some detachment on their own lives, yet not without the ability to elicit reader empathy.

Earl, the narrator of Ford's title story, shares many traits with Springsteen characters in such songs as "Stolen Car," "Used Cars," and, to a lesser degree, "Reason to Believe." Earl has served time in jail for a petty theft, and has also written some bad checks. Loading his girlfriend Edna and young daughter Cheryl in a Mercedes, stolen from the parking lot of a Whitefish, Montana doctor, he makes his way to the outskirts of Rock Springs. He plans to dump the car, which turns out to have engine trouble, at the edge of town and lift another ride. Explaining his thinking in taking the Mercedes, Earl recounts, "I stole it because I thought it would be comfortable over a long haul, because I thought it got good mileage, which it didn't, and because I'd never had a good car in my life ..." (2). Rock Springs, the town on the edges of which the story takes place, contains a large corporate gold mining plant, bordered by a vast mobile home park for the laborers, a makeshift neighborhood that may or may not be rife with prostitution. Neither the riches of the mine nor the seedy vice draws in Earl. Instead, he takes

Edna and Cheryl to what he deems to be a respectable Ramada Inn, so they can get food and rest while he plans his next theft. Edna announces her desire to abandon the journey, and the story closes with Earl prowling the parking lot. He asks:

> And I wondered, because it seemed funny, what would you think a man was doing if you saw him in the middle of the night looking in the windows of cars in the parking lot of the Ramada Inn? Would you think he was trying to get his head cleared? … Would you think his girlfriend was leaving him? Would you think he had a daughter? Would you think he was anybody like you? (27)

Like the unnamed first-person narrator of Springsteen's "Used Cars," Earl is fully conscious of his class position as well as his personal failings. The gold, the Mercedes, let alone a sense of personal security, well-being, and self-esteem, all belong to anonymous others, not to Earl or, in the Springsteen song, the grown man remembering his childhood. The Mercedes is a means to an end—he really does want to drive to Florida—but it also represents an alternative identity and, as such, a measure of alienation as well; even having ditched the Mercedes, which turns out to be just another bad used car, Earl registers at the Ramada as an ophthalmologist, a "mister" even less likely to be riding around in a used car than the "mister" apostrophized in "Used Cars" (Leder, "Men with Women" 116; Garman, *A Race of Singers* 210).

The parallels between "Rock Springs" and Springsteen's "Stolen Car" are even more evocative. Like "Rock Springs," "Stolen Car" is narrated by a man whose romantic life is in tatters; the "little girl" with whom he "settled down / In a little house out on the edge of town" has repudiated their love. The "stolen car" in which each man drives represents a profound sense of fugitive dis-ease, a literal and figurative false front. Yet, ironically, Ford's car thief and Springsteen's car thief fear the very thing that makes it possible to get away with the crime—invisibility. Springsteen's thief doesn't fear arrest, but rather "That in this darkness I will disappear" (Cullen 171-72), a sharpening of the fear presented in "Fade Away," the song which precedes "Stolen Car" on *The River* album. Ford's character shares the same existential dread (Walker, *Ford* 132), wondering, ultimately, not so much whether he will get caught, but whether his fellow human beings could see his humanity at all. Ford's ending is even more ambiguous than those of Springsteen's "Stolen Car" and "Reason to Believe." As in the latter song, the desperate situation "seemed funny," yet it is hard to tell which would be worse for Earl—being perceived as wholly different (a car thief) from "you" or being essentially like "you," someone who has to soldier on in the midst of personal crisis, in this case for the sake of his child.

Ford's story "Sweethearts" creates a more optimistic effect while working with a similar mix of legal crimes and crimes of the heart as Springsteen's work. A narrator named Russ describes the day he helps his girlfriend Arlene drive her ex-husband Bobby to the sheriff's office, so that Bobby can commence a long jail sentence. Bobby, like Earl in "Rock Springs," had written bad checks—in other words, he had committed the crime of imposture, pretending to be someone with money he didn't have—but supplemented this crime with the armed robbery of a convenience store. Bobby's bitterness is palpable but, in the story itself, contained to words. After a failed and relatively feeble attempt to bait his ex-wife into an argument, Bobby snaps, "I don't know why people came out here. ... The West is fucked up. It's ruined. I wish somebody would take me away from here," to which Arlene deadpans, "Somebody's going to, I guess" (56). Bobby's attempt to place his problems in a big frame doesn't fly. "The West" had failed to deliver anything but failure to Bobby, but he can't articulate why it should have been otherwise (Folks 145, 149). The grim awkwardness of an ex-wife, a daughter and a boyfriend taking Bobby to prison proceeds. This event occasions introspection, much of it unspoken, about the frailty of romantic relationships, culminating in Russ's silent reflection "I knew, then, how you became a criminal in the world and lost it all. Somehow, and for no apparent reason, your decisions got tipped over and you lost your hold. ... I knew what love was about. It was about not giving trouble or inviting it. It was about not leaving a woman for the thought of another one. . . . And it was not about being along. Never that. Never that" (Ford, *Rock Springs* 68).

In marked contrast to Russ, Sims, the protagonist in Ford's story "Empire," places himself exactly in the position Russ vows to avoid. The story is set in a train hurtling across the West and is told in the third person. Sims sneaks away from his wife and, after flirtatious rounds of drinks, has sex with another passenger, a female soldier looking for a good time. As he returns to his wife's sleeping compartment, he reflects, "This can do it ... this can finish you, this small thing." The story ends with a poignant image:

> Outside on the cold air, flames moved and divided and swarmed the sky. And Sims felt alone in a wide empire, removed and afloat, calmed, as if life was far away now, as if blackness was all around, as if stars held the only light. (148; Walker, *Ford* 129)

The grip of isolation, the fear of loneliness that Springsteen biographer Dave Marsh identifies as the principal quality and emotional fuel of Springsteen's *Nebraska* album is enacted on Ford's small stages nestled in a big country (Marsh, *Glory Days* 100; Cullen 1; Grondahl 66; Walker, *Ford* 100, 119). As Bobby in "Sweethearts" struggles to articulate, the West is not redeeming, but, for so many of Ford's characters, and some of Springsteen's, is a token of isolation, a portent of loneliness, experienced or avoided (Folks 143, 154). Although Springsteen's most searching exploration of the loneliness are found on the *Tunnel of Love* album, it is *Nebraska* that first forthrightly confronts the concept that the unlimited space of America's inland empire might not be quite the same thing as an empire of freedom (Marsh, *Glory Days* 133-39). In songs such as "Nebraska," "Johnny 99," and "Highway Patrolman," Springsteen explores the problem posed by Ford's Russ, "how you became a criminal in this world and lost it all." Springsteen's characters, like Ford's, live in an empire where they exercise little power except to perpetrate, or permit, some chilling act of violence (Cullen 21; Walker, *Ford* 127).

The title song, "Nebraska," follows the criminal journey across an explicitly Western landscape. The song heads into much darker places than Ford's stories, recounting, as it does, the killing spree carried out by Charles Starkweather and his girlfriend from Lincoln all the way into the "badlands of Wyoming" and ultimately to the electric chair. "Johnny 99," with its reference to Mahwah and a public defender, is ostensibly a modern New Jersey tale. Nonetheless, the song has the feel of an old-fashioned frontier drama, replete with the judge with the outsized personality, "Mean John Brown," and a courtroom brawl. The electric chair imagery at the end substitutes for the noose of old. By contrast, Ford's Western criminals in "Rock Springs" and "Sweethearts" are not hung at the end of rope or hooked up to a wire. In "Rock Springs," Edna may cruelly tease car-thief and ex-con Earl about going to the chair, but neither they nor Ford really sees this as a destination for his crimes—even if he were to be *seen* rather than *seen through*. As Springsteen himself has described his version of the Starkweather and "Johnny 99" murder spree tales, these songs contemplate what happens when someone becomes so thoroughly untethered as to feel no connections to community, to past, to code (Springsteen, *Songs* 138-39). It is a radical separation that at some level is fully understood as such, especially by his Starkweather (Marsh, *Glory Days* 98-99, 102, 132), while Ford's characters, even the less-than-sympathetic Bobby, know that they too are working the darkness at the edge of town, but without completely losing contact with social norms (Garman, *A Race of Singers* 207).

Ford's Western killers and would-be killers, in contrast to Springsteen's, are mature married fathers whose crimes are driven by sudden passion but whose targets are hardly random. Through these stories, Ford most powerfully explores emotional and physical distance at the edges of towns which themselves seem to teeter on the edge of nowhere. But in this cycle of stories, it is a son, reflecting back on adolescence, who tells the tale of the moment when his parents became fully alienated from one another, and he from both of them. The parents and their son are "Hungry Heart[s]" in the Springsteen mold—men and women who "took a wrong turn ... and just kept going"; the repeating theme of these Ford stories, like Springsteen's hungry-hearted lover who knew his romance was doomed from the start, enact a certain fatalism, from the readers' as well as the characters' perspective (Cullen 36). Yet Ford's boy narrator is even more of a fatalist than Springsteen's in that he seems even more ready to accept loneliness or at least isolation as part of the human condition. This resignation is heightened in Ford's work, in comparison to Springsteen, in part perhaps because mothers as well as fathers play crucial roles in provoking the child-parent rift (Leder, "Men with Women" 100-108; Walker, "Loneliness" 123-33), whereas in Springsteen's father-son songs, the mothers remain offstage.

In Ford's "Great Falls," "Optimists," and his novel *Wildlife*, the storyline involves an only male child, about age 16, whose parents' lives drift apart, a divided household where words are rarely exchanged between the inhabitants, and where the wife's disappointed hopes both for love and material comfort slip away as the father-husband pursues quixotic projects that fall far short of his initial promise to deliver the good life. Absent the marital strife and romantic trysts, it is, incidentally, striking how much such interiors of familial alienation mirror Bruce's stories of his father's grim, but largely internalized, sense of economic and psychological defeat (Folks 152). But in the Ford stories, it is not a long-haired teenager with a "god-damn guitar" (Springsteen, *Live*, disc 1, track 7) that is the provocateur, but rather the combination of a mother's unfaithfulness and the moment when the father slips the bonds of self-control. In "Great Falls" the father, Jack, an air-force base mechanic who illicitly sells geese to a local hotel in Great Falls, returns home to find a young recruit from the air-force base with his wife. The father confronts the recruit with a pistol on the lawn, and comes perilously close to blowing off the young man's head. The mother leaves town the next afternoon, and as the narrator describes his unemotional goodbye, he comments to the reader, "We were all of us on our own in this." At the end of the story, evoking the Western landscape, the narrator wonders whether the tale reflects "some coldness in us all" which "makes our existence seem like a border between two nothings" (Ford, *Rock Springs* 48, 49). If this is not quite "the meanness in this world" invoked at the end of "Nebraska," perhaps that is because the crimes detailed in Ford's stories were, ultimately, bloodless even when fatal.

Ford tills a similar plot in other stories, investigating the point at which independence and isolation become shockingly entangled. In "Optimists," the father Roy Brinson returns to his home after seeing a fellow laborer at the Great Northern Railway switchyard severed in half in a horrific accident, only to find his wife entertaining new friends—a couple and another man—in the living room. When one of the men, Boyd Mitchell, infuriates Roy by questioning him closely about why he didn't prevent the accident, Roy, in a sudden burst of rage, punches Boyd in the chest, inducing a fatal heart attack. In *Wildlife*, also set in Great Falls, the father, a teaching pro at a golf club who has been fired from his job, returns from a quixotic new passion for fighting forest fires to discover his wife's unfaithfulness, and comes close to burning the much nicer house of his wife's lover to the ground. Ultimately, Ford closes this version of estrangement with his parents living together again, the fires burned out and giving way to a cold, mysterious, truce (Walker, "Loneliness" 131, 135). In each of the stories, the boy narrator is a more or less passive witness to his parents' sins, their crimes of passion born of isolation and dashed dreams. The grown narrator in these stories does not ask for pity, but, in a plain, direct voice, reports the moment at which his path and that of his parents utterly diverge. For their part, the parents in these stories resemble the burned-out lovers in Springsteen's "The Promise," who took the highway to be a token of boundless possibility, only to find themselves trapped by their own imperfections and unrealizable dreams.[3]

---

[3]   Walker comments that, in many of Ford's stories, "the car ... suggests at once freedom and entrapment. " (*Ford* 126).

Like "Adam Raised a Cain," "My Father's House" and other Springsteen songs about fathers and sons, Ford's stories are about and by the son rather than the father. Despite the shared Biblical imagery of Ford's title "Great Falls" (Folks 144)—a reminder of man's original sin-induced expulsion from paradise—and Springsteen's "Adam Raised a Cain," Ford's tone and conclusions run closer to Springsteen's "My Father's House." In "Adam Raised a Cain," the near-screaming singer-narrator recalls "the same hot blood burning in our veins" unquenchable even by "relentless … rain" (Springsteen, *Songs* 68; Cullen 168-69). The "dark heart of a dream" has a much cooler, even sadder air in Ford's estranged Montana boy stories and in *Nebraska*'s "My Father's House" as sons kick over the traces of inescapable, yet ultimately remote, pasts. Despite, or because of, his becalmed voice, the narrator of "Great Falls" may trump either of Springsteen's characters, the break with his parents and his past being more decisive, as he sorts out the meaning of their misdeeds: perhaps "it is just low-life, some coldness in us all" which "makes us no more or less than animals who meet on the road—watchful, unforgiving, without patience or desire" (Ford, *Rock Springs* 49). Springsteen's screaming Cain and his brooding dreamer remain achingly human: one hot-blooded, the other drawn to "My father's house … shining hard and bright" even if it forever lies "cross this dark highway where our sins lie unatoned." Even without atonement, Springsteen's imagery offers heat, light, highways, sins—at once human and godly—in contrast to Ford's lone wolves circling each other on a Western road.

Just as many of Springsteen's son-singers refuse to let go of their fathers, or their fiery images, other Springsteen characters cling to the Western landscape. Thus, in the Springsteen canon, America's Badlands continue to reflect a mythic grandeur, if only because some of his most compelling songs invest it with big dreams. The dream of the West might even be soul-saving. The 1978 release "Badlands" bluntly lays out America's class-driven "facts": "Poor man wanna be rich / Rich man wanna be king / And a king ain't satisfied / Till he rules everything." But the dominant feel of the song is transcendent, rising "above these badlands" even spitting in the face of these realities, until, as the chorus intones "these badlands start treating us good."[4]

Six years later, Springsteen's ode to the liberating teenage rock and roll brotherhood, chronicled in "No Surrender," is filled with references to coming of age in New Jersey but leads into the final chorus with the proclamation: "I want to sleep beneath the peaceful skies in my lover's bed / With a wide open country in my eyes and these romantic dreams in my head." The dream of wide open spaces—the certainty that they exist—fuels rebellion and commitment, very much as it does in Springsteen's greatest road tribute, the triumphant "republican love song," "Born to Run" (Cullen 40).

---

[4]   Springsteen commented that "[t]he possibility of transcendence … felt a lot harder to come by" for the "characters" on the *Darkness on the Edge of Town* album (*Songs* 68), but that possibility, at least in "Badlands," remains quite palpable.

The song "This Hard Land"—recorded a decade later for the *Greatest Hits* album, though originally conceived much earlier (Cullen 130)—elaborates on "these romantic dreams" acknowledging their tenuousness yet elaborating on their seductiveness. The narrator "can hear a tape deck blastin' 'Home on the Range' / I can see them Bar-M choppers / Sweepin' low across the plains" prompting the singer to inform his running mate, "It's me and you, Frank, we're lookin' for lost cattle." So far, it's just a metaphor, but, in extending that metaphor, Springsteen breathes life into it. Springsteen invokes the "dream of this hard land," yet the images are so vivid and sincerely sung that one cannot say he is repudiating the romantic image of men defining themselves heroically against the hard and open spaces of a mythic West. Indeed, despite the failure of so many seeds that have failed to bear fruit, at the end of the song the singer urges, "Well if you can't make it / Stay hard, stay hungry, stay alive / If you can / And meet me in a dream of this hard land." "This Hard Land" finds a way to articulate what the prison-bound Bobby, in Ford's "Sweethearts," was unable to articulate. The song finds dreams to substitute for Bobby's and many other Ford and Springsteen characters' self-defeating acts. As Springsteen himself has written, the song "traces the search for 'home' against the restlessness and isolation that is at the heart of the American character" and offers "a shot of idealism" (*Songs* 263; see also, Cullen 130-31; Garman, *A Race of Singers* 253-57).

Most recently, in the 2005 album *Devils & Dust*, Springsteen democratizes this romance further, singing, in "Black Cowboys," of a young African-American hemmed in by the violence of the inner city.[5] Rainey Williams saves himself by traveling by train across America's inland empire. He is inspired by the storied black cowboys of Oklahoma, suggested to him by flickering images of old Westerns on a television screen and a book his mother gave him before she became a drug-worn shadow of her former self. The country that awaits him is ambiguous yet beguiling in its visual charms: Springsteen sings, "the towns gave way to muddy fields of green corn and cotton and an endless nothin' in between / Over the rutted hills of Oklahoma the red sun slipped and was gone / The moon rose and stripped the earth to its bone." Thus, the inland migrant finds himself transported by an American West—a beguiling and paradoxical dreamscape. His very name—Rainey—suggests the hope that he will coax the potentially barren landscape to be fruitful, lest, ironically, his dreams of liberation be washed away.

For Springsteen, the West remains compelling at the very least as a dream, even though historian Frederick Jackson Turner over a hundred years ago declared the frontier, the long-standing proving ground for American democracy, closed, and Hollywood (as well as Italy) long ago lost its preoccupation with the cinematic

---

[5]   Springsteen's cycle of songs about Mexican immigrants, bereft in the promised land of the southwest and California, first begun on *The Ghost of Tom Joad* and picked up again in "Matamoros Banks" on *Devils & Dust*, raises a set of issues related to Springsteen's Western landscapes, which might best be pursued in a separate essay; see Garman on "Springsteen's Democratic Vistas" regarding race on *Tom Joad* (241-44).

West. In Richard Ford's work, the West is no less compelling. His sensibility and storytelling, however, contain quieter dreams and more self-contained outbursts of failure than Springsteen generally portrays. The West is not so much an escape or a destination, but a place where people are often stranded. In Rainey Williams's "Black Cowboys" story, Springsteen has arrived at a coming-of-age moment that intriguingly resembles and diverges from Ford's model: it is the story of a child whose parents' misdeeds propelled him to a Western landscape where he will have to rely on himself alone. To quote another *Devils & Dust* composition, "Long Time Comin'," this new stance ensures that "your mistakes would be your own / Yea your sins would be your own." For Springsteen, as for Ford, owning your own sins on any landscape may be the very essence of that most vexed and most vital of concepts—independence (Ford, *Rock Springs* 98; Guagliardo "Marginal People" 5; Springsteen, "It Happened" 95). Both men explore independence in great and repeated depth, not only on the Great Plains, but also hard by the Jersey shore.

Declarations of Independence

The draw of "Independence Day," New Jersey-style, encourages an even more direct dialogue between the Americas of Springsteen and Ford—one that foregrounds the issues of fathers, sons, and coming of age even more intensively, while drawing on another set of classic American images. The Fourth of July is no ordinary day in either man's creative calendar. Ford's deft domestic story "Fireworks" takes place on the eve of the holiday. More famously, a young Bruce Springsteen set his farewell ode to the boardwalk scene of his youth on the Fourth of July, putting the day in the title quite purposefully. The man-made fireworks at the beginning of the song and nature's "aurora" in the chorus work to support the narrator's somewhat ambivalent declaration of the end of one life and the beginning of another.

Although the song pre-dates Springsteen's more self-conscious investigations into American history and its symbols, the metaphors are at once easy and appropriate. From the early days of the nation, the symbolism of the Fourth of July signaled a national rite of passage from youth to adulthood and adapted European styles of public celebration, such as processions and feasts, to do just that (Tavers 28-29, 41-55). Philadelphians in their 1788 Fourth of July celebration even marveled at the remarkable coincidence of their nation's birthday celebration and the appearance in the sky of the northern lights, the aurora borealis (Tavers 81). Springsteen's boardwalk youth is more preoccupied with talking Sandy into bed by making promises he is not sure he can or even wants to keep than he is concerned with historic symbolism. Yet this does not detract at all from the fact that the Fourth of July is almost the perfect setting, at least in song and story, for any American boy or girl to mark a passage from one state of mind, one set of self-defining characteristics, to another.

Seven years later, a more brooding singer returns to "Independence Day" to contemplate a rift more wrenching than summer romance and boardwalk life. The very fabric both of a household and a community is being called to account by the son in the song "Independence Day." A point of no return is declared, which, like the historic Declaration of Independence, signals a permanent rupture between past and future, between empire and colony, parent and child. But unlike the Fourth of July in "Sandy," let alone that of the Thirteen Colonies, the son's manifesto in "Independence Day" is full of dark foreboding, the decisive act of departure wearing the mantle of defeat at the hands of larger forces. "[T]he darkness of this house has got the best of us / There's a darkness in this town that's got us too," the son intones. The rite of passage language from boyhood to manhood is stronger than in "Sandy," the impulse toward nostalgia—so attractive in "Sandy," quashed by local and existential facts; as the singer explains, "it's Independence Day / All boys must run away" followed shortly by "All men must make their way come Independence Day."

While the declaring is in the hands of the boy/man, the song makes clear that the broader context is largely out of his control. The son explains what his father has refused to perceive, that the entire town is disintegrating, not like a Western town blown away with the tumbleweed, but by dimly identified social forces. Old haunts like "Frankie's joint" are abandoned; the old highway is "deserted clear down to Breaker's Point"; one type of person has left town, replaced by "different people coming down here now / And they see things in different ways / And soon everything we've know will just be swept away." This movement perhaps carries with it the implication of white working-class flight, without naming the phenomenon, in the face of a wave of black or Hispanic immigrants. Alternatively, the new people might be a sign gentrification, of people with money replacing ordinary, but wrung-out working men (Cullen 64-66). Springsteen is practicing song-craft not sociology, so the "different people" with their "different ways" don't need to be identified. The pivotal drama of the song involves the father and son, driven apart, as in "Adam Raised a Cain" not because father and son are different, but because "I guess that we were just too much of the same kind." The boy-man must leave before being worn down and worn out, powerless to shape or imagine, let alone seize a better future (Cullen 103, 151).[6]

Ford's *Independence Day* adapts to its own purposes the metaphor, landscape, and storyline of Springsteen's "Independence Day," "Sandy," and the New Jersey world of highways, beaches, cars, and people on the move. But Ford's genre and Ford's own particular set of personal and public concerns leads him to configure

---

[6]   As an aside, the song presents somewhat of a biographical paradox. In real life, it was the Springsteen parents who set out for California and a chance for a better life than the one in Freehold at the dawn of a post-industrial era. In real life, it is the singer who stays, deriving energy from old haunts at the long exuberant beginning to a career that makes him synonymous with the Jersey shore, yet repeatedly drawn to contemplate the personal and class dimensions of life in his "father's house."

both plotlines and landscape in ways that transfigure Springsteen's conventions. The most obvious reversal between the two Independence Days is that in Ford's story the father tells the tale and, moreover, he is traveling toward and ultimately with—not away from—his son. Writer turned real estate agent Frank Bascombe's voice and viewpoint predominates on the road and off. It is Frank's ill-fated and ill-conceived plan to use the holiday weekend not to say goodbye to his son Paul, who lives in Connecticut with his mother, but rather to reintroduce himself, or at least re-ingratiate himself.

In terms of social class dynamics, the novel occupies a much different stratum of New Jersey than Springsteen's work usually surveys. Frank Bascombe's New Jersey is one that is equally familiar and prototypically as American as Springsteen's working-class and beach world. Ford's tale is of suburban America, of the American Dream defined by owning a home and striking a profitable bargain (Cullen 54). Although it is almost impossible to imagine Springsteen singing about a relatively high-end real estate agent, or even the people to whom he sells, Springsteen is certainly alive to the meaning of house and home in his music, as evidenced by his songs "My Father's House" and "Mansion of the Hill." Clearly, he is aware that the homes we own and the homes we can't afford define and divide us as Americans. In later songs, Springsteen has indicated a further appreciation for the dreams and illusions delivered by homes: in "Ain't Got You" he's "got a house full of Rembrandt and priceless art"; in "57 Channels" he begins by explaining "I bought a bourgeois house in the Hollywood hills"; in "Souls of the Departed," the narrator responds to the horrors of foreign wars and domestic drive-by shootings by crying out "I want to build me a wall so high nothing can burn it down / Right here on my own piece of dirty ground." One might also note that Ford's book is set in the late 1980s, a period during which Springsteen's music largely revolved around domestic, interior themes rather than broadly public ones (Cullen 47-48). Nonetheless, the more prosaic world of upper-middle-class buying, selling, and striving is largely alien to Springsteen's canon, even if that may well be precisely the world that many of his fans occupy (Marsh, *Glory Days* 9; Cavicchi 17-18, 122, 148-49)

What is not alien to the Springsteen canon, however, is the sense of unease that plagues Ford's protagonist Frank Bascombe as he surveys the world around him. To paraphrase Springsteen, different people with different ways pop up everywhere in Ford's novel of late 1980s America. The placid surface of events even in the tonier parts of east coast suburbia suffer disturbances at the hands of simultaneously vague yet thinly veiled dangers (Folks 155; Guagliardo, "Marginal" 22). Frank lives in Ford's invented well-to-do town of Haddam, New Jersey, where recently roving youths, one of them Asian, have assaulted Frank on the street. Frank's downwardly mobile clients, the Markhams, balk at buying a home that shares a backyard fence with a penitentiary, albeit a minimum-security one, and only with great trepidation end up moving to Haddam's African-American neighborhood. Hispanic-looking highway robbers may be casing the hot dog stand that Frank owns. Frank is disturbed to learn that his business partner Karl Bemish, a retiree with an engineering background, has packed a shotgun behind the counter, in case he needs to take the law into his own hands. Frank's former girlfriend, a fellow real estate agent named Clair Devane, an African-American divorcee, has been brutally murdered by still unidentified suspects in a condo she was about to show. The perpetrators were never found. His current girlfriend was once married to a Vietnam veteran named Wally who, not long after his return to the US wandered away and completely disappeared, never to be heard from again—a self-induced fade-away of a kind that might stoke the existential fears of a number of other Ford and Springsteen characters. On his way to pick up his son, Paul, Frank stops at a Connecticut motel, only to discover that a murder has just taken place, apparently perpetrated by white youths preying mercilessly on a family from Utah who had unsuspectingly stopped for a night's rest.

Perhaps not coincidentally, Ford has set this story in the midst of the 1988 presidential election, his narrator, Frank, making frequent reference to the insipid George H.W. Bush and the hapless Michael Dukakis. Political buffs may recall that the deployment of flag-waving, the pledge of allegiance, and the image of black parolee-turned-recidivist murderer Willie Horton ultimately helped to put the first Bush in the White House. Even in respectable suburbia—the real thing and the one imagined by Ford—the American dream was taking on a foreboding cast. Although Ford casts Frank as a resolute Democrat, his character reflects, or at least records, the wary watchfulness of the day.

More than this watchfulness, what puts Ford's Bascombe in dialogue with the worlds inhabited by many Springsteen characters is the palliative that he concocts to quell his personal and social anxieties. Frank, like many Springsteen characters, is not seeking to solve the world's problems but his own and those of his loved ones, and his method is in keeping with Springsteen's American road lore. The perpetually optimistic, but easily distracted Frank decides to use the Independence Day weekend to take his troubled, alienated, and slovenly young teenage son on a road-trip. The road-trip is meant to renew the psychic kinship of father and son by visiting not one, but two sports Halls of Fame—basketball's shrine in Springfield, Massachusetts, and the ultimate twentieth-century icon of father-son historical memory, the Baseball Hall of Fame in Cooperstown, New York. And just in case his son doesn't get the point that history's lessons can be a cultural balm, Frank brings along Carl Becker's classic monograph on the Declaration of Independence and Ralph Waldo Emerson's famous monument to self-willed transcendence, "Self-Reliance." Further driving home, to the reader if not to Paul, the epically American nature of this weekend jaunt, Cooperstown is also the boyhood home of the progenitor of American Western epic fiction, James Fennimore Cooper. Indeed, Paul and Frank have hotel reservations at the Deerslayer which is named for one of Cooper's famous novels and a nickname for the Leatherstocking character who is the direct literary ancestor of Springsteen's beloved John Wayne character in John Ford's classic Western *The Searchers* (Slotkin, *The Fatal Environment*; Marsh, *Glory Days* 150, 183). In sum, the father-son dynamic set up by Frank is, in essence, Springsteen's "Independence Day" in reverse. Frank's plan is replete with much of the American dream of road-bound self-discovery communicated in some of Springsteen's greatest works, including "Born to Run," "Thunder Road," and "Rosalita," even as it is nestled in the divorced father's "Darkness of the Edge of Town" uncertainty about self and surroundings.

If Springsteen's biggest-selling, most famous album—the flag-draped *Born in the USA*—is not as literary in its allusions, it is just as insistent, like Ford's most famous work of fiction, in announcing its American purposes and images. The album is bracketed by the impassioned scream-song of the Vietnam veteran in the title track and the contemplative closing song "My Hometown," which reflects on race riots and urban decay. In between there is the America of highways, rock and roll forged friendships, trains, and chain-gangs. In the song "Darlington County" Springsteen offers up "Me and Wayne on the Fourth of July," New Yorkers on an erstwhile romp in Dixie's Darlington County; the final verse of this road-trip gone bad even ironically contains a wisp of "The Battle Hymn of the Republic": "Driving out of Darlington County / My eyes seen the glory of the coming of the Lord." One of the album's most popular songs, "Glory Days," begins by recounting the memories of a high-school baseball star. In short, Ford, Springsteen, Frank Bascombe, and a slew of unnamed *Born in the USA* protagonists are unafraid, indeed unashamed, to proclaim that their stories are American to the very core. *Born in the USA* and *Independence Day* are up-tempo compared with *Nebraska* songs and the *Rock Springs* stories, but, like those works, the stories here remain those of restless souls on the move. The abiding question in both Ford's *Independence Day* and Springsteen's *Born in the USA* is this: can the various protagonists draw on America's cultural resources and icons to cure what ails them?

It is not necessary to tell the whole tragi-comic 450-page saga set forth by Ford to understand why Frank's plan to heal the rift between divorced father and prematurely anxious son through such a road-trip is destined to fall well short of success. Springsteen's "Independence Day" poignantly illustrates how the independence metaphor speaks to the pronouncement of permanent rift between fathers and sons, not reunion. Frank is gamely committed to a more metaphorical project. He wants to teach his son Paul to find a path to independence from the anxieties that plague him—a litany of bad memories—all the while affirming the parental bond that Springsteen's and the Continental Congress's declarations of independence tore asunder. Frank's offering of Becker, Emerson, Halls of Fame, and deer-slaying proto-Western Cooperstown, all genuine made-in-the-USA materials, are unlikely to work for Paul.

If Frank could even get Paul to read, Emerson's "Self-Reliance," he might discover that the advice therein subverts the presumption of the father-son tour and, to some degree, Springsteen's restless journeyers as well. Emerson urges his nineteenth-century readers to stop trying to stand on the shoulders of giants, let alone emulate them. Self-reliance will mean casting off abeyance to the greats, be they founding fathers, ancient Greek philosophers, or Christian saints. Moreover, Emerson at one point cautions his audience about the folly of thinking that you can take to the road, that you can travel to the monuments of past greatness as a means of self-discovery. Emerson labels travel "a superstition" and a "fool's paradise," opining, "He who travels to be amused, or to get somewhat which he does not carry, travels away from himself, and grows old even in youth among old things" (Emerson 34-35).[7] The road is a false seduction for meaning-seekers, for those who would truly define themselves on their own terms. Emerson meant these statements as a call for Americans to contain their wanderings to native soil, not to rely on European models for artistic inspiration. But that was when America still fancied itself a young nation, before there were Halls of Fame and Deerslayer Inns to preserve the musty scent of glory days—to say nothing of America's self-defeating adventure in Vietnam, which Springsteen's "Born in the USA" so powerfully evokes.

The Bascombe father-son journey into America's mansions of faded glory is a farce until it becomes a near tragedy. Blocks from the baseball Hall of Fame, Paul is beaned in the eye by a pitching machine, after Frank practically shoves Paul into an automated batting cage. Neither gun-slinger, deer-slayer, nor bat-swinger, Paul is the near-victim of his father's own cloudy-eyed illusions about the healing power of Americana. If ultimately not as tragic as Springsteen's "Born in the USA" veteran, the sense of illusion and disillusion is analogous in the two stories. Wrapping oneself in the flag does not effectively staunch either old or fresh wounds. The situation in Ford's novel, Paul's eye trauma notwithstanding, is less forlorn. At the end of the novel, Frank winds up back where he started. He is alone in his adopted hometown, a participant-observer in the holiday celebration in Haddam, comforted by the way the community pulls together for the annual festivities and convinced that, despite everything, his son truly appreciated the effort, if not the execution, of their ill-fated journey.

What places the author and songwriter in dialogue, however, is not how plots resolve themselves, but rather the way in which each man's deployment of American imagery and icons seeks to get beneath the alternately placid and menacing surface of American life in the final decades of the twentieth century (Marsh, *Glory Days* 4). In some sense, for each author, the icons and symbols are that surface, the challenge for various protagonists is to pull back the flag, which is a curtain masking more difficult truths. In Springsteen's "Independence Day," and in his *Born in the USA* landscape, striking out on a journey seems to be the most efficacious response to the rift between past and present. As both the "Born in the USA" veteran and the father in "My Hometown" discover in different ways, the path either leads "nowhere" or right back to a personal past imperfectly expressed by symbols of American glory, freedom, and independence.

The upper-middle-class characters of Ford's *Independence Day* are shielded to a degree from the wounds suffered by Springsteen's characters, but Springsteen's characters, too, are tempted by American roads, American icons, and American homes. So too are Springsteen's listeners. As some critical appraisals of *Born in*

---

[7]   Special thanks to Marshall Kuresman for pointing out to me the disjuncture between Emerson's essays and Frank Bascombe's actions.

the USA have pointed out, the musical buoyancy of so many of the songs on the album cuts against the grain of the often depressive lyrics (Alterman, *It Ain't No Sin to Be Glad You're Alive* 155-56). Music is Springsteen's shield. Likewise, a native, humorously glib optimism and a well-padded bank account carry Ford's Frank Bascombe past even the worst dangers lurking in his world. Taken together, this set of American stories and American roads are not dead-ends. These highways do lead somewhere. But precisely how much liberating meaning these roads actually can bear in modern American lives, particularly the sort lived in the ultimate suburban state of New Jersey, is anything but self-evident.

Conclusion

Twenty years ago, Ford himself praised how Springsteen "dignifies small feelings with the gravity of real emotion, defines innocence in terms new to it, makes rote gestures seem heartbreaking, and gives a voice of consequence to the unlistened to." "It's what poets sometimes do," he commented (Ford, "Boss Observed" 328). With both temporal and scholarly distance, comparing the literary artistry of Ford and Springsteen creates the temptation of an even larger generalization: Springsteen can be fitted for the role of romantic poet; Ford can be seen as the practitioner of a more nuanced, but clinical, maybe even cynical, prose. Springsteen still celebrates the West that Ford sometimes aggressively deflates. But as this essay illustrates, such easy dichotomies can't stand up to the complexity, depth, and variety of either man's imagination. Springsteen's romantic open spaces sometimes give way to violence far more bloody than Ford's, while Ford's Frank Bascombe gives himself over, at the end of *Independence Day*, to the sentimental bonds of attachment enacted on the Fourth of July in a small New Jersey community (Wills 281-92; Edwards 53).

The problem of overgeneralization is compounded, moreover, by the fact that neither artist appears to be anywhere near finished. It would appear that, at least for the time being, clashes between fathers and sons will play a less prominent role in Ford's and Springsteen's exploration of American characters. Ford has declared himself likely done with the lonely Western youth stories (O'Rourke 202). Meanwhile, Springsteen's *Devils & Dust* features the maternal side of the oedipal triangle prominently, with "Jesus Was an Only Son," the aforementioned "Black Cowboys," and Springsteen's throwback boxer's confessional "The Hitter." The West isn't quite the same in either man's work over the last decade, though it is hardly a spent dramatic force. Ford's most recent collection, *A Multitude of Sins*, is largely an exploration of marital infidelity, set in places as diverse as Montreal, Maine, and Chicago. Yet the final story in the collection, "Abyss" deploys the Grand Canyon, a Western icon of monumental proportions, not only as a backdrop but as a critical element in the story's climax (Edwards 53-54). In Springsteen's *Devils & Dust*, as in its forerunner *Tom Joad*, the West achieves a stillness, a muted drama on a par with Ford's earlier Western sketches—the sexual isolation of "Reno" on the former and pensive reflection on lost love in "Dry Lightning" on the latter taking the place of crime-fueled car chases. Strikingly, over the past decade, Springsteen also has explored the lives of Mexican immigrants seeking an American dream that they already seem to know is unlikely to bring liberation or dignity.

The dialogue between artists like Springsteen and Ford as they assess their times, of course, can neither verify nor falsify the American dream, nor is their work meant to do so in any cut-and-dried fashion. Rather, their task has largely been to show us the dreamers, sometimes through narrowly etched domestic dramas, sometimes through expansive highway journeys, often using a common set of American terrains and national icons. Through a large and growing body of work, Springsteen and Ford help us to imagine the ways in which the American dream is experienced from "somewhere in the swamps of Jersey" to the half-mythic landscape of the Great Plains, and even south of the Rio Grande. That Springsteen and Ford operate creatively on similar terrains, working with similar plot elements, and deploying similar national icons is certain proof that Springsteen is not an author crying out alone in the wilderness when he asks, "Why ... the fulfillment of our promise as a people always seems to be just within grasp yet forever out of reach?" (Springsteen, "Chords"). Rather, Springsteen participates in a vibrant, ongoing, deeply creative artistic dialogue that asks the right questions even if, as Springsteen has acknowledged, the right answers are not easily come by.

Chapter 2

Dead Man's Town: "Born in the USA," Social History, and Working-Class Identity[1]

Jefferson Cowie and Lauren Boehm

In the summer of 1984, America's foremost working-class hero stood on stage, dwarfed by an enormous Patton-like flag, pounding the air with his fist like it mattered. Tens of thousands of voices united to chant the chorus of the most popular song of the summer, the year, and the decade: "Born in the USA." The audience's repeated cries of the famous chorus sometimes drowned out the E Street Band itself, bringing pitch to an event that was equal parts rock concert, spiritual revival, and nationalist rally. In place of the skinny greaser-poet of his earlier tours, Bruce Springsteen had been remade into a superhero version of himself, his new pumped-up body covered in exaggerated layers of denim and leather, his biceps working his '52 Fender Esquire like a jackhammer. Fists and flags were thrown into the air at the first hint of the famous melody as thousands of bodies shadow-boxed the empty space above the crowd to the rhythm of the song. Whether one chose to compare the spectacle to the horror of a Nuremburg Rally or the freedom of an Elvis Presley show, the intensity of the 1984 tour made rock and roll feel almost powerful again—more like a cause than an escape.

It is easy to understand why Springsteen's 1980s performances are typically seen as a continuation of backlash masculinity and whiteness that washed over popular culture in the 1970s and 1980s. "Like Reagan and Rambo," writes Bryan Garman, "the apparently working-class Springsteen was for many Americans a white hard-body hero whose masculinity confirmed the values of patriarchy and patriotism, the work ethic and rugged individualism, and who clearly demarcated the boundaries between men and women, black and white, heterosexual and homosexual" (*Race* 225). Many saw Springsteen as a packaged commodity, his performances little more than unthreatening nostalgia treats exuding the glory days of "white working-class masculinity associated with Fordist regimes of mass production and capital accumulation," according to Fred Pfeil (88). Indeed, Springsteen's politics, masculinity, whiteness, faith, patriotism, commercialization,

[1] For assistance and insights on earlier drafts, the authors also acknowledge Dan Bender, Joel Dinerstein, George Lipsitz, Lou Masur, Jamie May, Nick Salvatore, Bryant Simon, Tim Strangleman, Marita Sturken, and Robb Westbrook.

and sense of community have been much discussed in both the scholarly and popular literature.[2]

Beneath the fandom, the style, the reception, and all of what Christopher Small calls "musicking," however, "Born in the USA" can be read as something more profound and interesting than a genre piece (Small 20). Through a close reading of the song, we offer an intertextual and historically-embedded analysis in order to make a theoretical contribution to both working-class history and class theory. Rather than treating "Born in the USA" as a symptom or evidence of populist backlash, nostalgia, or retro-masculinity, this essay examines Springsteen's biggest and most controversial hit as a narrative of the transformation of white, male working-class identity.[3] We argue that this song—structured as fiction, crafted from reportage, and projected as anthem—can stand as a compelling explanation of the redefinition of civic identity for white, male workers from the early 1970s to the early 1980s. The tale Springsteen tells, looking back from "ten years burning down the road," works as a critical examination and lament of the coming of age of post-New Deal working-class politics.

Blue-collar themes permeated 1970s and 1980s popular culture—from musicians such as Merle Haggard, Johnny Paycheck, John Mellencamp, and Billy Joel to films such as *Saturday Night Fever*, *Blue Collar*, *Rocky*, *Norma Rae*, and *Flashdance*. Springsteen's work is unique, however, because he began to engage in the serious study of history and American letters through such works as Henry Steele Commager's and Allan Nevins's progressive *History of the United States*, the life of Woody Guthrie, country music—particularly Hank Williams—the stories of Flannery O'Connor, the novels of Walker Percy, film noir, and Robert Frank's photography among others. In the 1980s his rock and roll looked less to autobiography, his traditional source material, and began to experiment at the intersections between local stories and the forces of national history. As Mikal Gilmore argues, Springsteen began using music consciously and explicitly "as a means of *looking* at history, as a way of understanding how the lives of people in his songs had been shaped by the conditions surrounding them, and by forces beyond their control." In this sense, "Born in the USA" can be understood as the struggle of an organic intellectual to explain the transformations in the broader world around him (Gilmore, *Nightbeat* 212). [4]

A close reading of the song's narrative themes—and the cultural and political forces that gave rise to them—points toward an understanding of both working-

---

[2]   For Springsteen as cynical corporate creation, see Goodman (*Mansion on the Hill* 339-45). Much of the best writing on Springsteen is collected in Sawyers.

[3]   The working class, by any objective measure, is a gender-neutral, multiracial, multicultural category; see, for instance, the definition in Zweig. As David R. Roediger has argued, however, both workers and organized labor "in iconography, public discourse and historical writing ha[ve] often been assumed to be white and male" (181).

[4]   For the literary and artistic influence on Springsteen see his interview with Will Percy (Percy 36-43; Springsteen, *Songs*, 65-69, 136, 163-67).

class identity and community under siege in what can best be understood as a guerrilla war at home and abroad. The song's Vietnam/hometown metonymy is suggested through the song's unique musical structure, the anthemic chorus contrasted with the verses' desperate narrative. Springsteen reveals blue-collar America separated from an economic identity, sheltered only by the empty shell of a failed social patriotism, contained in a hometown under attack, and fighting in little but isolation and silence. The economic foundations of the industrial working class were disappearing, the politics that once offered some protection had all but disappeared, and what remained was a deafening but hollow national pride— "Born in the USA." The song helps to make sense of what sociologist David Halle identifies as the three levels of working-class identity: work experiences, neighborhood, and the nation-state—"a common bond between all Americans" (203). "Born in the USA" explores working-class America stripped of civic outlets for the first two and abandoned only to third: the imagined community of nationhood. Only the residual damages of guerrilla combat remain: an atomized and confused sense of self lost in the endlessly reverberating chorus of a nation.

Identity in Transition

Working-class identity, like any other, is never a given. While always present, its outlets vary and are constructed socially and politically in the historical moment. Class awareness does not emerge from the shop floor, the union hall, the neighborhood, the battlefield, or the voting booth in any automatic or obvious form, even though the tensions of power and conflict over material conditions remain very real. As political scientist Adolph Reed explains, those attempting understand workers need "to dispense with essentialist conceptions of working-class identity and recognize that there is no single route decreed by history, God, or any other force" (26). Working people resist any formulaic or singular representation of themselves, as Michael Frisch argues, "offering instead a more seamless web in which worlds of family, neighborhood, and community [are] woven together with work and workplace in their own identities" (214). When class identity becomes an inaccessible, illegitimate, or silenced aspect of people's lives, however, those tensions do not disappear along with the dismissal of their discursive referents. Class expressions are always in a practical dialogue with existing hierarchies, political regimes, and organizational outlets, but the shape that class does take in civic discourse often swings the cultural and political balance of the nation.

Blue-collar men once enjoyed a central place in both radical and mainstream political discourse that centered on the key questions of capitalism, their roles as wage-earners, and the justice due them. White workers even achieved a type of citizenship within the "culture of unity" of the 1930s, as they poured into the labor movement and formed the political backbone to Franklin Roosevelt's New Deal coalition (Cohen). While that economic citizenship was much celebrated by consensus Democrats and even by many labor historians, rank-and-file workers often found themselves in conflict with the stultifying power of the labor bureaucracy. Further, the failure of labor insurgencies focusing on civil rights in the immediate postwar period left working people enmeshed in a system that maintained skin privilege as a core aspect of working-class identity. Enter the new politics of the 1960s, when C. Wright Mills threw down the gauntlet by urging the New Left to get rid of its "labor metaphysic"—rejecting the idea that the power and will for society's emancipation burned in the breast of the proletariat (22). The new social movements flowered for minorities, for women, and against both liberal institutions and the war they created. In so doing, they struck important blows against white, male workers' provincial and often racist cultural authority.[5]

In the 1970s there emerged the possibility of combining the energy of the new social movements with the old class politics. The biggest wave of industrial unrest in postwar history rocked the nation between 1968 and 1974, including a series of wildcat strikes, democratization and reform movements within the unions, revolts against automation, and new organizing efforts that frequently built on a promising base of women, minorities, and students. For white workers, anti-bussing demonstrations and support for George Wallace and Richard Nixon competed against the lure of multiracial rank-and-file insurgency. Both backlash and protest often overlapped in their critiques of the liberal "consensus," whether for reasons of unfulfilling work, declining economic opportunity, the protection of traditional morality, or simple racial retrenchment. By the mid-to-late 1970s, however, the energy crisis, inflation, globalization, and deregulation had crushed the strike wave—and much of the industrial heartland along with it—ending hopes of a revival of a multicultural working-class agenda. While the reality of the working class in the 1970s was increasingly multiracial and multicultural by any objective measure, the *idea* of the working class in the popular idiom had, by the 1980s, devolved even further into a repository for patriarchy and racism (Cowie, "Vigorously Left," 75-106).

The new populist epithets for working-class white guys tended to be defined less by the profundity of structural need in deindustrializing America than by national leaders who talked tough but offered little economic sustenance: Nixon's "silent majority," the "Reagan Democrat," and, later, the "NASCAR Dad." So far had the white working class fallen from its place in liberal thought that political strategists such as Ruy Teixeira and Joel Rogers labeled them "America's forgotten majority" in the 1990s. The authors spent an entire book of the same title trying to legitimize their subject ("why the white working-class still matters" was the subtitle) as a potential progressive voice despite the fact that everybody thought of the working class as rednecks and Archie Bunkers out to roll back the gains of the civil rights and women's movements. By the 1980s "working class"—a term that had too long been defined as white and male in popular discourse despite the much

---

[5]   For an outline of the centrality of the "labor question," see Fraser. On the culture of unity, see Cohen. For postwar labor and civil rights, see Korstad and Lichtenstein (786-811).

more complex reality—had evolved into a label for a hardened form of white, male identity politics. The working class became, in essence, negatively defined: an "other," dwelling outside the new politics built by and upon minorities, women, youth, and sexuality. By the 1980s even the once militant worker champions like André Gorz were penning tracts like his famously provocative *Farewell to the Working Class*.

Just as the Left gave up, however, the New Right rushed in to try to fill the political void, placing blue-collar men at the center of a new political strategy. By the re-election of Ronald Reagan in 1984, flags, God, guns, heterosexuality, and whiteness had eclipsed the economic politics of labor rights, wages, unions, and working conditions as the focal points for enough of working-class identity to swing the balance of the nation. The short history of the post-Vietnam working-class, then, is the story of how blue-collar white guys moved from a somewhat vague and highly contested class identity to one of often militant cultural resentments. And as class was reified as a white, male construct, the problems of women and minorities tended to be isolated outside of the economics of class, limited to issues specific to relatively classless understandings of race and gender.[6] It is easy to read Springsteen and his hit as part of this transformation, but a closer examination reveals him trying to *explain* it through the dichotomous structure of the song: half social realist narrative and half national myth.

"Clearly the Words and the Music Didn't Go Together"

Amiri Baraka declares that "Springsteen is an American shouter, like the black country blues shouters from Leadbelly on, with an ear to James Brown and Wilson Pickett" (51). No minstrel, argues Baraka, Springsteen writes of authentic "victims, lonely, broke, and hungry" who are "yoked" to being born in the USA (80). Those shouts, however, are less connected to the African-American tradition of the "secular spiritual" that looks for grace in a mean world than they are linked to challenges to social status and a search for a new sociological and political footing (Cone 231-51). Most Springsteen songs hold the possibility of redemption; "Born in the USA" does not. It lacks the cinematic drama present in his other works[7]—a narrative that typically delivers the characters to the crossroads, where at least one direction might lead to a better day. The song is drained of all of the rich Catholic imagery that typically fills his lyrical world—baptism, rebirth, flowing waters, community, hope and faith are noticeably absent. The song, according to Springsteen, is about "a working-class man" in the midst of a "spiritual crisis, in

---

[6]   Dorothy Sue Cobble, among others, argues for a much more vibrant labor-based women's movement (180-222).

[7]   Ironically, given the song's departure from Springsteen's often-used cinematic structure, the song was originally supposed to be for a Paul Schrader film called *Born in the USA*, which Springsteen basically took from Schrader (Springsteen, *Songs* 163).

which man is left lost." He continues, "It's like he has nothing left to tie him into society anymore. He's isolated from the government. Isolated from his family;" his narrator has been driven "to the point where nothing makes sense" (qtd in Flippo 54-55). As loud as "Born in the USA" is, it is actually more of a song about silence—both existential and political.

The first twenty seconds of "Born in the USA" are all instrumental, structured around a straightforward rhythm and singsong tune that moves almost relentlessly through the entire piece. But the song's simplistic surface belies a structure built upon a series of dualities. The keyboards compete with the drums, and the vocals strain to be heard over the barrage of instrumentation. Though Springsteen seems to scream his voice hoarse, he barely manages to peek over the wall of sound, like a man caught in a musical cage, overpowered by the anthem of his own country. It is at once potent but overwhelmed, loud yet inaudible, compelling but as repetitive as an assembly line. The song's narrative, buried beneath the pounding music and the patriotic hollers of the chorus, explores a working-class man burning in the despair of deindustrialized, post-Vietnam America. Like the neo-patriotism of the Reagan era itself, the power of the national chorus dwarfs the pain below it. The narrative-chorus contrast of the song has been much fought over by rock critics, activists, and scholars. Was the song part of a patriotic revival or a tale of working-class betrayal? A symptom of Reagan's America or an antidote to it? Protest song or national anthem? Both sides assumed that the words and the music could not go together, and in picking one over the other, each disregarded the song's unity in favor of its individual parts.

Conservative columnist George Will fired the first shot in the Springsteen wars, claiming him as a repository of Republican values in a September 1984 opinion column. George Will's assessment of the song's conservatism was a product of his one-night stand with the E Street Band, a concert admittedly heard through ears packed with cotton. "I have not got a clue about Springsteen's politics, if any, but flags get waved at his concerts when he sings songs about hard times," Will explained in the *Washington Post*. "He is no whiner, and the recitation of closed factories and other problems always seems punctuated by a grand, cheerful, affirmation: 'Born in the USA!'" Casting this "working class hero" as a paragon of what workers should be—a little more patriotic, a lot more hardworking, and much more grown-up—he saw Springsteen as "vivid proof that the work ethic is alive and well" in the "hard times" of 1984. A few days later, when Will's informal advisee Ronald Reagan requested the song for his presidential campaign (and was turned down, politely), the President invoked Springsteen anyway during a campaign stop in the singer's home state of New Jersey (Marsh 259-60).

Liberals, leftists, and rock critics responded in kind and, ridiculing conservatives, claimed the song and the singer for their own. Democratic challenger Walter Mondale claimed (falsely) to have Springsteen's endorsement for the presidency. *Rolling Stone* cast the political "Phenomenon," as they called it, of "Born in the USA" as nothing more than a cynical, faintly villainous move against Springsteen and all that they claimed he stood for:

> … just maybe, the Phenomenon is subconsciously hostile to its subject. To make Springsteen something he's not, to make him a liar, is to get rid of him … It's no accident that the Reaganites tried to snatch Springsteen and haul him into the country club. They may have been ever so slightly worried. (Morley, "Phenomenon," 74-75)

His most devoted chroniclers (and fans), Jim Cullen and Dave Marsh, both claim that the song functioned more for the Right in the Reagan years, but with apologies:

> Released as it was in a time of chauvinism masquerading as patriotism, it was inevitable that "Born in the USA" would be misinterpreted, that the album would be heard as a celebration of "basic values," no matter how hard Springsteen pushed his side of the tale. (Marsh, *Glory Days* 232-33)

Lost to both the Right, celebrating the chorus, and the Left, pressing their ears to the narrative, was the fact that "Born in the USA" was consciously crafted as an indivisible, but inherently conflicted, whole. It was first written and recorded with a single acoustic guitar for *Nebraska* (1982)—a critically acclaimed collection of some of Springsteen's darkest and most haunting explorations of blue-collar despair, faith, and betrayal. Most of the lyrics of the original "Born" remain the same in the popular version, but the first recording lacks the pounding accompaniments and consequently any reason for pumping fists. In the original, the narrative comes to us in clear, bluesy storytelling, while the chorus is relegated to a reedy backdrop for the darkness that propels the song. Being "Born in the USA" in the earlier version was a cross to bear, not something to celebrate. The earlier "Born" was "*just* a protest song," Springsteen's producer Jon Landau claimed, and that was "the opposite of what Bruce wanted or needed" (Marsh, *Glory Days* 93).

The motivations of the ever-savvy Landau were certainly to help create the most popular (and lucrative) song he could, but the rocker's artistic impulses seemed to agree. "To me," Springsteen explained of the 1982 version, "it was a dead song … Clearly the words and the music didn't go together" (Marsh, *Two Hearts* 352). So the first draft was shelved, only to emerge again in much changed form, as the title track of its own album, *Born in the USA* (1984). In the intervening time, the song found its soul. As Landau explained, Springsteen had "discovered the key, which is that the words were right but they had to be in the right setting. It needed the turbulence and that scale—*there's* the song!" (Marsh, *Glory Days* 165). The electrification, amplification, and anthem-ification of the first draft placed the chorus-lyrics tension at the center of the song. For his project, then, the words of working-class desperation "went together" with the music of nationalism—the "protest" only worked within the framework of the "anthem." Springsteen explained that he could have made a clearer song with a different musical context, but that did not make artistic sense. "If I tried to undercut or change the music," he concluded, "I believe I would have had a record that might have been more easily understood, but not as good." And by "good," he did not mean popular (102).

Unlike the narratives of the Great Depression and World War II, the local stories of Vietnam and the hard times of the 1970s and early 1980s found no national narrative to make sense of them. Springsteen's dichotomous structure between narrative and chorus is not far from that of historian John Bodnar's conceptualization of patriotism in his *Remaking America*. Bodnar argues that a conflict exists between local, vernacular commemoration of the past and the patriotic formalism of official culture. "Normally," he writes, "vernacular expressions convey what social reality feels like rather than what it should be like." Historical experience is often more threatening to official structures than are odes and commemorations, and official patriotism is often rooted in the legitimization of power. By emphasizing the duties of nationhood over the rights of citizenship, official patriotism—more appropriately, nationalism—serves to quell local threats. Thus the official discourse on patriotism and war attempts to reinterpret social contradictions in a new and less threatening form (Bodnar 14-15).

For partisan critics looking for an anthem or a protest in 1984, "Born in the USA" had the right "words" in the wrong "setting" or vice versa. The artistic decision to juxtapose the song's two contrasting dimensions ought to be central to any approach to understanding the essence of "Born in the USA." The heart of the song rests at the *intersection*, not the selection, of its internal oppositions. Rather than understanding the chorus as a simple ironic lament, the seeming contradictions of the hit can be resolved by understanding the song—as well as the statement it makes about working-class identity—as a unified duality, jagged pieces to the puzzle of both the song and its subjects' social history. Far from an ode to blind patriotism and certainly not a straightforward protest song, "Born in the USA" stands as a conflicted statement about a conflicted identity.

The Vietnam-Hometown Metonymy

Although the entire narrative of "Born in the USA" is told by an American in the United States, it is the narrator's experience in Vietnam that both motivates and provides the story's thematic unity. In such a narrative structure, the "foreign land" comes to be identified with its supposed foil, the "hometown." The song's title may belie much of its content and point of reference, but does not contradict it. Instead, "Born in the USA" is further proof of how deeply the jungles of Vietnam have made their way into the ideological landscape of the United States. By some trick of mystic linguistics and still-warm history, the word "Vietnam" registers as an American one. The sounds of choppers and broad, blood-shined jungle leaves are as profoundly American as they are alien—just as "American" as footage of angry students, urban protests, Abbie Hoffman, and LBJ that join them in cultural representation and social memory. In "Born in the USA," the narrator's experience of economic, social, and political crises in his "hometown" is identified with the military crisis in "a foreign land." As in many other Vietnam narratives and late twentieth-century fiction and criticism broadly conceived, explains David W. Noble, "the boundaries established by the dominant culture are places of cultural dialogue rather than impervious walls" (234). The home drifts into the foreign, and the foreign into the home. Like Bobby Ann Mason's Springsteen-infused novel, *In Country*, the characters inhabit the United States while the title phrase famously refers to fighting in Vietnam.

What holds together the narrative divides—chorus/narrative, and domestic/foreign—is a guerrilla war, a working class under siege at home and abroad. The experience of the Vietnam War, the joblessness at the center of the post-Vietnam experience, and the beleaguered standing of hometown America from which both are experienced and remembered, offers a social history of the white, male working class in transformation. The Vietnam War, fought largely and disproportionately by working-class sons, was literally a guerrilla war. On the home front, workers entered an equally uncertain cultural war. By the mid-1970s, American workers faced direct assaults on their material well-being, but from abstract economic forces as wispy as the fog of jungle warfare. Wages steadily depreciated in the face of inflation, inequality simply rose, unions lost their power, and steel mills, electrical factories, textiles mills, and auto plants were shuttered by "them." A gun-shy Democratic Party offered little in the way of reinforcements. The first casualty of a guerrilla war, where enemies are hidden and unknown and even apparent allies can betray you, is one's sense of self.

As the historian Christian Appy explains, "Vietnam, more than any other American war in the twentieth century, was a working-class war" (7-8). The nation's military became younger and of lower socioeconomic class after changes in the institutional, bureaucratic, and political requirements for the draft, as well as the loopholes those changes created. The college draft exemption was the most infamous aspect of the 1960s class divide. In a society in which education is one of the best proxies for class, those in college generally did not serve. Other factors, including medical exemptions favoring the well informed and privileged, and the old-boy admissions of the National Guard and Reserve, contributed to making combatants disproportionately working-class (Appy 30).

Although subject to all such pressures, Springsteen's narrator is sent to Vietnam by a more localized, personalized, force: "Got in a little hometown jam / So they put a rifle in my hand." The specific and real-life referent of "hometown jam" was the choice between prison or enlistment that many judges offered young male offenders. In the context of the song, however, Springsteen's "hometown jam" is defined as much by its values and ideology as its street corners. Like Ron Kovic's 1976 autobiographical account of the war, *Born on the Fourth of July*—which Springsteen has cited as the most important influence on "Born in the USA"—the narrator of "Born" is so saturated in Americana, militarism, and misguided heroism as to have few choices. "For me," Kovic writes, "it began in 1946 when I was born on the fourth of July" (35). To read the sentence quickly, it seems as though Kovic is writing about the beginning of his life, his childhood—and, indeed, the chapter that follows chronicles just that. But the line is deceiving. Another narrative was "beginning" alongside of Kovic's life narrative. Read in the context of the title, "it" refers to the story of the war as well: the book is an explicit narrative of the Vietnam experience, not the story of Ron Kovic's life. What is striking about the sentence is what is striking about the book as a whole: the two stories—one of Americana, John Wayne, football, and firecrackers, and the other of Vietnam, death, paralysis, and depression—are embedded in one another. Springsteen's work picks up on that fusion but expands it toward larger circles of identity. As Springsteen once remarked on the guerrilla confusion of the era, "In the Seventies and Eighties, especially compared to the Sixties, it became awfully hard to identify an enemy" (Marsh, *Glory Days* 88).

Despite the traditional working-class affirmation of patriotism, courage, and fighting for one's country, there was *not* strong working-class support for the war itself within the United States (Appy 7). Popular images of disproportionately hawkish workers have been shown to have little (if any) basis in the historical record; the working class tended to be at least as dovish—or more so—than their middle- or upper-class counterparts. When anti-war protests rose up—often intermingled with a counter-culture too ready to reject all things "American"—working-class resentments were often, however, understandably severe, though generally voiced more in terms of class antagonisms than of foreign policy. As one anti-war working-class man who had lost a son in Vietnam said of the protestors: "My son didn't die so they can look filthy and talk filthy and insult everything we believe in and everyone—me and my wife here on this street, and the next street, and all over" (Appy 42). Here, class identity is cast as a coalescence of divergent local forces: place is more than location; "this street, and the next street" represent life—lost and living. The hometown is an ideological battleground, where values and voices clash at the very moment of their intersection. The working-class hometown, then, may be conceptualized as a kind of liminal identity structure, dependent on negative distinction in opposition to that which is outside of it in both geographical and ideological senses. The combination of a class-biased draft for an unpopular war and a growing cultural radicalism of the movement against that war served to further confuse the boundaries of working-class identity: anti-war but pro-America, anti-protestor but pro-tradition, a victim of place but "Born in the USA."[8]

The connection between working-class identity and an undefined "they" of the "hometown jam" is made even clearer in a work of similar origins—Tim O'Brien's classic treatment of the war, *The Things They Carried*. O'Brien's work is as iconic in literature as Springsteen's is in popular music. He, too, is sent to war "by" his hometown and by the role that hometown plays in his self-definition. His narrator has the advantage of speaking with a middle-class voice to working-class troubles—he is *summa cum laude* and has already been accepted into Harvard graduate school, but is working for the summer in the hometown meatpacking plant. O'Brien engages in the same ambiguity of Springsteen's second verse:

---

[8]　On workers' attitudes toward the war, see Levy ("New Left" 46-63); Koscielski (5-13).

"Certain blood was being shed for uncertain reasons. I saw no unity of purpose, no consensus … The very facts were shrouded in uncertainty … America was divided on these and a thousand other issues … The only certainty that summer was moral confusion" (40).

In the O'Brien chapter that occupies the same narrative place as Springsteen's "hometown jam" verse, both narrators have just been drafted and both are being forced into a war they neither understand nor see reason to fight. O'Brien's takes place on the Canadian border, where his narrator is intending to flee the country in order to escape the draft. But the place where he ends up, the Rainy River, comes to represent not only the boundaries of country, but also those of the narrator's identity. It is there, on the edges of self-definition and country, that O'Brien's "hometown jam" becomes more implicated in the draft than the foreign land. The strength of O'Brien's roots in a sense of place is revealed when it becomes evident that in order to escape the draft, he will have to leave not only his location, but also his sense of self that is intertwined with his social geography. Place has come to stand for an identity that is inescapable and essential.

Floating within a symbol of liminality—on a river between countries, identities, selves, and others—he chooses a side and makes a decision not to flee to Canada. "I would not swim away from my hometown and my country and my life," he explains as he sees chunks of his own hometown history flash before him:

> I saw a seven-year-old boy in a white cowboy hat … I saw my parents calling from the far [Minnesota] shoreline. I saw my brother and sister, all the townsfolk, the mayor and the entire Chamber of Commerce … Like some weird sporting event: everybody screaming from the sidelines, rooting me on … a million ferocious citizens waving flags … faces from my distant past and distant future. (58-59)

The phantasmagoria of Americana—waving flags, cheering family and town folk, and the town and nation—here coalesce into a single self. Everything he is, even everything he can think he will ever be is made of childhood, community, and family. It is there, on the edges of identity and national boundary, that O'Brien's "hometown jam" is held responsible for his draft. The football stadium of Americana becomes more "real than anything I would ever feel" and the single certainty in the song is one of the few certainties in the novel: the force of their respective "hometowns" overpowering the ambiguities and doubts of the war, the yell of "I was born in the USA!" drowning out everything else.

The ambiguity of place in "Born in the USA" continues in the same breath that relates to the "hometown jam:" "Sent me off to a foreign land / To go kill the yellow man." Springsteen's decision to use "foreign land" when a certain pronunciation of Viet-*nam* (rhymes with *ram*) actually fits better into the rhyme scheme is a striking choice. In the original acoustic version, what he called the "dead song," he chose to name the country. Along with pounding beats, it is the second verse's deliberate obfuscation of place that helped infuse the 1984 "Born in the USA" with what Springsteen called "life." In order for the idea of place to work properly, it had to go nameless. Rather than any concrete mention of the war's purpose or players, we have only unspecified, hazy categories of "a foreign land," "the yellow man," and "they." The entire verse is steeped in ambiguous identities of ally and enemy: both the hometown's forces ("jam") and those of the "foreign land" ("the yellow man") go unnamed, unidentified except by abstraction and indirection.

In the verse following the second chorus, Springsteen's soldier comes back to his hometown to find the same confusion that marked the war he has left

> Come back home to the refinery,
> Hiring man said 'Son, if it was up to me'
> Went down to see my VA man,
> He said 'Son, don't you understand'

The "hiring" and "VA" (Veteran's Administration) man represent the narrator's direct ties to institutional protection and aid within the crumbling powers of the economy and the liberal state. Neither, though, offers help, and there is no explanation. The murky quality of this verse recalls—even surpasses—that of the last. The "they" here is an implicit one, some incomprehensible higher-up casting shadows over the narrator's requests. Those requests not only go unanswered, but are also unheard in the song: only the VA/hiring men are given voice; the narrator never asks explicitly for aid but simply presents himself and is turned away. And the voices of the hometown—who gently call him "son"—answer in riddles and offer nothing. Supposed allies become suddenly uncertain, and the hometown takes on the same darkness as the guerrilla jungle it was previously defined against.

The next verse enacts a turn back to the *foreign* guerrilla war. Following the narrator's return from the "foreign land," he explains: "I had a brother at Khe Sanh / Fighting off the Viet Cong." For the first time Vietnam is explicit. Here, the previous ambiguities of "foreign land" and "yellow man" find their concrete answers. Here is the "certain blood" of both his brother and the North Vietnamese, shed at a highly specified place, not just Viet*nam* (rhymes with bomb) but Khe *Sanh*. Another implicit rhyme scheme choice, this one recalling a different pronunciation of Vietnam, reveals what the song previously kept hidden. It is here, in the return to Vietnam within American memory, that Springsteen completes— and complicates—his narrative of place-identity.

While the guerrilla jungle suddenly becomes lit with realities and specificities (fourth verse), hometown structures turn against their returning "son" for reasons he can only try to "understand" (third verse). The interplay between these verses represents the end of one uncertainty, in providing specific names for "a foreign land," and the beginning of another, more complex uncertainty: sources of hometown identity are not only kept anonymous, but are also both indicted and mourned within a setting of actual warfare.

While the syntax of the fourth verse positions the "they" to refer to the North Vietnamese, it simultaneously recalls the hometown "they" who "put a rifle in [his] hand" in the second verse. The first "they" could be the local draft board, but it more likely represents a broader, more abstract group of ideological/cultural origins—those we may imagine to comprise the "hometown jam." Indeed, the same collective pronouns—unhinged from their textual referents, named only as "they" and "them"—litter Kovic's account (72, 93, 126-27). Springsteen's fourth verse enacts a similar movement. The connection of the "theys" in the second and fourth verses ("they're still there") entwines the opposing identities of the Viet Cong and the hometown, making it disturbingly difficult to determine who is responsible for his brother's death.

This new uncertainty is emphasized with the bridge's structure, a three-line departure from the song's standard four-line verse, ending abruptly and leaving an unfulfilled anticipation on the part of the listener. After the fourth verse, the song itself breaks down—the anthem is being destroyed by its own progression; the martial drum solo stands in for the missing pieces of narrative. Rather than the satisfaction of a concluding line, Springsteen is silent as the instrumental fills in for the expected lyrics—like grief that cannot be answered with mere pride but is locked in its melody nonetheless. When the narrator has no words left, the backbeat and the keyboards are heard all the louder. Rather than a conclusion, these chords open another incomplete verse. The next fragment consists of only two lines to the normal four, and fittingly, for it inspires anything but certainty: "He had a woman he loved in Saigon / I got a picture of him in her arms now." The woman is not only connected with Vietnam (by way of logic as well as rhyme scheme) but with the narrator himself. She is the woman his brother loves, rooted in some of the most specific and compelling imagery of the song. What remains of the war effort is not pride, but a fading picture of an American soldier embracing a Vietnamese woman. That picture captures the blurring of distinctions between ally and enemy, self and other, hometowns and Saigon. The photograph turns the hometown jam on its head by uniting both the American working class and the Vietnamese as co-victims of some inexplicable "they."

Class War, Patriotism, and Politics

When Springsteen refers to one of the bloodiest and closely watched battles of the Vietnam War—Khe Sanh—he is also lamenting one of the most pointless. For seventy-seven relentless days, Americans fought off constant attacks from tens of thousands of North Vietnamese regulars who had burrowed into miles of trenches surrounding the American outpost. The high, barren plateau—often shrouded in an eerie fog in the winter of 1968—was a place of mass confusion. The siege forced the Americans to live in their own labyrinth of holes and trenches while waiting in fear of the moment when an estimated 20,000 enemy soldiers amassed outside of the perimeter would storm their position. As journalist Michael Herr explains, only the grunts themselves knew "the madness, the bitterness, the horror of it" (103). Two and a half months of constant attack ended with American carpet-bombing around Khe Sanh, turning the area around the fort into a sea of rat-chewed bodies, shrapnel, and twisted ordnance. Despite the heroism of the soldiers' stand, a mere two months after the battle General Westmoreland ordered the fort to be destroyed and abandoned. The gruesome defense was for naught. "A great many people," explains Herr, "wanted to know how the Khe Sanh Combat Base could have been the Western Anchor of our Defense one month and a worthless piece of ground the next, and they were simply told that the situation had changed" (163).

For Springsteen, Khe Sanh and deindustrialized places like Youngstown or Flint or Camden were not that far apart. A place like Detroit, once of such strategic national importance that it was known as the "Arsenal of Democracy," was left abandoned in the same manner as Khe Sanh (Sugrue 17). Springsteen's song was never a ballad of the foreign and faraway, after all, but an anthem of home. The confusion of allies and enemies, the confusion of identity, feeds another guerrilla war—this one fought at home, on the emerging Rustbelt and at the presidential polls. The enemy is no longer the "yellow man" and the site is not "Khe Sanh" but a war-torn land in which, economist Barry Bluestone explains, "entire communities" were forced "to compete for survival" (13).[9]

In the absence of any real material aid, one answer to the questions of lost wars, shuttered factories, and embattled hometowns, was to accept the New Right's retooled discourse of populist nationalism. That new populism, first drafted by segregationist George Wallace, then refined by Richard Nixon, and ultimately perfected by Ronald Reagan, was designed to provide symbolic sanctuary for a white working-class that felt itself embattled. Those leaders tapped into the material, social, and moral concerns of the white, male working class, but actively and strategically reformulated what it meant to be working class by seeking to move the ground of resentments away from the economics of class and onto social issues. At a time when the traditional working-class allies, the Democratic Party, offered precious little material comfort, the New Right offered to bolster morale on the basis of patriotism, whiteness, God, patriarchy, and nostalgia for community. But Reagan and his antecedents served a Janus-faced role in this transformation: they simultaneously offered discursive refuge from the economic trauma of the period while also being the central protagonists in the economic devastation that transformed the once-mighty industrial heartland. The soothing tonic for the injured pride and diminished material hopes for America's working men was mostly just that—pride but little substance. While "politics and identity" were being pulled "free from the gravity of class," as Seth Sanders and Mike O'Flaherty argue, the screaming chant of "Born in the USA" became the last refuge of identity as the national myth drowned out a place for lived working-class experience (81).

---

[9]   For a broader historical perspective, see the essays in Jefferson Cowie and Joseph Heathcott.

In the meantime, liberalism largely failed the material needs of blue-collar Americans. The institutionalization of the "rights revolution," while succeeding in modest efforts to open up opportunity to women and minorities, had absolutely no impact on the actual structure of the economy (Lichtenstein 207-11). Affirmative action, the Equal Employment Opportunity Commission, and the Bakke decision changed the complexion of the wealth and power pyramid, but they had no ability to affect its size or shape, thus sharpening intra-class conflict for jobs in a shrinking economy. Attempts to transform the economic structure through labor law reform, full employment legislation, or industrial planning either failed in Congress or failed to get to Congress. In 1978, after business lobbyists killed labor law reform efforts, United Auto Workers' President Doug Fraser announced that a "one-sided class war" was being waged on American workers. The failure of liberals and labor leaders to address a deeply flawed and legalistic labor relations regime or the deindustrialization crisis of the 1970s made them sadly complicit in those very problems.[10]

The inability of liberalism to match its social agenda with economic backbone made it an easy target for a well-organized opposition. The transformation of liberalism away from the basics of economic allocation and toward race, gender, and social issues, launched what Thomas and Mary Edsall call the "chain reaction" of race, rights, and taxes. The Democratic Party's particular historical problem— attempting to house both student protestors and yellow-ribboned machinists' wives, both bussed black students and the whites who "defended" local schools— was a unique one that paved the way for a sizable defection of white working-class voters away from the Democrats and toward a cross-class alliance with Republican elites. By the late 1970s Ronald Reagan had helped to shed the Republicans' elitist legacy by adopting a patina of common-man populism, declaring that "The New Republican Party I am speaking about is going to have room for the man and woman in the factories, for the farmer, for the cop on the beat, and for the millions of Americans who may never have thought of joining our party before, but whose interests coincide with those represented by principled Republicanism" (Reagan, *A Time for Choosing* 189).[11]

The tragedy was that just as class-based political discourse was shrinking, the real economic distinctions of class were growing for all Americans. Family income was falling for the first time since the Depression, stagflation unhinged the Keynesian success formula, global manufacturing and competition undermined American economic hegemony, deindustrialization and de-unionization shook the bedrock of working-class success, and a tax system that was losing its progressive structure justified a revolt against public spending. These factors led to profound

---

[10]   For further development of problems with "rights consciousness," see Lichtenstein (207-11) and Cowie ("One-Sided Class War" 307-14).

[11]   The manipulation of the blue-collar vote was understood by liberal and conservative strategists at the time: see Phillips; Scammon and Wattenberg; and Cowie ("Nixon's Class Struggle" 257-83).

sense of insecurity as the economic structure of blue-collar communities began to crumble. "Born down in a dead man's town," after all, is the first line of a song called "Born in the USA." The similarity of structure indicates a greater commonality between the two expressions: they are both an invocation, embodiment, and affirmation of working-class identity based specifically in *place*. The growing precariousness of that place in terms of its actual, material base mirrors the growing precariousness of that place as a source of identity. In this guerrilla working-class world, individuals are severed from their institutional allies and abandoned and abused by the figures that are meant to support them; they are propped up by new and uncertain allies on the Right—allies who promise only more chants of "Born in the USA."

The chorus "Born in the USA!" is an outcry of those hometown values, the search for a shared national identity, an echo of the social patriotism that once included a modest amount of equality and fraternity along with its allusions to liberty. Symbolic of the ally-enemy problem was August 1981, when President Reagan crushed the national strike of the Professional Air Traffic Controllers Organization (PATCO) and fired over 11,000 workers (the union ironically had endorsed Reagan). Even though the act was widely regarded as declaring open season on organized labor, the very next month, the President explained in an address to the United Brotherhood of Carpenters that "working people in America value family, work and neighborhood. These are things we have in common socially and politically" (Reagan, "Address," 189). At the moment when their material "hometowns" were under siege, national politics offered little more than the chorus stripped of its verses.

Just as the last vestiges of hope for a republic of wage-earners were collapsing, so was what Greil Marcus celebrated as the wild and eccentric "invisible republic" of people's music. Marcus invokes the idea of a strange, vibrant, inter-racial republican world of vinyl, where all of the wild and eccentric energy of America came together in popular music: "Here is a mystical body of the republic, a kind of public secret: a declaration of a weird but clearly recognizable America within the America of the exercise of institutional majoritarian power." In "Born in the USA," however, the "old weird America" seems to be coming to a close as the official trumps the mystical, the national smothers the local, and the majority drowns out the individual. The "ruling question of public life" is no longer what Marcus describes as "how people plumb their souls and then present their discoveries, their true selves to others" (Marcus, *Republic* 125) but, as Springsteen proclaims, how "you spend half your life just covering up."

At the end of the song's laments of the collapse of meaningful, shared, and vernacular social patriotism, there is a hidden eulogy to the roots of the invisible republic. As much as rock and roll is a product of a melding of African-American blues and white country music, Springsteen toys with both sides of the pop equation. At the end of the song, when he declares that he is "ten years burning down the road / Nowhere to run, Ain't got nowhere to go," he makes explicit the theme of being adrift by quoting Martha and the Vandellas' Motown hit, "Nowhere to

Run." In so doing, he unites black and white experiences—not in triumph or social unity, but in their shared but separate experiences of rootlessness within American culture. Springsteen, who never indulged in white racial victimization, suggests that politics—just like rock and roll—work best when integrated. He then turns to the country side of American pop, by invoking the great chronicler of loneliness and alienation, Hank Williams. As "Born in the USA" trails off, its narrator cites the title of a Williams tune when he declares, "I'm a long gone Daddy." As George Lipsitz has written, Hank Williams, with his "egalitarian, forgiving, and fatalistic worldview" sought to create "a music that underscored the connections between whites and blacks, that lamented the schisms between men and women, and that cried out for a more just and more loving existence for ordinary men and women" (*Rainbow at Midnight* 29). The lament is bitterly transformed in the following line, "I'm a cool rocking daddy in the USA." The narrator, "long gone" in social, economic, political, and even human senses, clings to the "cool"—a bit of culture flotsam left over from the glory days of postwar triumph.

The song ends with the narrator's sense of self growing more violent, more confused, and ultimately more detached from place. In the closing verse, we are left with a frantic character speeding down roads that lead nowhere, not in the long American tradition of the road chronicled by Whitman, Kerouac, or even "Born to Run," but in desperation and without alternatives. Rising above the concluding drum solo are sounds of the narrator taking punches as physical brutality is added to the confusion. The rootless worker is caught between two images: the refinery that will not offer him employment and the penitentiary that may hold his fate. With uncertain allies on all sides, with conservative populism poised to take over, class enemy becomes questionable ally. Shut out of all institutions of aid, Springsteen's narrator is subject to larger forces made even more uncontrollable by their mysteriousness. In a guerrilla hometown stripped of its material base, self/ other, ally/enemy are indistinguishable. As George Lipsitz argues in his article "Dilemmas of Beset Nationhood," the "'new patriotism' often seems strangely defensive, embattled and insecure," based as it is in "powerlessness, humiliation, and social disintegration" (255, 260).

Thirty-Years Burning Down the Road

Springsteen's producer, Jon Landau, once remarked that the narrator of "Born in the USA" is "disconnected from his past but not yet connected to any imaginable future beyond mere survival" (Marsh, *Two Hearts* 402). Rather than leading toward the fertile lands of redemption, however, the post-1980s working-class search for community and meaning has been further lost in the acidic soils of nationalism. Springsteen's song is therefore useful for exploring not simply a mid-1980s cultural moment, but also a larger cultural paradigm that continues to resonate—even strengthen—decades later. The withering of the economic dimensions of class, the destruction and demoralization of the politics of place, the betrayal of institutions designed to protect workers, and the amplification and mobilization of cultural nationalism to make it all palatable have only increased since "Born in the USA" dominated the airwaves in the middle of the Reagan years. Indeed, understanding a nationalist mythology that promises very little in terms of material security, social well-being, or community strength has become a core political and intellectual problem of the new millennium. Consider, for instance, sociologist Arlie Hochschild's explanation of the effectiveness of the George W. Bush administration's "Let Them Eat War" strategy for white, blue-collar men, or the thesis of Thomas Frank's *What's the Matter with Kansas?* in which he finds cultural values serving as political cover for the economic devastation of the heartland (Hochschild; Frank).

One of the most compelling explorations of the themes of "Born in the USA" is Dean Bakopoulos's 2005 novel *Please Don't Come Back from the Moon*. A story about aimless, violent, white working-class youths in a blue-collar suburb of Detroit, it effectively carries the issues of "Born in the USA" to the next generation. The youths live in a world without fathers, who, like Springsteen's narrator, have given up and vanished from the hometown—"gone to the moon"— rather than face the joblessness, the meaninglessness, the daily humiliation that replaced their once-stable lives. The guerrilla wars have ended, and the working-class veterans are placeless, floating away in magic-realist redemption from the class-degradation of a postindustrial world. As their sons mature into adulthood, they struggle to stay grounded and responsible in a world that promises them little more than dismal, weightless futures in the low-wage service sector.

For a moment in the book, however, all is not lost. After sneaking into a college labor history class, the charismatic Nick decides to lead his demeaned co-workers at the local mall into a sit-down strike during the opening of the Christmas shopping season. At a very rare political party on the night of the 2000 election—just a couple of weeks before the sit-down is to take place—Nick declares as he might at any other meaningless party, "We're dry! We need more beer!" The narrator reflects, "It was strange to hear him shout this phrase, one I had heard him shout so many times in our lives, on this night infused with politics and history and vision. I almost wished the whole sit-down campaign would stop." The momentum toward working-class justice did not make sense in the narrative of his life. "It felt like we were being people we were not," he explained, "people we had no right to be" (184-85). The plan failed to get off the ground. Bakopoulos's workers may be too street-smart and jaded to believe in nationalist myths, but they also explicitly refuse to avail themselves of an identity that may actually offer them agency.

Since the events of September 11, 2001, the culture of nationalism has become all the more pronounced. Journalist Dale Maharidge and photographer Michael Williamson, famous for their studies of the rustbelt—including inspiring the Springsteen song "Youngstown"—suggest that the problem has become greatly exacerbated since Springsteen first projected the issue. Back in the 1980s the two journalists refused to believe that workers would take the destruction of the economic heartland lying down. Surely, the old class politics of the CIO era, they believed, were right around the corner. In *Homeland* (2004), which recounts their tour of post-9/11 America, however, they return to find that a Weimar-like culture of nationalism has become not the voice that masks or drowns out class discontent as Springsteen portrayed it, but the actual *way* in which discontent is expressed in a nation mobilized for war. Nationalism simultaneously voices and distorts expressions of working-class pain that rise from the terminally wounded brick-and-mortar world of the many American hometowns. "Even though I'd lived through years of witnessing anger and despair among the American working class," recalls Maharidge, "I couldn't imagine an event that would unleash a sinister genie that would put us over the edge into a battle between the good of tolerance and the force of dark nationalism" (156).

As Maharidge and other chroniclers of blue-collar America report, whatever voices that remain calling from the "dead man's town[s]" remain voices besieged—voices that continue to be lost under even larger and more numerous American flags. While the dichotomy between patriotic rhetoric and the reality of the post-New Deal working-class experience is stark, the narrative of nationhood is the one available—the narrative onto which working people can graft their hopes. Patriotism is the stronger—and louder—of the many competing voices, and its power dwarfs the material concerns, the capacity for love, the meanings of neighborhood and community, and the sacrifice of war that give shape to blue-collar life. Springsteen's song is ultimately about the search for those qualities in a national culture devoid of them, and its nationalist themes serve as both cover and point of hopeful identification for a working class lost in neo-liberal America. As he once explained, the narrator of "Born in the USA" longs "to strip away that mythic America which was Reagan's image of America. He wants to find something real, and connecting. He's looking for a home in his country" (qtd in Alterman, *It Ain't No Sin to Be Glad You're Alive* 157).

After the "Born in the USA" furor of the mid-1980s subsided, Bruce Springsteen attempted to be more explicit about his politics, with edgier and more provocative renditions of his hit. The discomforting chill of an acoustic twelve-string often replaced the power of his trademark Fender Esquire, and the new versions frequently moved the narrative to the foreground and relegated the once dominant chorus to a haunting echo. Then, in 2004, twenty years after the release of his song, Springsteen made a series of campaign appearances on behalf of the floundering Democratic presidential ticket. His stump appearances attempted to reverse the logic of "Born in the USA," calling for a "deeper patriotism" based not on the politics of mythology, but on the way in which the nation treated its citizens. "The country we carry in our hearts," he declared, "is waiting."[12] Springsteen's criticism of the Iraq war, his reinterpretations of his hit, and his overt political affiliations made his positions perfectly clear, though at times less popular, to anyone who cared to listen.

---

[12] Springsteen used these words in many campaign appearances, as well as in the specific op-ed quoted here.

While those on the Left may have felt vindicated—and those on the Right betrayed—by the seemingly explicit politics of Springsteen's new performances, it is the full pop presentation of 1984 that manages to transcend simple partisanship in its use of art and history. The "Born in the USA" that still finds airtime tells the story of a man dwarfed by a sonic wall of nationalism and abandoned to the confusion of guerrilla wars. Until the birthright of being born in USA is fulfilled by more than triumphant rhetoric, the country we carry in our hearts will remain there. In that nation's absence, fists and flags are all that rise above dead man's towns.

Chapter 3

"Believe Me, Mister": The Tradition of Woody Guthrie's Hurt Song in Springsteen's *The Rising* and *Devils & Dust*

Donna M. Dolphin

Introduction

Woody Guthrie makes an attractive role model for a young musician who wants to change the world and become famous. Guthrie had it all: popularity, a romanticized vagabond lifestyle, a magnanimous personality, and the power to affect policy and create change, all expressed through music which was truly timeless—so "timeless," in fact, that it often encompassed the past, present and future. Simultaneously historic and original, Guthrie's music spoke to a better future. Whether he was "borrowing" from an old tune or revising history, his music made connections. He connected the present moment to human history in a way that made listeners aware of what might be yet to come.

Guthrie's words and music were simple but the images they evoked were poignant. He was the voice that uttered the pain and pointed to the injustices for so many who could not be heard on their own. More than that, he spoke of basic human dignity. Guthrie's connection to John Steinbeck's classic work *The Grapes of Wrath* is well known and indelible. He once wrote in an autobiographical explanation: "I made twelve records called 'Dust Bowl Ballads' for Victor after I seen *Grapes of Wrath* a couple or three times in a row" (*Pastures* 9). Springsteen's album *The Ghost of Tom Joad* is an obvious link, both by name and by content. In this instance, both Steinbeck and Guthrie employed popular culture to perform the important cultural work of revealing the injustices endured by the displaced farmers known as Dustbowl Refugees in 1930's America.

The Hurt Song

"Written in working-class language, hurt songs express the collective pain, suffering, and injustice working people have historically suffered, and articulate their collective hopes and dreams for a less oppressive future" (Garman, "The Ghost" 70-71). They are about community. The individual experience of suffering is connected to the larger human experience. Hurt songs suggest an historical time when people were more kind to each other. It is this memory that supports the "hopes and dreams for a less oppressive future." Narrators and agents of hurt songs invariably strive to retain their dignity, and it is through this dignity that hope and promise is often expressed.

Consider the narrator of Guthrie's "Blowin' Down the Road" ("I Ain't Gonna Be Treated This Way"):

> It takes a ten dollar shoe to fit my foot
> It takes a ten dollar shoe to fit my foot
> It takes a ten dollar shoe to fit my foot, Lord, Lord
> And I ain't gonna be treated this-a-way.
> Your two dollar shoes hurt my feet
> Your two dollar shoes hurt my feet
> Your two dollar shoes hurt my feet, Lord, Lord
> And I ain't gonna be treated this-a-way. (*DustBowl Ballads*)

In two simple verses about the cost and fit of shoes, Guthrie expresses the loss of dignity that was associated with government relief aid. The cheaply made relief shoes are ill-fitting and impede the man's ability to do a good day's work. He doesn't want charity; he wants to be treated correctly. The song goes on, "I'm lookin' for an honest job at honest pay / And I ain't gonna be treated this-a-way" (Guthrie, *Dustbowl Ballads*).

Though the agents of hurt songs may often, but not always, have strayed to the wrong side of the law, they are always victims of injustice themselves. If, in fact, they do exist outside of the law, it is the lack of community which has driven them there. The hurt song seeks to frame them sympathetically, and to look for larger social and political causes for the injustice. The working-class language in which they are written serves to reinforce the notion of the common man standing against the powerful institution, the worker against big business, the citizen against the corrupt government, the righteous against evil.

Guthrie believed in the power of music to heal. His own life experiences had shown him this first-hand. As a boy, his family had been affluent and influential but had lost nearly everything to hard times and the bad decisions of his colorful and violent father. His sister was killed in a house fire. He watched his mother's slow deterioration from Huntington's chorea (the same disease that would take his own life in 1967). However, his mother was not correctly diagnosed with this disease of the central nervous system at the time and was generally believed to be mentally unstable. Yet, whether providing the soundtrack for good times or bad, music was always part of the experience, with the type and tone changing to match the road that the Guthries were on at any given time (Klein; Guthrie, *Bound*).

When Woody Guthrie took to the road as a boy in his teens, his musical education continued (Guthrie, *Bound*; *Pastures* 5). When Alan Lomax recorded Woody Guthrie's music for the Library of Congress in 1940, he included Guthrie's explanations of how he had come to write each song. This often involved historic background about how Woody learned the root song on which his own music was often based (Guthrie, *Library of Congress*).

Guthrie came to believe in the power of music to affect change:

> Woody really fulfilled Whitman's ideals for a poet who would walk the roads of the country and sing the American story in the language of the people. He felt that songs should wake people up, help them understand their environment better and be more willing to do something about it. (A. Lomax, qtd in *A Vision Shared*).

Guthrie explained why he

> ... had to keep to going around and around with my guitar making up songs and singing. I never did really know that the human race was this big before. I never did really know that the fight had been going on so long and so bad. I never had been able to look out over and across the slum section nor a sharecropper farm and connect it up with the owner and the landlord and guards and the police and the dicks and the bulls and the vigilante men with their black sedans and sawed off shot guns. (*Pastures* 9)

Harold Leventhal, one of the managers of Pete Seeger's group, The Weavers, spoke in 1988 about the power of Guthrie's hurt songs:

> I think the important thing is the fact that Woody's music, written 40 years ago or more, is relevant today. Take the song "I Ain't Got No Home." When Woody wrote this he dealt about the people who were homeless during the Depression. Now we're talking some time ago. ... and the song is as valid today as when Woody wrote it. (qtd in *A Vision Shared*)

Many musicians have since invited comparison of their own work to that of Woody Guthrie. So many tributes to his life's work have been performed that include a collection of artists from across genres. The 1988 documentary *A Vision Shared: A Tribute to Woody Guthrie and Leadbelly* includes performances of Guthrie's work by Bruce Springsteen, John Mellencamp, U2, Sweet Honey in The Rock, Pete Seeger, Arlo Guthrie, and Emmylou Harris (*A Vision Shared*). The documentary is a collection of performance intermingled with statements from the musicians regarding the impact of Guthrie's work on their own (and Leadbelly's, though his work is not germane to this chapter at this time). John Mellencamp states:

> Anybody that even thinks they're writing songs, they have got to admit that Woody Guthrie was an influence on them because you just trace the trail back. What was Bob Dylan doing actually in the beginning but playing like he was Woody Guthrie? (qtd in *A Vision Shared*).

Bob Dylan's self-conscious pose is undeniable. He states, "I was completely taken over by him, by his spirit or whatever" (qtd in *A Vision Shared*). The well-known photographs from the early days of Dylan's folk music career in which he imitates Guthrie's costume, gesture, and even hairstyle are wryly amusing. As Dylan explained, "He had a particular sound and besides that, he said something to go along with his sound. I liked the way he played and sang. And I liked the things he said when he sang. ... You could listen to his sounds and actually learn how to live" (qtd in *A Vision Shared*). The career Dylan fashioned himself, based on the spirit of Woody Guthrie, served not only to bring success to Bob Dylan, but also to revitalize the hurt song and Guthrie's work. In the introduction to Guthrie's *Pastures of Plenty*, Dave Marsh writes, "without Woody Guthrie there would have been no Bob Dylan, and without Bob Dylan, no popular music as we know it today" (xxii). Dylan's homage to Guthrie, though relatively self-serving and short-lived, did the important cultural work of re-establishing the vitality of the hurt song and bringing to Guthrie's work a popularity it had not previously known (*A Vision Shared*; Garman, *A Race* 135, 146-50).

What is it that makes Guthrie's hurt song so uniquely powerful? Perhaps it's the compassion, the demand for community, so simply expressed. Bruce Springsteen said, "I think [in Guthrie's work there was] just a dream for more justice, less oppression, less racism, less hatred. Period. Less hatred" (qtd in *A Vision Shared*). In the introduction to a book of folk songs, called *Hard Hitting Songs for Hard Hit People*, collected by Guthrie, Alan Lomax, and Pete Seeger, Guthrie wrote, "thank heaven, one day we'll all find out that all of our songs was just little notes in a great big fog, and the poor will vanish like a drunkard's dream. ..." (*Pastures* 65). But, for Guthrie himself, it was the blues that meant the most:

> The blues are my favorite, because the blues are the saddest and lonesomest, and say the right thing in a way that most preachers ought to pattern after. All honky tonk and dance hall blues had parents, and those parents was the blues that came from the workers in the factories, mills, mines, crops, orchards, and oil fields— but by the time a blues reaches a honky tonk music box, it is changed from chains to kisses, and from a cold prison cell to a warm bed with a hot mama, and from sunstroke on a chain gang, to a chock house song, or a new baby and a bottle of gin. (Guthrie, *Pastures* 62)

Guthrie insisted that the words and music remain uncomplicated: "The fancier it is, the worse it is. The plainer it is the easier it is, and the easier it is, the better it is—and the words don't even have to be spelt right" (*Pastures* 64). In his formalized definition of a hurt song, Garman includes the need for working-class language (*The Ghost* 70).

Springsteen has often been compared to Woody Guthrie, and justifiably so. He has certainly invited that comparison overtly with his album *The Ghost of Tom Joad* (1995). Garman's 1996 article traces Springsteen's connection to Guthrie's hurt song and presents a deconstruction of *The Ghost of Tom Joad* based on that analysis. In the tradition of Woody Guthrie, *The Ghost of Tom Joad* connects the present moment to human history and suggests that all of human dignity is at stake. In his article, "The Ghost of History: Bruce Springsteen, Woody Guthrie, and the Hurt Song," Bryan Garman describes Springsteen performing in concert during the *Ghost* tour (1996). During the performance, Springsteen "acknowledges his artistic debt" to *The Grapes of Wrath* (1940) film director, John Ford, describing in detail a climactic scene from the film based on Steinbeck's novel (Garman, *The Ghost* 103). Springsteen's intention seems pretty clear, as far as cultural work is concerned; he is connecting with that "one big soul."

As Garman notes:

> Employing the language and representational strategies of the hurt song, Springsteen reclaims popular music as a cultural space in which class relations are both taken seriously and historicized. He places his work in the context of a recognizable cultural and political tradition which affords his characters dignity and opens possibilities for social change. (*The Ghost* 71).

Hurt songs are more than an expression of pain and hope; they are a call to action. Guthrie knew this as well, and used his music as cultural work to attempt to bring about social reform. "There's several ways of saying what's on your mind," he wrote. "One of the mainest ways is by singing" (*Pastures* 78). Garman's 1996 article presents a thorough record of Springsteen's musical education vis-à-vis Guthrie: "For me Woody was that sense of idealism," Springsteen recalled, "along with a sense of realism that said, 'well, maybe you can't save the world, but you can change the world'" (qtd in *A Vision Shared*).

Though Bob Dylan felt he was "completely taken over" by Guthrie's "spirit or whatever," it is Bruce Springsteen who seems to understand the hurt song's function in community-building as cultural work. Speaking in reference to Guthrie's *Dust Bowl Ballad*, "I Ain't Got No Home," Springsteen said:

> I think that the heart of that song cries out for some sort of belief and reckoning with the idea of universal family, which is something people long for, you know, everybody longs for that. And that's why it is so resonant, and it will always be so resonant. It reaches down and pulls out that part of you that thinks of the next guy. I think that was embedded in every song he wrote and every story he told. (qtd in *A Vision Shared*)

Springsteen continues a rich tradition of cultural work with *The Rising* (2002) and *Devils & Dust* (2005). The very titles suggest that these albums are collections of hurt songs. In post-9/11 America, Springsteen uses the hurt song to cross class boundaries and confront xenophobia. In the face of national hysteria over terrorism and government-sanctioned hatred in the guise of national security, he presents two collections of songs about the universality of loss and the need for human contact. As Garman said about *Ghost*, once again, "in the tradition of the hurt song, Springsteen locates and preserves the political potential of a usable past, and demonstrates an awareness of how his status as a popular musician circumscribes this potential" (*The Ghost* 71).

The Rising is a perfect example of a collection of hurt songs. While the album was embraced by the nation for its healing tones, it spoke particularly to those audiences who experienced the September 11 tragedy first-hand, most particularly residents of New York and New Jersey. The nature of the hurt song is that it deals with the experiences of the working class. Garman observes that:

> ... as Springsteen's characters tell their stories, they speak in a working-class language which locates them in a specific social space, but also empowers them to push against the boundaries that delineate this space.... The use of nonstandard English represents the unequal educational opportunities afforded to working people and corresponds to the lack of political and cultural power and influence that they wield in the vast social spaces claimed by the middle class. (*The Ghost* 87)

This is certainly true regarding Springsteen's work up until *Ghost*. But *The Rising* represents a variation from this use of colloquialism. The song "Into the Fire" is about the firefighters and police officers who lost their lives in the World Trade Center. The narrator of the song is a bereaved lover, but the real power of this hurt song is that it presents two perspectives simultaneously. We share in the pain of loss in being left behind. The severed connection is so sudden, the relationship so strong, that we also experience the moments leading to death. "I heard you calling me, then you disappeared / into the dust" references the numerous cellphone conversations that ended abruptly at that tragic moment when the towers fell. These lines connect the song not just to history, but to an historic moment, and, for many, a personal historic moment. Springsteen goes on to present both perspectives with, "It was dark, too dark to see, you held me in the light you gave / You lay your hand on me / Then walked into the darkness of your smoky grave / Up the stairs, into the fire." We feel the pain of loss and bereavement, but we also get a glimpse of the bravery required of the rescue workers that day. While everyone else was trying to leave the burning building, firefighters and other rescue workers were trying to enter it. Springsteen uses "Into the Fire" to frame their heroism in human terms without jingoism. His frame is inclusive in that it recognizes a human chain and acknowledges the heroism of the family and even the larger community. "I need your kiss but love and duty called you someplace higher / Somewhere up the stairs into the fire."

True to its form as a hurt song, "Into the Fire" articulates a "hope for a less oppressive future." The refrain of this painfully evocative song is, "May your strength give us strength / May your faith give us faith / May your hope give us hope / May your love give us love." Despite the lyrics, this is not a maudlin song. Ending with the refrain, "Into the Fire" is a complex and dignified glimpse into the sacrifice required for heroic bravery. Prayerful in tone, language and meter, as

Woody Guthrie said the best songs should be, it "says the right thing in a way most preachers ought to pattern after" (Guthrie, *Pastures* 62).

Two other tracks which deal obviously with loss and sorrow associated with September 11 are "Empty Sky" and "You're Missing," both of which speak to the experience of dealing with recent loss. Neither of these songs is strikingly colloquial nor working-class, yet both are valid hurt songs. "You're Missing" is a poignant song which deals with the everyday intimacies of loss, such as "Shirts in the closet, shoes in the hall." The narrator recites a litany of everyday intimate scenes which could come from almost any family household. The images are vivid in their simplicity: "Coffee cups on the counter, jackets on the chair / Papers on the doorstep, but you're not there / Everything is everything / Everything is everything / But you're missing." Clearly, Springsteen has taken to heart Guthrie's admonishment, "the fancier it is, the worse it is. The plainer it is …" the better, the more poignant (*Pastures* 64). "You're Missing" is not overtly working-class. Although the language is informal, it is not all that colloquial. But it is plain, and beautifully so. The song goes on to speak of the children left behind and then of the narrator's empty bed, both intimate scenes and intimate pains. But while those pains are intimate, they were experienced simultaneously on September 11 by thousands of families. Springsteen links his narrator to that historic community of loss and links the subject of this song to that historic community of missing persons. In so doing, he connects a solitary suffering to an historic community of survivors.

Springsteen's ability to employ the hurt song in the performance of important cultural work across class boundaries is better appreciated when one understands more clearly the demographics of the New Jersey community in which he resides and the particular demands of citizenship that community places upon him. While much is made of Springsteen's own working-class background, the small community where he lives enjoys an upper-middle-class standard of living (*NJ Municipal Data Book (2005)*, 439). Some of the neighboring communities are similar in terms of demographics. Many of the people who lost their lives on September 11 were from these communities, and left behind loved ones (see www.september11victims.com/september11victims/victims-list.htm). While "Into the Fire" is specifically about the loss of working-class lives, "You're Missing" and "Empty Sky" are more class-vague, allowing listeners from across classes to write themselves into the community of pain and suffering, and, by extension, history and healing. Connected to history, all of this pain and suffering came from the same place.

Garman writes about the ways in which Springsteen employs working-class geographies in his music—that is, "physical places and cultural spaces in which working-class people both experience and shape the material conditions and social relationships that define class. … These geographies are … places of work … and any number of places significant to working-class communities. …" (*The Ghost* 85). In *The Rising* and *Devils & Dust*, Springsteen adds a dimension of hurt geography to the already established working-class geographies. This new dimension of hurt geography includes more intimate spaces, such as those occupied by personal belongings, as in "You're Missing," and, of course, beds. Garman writes that "Springsteen's working-class geographies illustrate the dissolution of working-class communities" (*The Ghost* 85). They come to signify the loss identity rather than the bonds of community. A similar argument can be made for the intimate spaces of the hurt geography. Empty places in bed, coffee cups, unworn shirts, family photographs—the mundane detritus of intimacy leaves the narrators in Springsteen's songs at a loss to know who they are.

The title track on this album, "The Rising" and the song "My City of Ruins" are both hurt songs in the pure Guthrie tradition. "The Rising" is spoken in working-class language by a masculine narrator. "Left the house this morning / Bells ringing filled the air / Wearing' the cross of my calling / On wheels of fire I come rollin' down here" locates "The Rising" in traditional working-class geography. Evoking September 11 imagery, a call-and-answer style verse answers each statement of tragedy with a statement of hope:

> Sky of blackness and sorrow (a dream of life)
> Sky of love, sky of tears (a dream of life)
> Sky of glory and sadness (a dream of life)
> Sky of memory and shadow (a dream of life)
> Your burnin' wind fills my arms tonight
> Sky of longing and emptiness (a dream of life)
> Sky of fullness, sky of blessed life

Although "My City of Ruins" does not reference work directly, it is located in those places which help to define the working-class desolation that Springsteen depicts so vividly, namely street corners and boarded-up buildings. The narrator of this song is connected to the "one big soul" that is the community and feels the loss. "My soul is lost, my friend / Tell me how do I begin again? / My city's in ruins." The hope for a better future seems to lie in the entire community. In another call-and-answer-style verse, the phrase "With these hands, With these hands" is repeated again and again, suggesting that the ruined community will only "rise up" with prayer and hard work—the work of every member's hands.

In *Devils & Dust* Springsteen continues to use the hurt song to give voice to the experiences of people who have been pushed outside the boundaries of community. On the DVD side of this DualDisc, Springsteen explains his connection to the characters he writes about:

> The people that are interesting are the people that have something eating at them and they're not exactly sure what that thing is. The characters on this record are all trying to find their way through that, through those questions and some do it somewhat successfully and some come to tragic ends. (qtd in Clinch)

The Western landscapes and isolated individuals of *Devils & Dust* are reminiscent of *Ghost*, and perhaps that should come as no surprise. In a review of the album, Edna Gunderson points out, "aside from the title track (written at the outset of the Iraq invasion), *Devils* tunes were written during a creative burst after *Joad*. They reflect views held then and now" (Gunderson). But the landscapes aren't the only similarities between these two albums. She quotes Springsteen in the same article, "we do triage on the citizenry and decide there are certain dreams and lives that are expendable and others that aren't. We're never going to fulfill our promise as a country until we deal with that fundamental hole in the middle of our souls …" (Gunderson).

The title track "Devils & Dust" depicts an American soldier in fighting in Iraq. The pain he articulates is the confusion of fighting in a war of questionable justice and of the loss of his own humanity which is required in order for him to be able to do the job asked of him by his government. "I got my finger on the trigger / But I don't know who to trust." Springsteen is, once again, singing about an individual struggling with a desire to stay connected to the institution that has betrayed him. The hurt geography here is both traditional working-class and personal: "Well I've got God on my side / And I'm just trying to survive / What if what you do to survive / Kills the things you love / Fear's a dangerous thing / It can turn your heart black you can trust / It'll take your God filled soul / Fill it with devils and dust." This song also stresses the need to connect to community. "We're a long, long way from home, Bobbie / Home's a long, long way from us."

Remembering that hurt songs assert hope for a better future, there are two important points to make regarding the song "Devils & Dust." First is the dignity of the narrator of this song who says, "I've got God on my side / I'm just trying to survive." This individual struggles to maintain their humanity as well as their dignity. The second point involves a belief in the basic goodness of people:

> Now every woman and every man
> They want to take a righteous stand
> Find the love that God wills
> And the faith that He commands.
> I've got my finger on the trigger
> And tonight faith just ain't enough
> When I look inside my heart
> There's just devils and dust.

"Devils & Dust" provides a poignant narrative about an individual slowly losing their foothold in the human community: "Fear's a powerful thing / It'll turn your heart black you can trust" Springsteen warns us all.

"Matamoros Banks" offers a hurt song reminiscent of Guthrie's "Deportees." Both songs are taken from the headlines of the day. Guthrie's "Deportees" is a heartfelt song about illegal Mexican migrant workers killed in a plane crash while being deported from the United States. The news reports failed to identify the victims by name, calling them only deportees. Regarding "Matamoros Banks," Springsteen writes in the liner notes of *Devils & Dust*:

> Each year many die crossing the deserts, mountains, and rivers of our southern border in search of a better life. Here I follow the journey backwards, from the body at the river bottom, to the man walking across the desert towards the banks of the Rio Grande.

"Matamoros Banks" centers itself in the intimate geographies of hurt. Rather than focus on the social and institutional causes which propel so many people across the Mexican border into danger, uncertainty, and working-class poverty, Springsteen gives a voice to the bereaved lover left behind. "I long, my darling, for your kiss, for your sweet love I give God thanks / The touch of your loving fingertips." Though the characters are nameless, they are joined to the human community via experience and history. The force that propels them, though also unnamed in this song, is strong enough to cause history to repeat. Despite the annihilation of the song's subject—"Your clothes give way to the current and river stone / 'Till every trace of who you ever were is gone"— the narrator will follow the same path and take the same risks: "Your sweet memory comes on the evenin' wind / I sleep and dream of holding you in my arms again / The lights of Brownsville, across the river shine / A shout rings out and into the silty red river I dive." Just as Guthrie sought to give the nameless "deportees" their identities back, Springsteen seeks to rejoin the nameless dead on the Matamoros to the human community and to all of history. By connecting his subject to Guthrie's and to the greater social problem, he succeeds in connecting to history. And furthermore, by connecting to the human community, especially via the familiar territory of working-class need and the intimate geography of bereavement, he succeeds in connecting to the one big soul, and in asserting hope for a less oppressive future.

"Black Cowboys" and "The Hitter" are both songs about the chain of betrayal which is so much a part of the working-class geography. In both songs, the main character was betrayed as a boy by a mother who was betrayed by a community which had been betrayed by the socioeconomic institutions of government. In each song, Springsteen uses this complex chain to link each character to history and to suggest possibilities for the future. "Black Cowboys" addresses race, as well as class, in telling the story of a boy growing up in a neighborhood where "names and photos of young black faces / whose death and blood consecrated these places" commonly decorate the streets. The song goes on to depict a close relationship between mother and son. The boy, Rainey, watched Western movies on TV each day, so his mother brought him books about black cowboys and Seminole Calvary Scouts. She nurtured him in every way, including his dignity, until she became involved with the sort of man from whom she is protecting Rainey. Drawing upon the dignity and sense of self preservation that his mother provided before succumbing to the evils of the abandoned community, Rainey leaves his mother and takes a train to the West, becoming a black cowboy himself, asserting the possibility of a better future, or at least some sort of future, and joining history by doubling back upon it.

"The Hitter" is narrated in the first person by a boxer addressing the mother with whom he has had no contact in many years. He asks for nothing but a few hours of asylum. He reflects upon a life of violence and fleeting success since she put him on the road as a child to hide from the police for an unknown crime:

> Understand, in the end, Ma, every man plays the game
> If you know me one different then speak out his name
> Ma, if my voice now you don't recognize
> Then just open the door and look into your dark eyes
> I ask of you nothin', not a kiss not a smile,
> Just open the door and let me lie down for while.

Written in working-class language which is much more characteristic of Springsteen's earlier work, this evocative song ultimately reveals that this narrator has had to quite literally fight his way all of his life. He speaks knowingly of the things he has done wrong but is not apologetic: "If you're a better man than me then just step to the line / Show me your money and speak out your crime." "The Hitter" addresses the collective pain of the working class without much hope for a better future. The only hope can be found in the dignity and endurance of the character.

> Tonight in the shipyard a man draws a circle in the dirt
> I move to the center and I take off my shirt
> I study him for the cuts, the scars, the pain,
> Man nor time can erase
> I move hard to the left and I strike to the face.

The hitter recognizes the soft spots in others, and he is so hardened by life that he strikes at those. He lists a string of places that he has been, and even now, in fact, he just wants to lie down for a while and then be on his way again. There has been no nurturing mother, no supportive community to soften life's hard blows for this man.

Relationships between mothers and sons permeate *Devils & Dust*; four of the album's twelve songs deal directly with the subject. In addition to the two discussed above—"The Hitter" and "Black Cowboys"—"Silver Palomino" and "Jesus Was an Only Son" draw upon mother-son relationship and place the pain and suffering which each song articulates within the geography of the intimate.

"Jesus Was an Only Son" is particularly interesting to consider as a hurt song. It takes the divinity of Jesus of Nazareth and anchors it squarely in human experience, connecting the historic person Jesus to all of human history by focusing on the pain and bereavement of his mother. Jesus is part of the human community because his mother suffered the anxieties of motherhood and, ultimately, the pain of losing her son. "A mother prays, 'Sleep tight, my child, sleep well / For I'll be at your side / That no shadow, no darkness, no tolling bell, / Shall pierce your dreams this night."

This song, too, is reminiscent of Guthrie. Guthrie's "They Laid Jesus Christ in His Grave," a song about contemporary society's apparent rejection of Christ's message, took as its subject the death of Jesus in a contemporary, humanist setting, as does Springsteen's "Jesus Was an Only Son." As with the song "The Ghost of Tom Joad" and "Matamoros Banks," Springsteen simultaneously pays homage to Guthrie and becomes part of that one big soul by connecting to history via his cultural work. The words "Jesus was an only son / As he walked up Calvary Hill / His mother Mary walking beside him / In the path where his blood spilled" connect Jesus and his mother to the community of mothers and sons who have been separated by institutionalized human violence. "Now there's a loss that can never be replaced / A destination that can never be reached / A light you'll never find in another's face" could be sung by a million mothers about a million sons. Ever the humanist, Springsteen employs the hurt song to take power away from the established institutions and place it squarely in the community: "Well Jesus kissed his mother's hands / Whispered, 'Mother, still your tears, / For remember the soul of the universe / Willed a world and it appeared." Clearly, Springsteen denies the creationist argument here, while simultaneously connecting to that historic one big soul and lending the reputations of Jesus and his mother to the argument. In so doing, the ghost of Tom Joad appears once more, suggesting another conversation regarding the universe's soul between another son and his mother. As Steinbeck's Tom Joad is about to take to the road to escape the police and the vigilantes, he explains to his mother the idea he learned from Preacher Casy: maybe "a fella ain't got a soul of his own, but on'y a piece of a big soul—the one big soul that belongs to ever'body" (*The Grapes of Wrath* 419). Joad tells his mother to still her tears as well, and that she will see him everywhere she sees people fighting for justice in the name of the community.

Bruce Springsteen is clearly using the traditions of Woody Guthrie and the hurt song to do important cultural work. Much of that work is connected to Guthrie's historic traditions in a self-conscious and intentional way. But Guthrie himself was connected to history not only in the (re)presentation of some of his music, or the historic reference and connection to working-class hurt geographies, but also in the sense that he fulfilled, as Alan Lomax stated, "Walt Whitman's ideals for a poet who would walk the roads of the country and sing the American story in the language of the people" (qtd. in *A Vision Shared*).

Adhesiveness

In his book, *A Race of Singers: Whitman's Working-Class Hero from Guthrie to Springsteen*, Bryan Garman uncovers the traditions of Whitman's ideals that are at the root of some of the most important American popular music. At the foundation of Whitman's ideal is the notion of adhesiveness, or men protecting the interests of other men. Garman explains:

> Whitman argued that if Americans were to create a previously unimagined democracy, they would have to forge an unforeseen love and respect for political equals, that is, other white men. Rooted in the homosocial and often homoerotic culture of the artisan workshop, adhesiveness promised that the exchange of sexual pleasure between men would reconcile individual freedom and social equality and promote a radical democracy. Although adhesive love presented the possibility for a gay male identity and had the potential to erode the masculine competitiveness that characterized the marketplace, it also allowed men to strengthen the masculine bonds they formed on the job, prohibited women from engaging in same-sex love, and took for granted both women's participation in the domestic economy and their exclusion from male leisure and work places. (9)

Though presented as the working-class artisan male's defense against industrialization, adhesiveness was *de facto* classist, racist, and sexist discrimination.

Though radical in so many other ways, Guthrie's music was sexist at the core. His narrator was most often masculine, and spoke of masculine work or pain. He sang from a masculine perspective because he sang from masculine experience. His autobiography, *Bound for Glory*, is a collection of adhesive male bonding experiences which take place in railroad boxcars and vacant lots across the South and West. A simple deconstruction of his music reveals that he is speaking from a masculine perspective, and it is one which often suggests that the male narrator is speaking to a male audience of listeners—that he is, essentially, looking for validation of his painful experience from other men. His song "Talking Dustbowl Blues," in which the narrator tells the story of losing the farm to the dust storms, packing all of the family belongings into the Ford truck and heading to California, is one such example. Along the way "there was a hairpin turn / and I didn't make it / … Scattered wives and childrens all over the side of that mountain" (Guthrie, *Library of Congress*). It is wives and children who got scattered by the driver, who by deduction must be husband and father. The song also speaks of the inability to keep the farm/job and the house and of experiencing engine trouble, all traditionally masculine areas of responsibility. The heart-wrenching "I Ain't Got No Home" is another example of the masculine voice in Guthrie's music. The narrator reveals his identity with the line, "and my darlin' wife / to heaven she has flown." He also mentions raising six children, identifying the narrator as husband and father.

Springsteen uses many of the same devices in his music. Although some songs from *The Rising* and *Devils & Dust* attempt to represent or acknowledge the experiences of working-class women, Springsteen's hurt songs carry on the tradition of Whitman's adhesiveness. If, as Garman writes, adhesiveness "allowed men to strengthen bonds they formed on the job … [and] took for granted both women's participation in the domestic economy and their exclusion from male leisure and work places," then many of the songs on both of these albums produce a duality of experience for women listeners (*A Race* 9). While they work to include women's experience in the community of pain and hardship, they simultaneously exclude women from the traditional masculine geographies.

"The Rising" serves as a case in point. The narrator is a fire and rescue worker, presumably at the World Trade Center on September 11. Details of the psychological and physical hardships of that traditionally masculine working-class work are evocatively included in the song. The gender of the narrator is only presumed until the lines, "I see you Mary in the garden / In the garden of a thousand sighs / There's holy pictures of our children." Although it is a heterosexual presumption, it seems clear that Springsteen's intention is to give voice to a fire*man*, one who is both husband and father. Since the song honors the memory and sacrifice of those workers, the presumption is that they are men. Therefore women are excluded from this workplace. Furthermore, the narrator "Left the house this morning" to go to work, but sees "Mary in the garden" as he is dying. It's not much of a stretch to see Mary as responsible for the domestic realm.

"You're Missing" doesn't provide any specific work clues or gendered names, yet the narrator seems to be female. Also apparently about September 11, the narrator talks about the everyday ways in which a loved one is missing from the home. The remnants of the life, "Shirts in the closet, shoes in the hall" and "Coffee cups on the counter," "Papers on the doorsteps," while not specifically masculine, are also not overtly feminine, nor do they seem to be the sort of feminine details one might expect to hear described. They are shirts, not dresses. Coffee cups and newspapers evoke a traditional image of Dad at the breakfast table, and the "Children are asking if it's alright / Will you be in our arms tonight?" The subject of the song leaves for work every morning and returns every evening, but the children and the narrator are accustomed to being in the home during the day. It is a scene of domesticity, with the implication that this narrator participates in the domestic economy while the subject has been meaningfully employed, elsewhere. While this haunting song seems to articulate women's pain, it is also traditionally adhesive in that it excludes women's participation from male work and takes for granted women's participation in the domestic economy.

Similar arguments can be made for other songs on the album. "Further On (Up the Road)" is a good example of the way in which Springsteen often addresses a specifically male audience. "If there's a light up ahead, well *brother* I don't know" is typical of the way he uses working-class colloquialisms of address to personalize his narratives. While they help to establish class, they also function to establish the nature of the audience. The narrator in this song has "Got on my dead man's suit" and is speaking to another man. Once again, this analysis presumes heterosexuality, but accepting that, there is no place for women "Further On (Up the Road)."

The women in *Devils & Dust* are mothers and sex partners. Arguably, sex partners have found a place in men's leisure, but not in men's leisure community.

Mothering is certainly an established element of the domestic economy. Failed by the community, the mother in "The Hitter" is such a poor nurturer that she doesn't recognize her own son, yet "Ma" is all she is. He has agency, and she has no part in his work or leisure. Rainey's mother in "Black Cowboys" takes a more active and positive role in his young life, but fails as a mother when the community fails her. Her agency in the narrative is limited, however, to the domestic realm. "Along a street of stray bullets he made his way, / To the warmth of her arms at the end of each day." When she fails to nurture him, Rainey leaves home and she is written out of the narrative altogether. "Then she got lost in the days / The smile Rainey depended on dusted away / The arms that held him were no more his home. " In "Jesus Was an Only Son," the good mother is given a voice to articulate a prayer for her child's safety, and all of her other actions involve childrearing as well. In the final verse her grown son tells her that she can't interfere with his work: "… Mother, still your tears, / For remember the soul of the universe / Willed a world and it appeared." While this moment between Jesus and Mary reminds us, very much, of the conversation between Tom Joad and Ma, it also reminds us that, for Walt Whitman, there were masculine and feminine geographies. One of the functions of adhesiveness was to maintain those geographies.

Arguably, the points regarding adhesiveness in Springsteen's work are constructed from a heterosexual position, with a patriarchal definition of domesticity and work. It would be valuable to make a more complete reading of Springsteen's work—one that is not limited to *The Rising* and *Devils & Dust*, and also one that is made from a more inclusive perspective. Springsteen continues the tradition of Woody Guthrie's hurt song in *The Rising* and *Devils & Dust*. Several songs on both albums articulate the collective pain and suffering of the working class. These songs are either written in working-class language, or deal with working-class geographies. They maintain hope for a less oppressive future, through the direct assertion of looking for a better day, or else in the assertion of the dignity of the song's characters. Like Guthrie, Springsteen's hurt songs connect the present narrative moment to human history. And, like Guthrie's, Springsteen's hurt songs express the value of human community. Although a number of the hurt songs on *The Rising* and *Devils & Dust* acknowledge the experience of women, for the most part these songs are written in the tradition of Whitman's notion of adhesiveness—that is, the working man protecting the interests of the working man, and taking for granted women's participation in the domestic economy.

Chapter 4

"Where Dreams are Found and Lost": Springsteen, Nostalgia, and Identity

Elizabeth M. Seymour

One of modernity's permanent laments concerns the loss of a better past, the memory of living in a securely circumscribed place, with a sense of stable boundaries and a place-bound culture with its regular flow of time and a core of permanent relations. Perhaps such days have always been a dream rather than a reality, a phantasmagoria of loss generated by modernity itself rather than its prehistory. But the dream does have staying power.

Andreas Huyssen, "Present Pasts: Media, Politics, Amnesia"

Is a dream a lie that don't come true
Or is it something worse?

Bruce Springsteen, "The River"

Bruce Springsteen is closely identified with the working-class hero of American culture. He was born in the working class, has always identified personally with that group, and has chosen to write their narratives in his art for the last 35 years. These narratives are often intimate and personal in nature, and his persona continues to be identified with this class. Many people from different backgrounds and with entirely different political perspectives have attempted to appropriate his image and so grab the cultural authenticity of the working class. It is a powerful icon, full of contradictory and conflicting components that make it easy for appropriation from many different directions and also difficult for the artist himself to control. Working-class heroes epitomize the American Dream which promises that, with hard work and perseverance, everyone can pick themselves up by their bootstraps and raise their, or at least their children's, social standing.

As the turmoil of the 1960s confronted the economic reality of the 1970s, this dream was brought into serious question. This is the period during which Springsteen's identity as a narrator for the working class solidified, and, within these changing times, different nostalgic discourses started to appear in his work. From the 1970s through to the present, Springsteen continued to employ a variety of nostalgic elements. This chapter will focus on the changing construction of masculinity and the working-class hero in Springsteen's nostalgic moments, contextualizing them within the broader socioeconomic changes in American society.

To understand nostalgia we need to recognize that it does not occur at just any particular moment in time or in every society. Nostalgia, or a longing for a past, requires both a sense of linear time and a sense of loss. Nostalgic discourses flourish when the present is compared to the past and marked as a moment of decline, such as the fall of an empire, the loss of power of a particular group, migration to a new land, or other societal changes. Fred Davis notes that nostalgia is sparked by transition or discontinuity (49). Capitalism and the socioeconomic changes it wrought made Western cultures ripe for the development of nostalgic discourses, as we try to understand and come to terms with our disrupted daily lives. Nostalgic discourses become part of how we invent traditions in our nationalist discourses for our pasts, enabling us to come to terms with and live with our presents (Hobsbawm, *Invention*).

Stewart states that nostalgia was first discussed in Western culture as a social disease (23). It was originally identified in the 1680s as a sickness affecting Swiss mercenaries fighting far away from their homes. This medical/psychological approach dominated until the nineteenth century when, under the influence of romanticism, nostalgia became intimately tied with melancholia. Bryan S. Turner describes this new nostalgia as an outlook dwelling on the passage of time, the fragility of things, and the loss associated with social change (117). This change of perspective occurs at a time when social relations of workers in artisanal guilds are breaking down as a result of industrial capitalism and the move to mechanization and factory production. Turner argues that social thought in the West has been strongly affected by this nostalgic turn. First, there is a strong sense of history as a cyclical pattern of decline and fall, with a sense of a lost home or community relations. Second, there is an awareness of fragmentation, a loss of wholeness, cohesion, and certainty in this changing world (often seen as the erosion of moral values in the face of social change). Third, there is a perceived loss of autonomy (as workers in guilds no longer control their means of production but, rather, have to rely on paid labor and bureaucracies). Finally, there is dismay over the loss of world-views and ways of life that are considered authentic (as seen in the validation of native cultural artifacts and the disdain for popular culture).

In fact, it is hard to imagine much of the critical tradition in Western thought, including Marx and the Frankfurt School (Benjamin, Durkheim, Tonnies, Simmel, and Weber), without the influence of nostalgia (Bissell 223). As Robertson states, "the will to nostalgia is indeed a distinctive issue of modernity" (49). Many of the structural oppositions that we use to analyze social change come from this nostalgic view of the world: tradition/modernity, authentic/inauthentic, *Gemeinschaft/Gesellschaft*, organic/mechanical, status/contract, and use value/exchange value (Frow 81). Nostalgia and the imagined or real loss of home, moral values, and social relations are all a part of our world-view today.

Starting in the 1960s and still continuing, nostalgia theory became important in culture studies, literary and film theory as various scholars (Harper, Davis, Coontz, Boym) started to focus on mass culture and the media landscape. For Springsteen and his work, nostalgia became an overt issue during the 1980s when various conservative groups attempted to appropriate his music and image for their own political causes. In the West, the 1980s was a period in which expressions of nostalgia became a familiar part of mass media and nationalist discourses. Springsteen was already responding to some of this nationalistic nostalgia in his lyrics, and was forced to distance himself publicly from these types of appropriation (Marsh, *Glory Days*). He responded to this nostalgic turn by writing narratives of working-class America that were critical of these romantic nostalgic discourses of the American Dream.

As this chapter will demonstrate, Springsteen's lyrics contain multiple levels of nostalgia, and his overt nostalgic moments change dramatically in character over the course of his career. In particular, I will use Boym's typology of nostalgia as restorative and reflective to help understand the complexity and multilayered nature of nostalgia in his songs. Restorative nostalgia stresses *nostos* (return home) and attempts a reconstruction of a lost home. It doesn't think of itself as nostalgia, but rather as truth and tradition. It is at the core of national and religious movements, protects the truth and rarely questions the assumptions on which it is based. It is the nostalgia containing a single plot trying to create a national identity. Reflective nostalgia stresses *algia* (longing) and delays the homecoming—tending to be more wistful, ironic, and sometimes desperate. It dwells in the ambivalence of human longing and belonging and does not shy away from discussing the contradictions of modernity. It often does not follow a single plot, but loves exploring many different spaces. It loves details and not symbols, and it is the nostalgia of social memory, with collective frameworks that mark, but might not define, individual memory (Boym 49).

I will analyze the way in which Springsteen either overtly or implicitly uses nostalgia to construct masculinity and his working-class male characters throughout his career. Gender is an important way of thinking about identity, and is central to the American idea of the working-class hero. Springsteen's masculine male is buff, white, sexual, and very virile. He controls his emotions, works hard and honestly in public, plays just as hard at night, and is often a loner. The loner ideal looks back to the nostalgic past of heroes and cowboys—men who controlled nature and their environment and are often found in open spaces. For Springsteen, these open spaces are located on the urban and suburban streets of the Northeast or the wide open spaces of the American West. This cowboy-pilgrim lives in the streets where, in the early days, he finds freedom from the confinement of parents and authority in a car or with a band. As he matures, he gets lonely. He needs a woman for sex, but also for that emotional attachment lacking in modern capitalism's working world. These later relationships start to include themes of partnership between lovers, reflecting changing attitudes in American society toward women, particularly in the middle and upper classes. For the characters Springsteen creates, women come to offer the promise of redemption from the failures of age and the difficulties of being successful in modern America.

Females are constructed in a variety of ways in Springsteen's songs over the years. They start out as sex objects, foils, and avenues of escape and then end up as love objects, avenues of redemption, partners and, sometimes, prostitutes. The feminine is located predominantly in the private sphere, or the domestic. As teens they roam the streets, but as women they eventually provide the connection men need with family and community. They give men back the humanity lost in the brutal working world which ultimately dashes his working-class heroes' dreams.

The masculine for Springsteen follows much the same pattern as his feminine counterpart, providing the perfect foil for his male characters. In the early years, Springsteen's male characters roam the streets in cars or sit on the beaches looking for pretty girls to fulfill their needs. But they are loners—posers, imitating their favorite heroes from cinema and music. As these boys grow up into men, the American Dream promises that hard work will provide them and their families with a good middle-class life. Their fundamental role is as saviors. While these themes become more mixed and more complicated in the later songs, men are still responsible for taking care of women and their families. But, when the economy changes, these dreams are broken, too. This emasculates the male hero, who, by the early 1980s, reacts with violence. Men roam the public sphere, but without decent paychecks, what can they do except strike out at the society that is causing their problems? As Springsteen's hero matures, he learns to live with these lost dreams by looking to a good woman and a band of brothers to provide support, to balance his individual freedom, so important in his youth, with the community that he now sees as the key to survival. The male, for Springsteen, then becomes a bit more sensitive, understanding, and ambivalent in order to accommodate the changes that must be made.

Work is a key component in Springsteen's definition of masculinity. In the American Dream, hard work earns you a better living than your parents had. People enjoy individual freedom. However, changing economic times limit these possibilities, making the dream difficult to achieve. But the band of brothers and the male hero form a strong artisanal bond of trust that allows them to survive in this new, mean world. These are the new links men rely on to make them strong. They can no longer do it on their own, and many of Springsteen's songs explore these themes of friends working together, and the importance of family helping the individual through this world. Redemption or salvation is found in three places: music, religion, and community (especially romantic love and blood brothers). Depending on the period of his songs, these provide the means for finding your way through a treacherous world. For Springsteen, it isn't just society that has gone astray; there is also a fundamental darkness in our souls that we must fight against in order to lead good, honorable lives.

But, ultimately, society has a problem. Greedy capitalism means that business owners, capitalists, and politicians don't care about working people and will leave the community in pursuit of more profit. Thus, people need to help each other and stand together in order to build a better society. Springsteen never articulates how this will happen; he explicitly sees himself as an artist and not an activist (Marsh, *Glory Days*). He also never questions the economic and political bases of American capitalism. This is the structural problem that allows Springsteen to explicitly critique society with reflective nostalgic discourses while simultaneously implicitly retaining a restorative nostalgia that refers back to the golden age of preindustrial capitalism and artisanal solidarity between workers.

Not only does Springsteen's nostalgic vision change over time as he grows older and gains experience, but he also uses multiple nostalgic discourses in his lyrics for any given period. Some of these nostalgic discourses are obviously and clearly stated, while others are implied or merely hinted at by the unstated perspective of his world-view. His vision also reflects, and has a discursive relationship with, the changing socioeconomic and political culture of modern America. Springsteen identifies himself as a poet and artist who writes about the core of America—the working-class hero—following in the footsteps of Whitman and Guthrie (Garman, *A Race* 12). Unlike Guthrie and more like Whitman, he is lyrically more of an idealist, without the socialist and more radical politics of Guthrie (Garman, *A Race* 249). Like Whitman, he believes that, as a poet, his role is to talk to working-class America, bringing the true American spirit out as we come together focused on community and healing, rather than competitive, greedy, consumptive capitalism. Today is a different time than Guthrie's, and the search for community may be as crucial as socialism and union organizing was in Guthrie's day (Putnam).

Springsteen's embrace of the working-class hero runs counter to most of our twentieth-century popular culture, which has increasingly demonized working-class characters, painting them as slovenly, lazy, and corrupt. Rather, the white-collar male is lionized: always saving the day, getting the girl, and, in today's modern world, riding off in the Beemer (Butsch 575). Springsteen fights this bias by consistently writing nuanced narratives about working-class characters, thereby giving them a depth rarely found in popular culture. I think he and his audience feel the need for truer characterizations of working Americans, and that this is part of the reason for his legendary popularity and his continued need to stay true to their stories. However, this places him in a bind: his need to embrace the working class makes it more difficult for him to recognize many of the contradictions in these characters, including the sexist and racist nature of the American construction of working-class men.

This mixed history of working-class Americans made Springsteen an obvious target for Reagan and others to appropriate in the 1980s, even though his lyrics at the time explicitly criticized the direction America was taking. He overcomes some of this contradiction by the late 1980s and early 1990s by writing more sophisticated narratives embracing the perspectives of people of color and women. However, this is a difficult contradiction for him to resolve. He never fully distances himself from a fairly rigid portrayal of men and women, with men more comfortably placed in the public sphere and women at home (or in the church), in charge of nurturing their working-class heroes. The main reason for this is that he is never fully able to examine the deep contradictions inherent in American culture, between the desire for individual freedom and the desire for strong communities. Like Whitman, he envisions the solution to lie in a return to a more artisanal fraternity of democratic individuals, who work together, as a band of brothers, to overcome the greedy nature of capitalism (Garman *A Race* 237). This artisanal democracy is at the heart of his working-class restorative nostalgia, in which he never really questions the political and economic structures that underpin the American Dream/Nightmare.

Springsteen never really addresses the fundamental conflict at its heart—between individual freedom and community, though he does try to heal the rupture, as is typical in our society, with romantic love (Coontz 43). However, the gender roles in this construction reinforce the stereotype of the white, male working-class hero, with women looked upon to provide the nurturing and healing the community needs. Women are viewed as the keepers of community (family, church) with men in the marketplace, existing as free individuals. In the following, I identify five distinct periods in which Springsteen's layered nostalgia changes over the course of his career.

Period One: Setting the Scene

In this period, Springsteen figures out what he wants to talk about, establishing the background of the characters that continue throughout his music (Marsh, *Born*). In his first two albums, Springsteen finds his voice, or his muse: a focus on working-class individuals he follows in one form or another for the rest of his career. It is during this period that he and the band establish the E Street sound, and he, with the help of Landau, starts to explicitly refine his vision and write directed narratives about these kids in New York and New Jersey (Marsh, *Born*). The songs on *Greetings From Asbury Park, NJ* and *The Wild* celebrate the life of these kids as they start to find their way in the world, leaving their parents and racing in the street. Springsteen paints a largely restorative nostalgia for the working-class street life he experienced. He paints a romantic image of nightlife on the streets, with kids running from their parents and authorities in search of romance, adventure, and cars. There are few practical moments; Springsteen's geography is outside, in the streets, on the beach, and away from authority and responsibility. Work is almost never mentioned, but trying to find a good ride, either mechanical or female, is.

It is during this period that Springsteen introduces and establishes both cars and female bodies as prisms through which he looks at the nostalgic past. Even though these kids aren't rich, there is a sense of wealth in the form of hope and the promise that they will find their way into an American dream. This perspective reflects the improved economic status of many Americans during the 1950s and 1960s and the promise of a better future. Even though there were problems during this period, including racial tension, the Vietnam War, and social conflicts, darker themes do not appear in these early works. They begin to appear on *Born to Run* and increase in the late 1970s and early 1980s as Springsteen's nostalgic vision gets darker, more personal, and more reflective. In this early period he is writing party songs, bar band music and solid rock with classic anti-authoritarian themes that aren't dark and introspective. It is the voice of adolescents avoiding and rebelling from authority so that they can go out and have some fun—a truly 1950s-1960s theme.

It is during this period that Springsteen begins to develop themes of fraternal togetherness of the band. This is a continuing and powerful theme in his work, the band of blood brothers being central to Springsteen's sense of community. The band of brothers provides support against parents and authority and, later, against bad bosses and harsh economic downturns. It offers the support needed to carry on through broken relationships. Later, this redemptive theme is expanded to include women as well, particularly as romantic love becomes the primary means of coping with the vagaries of this harsh and changing world. In "Rosalita," women are the vehicle for much of this romantic nostalgia:

> Now I know your mama she don't like me 'cause I play in a rock and roll band
> And I know your daddy he don't dig me but he never did understand
> Papa lowered the boom, he locked you in your room
> I'm coming in to lend a hand
> I'm coming to liberate you, confiscate you, I want to be your man
> Someday we'll look back on this and it will all seem funny
> But now you're sad, your mama's mad
> And your papa says he knows I don't have any money
> Tell him this is last chance to get his daughter in a fine romance
> Because a record company, Rosie, just gave me a big advance

This gender construction is established in post-World War II America (Coontz 25). It positions the man as the provider, and the woman as the object of desire in need of rescue by her working-class hero. He wants to liberate her from her father's tyranny. As with most adolescent dreams, escape in early Springsteen means escape from parental authority, with the girl trading one man for another.

He also establishes the geography of his characters—the outdoors, suburban boardwalk life, and urban landscapes, with cars, open roads, and strong images of young, dark, loner men searching for their ideal car and girl. His men are young, vibrant, posers mimicking Hollywood heroes such as Brando, Casanova, and Dean. They all strut and preen across these urban or beach landscapes. They are usually white, though sometimes Latino, and Catholic. Springsteen's women are love objects of his Casanova dreams with very little voice or action of their own during this early period. They are literally the objects of the male actor's affections and only act to pleasure or thwart the male hero. It is a very adolescent view of women, with them controlling sexual access.

Springsteen's characters in this period are hard-playing, hard-loving, working-class heroes with restless dreams of roaming the night-time highways. These dreams are all nostalgic. It is at this point that Springsteen starts to employ a code in his lyrics that comes to mark many of his obvious nostalgic transitions. Within the transition, the character dreams of a past event only to awaken and return to the horror of daily life. It is through this narrative shift that he draws attention to the broken nature of these dreams and employs a more reflective nostalgia to critique the present.

Major Transition: *Born to Run*

Born to Run is a transition album and one that Springsteen consciously identified as such (Marsh, *Born*). In it, he explicitly pulls together and clarifies some of the images, narratives, and themes from the first two albums and starts to develop more of a critical distance from his stories. The basic nostalgia, very romantic and restorative, remains the same as the previous two albums, though we begin to get hints of a more complicated, reflective, mixed nostalgia. The reality of working comes into play for the first time in "Night," and other darker themes, more real violence and its consequences are portrayed in songs like "Thunder Road," "Backstreets," "Meeting across the River," and "Jungleland." Even more explicitly, the road and cars begin to provide the literal vehicle for a possible means of escape from these mean streets where romantic love is established as the main redemption for the loneliness, isolation, and poverty of modern society. Romantic love becomes crucial for healing the community as it fractures under the weight of the collapse of industrial production in the Northeast during the 1970s. Springsteen opens *Born to Run* with "Thunder Road" because he envisions it as his invitation to his fans to join in this new, more explicit exploration of his narratives (*VH1 Storytellers*):

> The screen door slams
> Mary's dress waves
> Like a vision she dances across the porch
> As the radio plays
> Roy Orbison singing for the lonely
> Hey that's me and I want you only
> Don't turn me home again
> I just can't face myself alone again
> Don't run back inside
> darling you know just what I'm here for
> So you're scared and you're thinking
> That maybe we ain't that young anymore
> Show a little faith, there's magic in the night
> You ain't a beauty, but hey you're alright
> Oh and that's alright with me

Period Two: Darkness Creeps In

Starting with *Born to Run*, but gaining momentum in *Darkness on the Edge of Town* and *The River*, Springsteen paints a much darker view of the world. For the first time, extensive Biblical imagery is used to explore these darker themes. They address the realization that, by the late 1970s, many of the hopes and dreams of the 1960s have been shattered and the American Dream is no longer available to all. In reacting to some of these economic changes, Springsteen starts delving into patriarchal power as symbolized by his difficult relationship with his own father and makes explicit mention of the sharp class distinctions in America. This era, 1975-1980, marks a real shift in the United States, a new depression and lethargy sparked by the loss of the Vietnam War, Watergate, and the general downturn and contraction of the American economy after the boom that followed World War II. The idea that hard work would lead to a better life was in doubt; dreams had been dashed. Springsteen addresses this reality in "Racing in the Street" with a darker, more reflective, personal and contradictory nostalgia:

> We take all of the action we can meet
> And we cover all the northeast state
> When the strip shuts down we run 'em in the street
> From the fire roads to the interstate
> Some guys they just give up living
> And start dying little by little, piece by piece
> Some guys come home from work and wash up
> And go racin' in the street.

In "Racing in the Street," Springsteen inserts two of his most commonly used prisms into his nostalgia: a love object in the form of a woman and a car. These are two powerful images of freedom and emancipation in his earlier work, but in this period they are used to focus our attention on the falling apart of life's expectations. His earlier dream of escaping with his love on the open streets of the highway has turned into a more jaded nostalgic vision in which his dreams of freedom are lost. He uses the female character, in particular, to show how the man's personal dream of freedom and community does not enhance the life of the woman. She is left with her dreams "torn," sitting on his porch thinking about what could, or should, have been. His vision of success and redemption has failed her, and he realizes it. While the lyrics could be read as romanticizing this life of hot-rodding on the street, the music is much more dirge-like and, with Springsteen's delivery, it leaves little doubt that his dream has not been found. This song can be read as an extension of *Born to Run*, in which the dream of finding love and hot-rodding it out of town to a better place in the sun is unfulfilled.

As for the relationship between the sexes and masculinity, the feminine in this song has become much more complex and less just an object of the narrator's affection. She now has her own concerns and worries. The male lead is growing up, too. He is no longer just a hot loner, riding along in his car. In fact, he now explicitly needs the love of a good woman and the bonding experience of his male friends whom he works with—that artisanal sense of working-class maleness. Part of this is due to the fact that he is aging. While being a lone male is cool in your twenties, by your thirties you just end up being lonely. This song still shows the camaraderie between men that exists in the public sphere, and that more romantic and positive nostalgia remains intact. So we have two levels of nostalgia present in this song, painting a personal and complex picture of the past, some of which is restorative, but much of which is reflective. These different types of nostalgia are representative of Springsteen's attempt, during this period, to try to understand what is going on in the world and why things aren't exactly working out the way they are supposed to for the working class and his male heroes.

Another theme Springsteen focuses on during this period is the collapse of the economy in the late 1970s. In no song does he bring these images together better, and in a more explicitly nostalgic fashion, than in *The River*. While *The River* is largely a more upbeat and varied album than *Darkness*, several songs, such as the title track, really sum up the lost dreams of Springsteen's characters. "The River" exemplifies much of the frustration and pain Springsteen feels when thinking about the nostalgic past and the broken promises made between individuals and to the working class. Two of his main prisms for viewing this reflective and personal nostalgia involve a woman and a car. Both take us back to the past and the romantic nostalgia of youth and falling in love, epitomized by her body, "tan and wet," down at the reservoir, and then to the present of the reality of how these dreams have come crashing down. In this song Springsteen expresses probably one of his harshest cries, which is the idea that a dream that doesn't come true might be worse than a lie—that there might be something else fundamentally wrong with the way we are living our lives. He doesn't offer an answer, but he does bring our attention to the fact that something is deeply wrong, and that our dreams become the physical manifestations of our nostalgia. They are our way of looking back at the past to tell us what is right, wrong, and working in our present. This overt reflective nostalgia is broken for Springsteen by this point, or at least the nostalgia that he openly talks about. But there is that basic, unspoken nostalgia still present, which he begins to come back to later. For Springsteen, the dreams of the 1960s were worse than a lie; the car is no longer the way to get out of this hell and neither is the woman. She is also trapped with him in the broken dream, and the car can't take them anywhere but to a dried-up memory—a lie that was a dream.

Period Three: Deep Despair

A much darker period dawns with *Nebraska* and, in many ways, continues with *Born in the USA*, though the latter has lighter musical arrangements. With the 1980s and Reagan, a romantic militaristic nostalgia gripped the American nation—a vision involving militant cowboys winning wars that were just and good. These images jarred with many of Springsteen's harsh lyrics, reflecting the conflicting and plummeting reality of working-class America. Consequently, Springsteen's nostalgic vision can be read as opposed to, and dialogic with, this much broader patriotic vision espoused by the Reagan administration. Part of creating a romantic nostalgia to counter the lethargy and emasculation felt by Americans during the Carter era was to retrieve the Vietnam veteran as an heroic character. Films such as *Rambo* (and, in a different way, *Platoon*) tried to tap into this strongly restorative nostalgia.

In this period Springsteen starts to address much of this appropriation of working-class veterans by the Reagan administration by explicitly writing stories about these characters. His veterans are not happy, employed, white-collar workers. In fact, they are working-class characters that can't find jobs in Reagan's new economy and are left out of the growth and expanded consumer economy of the 1980s. This much more reflective nostalgia conflicts sharply with Reagan's nostalgic vision, even as Reagan tried to appropriate the very masculine image of Springsteen in order to be identified with working Americans.

By the 1980s a new white-collar economy had convincingly left out Springsteen's working-class heroes, who continue to lose their jobs, their families, their manhood, and their lives. *Nebraska* is Springsteen's bleakest and darkest album; it explores the despair his characters experience in a much more explicitly narrative sense than before. The spare arrangements and repeated lines unify the album, making it a much more mournful work. It is also filled with criminality and violence, with men lashing out against society and whoever else is around, often taking their women down with them or leaving them behind. Men are the primary actors in these narratives, though for the first time they start to express self-doubt in ways not really seen in Springsteen's earlier work. *Nebraska* is full of loners, and this is reinforced by the fact that this album is a solo effort by Springsteen; he is the loner without his usual band of brothers there to support him. As Springsteen sings in "Used Cars":

> Now, the neighbors come from near and far
> As we pull up in our brand new used car
> I wish he'd just hit the gas and let out a cry and tell 'em all they can kiss our asses goodbye
> My dad, he sweats the same job from mornin' to morn
> Me, I walk home on the same dirty streets where I was born
> Up the block I can hear my little sister in the front seat blowin' that horn
> The sounds echoin' all down Michigan Avenue
> Now, mister, the day my number comes in I ain't ever gonna ride in no used car again.

"Used Car" explores many of the much darker nostalgic themes during this period. The car again is used as the vehicle through which we look at the past, and the vision of 1950s and 1960s America differs dramatically from the one romanticized during this period by the Reagan administration. Here, we see that our hero has been embittered by his poverty and the sense of helplessness that he will never be able to escape from the dirty streets on which he, and by extension his father, was born. This falsifies the idea that hard work will get you out of poverty. His father works hard but is continually humiliated by his inability to get out of the same dirty life that he has led. And there is little romantic about the love between his parents. They do not seem particularly close or happy, but rather each continues to play out the role they were given. By extension, we feel the hopelessness of the lead character's life continuing the same way. The boy is trapped in the same dead-end job and town in which his dad was born, and must continue to act out the same masculine tale, humiliation and all. This nostalgic vision is a dark one, very personal and conflicted, and at odds with the romantic, restorative nostalgia about the 1950s and 1960s that was popular at this time.

Born in the USA continues with many of the same themes, though set to a rockier, more anthemic sound. The band is back to support Springsteen, and some of the rays of personal responsibility and hope that start to emerge on the album reflect this camaraderie and return to community. By contrast, *Nebraska*, in its own way, is an exploration in individual freedom when taken to the exclusion of the community and anything else. So the characters have more hope on *Born in the USA*, or are at least willing to continue plugging along. The analysis of class differences and the critique of capitalism are also weaker on this album, as people come to accept that they must make do with what they have. In that sense, it is a more defeatist album. Part of this is reflected in a stronger sense of romantic nostalgia on *Born in the USA*—an element that is missing on *Nebraska*. Springsteen's nostalgic elements continue to be complex and multilayered, though the underlying nostalgia continues to be restorative with romantic and brotherly love are presented once again as means of redemption—means through which the community can be resurrected and individuals supported through tough times.

"No Surrender" from *Born in the USA* is an explicit statement of the romantic nostalgia that Springsteen articulates. It focuses on the importance of friendship and camaraderie among a band of brothers working together, doing their craft, and maintaining the community. In this particular song, the elements are very masculine and nostalgic; it is a view back to the past of a couple of kids who bond together to protect themselves from their mean peers and authority. These same brothers remain committed to supporting each other through all they encounter, even if their dreams break down. The song also alludes to the fact that something darker has crept into their lives; their romantic dreams have broken down, though the singer calls for these dreams to continue with the support of his lover, if not of his blood brother. The images are strongly masculine, and the language is quite militant as the two blood brothers refuse to surrender and continue, like soldiers, to never forget the fight. Youth is an important element of this romantic nostalgia–a lost innocence that allowed the two of them to continue the good fight before they realized their dreams might fail. While some elements are a bit ambiguous in this nostalgia for the past, fundamentally the song intimates that both romantic love and the camaraderie of companions are key to survival in this mean world. In the next period, the main focus will shift to exploring the complexities of romantic love and the important redemptive role that women provide for the working-class hero.

Period Four: Romantic Love

In this period, there is a radical change in Springsteen's lyrics and music. He is no longer performing with the E Street Band, so many of his anthems and bar-room songs are gone. He also has divorced, remarried and had children, so his songs are often less narrative in structure and focus instead on the complexity of marriage, relationships, and the responsibility of being a father. This period sees real changes in the way Springsteen deals with the hyper-masculine image—the often rather boastful and violent nature of men on his earlier albums. His men in these later works are more thoughtful, emotional, conflicted, and generous to the women in their lives. They are searching for an answer to what life means, and part of this answer is life with a family. But there is also enough cynicism tied to this concept of romantic love and domestic bliss that it won't just be a simple answer of finding the perfect person and living happily ever after. There is a new understanding that relationships are difficult to keep going, and that we often lose each other along the way.

At the same time, the nostalgic turns on these albums—particularly on *The Ghost of Tom Joad* and *Devils & Dust*—are much less obvious and less frequent than in the works of the middle two periods. Lyrically, they deal much more with the emotions involved with family life and love than with issues of the past. Indeed, much of the material on these albums is more personal than on many of Springsteen's earlier works, reflecting his own personal concerns rather than commenting directly on larger societal issues. There are also fewer songs invoking artisanal nostalgia in the form of the band of brothers. The absence of these themes may be due to the fact that Springsteen recorded the songs without most of his prototypical band of brothers, the E Street Band, during a period when he was exploring love and family life. While his male characters in these albums continue to work hard, class issues and the working life are downplayed. Men are still the public face of the family, with women almost exclusively located in the home. But it is this home life that is the focus of the majority of these songs.

There is a real shift in the construction of masculinity. Male characters are more mature. They posture and pose less, and are more eager to try to develop a complex relationship with a woman. Men are no longer lashing out as much or as violently, nor do they seek the open road. They are ready to settle down and find a partner. Jealousy and doubt are much stronger themes on these albums, as men wrestle with more complex relationships. Women are more often seen as teachers or as guides for men through turbulent times. But they are instructors in emotion. They do not have careers outside of the home unless it is as prostitutes or waitresses. Their primary responsibility is as mothers and wives—as the person who provides the emotional core for the family. They provide men with the means for emotional and spiritual survival in a difficult world.

The car is no longer one of the main vehicles for emancipation or nostalgia. In many of the songs of this period the nostalgic moments are still triggered by females, though places also play a role as our heroes explore the memories of their pasts. As Springsteen sings in "Walk Like a Man":

> I remember how rough your hand felt on mine
> On my wedding day
> And the tears cried on my shoulder
> I couldn't turn away
> Well so much has happened to me
> That I don't understand
> All I can think of is being five years old following behind you at the beach
> Tracing your footsteps in the sand
> Trying to walk like a man

This nostalgia is still personal, but it has lost most of the latent sense of darkness characteristic of the earlier periods. It is a questioning nostalgia, one in which some of the romantic framework of the past still exists, but carrying a doubt that relationships and dreams will come to fruition the way that we hope. However, there is no hopelessness. These characters are still hoping that, with a little help, they will be able to make it through, even if they have problems and failures. There is a strong sense that, with a little luck, it is now possible to succeed. While the masculine tone is still quite virile, men are much more doubtful of what the future will bring. With maturity has come more of an understanding of the problems faced by Springsteen's father and how he had to cope with some of the challenges life sent his way.

Period Five: Ambivalent Darkness

In Springsteen's most recent period we see a mix of images in his music. While he still explores the complexity of romantic love in American society, he has moved back to some of the darker themes that haunted his earlier work. Starting with *The Ghost of Tom Joad*, Springsteen returns to the sparser arrangements and the more detailed narratives he used on *Nebraska*. While most of the themes in *Tom Joad* are dark, the stories are more nuanced and contain less despair than those on *Nebraska*.

For the first time Springsteen writes detailed narratives of working-class male heroes who aren't white. Several of his characters are Latino, and he follows a new theme on these albums, involving tracing the new and expanded waves of immigration to the United States in the 1990s. He describes a different American Dream—the one belonging to immigrants coming to America in search of streets paved with gold. But the reality of this new life for Latinos isn't a prosperous one. They are hired in low-wage jobs and hunted by the INS (*la migra*). Much like the 1980s and the booming American economy that included some but left out many others, the high-tech boom of the 1990s excluded many of Springsteen's working-class heroes. During this period he expands his working-class hero to include men of color, something he rarely did in his earlier work. It is indeed a new era.

While Springsteen employs more overt nostalgia in this period than in the previous one, he uses less than he did in the early 1980s. Most of the current narratives take place in the present, and when they do have a deeper time construct they often employ a more historical approach (as in "Youngstown") than in earlier periods. When Springsteen does overtly use nostalgia, it is reflective in nature and not particularly romantic. As in the previous period, cars are no longer the prism through which he establishes these reflective nostalgic discourses. However, women remain a crucial prism for his nostalgia, reflecting their primary role as redemptive figures for his working-class men. These nostalgic turns are often transitioned through the use of dream periods.

Two themes that are much more common are the overt use of religious imagery and military references. Although religious imagery has been present in Springsteen's music since the mid-1970s, many of these later songs explore religious images much more explicitly. His songs also now feature military figures from the Gulf War, Bosnia, and the Iraq War, reflecting the increased number of American military engagements and the consequent increase in militarism in American culture. Springsteen explicitly reflects upon such themes in "The Hitter":

> Now the gray rain's fallin' and my ring fightin's done
> So in the work fields and alleys I take all who'll come
> If you're a better man than me then just step to the line
> Show me your money and speak out your crime
> Now there's nothin' I want, Ma, nothin' that you need say
> Just let me lie down for a while and I'll be on my way
>
> Tonight in the shipyard a man draws a circle in the dirt
> I move to the center and I take off my shirt
> I study him for the cuts, the scars, the pain,
> Man nor time can erase
> I move hard to the left and I strike to the face.

In "The Hitter," the critical nostalgia contains dark references and unromantic images of a dark, antisocial man. This socially broken loner is positioned against the unspoken nostalgia of a community that functions well, with cooperation between men who have the love of fine women. This restorative nostalgia looks back to a prior utopia in which artisans worked hard and maintained brotherly relationships. It contains a strong notion that a return to this more authentic, brotherly relationship between workers will help rebuild and heal the rifts in the community, our democracy, and America in general.

This restorative nostalgia has become more common in Springsteen's lyrics at a time when he explicitly re-explores darker themes, with a more explicit reflective nostalgia. This tension between conflicting nostalgic discourses, while present throughout most of his career, becomes even more starkly drawn in this current period.

Conclusion

The evolution of Springsteen's use of nostalgia through these five periods has reflected his growing authority as a voice for the working class and as a critic of modern American capitalism. However, he now finds himself caught in a contradiction caused by his inability to critique the underlying constructions of American capitalism and working-class Americans. Without being able to articulate a critique of a system that exploits his working-class hero and leaves him out of the American Dream, he has to rely on this preindustrial vision of fraternal community for hope. But with the vision of a band of artisans working together to create both capitalistic relations and community bonds comes cultural baggage, including a narrow role for women and minorities in America. In addition, this vision includes the fundamental contradiction inherent in capitalism—that of individual freedom and community values and of maximizing profit without exploiting workers. This unresolved tension is reflected in the multiple nostalgic discourses present in Springsteen's lyrics as he tries to come to terms with the reality of working-class Americans by applying a utopian vision of capitalism that perpetuates the same fundamental inequalities he critiques.

PART II
"There's a Sadness Hidden in that Pretty Face": Springsteen and Gender Identity

Chapter 5

"Come to the Door, Ma": Mothers, Women and Home in Springsteen's *Devils & Dust*

Liza Zitelli

Introduction: Everybody Wants to Have a Home

In a televised interview, Sweden's rock journalist Per Sinding-Larsen asked Bruce Springsteen about the prevalence of mothers and sons on his then most recent full-length album release, 2005's *Devils & Dust*. Larsen's line of inquiry was astute; on no other album or set of songs by Springsteen is the presence of the mother so strong. Springsteen, at first, made a joke of it: "I don't know, maybe it was just time it came along," he said, chuckling (Springsteen, "On his Mother"). Certainly, his joking comment made reference to the great weight that he has given to fathers in his work and the relative lack of attention he has, in contrast, given to mothers. Indeed, fathers have always been a strong presence in Springsteen's work: "Independence Day," "Adam Raised a Cain," "Factory," and "Walk Like a Man," to name only a few, are stories that ponder the relationship between fathers and sons as a means of understanding masculinity, tradition, and self-identity. In contrast, songs by Springsteen that revolve around mother-child relationships, have been minimal.

Yet, as Larsen noticed, on *Devils & Dust*, narrative representations of motherhood, the mother's body, and mother-child relationships fill more of the lyrical and narrative space than any other thematic element on the album. In the interview, as Springsteen continued his train of thought about why mothers became a forceful trope on the album, he worked his way inductively towards some bit of insight that would help answer the question:

> Home. The sense of home is embodied in the mother's voice, and in her body, and in her hair—the scent of her hair, and skin. I think everyone's real sense of home and place and their essential elemental beginning goes back to the experience they had with their mother. That's why it's so primal and so fundamental, and everyone instantly understands the drama that you're singing about when they hear it. (Springsteen, "On his Mother")

These insightful words by Springsteen begin to hone in on the meaning and significance of the image of the mother on the album. In what follows, I examine how and why Springsteen, after largely neglecting mothers and motherhood in most of his writing, finally turns to the image of the mother in *Devils & Dust*. Examining his songs as cultural texts, and using a gender studies framework, I hope to demonstrate that Springsteen's use of the mother as a trope reflects a cultural desire to understand, and perhaps reconnect with, the roots and origin of our identities, at a time in our history—as we were evaluating our recovery from 9/11—when our national, personal, and cultural identities had been shaken to their core.

"Papa Go to Bed Now": Founding Fathers and Mothers

Prior to *Devils & Dust*, Springsteen's work focused more on the sense of identity derived from our fathers than the identity derived from our mothers. A quintessential example of a song that examines the father-child relationship appears on *The River*, released in 1980. In "Independence Day," a son talks to his father about growing up, getting out, and moving on, saying, "They ain't gonna do to me / What I watched them do to you." The "they" and "them" in the song refer abstractly to the patriarchal system of power that governs us, dividing us and entrenching us into class and gender roles, shaping us into people we didn't necessarily want or choose to be. The song captures the feelings of pain, confusion, and regret as a son reflects on the differences between him and his father: "Now I don't know what it always was with us / We chose the words, and yeah, we drew the lines / There was just no way this house could hold the two of us / I guess that we were just too much of the same kind." These lines reflect the inevitable emotional conflicts that exist in this patriarchal American culture, as sons must make emotional breaks from their fathers and their childhood homes in order to move forward, set up their own household, and become entrenched in the roles the system has set up for them. Choice and liberty seems limited in this system, though the narrator breaks away still hoping for a chance of freedom and self-determination.

With its title alluding to the national holiday, the song "Independence Day" examines becoming a man in American culture; it explores what it is to have been raised by an American father, both in the familial sense and in the metaphorical sense of a nation whose ideas of masculinity are embedded in its narrative origins of the "founding fathers." There is grief, and understanding, in the song, but there is no real resolution—just resignation to the way things are and have always been: "All men must make their way, come Independence Day." The reference to the holiday Independence Day, America's birthday, aligns manhood and masculinity with the narrative of America itself, as Springsteen shrewdly suggests that American masculine identity is closely tied to the entrenched ideological structures and social roles that formed our nation. The image of the house that cannot hold more than one grown man is a representation of the limitations of this patriarchal system in which a man cannot express himself fully: "Papa now I know the things you wanted that you could not say." With its haunting melody and somber instrumentation, the song laments the way in which men must become men in American culture.

After years of scrutinizing the father's impact on our identity formation, Springsteen finally turns to narratives about the mother in order to view an alternative origin story for our identities. In *Devils & Dust*, the common thread that links each male character in his search for identity is that he is trying to locate what is familiar inside of him after having been, in many ways, fragmented, shattered, or removed from what he loves or has loved. Springsteen's turn to the mother's body reflects not only a nostalgic desire for something familiar, but also a primal desire for some essential recognition of the self. The title track on *Devils & Dust* seems to suggest that this search for something primal and essential in the self may just be a phantom, despite the many ways in which we may try to represent our own essence to ourselves. However, the rest of the album offers a counter-position to the idea of this phantom core of humanity and goodness that we may fabricate for ourselves. Indeed, the album as a whole calls attention to the embodied experience of having, in some way or another, *come from* our mother's body. Through narrative, Springsteen emphasizes the uniqueness of this experience, rather than looking at the mother-child relationship as a broad monolithic and disembodied cultural category of social relationship. The album ponders the cultural value of the universality of this embodied experience. *Devils & Dust* depicts the mother-child relationship as one that has essential value in contributing to our identities as individuals, as gender populations, and as a nation.

Most fans and critics think of *Devils & Dust* as a collection of folk-style songs—some written for the album, some written at previous points in Springsteen's career but never released—that were collected on this record. It is true that the songs from *Devils & Dust* were not written all at once. A few songs, such as "The Hitter," "Long Time Comin'," and "All the Way Home," had been written previously, some during the mid-1990s when Springsteen was writing *The Ghost of Tom Joad*. These songs "found a nice home" on *Devils*, as Springsteen tells his audience at a *Devils & Dust* tour rehearsal show (Pirttijärvi, "Intro to 'Long Time Comin'"). But despite the scope in chronology that the songs represent, the album does project a coherent exploration of home, through a re-visioning of the woman-as-mother that was important to Springsteen's vision of both himself and the community at large at the time of its release. It is telling that Springsteen uses the phrase "found a home" about the songs on *Devils & Dust*—the album is, after all, about what happens when we lose connection to, and our identification with, our sense of home.

But what does it mean, from a gender studies point of view, for a woman's body—a mother's body—to be seen as the embodiment of home? I believe that there are cultural consequences (be these consequences valuable or limiting, or both) to equating any cultural group symbolically to a concept. But, in particular, what are the consequences of envisioning the figure of the mother as symbolic of the home? In stark contrast to the portraits of women as mysteries in the night and out on the road on earlier albums, *Devils & Dust* meditates on woman as mothers, in relation to homes, childhood, and images of domestic life. The audience does not imagine "pretty little girls" in "blue jeans so tight" on *Devils & Dust*. In contrast to the images of girls and women on, for example, albums from *Greetings From Asbury Park, NJ* to *Born in the USA*, the images of women on *Devils & Dust* call forth portraits of working women, middle-aged, having gone through experiences in their lives that may have grayed their hair or made them slightly careworn.

Yet there is beauty in the care with which the men on *Devils & Dust* talk about, remember, and describe their relationships, lives, and homes with their women. In "Long Time Comin'," the character's partner is pregnant, and the narrator takes pleasure in feeling the life inside her as he "lay[s] [his] hands across [her] belly." In "Maria's Bed" and "Leah" there is the sense of longing for, and contentment in, domesticity, as the character expresses the value and pleasure in being in an intimate, private space with his partner—in building a home. These songs, though told from a male perspective, depict characters who understand women as subjects rather than objects.

The songs that deal explicitly with mother-son relationships constitute the heart of the album, portraying a collection of voices belonging to subjects who have been protected, failed, and loved by mothers. "Black Cowboys" explores a son's diminishing relationship to his mother as he grows older. "Silver Palomino" reflects on the death of a young boy's mother. "Jesus Was an Only Son" examines the reciprocal nature of a mother-child relationship, celebrating both the gifts a mother gives to her child as well as those that a child gives to his mother. In "The Hitter," a boxer returns home at the end of his sinful life, searching for redemption in a conversation with his mother. The central image of the album is the home, and that image is created and embodied by the image of the mother. Through a close reading of these and the other songs on the album, I hope to reveal Springsteen's contribution to our cultural understanding of the mother's role in the creation of our personal, social, national, and global identities.

Critical Positions and Backgrounds

The reception, both popular and critical, of *Devils & Dust* at the time of its release was mixed. The review from *Paste* magazine praised the album: "*Devils & Dust* is remarkably self-contained and perfectly linear: here is the aftermath of *The Rising*, when the plains go quiet, the windows shut and we pray, pause, and plot our next move" (Petrusich para. 10). *Rolling Stone* gave the album 3.5 stars out of 5, in contrast to the many 5-star ratings it has awarded Springsteen's work. *The Village Voice* called it "long and boring and preachy" (Phillips para. 3). The mixed reviews paralleled the lukewarm reception of the release, relative to other Springsteen releases, by the Springsteen fanbase. This kind of reception undermined the important contribution that the album makes in terms of reflecting important gender and identity politics that were going on at the time of the release. The songs on *Devils & Dust* are Springsteen's first collective attempt to use the narrative elements of his songwriting to create mothers and their children as embodied subjects with agency, history, and voice. The album's strides in creating this narrative picture of the role of motherhood in a nation which strongly identifies with the images of its founding fathers warrants further attention by fans, critics, and scholars alike.

Although *Devils & Dust* has been in no way ignored by recent scholarship on Springsteen, there have been few sustained readings or arguments made about the album's portrayal of gender that would help position it as an essential and transformative contribution to Springsteen's body of work. Most of the critical conversation about *Devils & Dust* has centered on the spiritual images and narratives on the album. For example, framed in an analysis of parallels and intersections between Springsteen and Flannery O'Connor's work, Irwin Streight insightfully discusses the internal spiritual struggles and Catholic imagery on the album, asserting that the album provides us with Springsteen's "most Catholic collection" of his songs (72). Michael Kobre refers to *Devils & Dust* in his discussion about parallel narratives of faith in the works of Springsteen and Walker Percy (Kobre). Past discussions about gender and Springsteen have either been written before *Devils & Dust* was released or have not addressed the significance of the way in which women are figured on this album. This study aims to position *Devils & Dust* as essential to understanding gender in the evolution of Springsteen's works.

Journalistic responses to *Devils & Dust* also focused on its return to a more introspective and folk sound after the uplifting, full-band response to 9/11, *The Rising*. Often, critics and journalist group this album with Springsteen's two other "folk" albums, *Nebraska* and *The Ghost of Tom Joad*, viewing each as introspective narratives that contribute both musically and lyrically to the story of American identity.

There was also some discussion by journalists, at the time of the album's release, about the spiritual themes in the album. In his *New York Times* article, published in conjunction with the release of *Devils & Dust*, Jon Pareles wrote, "Soul and spirit, God and family; that's what's on his mind in the quiet, folky songs on *Devils & Dust*" ("Bruce Almighty" para. 1). Pareles' assessment links *Devils & Dust*'s spiritual themes with the images of family and motherhood on the album. He asserted that "*Devils & Dust* is Mr. Springsteen's family-values album, filled with reflections on God, motherhood and the meaning of home" (para. 5). Pareles also addressed "the other kind of love" on the album: the love between a mother and son: "Half the songs on the album, like 'Jesus Was an Only Son,' ponder relationships between mothers and sons. Mr. Springsteen has written often about his uneasy ties to his father, who died in 1998, but rarely about his mother, who is still, he said, 'alive and kicking'" (para. 22).

Pareles' biographical reference to Springsteen's parents highlights the imbalance of songs about fathers and mothers in Springsteen's work. His comment implicitly wonders if Springsteen's turn to the mother as a trope had to do in some way with Springsteen working out his own personal issues as a son to his mother, after so many years of emotionally and psychologically working out issues with his father through his songs. Indeed, there are only a handful of songs in Springsteen's body of work that are written directly about his own mother. One such song is "The Wish," released on *Tracks* in 1998. This song was famously written as a thank-you to Springsteen's own mother, with Springsteen implicitly admitting that songs about his father or fathers in general showed up everywhere in his music, but that there were no songs for his mother.

"The Wish" chronicles the daily life and grind of a typical New Jersey working mother (not a Jersey housewife) living in the 1960s, from the perspective of a loving and admiring son. It's a quiet, wistful, and graceful song, set at Christmas time, and stands as a type of love song that is rare—one to someone other than a romantic partner. Springsteen tributes his mother as offering him protection from the world's harshness and cruelty: "If pa's eyes were windows into a world so deadly and true / You couldn't stop me from looking but you kept me from crawlin' through." With its simple melody and lyrics that are at times almost spoken rather than sung, "The Wish" gives a heartfelt and romanticized portrait of a woman through the eyes of her son:

> I remember in the morning, ma, hearing your alarm clock ring
> I'd lie in bed and listen to you gettin' ready for work
> The sound of your makeup case on the sink
> And the ladies at the office, all lipstick, perfume and rustlin' skirts
> And how proud and happy you always looked walking home from work.

"The Wish," openly autobiographical, also reflects the limitations and emotions evoked by the distinct roles designated by American society to fathers and mothers. To the child, the father seems to represent the real world—the one that the child will one day face—whereas the mother represents a promise of hope and brightness. The mother is the quiet protector, buffering reality, keeping the home an ideal and hopeful place. Though the song portrays a mother who works outside the home, the narrator's memories of his home are filled with images and sounds of his mother.

Although "The Wish" does devote itself to the mother's role in a family and son's life, it is only one song and was not included on any formal album release; it was finally made available to the public on *Tracks*, a collection of out-takes from numerous recording sessions throughout Springsteen's career. Springsteen's use of the mother on *Devils & Dust* continues the discourse on mothers that was begun by "The Wish," yet the coherent presence of mothers on *Devils & Dust* makes it unique among Springsteen's previous and later albums. In contrast to the portrait of mothers in "The Wish," the depiction of motherhood on *Devils & Dust* is not characterized by romanticized and nostalgic notions of the mother. Rather, the album creates real characters whose interactions with mothers deepen our ability to see the mother-child relationship not simply as a broad socially constructed ideological concept, but also as a real and embodied unique interaction between two people, with real emotional, physical, and psychological consequences that shape an individual's vision of himself and his world. The album reflects a larger cultural desire to find a common and embodied sense of humanness in our journey from birth to adulthood.

"Devils & Dust": A Long Way from Home

Although the heart of the album consists of an overarching narrative about mothers and homes, the title track is set in a place described as "long long way from home" and lacks any direct image of a mother. However, this absence serves an important purpose in relation to the album as a whole, as Springsteen's character is faced with the numbing and disembodied experience a man feels when he no longer can feel a connection to the basic sense of humanity inside him. "Devils & Dust," often interpreted by reviewers and commentators as a response to the war in Iraq, reflects the internal disconnection to humanness and home that a soldier experiences when at war. Any soldier, man or woman—even those with the strongest connections to a sense of faith, home, family, and morality—may lose his or her connection to those things in the midst of war. "We're a long, long way from home, Bobbie / Home's a long, long way from us." The speaker confesses that he doesn't know who to trust. He wants to "take a righteous stand," but there is no recognition of any familiar values or humanity here at war: "When I look into your eyes / There's just devils and dust." The solider turns to the idea of God, but realizes that the fear he is feeling overwhelms anything that resembles his faith: "Fear's a powerful thing / It can turn your heart black you can trust / It'll take your God filled soul / And fill it with devils and dust." It is with this dismal image that the song ends, seemingly without hope that the soul can exist in a space not only so far from home, but also so completely disconnected from home.

However, despite the song's bleak lyrics, the music helps narrate a different side of the story. The song begins with a resonant bass sound which is then accompanied by an acoustic guitar as the story is told. Slowly, the story builds with a community of instruments, as the sounds of organ, strings, and finally a harmonica contribute to a surprisingly resounding and resolved ending. The music's build, in contrast to the lyric's grim outlook on the soul's survival, harkens to the sense of hope and salvation that are evoked in the images of home songs that follow it on the album.

Building Homes

In "All the Way Home," the second song on the album after "Devils & Dust," the premise of "home" plays a dominant role in the impetus of the song. Although written in 1991, fourteen years before the album's release, the song coheres with the album's fearless examination of a man's desire to establish a home. In the song, the character yearns for a second chance at love. His "old fears and failures" haunt him. He postulates that similar fears and failures haunt the woman he is serenading, too, alluding to the "shadow of that ring / That was on [her] finger." The image of the shadow of the ring references the failure of domestic partnership—perhaps manifesting in divorce or separation—that has become a sad hallmark of a generation's attempt at building families and homes.

The use of the tambora, sitar, steel guitar, and electric sarangi—an Indian instrument that is known to resemble the sound of a human voice— slightly dislocates the album version of the song from its Jersey shore roots,[1] which complicates the notion of "home" in the title of the album. The song plays like a fun bar song, with driving percussion and lyrics about a band trashing a Stones' song, but its thematic impulse affirms the underlying desire expressed by the narrator as well as the other male characters on the album: to find his way to what he imagines as "home," alongside a partner with whom he wants to share that home.

"Leah" is about starting a life. The images are domestic: there is the image of climbing the stairs, building a house, and starting a life. Though "Leah" isn't explicitly about mothers, the driving image of the song is the home that the narrator wants to build with his partner: "I wanna live in the same house, beneath the same roof / Sleep in the same bed, search for the same proof / As Leah." Like the earlier songs from *Tunnel of Love*, *Human Touch*, and *Lucky Town*, this song focuses on building love within the home, not searching for it on the wild and unpredictable thunder-roads. As Springsteen put it, "Well, in life and in love we are moved to create and to destroy ... and uh, you gotta get that balance right (chuckles) before anything starts working and, uh, this is a story about somebody just trying to get there, just trying to get to that place ..." (Pirttijärvi, "Intro to 'Leah'"). The final lines of the song resonate with the imagery of salvation: "tonight I feel the light I say the prayer/ I open the door, I climb the stairs ..." There is an ascent into light that evokes the feeling of spiritual uplift that the narrator is experiencing.

Another song on the album that depicts the desire to return home to a domestic partner is "All I'm Thinkin' About." Sung in Springsteen's almost haunting falsetto voice and loaded with images of rural America, the song invites us on the road with a character who can't stop thinking about getting home to his lover. The repeated phrase of "Mama go to church now, mama go to church now," followed by "Friday night daddy's shirt is torn/ Daddy's goin' downtown, daddy's goin' downtown," suggests that the domestic world from which this young adult comes may not be ideal. He knows that his mother is a church-going woman, and he alludes to his father's wild nights in town. The narrator perceives his mother's life as an attempt at virtue, but also gives hints at his father's less than virtuous life. Here, Springsteen references the stratification between men and women in the current binary gender system by which our behaviors and thoughts about ourselves are governed. The narrator's falsetto voice destabilizes the binary of gender roles, creating a character who embodies both the male and the female spirits.

---

[1]   Southside Johnny has covered the song in performance.

In "Maria's Bed," again, it is the home that is the centralized image. The hurdy gurdy in the song gives it a sweet, twangy, folky sound, and the violin and female and male background vocals contribute to its swinging country vibe, which musically references the iconic familiarity and rootedness of the American heartland. Lyrically, the bed—a symbol of sexual intimacy and domesticity—is the focus; it highlights the desire to unite with a woman not in a car or on the road, but in the home.

In the song, the driver has been on a long road-trip and is finally returning home. He sings, "Been on a barbed wire highway 40 days and nights," a length of time that alludes to the time Jesus spent fasting in the desert before he began his public ministry, a period of time during which he resisted temptations by the devil. Springsteen's reference is made playfully, but the analogy suggests that on our spiritual journeys we often leave home only to come back to it in the end. Jesus's time in the desert was necessary for him to find the meaning and purpose in his life, and allusions to 40 days and 40 nights often evoke the sense of a trying, but necessary, time in a person's life that tests the soul.

Of all the songs on *Devils & Dust*, the alignment between the female body, the home, and salvation is most prominently presented in "Maria's Bed." Springsteen often associates salvation with the female body, locating it in romantic relationships, love, and sex, as if his characters can, or at least believe they can, be redeemed through a meaningful intimate encounter with a female. In this song, the association is explicit: "I keep my soul in Maria's bed," says the narrator, suggesting that while the body may leave the home, his soul remains in his home, with the female. He goes on to say that he "drank the cool clear waters from Maria's bed," eliciting an image of the purifying and baptismal power of a woman. In addition, he says "she'll take you, mister, to the upper room," creating the idea that a woman will lead a man to heaven. The song is a man's testimony for the redeeming powers of a woman: "I was burned by the angels, sold wings of lead / Then I fell in the roses and sweet salvation of Maria's bed." I believe that Springsteen's project explores females in this way—that is, as a means to salvation—in order to critique the stratifying patriarchal structure to which our society adheres.

The man's journey of 40 days and 40 nights on the road as a truck driver rewards him with "the light of Maria's bed." The man was "Siftin' through the dust for fools [*sic*] gold, looking for a sign," and then hears from a "holy man" who gives him hope about the salvation that lies on the path ahead: "Holy man said, 'Hold on, brother, there's a light up ahead.'" He ultimately finds what he is searching for in Maria's arms: "Ain't nothin' like the light that shines on me in Maria's bed," he says, and claims, "I take my blessings at the riverhead/ I'm living in the light of Maria's bed." But what does it mean for a character to be so fully invested in the idea that he can find salvation in a woman's bed? What does that reflect about our society? The song imagines the arc of a human soul, struggling to do the right thing in the face of a difficult life and one day finding meaning and redemption by reconciling these hardships and struggles with the pleasures and fulfillment of a loving partnership with another human being. He had "run out'a luck and gave [himself] up for dead," but then got a second chance at life—a rebirth—after he "drank the cool clear waters from Maria's bed." This image of being baptized by a woman inverts the patriarchal structure embedded in Western religious traditions, in which the man and the heavenly father provide salvation. Springsteen's playful inversions suggest that there are viable alternatives to the stratifying and sometimes dispiriting gender rules which govern our society.

Being Reborn: Earth as Mother

The theme of building homes is continued in the song "Long Time Comin'." Introducing the song to his audience during a public rehearsal for the tour, Springsteen said:

> I['m] past the point of thinking I'm not gonna make some of the same mistakes that my folks made with me and, uh, uh … who the hell did I think I was? (chuckles) But kids are great because they do give you, uh, second chances of kind of sorting out the stuff from your childhood and we honor our parents by holding on to the good things and setting down the, uh, the things that may not have went so well for us, you know, that's what this song is about, it's a song called "Long Time Comin'" and uh … wrote this one a while back and it's finally found a nice home on, on the new record and uh … I'll dedicate this one to my lovely mother, this is for you … you of course are perfect (chuckles)." (Pirttijärvi, "Intro to 'Long Time Comin'"")

Springsteen's introduction illuminates his themes of second chances—perhaps even a kind of redemption—that can be created in the process of having children and building a family of one's own. A light acoustic guitar opens the song, and a reverberant voice describes earthy, rejuvenating images of the land that create the sense of possibility of new things to come. There is a joyful sense of rejuvenation in these opening lines: "Out where the creek turns shallow and sandy/ And the moon comes skimming away the stars/ The wind in the mesquite comes rushin' over the hilltops/ Straight into my arms." The narrator is encountering nature—and finding a sense of home in this encounter.

This is the first song on the album that begins to reclaim and re-imagine the earth as something motherly, fruitful, and pregnant with life—an earth that embraces and protects humanity as its children rather than an earth that leaves humanity to fend for itself. The image of the mother earth resonates here, in contrast to the barren and almost post-apocalyptic "fields of blood and stone" and "dirty wind" that appear in the album opener "Devils & Dust." In "Long Time Comin'," the song's main thematic motif is rebirth: the narrator says he will get "birth naked" and "bury my old soul / And dance on its grave," as lush female vocals sustain in the background. He is ready to celebrate a new beginning.

Although the narrator celebrates images of a motherly terrain, he also tells us, "Well, my daddy, he was just a stranger/ Lived in a hotel downtown." From this image, the audience envisions a home without a father—a home from which the father figure has been separated. "When I was a kid," he sings, "he was just somebody/ Somebody I'd see around." However, the narrator does not want to perpetuate this narrative of the absent father: "Well if I had one wish in this god forsaken world, kids/ It'd be that your mistakes would be your own/ Yea your sins would be your own." He wants to create his sense of parenthood from something natural, not from what he learned from his father's absence but from a place deep within himself. He wants to figure out parenthood using a "fresh map," not retracing the mistakes of the past, and not passing down his sins to his children.

These lines examine the consequences of a domestic setting in which the father is absent and also imagine a father who can be present in his children's lives, working as a unit with the mother instead of in a separate sphere. The character is exploring a kind of family structure that is not based on the separation of male and female but is based instead on a more all-encompassing unified spirit.

The juxtaposition in the song of the absent father with images of the motherly earth illuminates what some scholars of mythology see as a major flaw in modern society: the entrenchment of the binary division between male and female gender roles. Modern Western culture, surmise scholars, is lacking a sense of wholeness of which ancient peoples once had a grasp—a multi-dimensional, all-encompassing religion that embraces all binary forces, including male and female energies. The ancient religions of India, Africa, North America, and even Northern Europe (Celtic, Nordic) had deities that represented the full scale of the human psyche and worshipped the female gender in a way different from, but equal to, that of the male, most often in the form of a mother Earth Goddess—who, because she could bear life, represented both sexes (Leeming and Page 7).

Springsteen's *Devils & Dust* explores many Catholic images, but in "Long Time Comin'" there is divinity in the land itself. The character's reverence toward the earthly sphere in this song tunes us into a divine spirit older and more all-encompassing than the fatherly Judeo-Christian God that exists in Western consciousness—the divine mother Earth. Scholars of cultural myth and anthropological folklore consistently associate the Earth Goddess with wholeness, and see her as representing both sides of universal binaries more naturally than the patriarchal system. In their study entitled *Goddess: Myths of the Female Divine*, Leeming and Page write, "We are emerging today from the artificial polarities of the male God religions in search within ourselves and our world of the ecological wholeness of Goddess, who contains and celebrates light and dark, life and death, male and female, and whose source is in the inner depths rather than the airy heights" (3). The Goddess is described as "more than a mother goddess or fertility goddess—she appears to have been Earth and nature itself, an immense organic, ecological, and conscious whole—one with which we humans would eventually lose touch" (7). In "Long Time Comin'," Springsteen's images of a kind, nurturing earth, and a man next to his pregnant wife camping under the stars with their children, celebrate this wholeness and sense unity between man, woman, child, earth, and sky.

Springsteen's images on *Devils & Dust* continuously provide the audience with a contrast between the religions that honor the body and the female spirit and the religion that neglects the body and subordinates the female. The rigidity of Western cultures and such religions as Catholicism and Judaism can be viewed as shutting out women, setting up a society in which males are the superior sex. Fathers, brothers and sons dominate the household. The mother sacrifices, the wife serves, the daughter obeys. Scholars of myth suggest that, by neglecting to worship and appreciate and acknowledge a female divine energy in our culture, we are subconsciously reducing the status of woman in society. The Earth Goddess has disappeared from the collective consciousness of modern human culture in the West—or, to be more precise, has entered the realm of the collective unconscious. Yet, scholars suggest, "[B]y examining that life [of the Goddess], we can perhaps contribute to a reestablishment of balance within ourselves and our world" (Leeming and Page 4). Springsteen's song "Long Time Comin'" represents a yearning for this kind of balance.

These allusions to a non-Western, matriarchal divinity offer an alternative to the damaging and divisive patriarchal structures by which the Western world is governed today. The imagery in "Long Time Comin'" harks back to Native American images in which the Earth Mother, rather than a father in heaven, is honored. The image of dancing on the grave, alongside the images of an unsettled, wild American land, with its creeks and "wind in the mesquite over the hilltops" evokes the sense of ancient American landscapes, untouched and unsettled by Christian Europeans and Western social structures in which women are subordinate to men. Indeed, the Hopi Indians, of the North American Southwest, for example, use dance to "get in touch with the forces of nature that govern the world" (Jonas 26) and believed that "dance was good for the body and good for the spirit and essential to integrating the two" (26). Like the Hopi Indians—who honor a gender-balanced perspective of the universe through their own primal dance, the character in "Long Time Comin'" honors the Earth Mother.

The song's broad sweeping portraits of the starry, constellated sky create a sense of the continuity between the earthly human bodies of the man and woman and the sky above them, once again reinforcing a connection, rather than separation, between the two sexes. "Out 'neath the arms of Cassiopeia / Where the sword of Orion sweep s/ It's me and you Rosie, cracklin' like crossed wires." Even the constellations Springsteen refers to are one female and one male, creating a further allusion to the fictional narratives of gender we create in an attempt to organize our social interactions.

The man and "Rosie" are camping under the stars, in their makeshift bed, the kids are sleeping in a sleeping bag, and Rosie is pregnant. The narrator reverently observes the life inside his wife: her "breathing in [her] sleep" and the new child growing inside her. He sings, "I reach 'neath your shirt, lay my hands across your belly / And feel another one kickin' inside / I ain't gonna fuck it up this time." The images of birth, rebirth, second chances, and change are strong here. Moreover, the song creates the image of domesticity, although it is not home-based—the family is out in the wilderness, roughing it, camping, away from Western structures of society and culture. The lines almost give the sense of a new Eden: a revised Adam and Eve, creating a family, trying not to pass down the sins from the past. This new start has been, Springsteen suggests, "a long time comin'."

Exploring the Anti-Home/Anti-Mother

The analysis of mothers in *Devils & Dust* exposes many culturally relevant ideas about identity, a sense of home, bodies, gender, and even sexuality. The sexuality on *Devils & Dust* centers on intimacy, or desire for intimacy, in the home, as in songs such as "Leah," "All the Way Home," "All I'm Thinkin' About is You," "Maria's Bed," and "Long Time Comin'." However, there is one song in which sexuality is explored in a space far away from this centralized image of home. In "Reno," Springsteen's most explicitly and unapologetically sexual song in his entire song-set, a man and a prostitute have sexual relations in a hotel. On an album on which the mother emerges as the predominantly represented cultural and social figure, the song engenders especially distinct contrasting emotions and images in the mind.

As in "Maria's Bed" and "Leah," the idea of achieving salvation through sexual intimacy is still prevalent in "Reno," but the song depicts the failures of that idea rather than its power. With this song, Springsteen critiques our cultural desire to make sex and love something spiritual. He often associates the female body, or encounters with the female body, with salvation, or promises of redemption. His characters often express an implied belief that the female body offers or represents salvation. In "Reno," he shows the failures of this belief.

The opening lines of the song, "She took off her stockings/ I held them to my face / She had your ankles, I felt filled with grace," tells us that the narrator is relating his encounter with a prostitute in a hotel room to another woman. This narrative dynamic is, at first, uncomfortable for the listener; we do not often give accounts of our sexual affairs with other people to our romantic partners. Yet, as the song moves along, the man's words and images suggest the possibility that the song may be a sort of confessional prayer to his true love, Maria, from whom he is separated at least for the time being, or maybe forever. When he is reminded of Maria's body by the prostitute's similarly shaped ankles, he feels "filled with grace," suggesting ironically that, although he has found himself with a prostitute in a hotel room in Reno, his search for redemption culminates in nostalgia for intimacy with his old lover.

In contrast to the lush pastoral landscape in "Long Time Comin'," the imagery of the landscape in "Reno" is one of postmodern violence: "The sun bloodied the sky / And sliced through the hotel blinds." The bloodied sky evokes the feeling of something killed, gored to death, and the verb "sliced" evokes the sense of something severed or cut. The setting of the hotel room creates the feeling of transience, or impermanence—in contrast to the many representations of home on the album. Before his April 28, 2005 performance in Dallas, Texas, Springsteen explained, "this is a love song, it's also about not being able to handle the real thing … so you, uh … settle for something else … that doesn't work out that good either" (Pirttijärvi, "Intro to 'Reno'").

The man is realizing that this tryst in a hotel room is not satisfying—"not even close" to the best he ever had. There is a longing, there, for something else—for something he cannot get in this hotel room in Reno. The experience of the character in this story-song reflects what might happen to characters in the other songs on the album as they depart from home. He ran away from home and did not find what he was looking for.

Loss of Mother/Loss of Child

Another aspect of mother-child relationships that Springsteen explores on *Devils & Dust* is death and loss. In "Silver Palomino" the mother is represented as an angel figure in the form of a silver palomino horse. In the lyric booklet that accompanied with the CD release, under the title of the song, it reads: "A mother dies, leaving her young son to come to terms with the loss. In remembrance of Fiona Chappel, for her sons Tyler and Oliver" (9). In his rehearsal tour banter, Springsteen elaborates on the real-life family that inspired the song:

> … we had a … two best friends of my boys had a young mother and, uh, passed away at a real young age and I wanted to write a song for the two of them … uh, I wasn't quite sure how to go about it so this is kind of a song that I set in Texas and, uh, it's about a young son who loses his mom and he believes that she comes back to him at night in the form of this palomino that comes out of the mountains as he goes to bed, this is called, uh, "Silver Palomino" … (Pirttijärvi, "Intro to 'Silver Palomino'")

"Silver Palomino" is a response to the struggle to understand the loss of a mother, something that often leaves an individual wondering about the significance of their birth as well as the mysteries of death. The song explores the idea that when an individual loses his or her mother, he or she has the desire to re-create an embodied version of her. The body of the mother reigns as an all-important symbol of identity for an individual, and when the mother is lost, however early or late in life, we yearn to reconstruct that body in other ways. This song portrays a manifestation of that desire. The imagery in the song suggests that a mother's impact on a child outlives her biological existence: "The scent of your skin, mother, fills the air / 'Midst the harsh scrub pine that grows / I watch the silver palomino."

"Jesus Was an Only Son" is another song on the album that examines the impact of the relationship between a mother and child. Springsteen said:

I was sort of interested in … in Jesus as somebody's boy, Mary's, Mary's boy, what that … was like, that particular loss and, uh, also about the way that will, the human will shapes the world and, uh … and as parents, of course we always wanna protect our children from all harm and we realize pretty early on that that's an impossible job … you still do your best but, uh … I was trying to get at something … something in the human side in the story of Jesus. (Pirttijärvi, "Intro to 'Jesus Was an Only Son'")

In Springsteen's representation of mothers and sons on *Devils & Dust*, "Jesus Was an Only Son" contributes to the album's meditation on that particular relationship by attempting to humanize the hugely iconic mother-son relationship of Mary and Jesus. "A mother prays, 'Sleep tight, my child, sleep well / For I'll be at your side / That no shadow, no darkness, no tolling bell / Shall pierce your dreams this night.'" The song considers the mother's loss of a child, and observes, "Now there's a loss that can never be replaced." At the end of the song, the son offers comfort to his mother instead of the other way round: "Well Jesus kissed his mother's hands / Whispered, 'Mother, still your tears, / For remember the soul of the universe / Willed a world and it appeared.'"

Leaving Home: Severing Ties with the Mother

"Black Cowboys" is a hard-hitting song that scrutinizes the limits of the love between a mother and child in a world of harsh uncertainties. Its dark minor chords and muted guitar strums create an atmosphere of loss and sadness. The main character, Rainey Williams, is growing up "along a street of stray bullets," where kids just like him died everyday, whose "death and blood" had tragically "consecrated" his neighborhood. His mother, Lynette, tries, at first desperately, to keep him safe. The beginning verses paint a rosy picture of a dedicated mother: Rainey "always had his mother's smile to depend on," and he came home to the "warmth of her arms at the end of each day." Inside his mother's home, he is safe from the war of the inner city streets outside.

In addition to the shelter of her own body and her home, Lynette also tried to give Rainey the tools to protect himself, at least internally. She tunes him into a TV channel that "showed a Western movie everyday" and brings him "books on the black cowboys of the Oklahoma range / And the Seminole/ scouts who fought the tribes of the Great Plains." Her efforts provided an alternative world to imagine so that Rainey could escape, psychologically, the terror of his dangerous neighborhood, and perhaps dream of other possible landscapes.

We hear Lynette's voice—"Rainey, stay at my side"—but eventually he can no longer stay at her side, because she abandons her duties as a mother. The imagery darkens: "Come the fall, the rain flooded these homes / Here in Ezekiel's valley of dry bones It fell hard and dark to the ground / It fell without a sound." The landscape here is once again barren, as if preparing the audience for a mother's turn away from her child. The lyrics tell the audience that "the arms that held him were no more his home," as Lynette lets a drug dealer become the dominant figure in her home. She "took up with a man whose business was the boulevard," and her smile that Rainey had once depended on gets "dusted away." As in "Devils & Dust," the image of dust recurs in this song, suggesting that the woman and her home become ruined and destroyed; she gets "lost in the days," probably addicted to drugs herself, and becomes devoted to her lover and the substances he provides to her rather than to her son.

In a preamble to the song on tour, Springsteen said that Rainey's mother "fails him at the end" (Pirttijärvi, "Intro to 'Black Cowboys'"). The story is one of a man having to deal with the failure of his mother to keep him safe, and having to reconcile her early attempts to protect him with her eventual failure to do so. But Rainey never blames his mother: when he leaves, he stands "in the dark at his mother's bed," and kisses her goodbye. This kiss is a proclamation of forgiveness, of understanding, and of love.

The Chain-Locked Door: Barriers between Mother and Child

"The Hitter," which appears as the tenth track on *Devils & Dust*, opens with the narrator at the door of his childhood home, saying "Come to the door, Ma, and unlock the chain." It is a plea to be let into his home once again after having grown up, moved on, and become a champion boxer. He follows up with an attempt to persuade, saying, "There's nothin' I want, nothin' that you need say / Just let me lie down for a while and I'll be on my way."

Despite the claim "There's nothin' I want," these powerful opening lines create a dramatic story of a man wanting to return to a home that may not want him back. There is familiarity in the way he calls his mother "Ma," but it is almost a forced familiarity, as if by using the shortened version of the name he might fabricate an intimacy that isn't truly there. The imperative statements of "Come to the door" and "unlock the chain" sound like understated commands, evoking the sense of a man trying to exert dominance, while also inciting the quiet urgency and desperation of a man in need of approval, or even redemption. The chain-lock evokes the image of an urban home, trying feebly but earnestly to lock out strangers and predators. The man asks to be let in to "lie down for a while," saying that there is nothing more he wants, and nothing that his mother needs to say to him. The repeated image of taking his earthly rest—"Just let me lie down for a while"—suggests that the son has returned to his mother's home to die.

Along with "Black Cowboys," "The Hitter" references the moment in a son's life, and those moments that followed after, when his mother no longer provided shelter for him. In "The Hitter," the boxer says, "Restraint and mercy, Ma, were always strangers to me," and there is a slight sense of accusation here, as if he never had the opportunity to see these virtuous qualities as a child growing up. These qualities were "strangers" to him, as if he was raised in the absence of them.

"The Hitter" is a confession of a son to his mother. The sense of confession is created by the image of the mother behind the chain-locked door, listening to her son on the other side, only a thin strip of their faces visible through the crack in the door. The mother, then, is placed in the role of the priest, who must offer forgiveness or condemn the man. The man is ready to die—"My ring fighting's done," he laments—but does not know where his soul will rest. The monologue becomes a defense of his actions over the course of his life.

Springsteen commented on "The Hitter" at a public rehearsal show at the Paramount Theater, April 21, 2005:

> This is a story about a young, young kid, he, uh, gets in some trouble and he leaves home, becomes a, a boxer and becomes quite a champion and uh … shorts himself, shorts himself in the end … uh … you know, we can keep it or we can throw it away … a lot of people throw 'em away, throw 'em away, uh … I suppose it's easy to do that but, uh, anyway, so this is, uh … once again it's a song about mothers and sons, the son, he comes back through town towards the end of his life … and, uh, he has no place left to go and he goes back to his mother's house … and the whole song is a conversation that he has with his mother through a locked door … this is called "The Hitter". (Pirttijärvi, "Intro to 'The Hitter'")

In the monologue addressed to his mother, the man says, "I was no more than a kid when you put me on the Southern Queen / With the police on my back I fled to New Orleans." Here, there is a sense that he is identifying a point in his life when his mother cut ties and sent him off to become a man, without her guidance. Is there a sense of blame here? Lamentation? The fact that he was "no more than a kid" makes it seem like he was perhaps too young, in his retrospective look at his life, to be left to his own devices without his mother. As in "Black Cowboys" there is no present father figure in the man's life. He goes on to say, "I knew the fight was my home and blood was my trade." Forsaken by his mother, he can only identify "the fight" as his home. This identification is a powerful and moving image in Springsteen's song. When you can no longer identify yourself with a real place as a home, Springsteen seems to suggest, you begin to identify with actions, behaviors, and events that come to define your daily life. Springsteen's song allows us, through this dramatic encounter between a mother and son, to examine the possible consequences of the loss or lack of identification with a real, tangible home.

"Matamoros Banks": Borders, Gender and Identity

The final song of the album, "Matamoros Banks," tells the story of a man leaving one home, but imagining a new home for himself on the other side of the border. Springsteen tells the story chronologically backwards, as the man's body rises from the bottom of the river in which he has drowned. Though the song does not explicitly refer to motherhood or mothers, the imagery of the earth's relationship to the body and the soul suggest the possibility of a motherly divinity embracing the body of the man. The man gives thanks to "God" in each verse, and yet he does not speak of meeting his lover in heaven; he says, "Meet me on the Matamoros Banks." Like the images of the nurturing terrain in "Long Time Comin'," the imagery in "Matamoros Banks" subverts the image of a body rising to heaven and instead imagines the meeting of the man and woman's soul on the river bank—on the earth itself. Despite the tragedy depicted in the song, it ultimately reverberates with the image of Mother Earth embracing one of her own. The narration is told in reverse; in the first verse, the man attempting to cross the border has already drowned in the river, and his dead body has risen to the top. Then, each verse of the song traces his journey backwards, to his initial hope of crossing the border, entering a land where opportunity would abound, and reuniting with his lover. The backwards narration inverts the narrative of the American Dream, exposing it as a fictional tale, and empowering us to see it as such, rather than remaining unaware of its fiction.

Unlocking the Chain: Revising American Identity

Devils & Dust provides a counter-narrative to the illusive, and elusive, narrative of the American Dream—go West, find your opportunity, and become rich. On this album, the West is not depicted as a magical and abstract place of opportunity, but rather as a real space in which relationships are had and lost, where characters—drifters, victims, people who have lost much—can only continue, not begin, their internal search for meaning in their lives.

In *Devils & Dust*, Springsteen critiques the double-edged sword of our society's patriarchal structure by illustrating the consequences of not only the loss of the relationship with the mother/home, but also the inability to let go of the mother/home and become a self-reliant individual. Reflecting a time when American identity was being transformed and challenged by America's international politics and global economic and cultural role, *Devils & Dust* uses the mother figure as a way of representing an embodiment of home. Springsteen's turn to the use of the mother as an embodiment of home, origins, and beginnings provides an alternative to the patriarchal origin narrative to which most of Springsteen's vision has previously adhered and explored. The album's songs use multiple narratives about mothers, lovers, and journeys home, all of which express, collectively, the desire to find, and understand, the body and soul's connection to an original life source. Even in the senseless aftermath of 9/11, portraying the voices of Americans sifting through the rubble of terror and war to regain a sense of their identities, this album's exploration of mothers' and their children's journeys epitomizes the life-affirming promise and vision of Springsteen's works.

Chapter 6

Bruce Zirilli: The Italian Sides of Bruce Springsteen

Samuele F.S. Pardini

Harlem is still filled with Negroes, Italians, Puerto Ricans, Jews.

Time Magazine, 1948

What the English occasionally have the refined sensibilities to overcome, we Irish and Italians have no such problem. We come through the door fists and hearts first.

Bruce Springsteen, Rock and Roll Hall of Fame, March 2005

On June 28, 2003 Bruce Springsteen and the E Street Band closed the European leg of *The Rising Tour* in front of 60,000 people at Giuseppe Meazza San Siro Stadium in Milan. On the third level of the stadium one could spot two big signs hung by the fans. The first, written in Italian, read "Grazie Adele." The second, in English, read "This land is your land," the title of Woody Guthrie's anthem celebrating the ideal of a free and equal America that is so dear to Bruce Springsteen. Both signs recalled the fact that Springsteen is also of Italian origin. While his last name betrays the Dutch and Irish (and possibly Jewish) traces of his father's family history, his mother, Adele Zirilli, is the daughter of Italians who emigrated to the United States from the Naples area. Maternal family history is not the only Italian sign in Bruce Springsteen and his world. Three out of nine members of the E Street Band, Steven Van Zandt, Danny Federici, and Springsteen's wife Patti Scialfa are also of Italian origin. Italian blood runs in a few of Springsteen's acknowledged major musical influences: Dion and the Belmonts in the first place, but also The Young Rascals, Frankie Valli, Mitch Ryder, and, last but not least, the man himself, Frank Sinatra, the singer from New Jersey, as mama Adele pointed out to young Bruce when for the first time he heard Ol' Blue Eyes's voice coming out of a bar's juke-box in his native Freehold, New Jersey. Springsteen calls the music he makes with the E Street Band Italian. Italian is the rhythm of the diction when he sings songs such as the studio version of "Backstreets." Italian is his body language.

However, none of these signs identifies this side of Springsteen's heritage as much as his Catholic upbringing does. For if Bob Dylan has always been mythically Jewish no matter the number of conversions he has undertaken, Springsteen has always been culturally Italian. One only needs to consider the redeeming symbolism he assigns to water and light in his lyrics. An Irish-American writer of Catholic upbringing would struggle to use them in the way Springsteen does. In

F. Scott Fitzgerald's *The Great Gatsby*, Myrtle Wilson is killed during daylight, while Gatsby is found shot dead in his swimming pool. It is something that Springsteen could hardly conceive, I think. In "Matamoros Bank," the song that closes *Devils & Dust* and one of the most graphic and disillusioned songs in his entire catalog, he tells the story of a dead immigrant starting from the end in order to turn the river that killed this immigrant at the beginning from a symbol of death into the symbol of the promise of a better life in the final section.

Being Italian-American, however, pertains to Springsteen's cultural imagination as much as it belongs to American history. That is, it belongs to the way in which it defines his politics. This I see embodied in Springsteen's subverted representation of his prime *female* character of choice, the one who carries the name of the Catholic archetypical figure *par excellence*, Mary. Mary constantly recurs in an interconnected and interrelated number of linguistic variations in his songs: from the Mary of "Mary Queen of Arkansas" and the Mary Lou of "Does This Bus Stop at 82nd Street?" to the Mary who launched Springsteen's career, the Mary of "Thunder Road," originally an Italian character as we shall see, via the Mary of "The River," the Maria of "Highway Patrolmen," that of "Maria's Bed," and a few more that I will mention along with some other female characters. This woman is the center of Springsteen's politics summed up by the words on the two signs at San Sirio Stadium. It is the politics of sharing ("This land is your land"), recognition of the Other, especially the female other ("Grazie Adele"), and historical memory (Woody Guthrie and Springsteen's Italian heritage as symbols of musical traditions, working-class origins, and immigrants' struggles in America). Mary embodies that open community of different and equal people that Springsteen has been creating over the years. Gradually, he has intertwined it with the historical memory of his native country in the forms of the musical references, the places, and the character of his music. Through the Mary character, he has given voice and visibility to a different class of people, who represent the (re)construction of a set of causal relations that recalls the personal and collective history evoked by those two signs at San Siro Stadium. It is the history of the subaltern and the dispossessed whose human condition bridges the subjective differences without denying them. As such, it is also one that subverts the established American identity traditionally based on the paternalistic, male myths of independence as individualism, unconditioned social mobility, and political equality that supposedly all Americans would share—and, which historically originates in the polished version of the myth of the frontier that gave birth to the myth of the self-made man.

In a nutshell, this vision of a different country and a plural identity represented by the Mary character has been manifest ever since Springsteen's early recording career. Starting with *Greetings From Asbury Park, NJ*, Springsteen has used a Mary character in ways that either consciously or unconsciously clashed with (and thus challenged) the established identity of the Protestant white British heritage which favors men over women and traditionally portrays women as either wounded or wounding creatures, but hardly as autonomous, complex, and fully mature subjects. He did this first of all by subverting the sexually annihilated and socially elevated image of Mary that dates back to feudal European aristocratic Catholicism and has entered the collective psyche of the West through a myriad paintings and sculptures. In "Mary Queen of Arkansas," the boy-speaker, a lonely acrobat who foreshadows the lonely rider of "Born to Run," sings *to* Mary that she was not born for acting like a queen, the *locus classicus* that a male-controlled Catholic Church assigned to Mary in order to neutralize her gender and secure its power over the centuries (Hamington).

Through the devaluation of Mary's classic role, Springsteen re-inscribes and re-evaluates in her the one element that makes her queen in the first place—her hidden womanhood. Mary is no longer a desexualized, romanticized queen. The subversion of her classic trope humanizes her and allows Springsteen to challenge fixed notions of gender that would strike fear into any institutional Catholic, especially men. No longer wrapped around and trapped in a sentimentalized status, no longer sexually neutralized, Mary is said to be neither "man enough" for him "to hate" nor "woman enough for kissing" (Springsteen, *Songs* 11). In an almost Manichean fashion, Springsteen divides ethics and genders—two elements that, along with work, will persistently recur throughout the songs that present a Mary character as well as throughout his production as a whole. On one side, he assigns a negative abstract connotation to men; on the other, he pairs women with the kiss, the prime symbol of physical unity between two human beings and usually the act that precedes and leads toward sexual union, as well as the symbol of male betrayal in the Christian tradition. It is as if the origin of togetherness, of unity, both spiritual and physical, which stands at the heart of any community, beginning with the micro-community represented by a couple, held a feminine gene for Springsteen.

Yet this picture is presented from a male standpoint. Rather than being shared, power and responsibility are still in male hands. In "Mary Queen of Arkansas," the decision to either hate or kiss is the boy's. In addition, the song ends with a traditional American image of male escapism that genders work and responsibility while it relegates Mary to the margins, denying her both subjectivity and freedom. The boy sings that *he* can get a good job in Mexico, of all places, so that *they* will be able to honestly start anew. Here, Mary's humanization does liberate her of a traditional trope of both high and popular culture. Nonetheless this change is at the service of male escapism, although in the form of a search for unity that Springsteen locates somewhere outside the boy's original space, across a geographical national border that is also a border of his human condition which he equates in turn with a good job that only escape seems to be able to guarantee. This Springsteen presents as a given fact rather than as an ideological construct, which is what makes it an ideological position in the first place.

The same interconnected dichotomy returns in "Does This Bus Stop at 82nd Street?" The song begins with the narrator telling the bus driver not to trust adult men who walk with canes, objects that traditionally indicate phallic power, rigid order, and masculinity (Faulkner's final scenes of *Sanctuary* come to mind), as if men somehow embodied a dangerous force. Here, however, Springsteen begins to empower and differentiate the Mary character, inscribing into it multiple identities and an urban working-class environment. He overlaps it with ethnic identities that signal both Mary's and her men's working-class environment. Mary is first a Broadway Mary and then a Hispanic Mary Lou who lives in an urban space—specifically, in New York City's Harlem, the racially and ethnically diverse working-class district originally inhabited for the most part by Italians, Puerto Ricans, and African-Americans, and later by African-Americans and Hispanics. The ethnic and racial composition changes, but the working-class condition remains because the latter identifies the former in America. The dream of a good job in Mexico of "Mary Queen of Arkansas" is now the job of dock workers who dream. At the same time, Springsteen turns Mary Lou into the messenger of hope, a secular affirmation of life. To the *Daily News* which asks her for dope she replies that the dope is the very fact that hope is still alive, as Reverend Jesse Jackson would have it. Then she throws a rose—the ultimate Catholic symbol of hope that has been paired with a woman by Western culture at least since Dante— to a young matador.

   The alignment of men with escapism and hate seems to spring from these men's marginal existence, either dreamed or lived, which is always uncertain and contains no certain promise, as well as from their working lives that seem to cause, or at least to be a fundamental part of, this instability. Springsteen will make its meaning fully explicit in his fourth album, *Darkness on the Edge of Town*, a title that combines the metaphorical Catholic darkness of a working-class existence with the liminal, urban space of a community in which instability is the permanent starting point. Later works, such as *The River* and *Nebraska*, will deepen this concept almost to the point of the community's complete disintegration. Here, the metaphorical darkness first takes the form of geographical otherness, of Mexico, and then of the representation of the harbor front (or the working-class and partly Italian-American *On the Waterfront*?) as a working site. What highlights this sense of otherness are the different ethnicities of a woman named Mary, Mary Lou or Maria, who is empowered with a secular hope for salvation and freedom that resides neither in the liminal space inhabited by men nor in male escapism. It lies in either a Hispanic Mary Lou or a sexualized Mary whose deceiving feature is her color rather than her gender. In fact, what makes Mary deceiving in "Mary Queen of Arkansas" is precisely the white color of her skin. Though she is initially marginalized, she carries within herself, within her identity, the multiple origins of an otherness that, in terms of both history and geography, in terms of identity, originates from an historical outside that lives inside America rather than a geographical, spatial outside that leaves her. Springsteen, the grandchild of southern Italian immigrants, brings this otherness into his own universe through the Mary character with whom he has just started to build his own community. In both songs she stands in opposition to the liminal space that the male characters would like to cross. In "Mary Queen of Arkansas" she is still at the margins; in "Does This Bus Stop at 82nd Street?" she occupies a central position that seems to define the male liminal space by way of contrast. Whereas the male narrators seek to go beyond their original geographical and working space, she comes from outside and becomes the center of the space which they share and which the men want to abandon.

These same themes and contexts return in "Thunder Road," the song Springsteen called an invitation to the journey of his music and the song that really turned Mary into a central character in the work of the New Jersey native. It is *this* Mary that Springsteen would develop in the years ahead. At first, there would seem to be no trace of any plural otherness or centrality whatsoever in this Mary. What seems to prevail in the song is a language heavily charged with words such as "vision," "crosses," "saviors," and "redemption" whose parataxis denotes a Catholic imagery. However, the Mary of "Thunder Road" was in fact initially called Angelina, an Italian name widespread among the lower classes of Southern Italy, especially of the Neapolitan area where Springsteen's Italian family originates from. The religious trace of the name, the "angel" of the first part of the name, notoriously conceals sex, while the diminutive "—ina" indicates both her youth and marginal hierarchical position within her family. The Italian-American female writers Gigi Marino and Maria Mazziotti Gillan each used the same name as the title for one of their stories, focused on lower-class Italian-American women, family, gender, and historical memory. Angelina characters also appear in various classics of Italian-American literature such as *Christ in Concrete* by Pietro Di Donato, *Mount Allegro* by Jerre Mangione, and that forgotten masterpiece titled *Maria* (indeed!) by Michael De Capite. The same name is in use among African-Americans. Paul Laurence Dunbar, whose poem "We Wear the Mask" would later serve as a kind of inspirational subtext to Springsteen's "American Skin (41 Shots)," wrote a "poem" titled "Angelina" which celebrates the subverting and redeeming power of music and dance, of festive times, and receives the blessings of the Lord. Springsteen's main tradition, however, is that of popular music. Thus one would be inclined to think that he took the name from Dylan's "Farewell Angelina." Or perhaps from "Angelina," a song that saw the light of day on *The Bootleg Series*, where the Jokerman sings that he knows what has drawn him to Angelina's door. One of Harry Belafonte's calypso songs is also titled "Angelina." Yet Angelina is also the name of the waitress at the pizzeria in the hit by the same title that entered millions of American households through the radio in the 1950s and 1960s, sung by the dean of Italian-American singers, the king and disseminator of swing and Elvis's acknowledged prime source of inspiration, Louis Prima.

I do not know whether Springsteen was aware of this "musical tradition" of Angelina when he composed "Thunder Road.". Though I suspect he was, it nonetheless seems to me to be of no relevance. What matters is that the woman who he is about to turn into the most important female character of his songwriting career is a figure that once again carries within herself a plurality of historical identities in terms of ethnicity, race, and social conditions identified by the tradition of popular culture and music she belongs to. She belongs to history before she belongs to religion and myth.

Through the transformation of Angelina into Mary, which he accompanies and operates with a rhetoric that betrays a Catholic background, Springsteen has Mary taking upon herself an interrelated double function. On the one hand, she identifies his historical heritage and class status as a set of social relations that belong to the lower classes. On the other hand, she embodies an historical memory rooted in the history of popular music produced by those same classes and racial and ethnic groups, which in turn marks and inspires Springsteen's music. It is this combination that will allow him to employ this character to reach beyond his own heritage and resist assimilation into the male, bourgeois, individualist world of the self-made man, which was canonized by Benjamin Franklin's autobiography at the outset of the formation of the identity of the Republic, and which has appealed to a broad range of authors and people, from Frederick Douglass to numerous immigrants or immigrants' children.

Ironically—and irony is mark of personal and collective history—this process, vaguely present in "Mary Queen of Arkansas" and "Does This Bus Stop at 82nd Street?," is set in motion by the subversive use of Catholic symbols that an Italian-American singer nicknamed "The Boss" applies to the archetypical Catholic woman. If he previously had sung of pregnant nuns in the Vatican, here, in "Thunder Road," he goes even further because there is no irony or satire in the rhetoric. There is subversion or, perhaps, a true understanding of the message of Catholicism, which in a concrete way would be the same thing. The male narrator of "Thunder Road" and of *Born to Run* as a whole (whom Melissa Etheridge's cover of the record's title track turned into a female homosexual opening up new hermeneutic possibilities) tells a woman called Mary that she can pray in vain for a savior to rise from the street—hardly a sign of conventional Catholicism. Springsteen does not (and never will) attach to her the typical traits that historically bind American Protestantism and Catholicism. She is neither a desexualized mother nor an evil whore, as the Mary of "The River" further demonstrates. Mary does not represent the so-called petticoat government so familiar (and dear) to too many American writers, such as James Fennimore Cooper or Pietro Di Donato, the latter a writer who otherwise shares many similarities with Springsteen beside his Italian heritage. Nor do any of Springsteen's songs that present the Mary character, beginning with "Thunder Road," show any trace of classic Italian-American authoritarian paternalism. Seen under this light, Springsteen's Mary and the rhetoric he employs subvert both such a tradition and the myth of the self-sufficient, self-made-man of Protestant origins that favors individualism over equality by separating them, by making them incompatible.

In "Thunder Road" Mary resembles a vision that the narrator implores to come with him because he does not want to go back to the solitude of his home, which stands for his home, for post-Vietnam and Watergate America, and even, if not especially, for the empty home of 1975 rock and roll that has been deprived of many of its icons and no longer has Roy Orbison to heal the lonely on the radio, his heyday having long since passed. In its place there is now a "love … filled with defeat" as "Backstreets" has it (Springsteen, *Songs* 52). Leaving home—the place white men traditionally escape to become Americans—is the goal of this somewhat hopeless, disillusioned, fundamentally angry narrator who believes he has one last chance to get to the promised land by leaving behind a town (and a country one would think) that has nothing to offer but losers. Unlike him, Mary is not hopeless nor does she intend to escape. Not only does she dance, the one action that always symbolizes hope and liberation as it does in Dunbar's poem mentioned above, but she does it across the porch, the frontier, so to speak, that stands between her home—the one place that Springsteen the participant-observer often assigns to his women for reasons that I hope to make clear before I am through—and the outer space where he initially places the possibility of finding the promised land. In the male narrator's eyes, all Mary needs to do is to cross that border and climb in his car. Like a modern, urban Huck Finn at the steering wheel of the prime American symbol of male escapism (disguised as freedom), the automobile, he wants to light out for the territory ahead and find a heaven for the two of them.

The invitation to Mary does carries no signs of machismo. The character makes it clear that he is no hero and that is Mary is no beauty. His redemption lies underneath the hood of his car, on the tangible earth, in the hidden work of the engine so to speak, not in the heavenly and intangible sky. He has no money or illusionary shelters such as the isolated bourgeois house on a hill to offer as he will in "57 Channels and Nothin' On." What his escape anxiously announces is a need for companionship, some togetherness, a human connection, or, as Springsteen would put it once he became a father, a human touch. Yet, ultimately, this anxious invitation subscribes to the myth of the isolated winner that subjugates freedom to exchange by requiring a price to pay. The song closes with a division between winners and losers, whose individualist meaning John Mellencamp would empty out in "Pink Houses," in which he sings of the futility of dividing people between winners and losers. Springsteen himself was to turn this same image into a metaphor of class division and its ethical consequences years later in "Atlantic City."

What underlies the narrator's search for companionship is a fundamentally unresolved dilemma that somehow already betrays the insufficiency of one's individual effort. Mary's presence and location within the lyrics makes manifest this kind of insufficiency, the limits of a partial freedom. The song takes the man's perspective. Mary has no voice in it. Nonetheless, she finds another way to speak. Daniel Wolf noted in *4th of July, Asbury Park* that when the song ends Mary is still on the porch, still on home ground—perhaps still dancing, I would add. She resists the narrator's call. In other words, she says "no." However, just as importantly, in my view, halfway through the song the subject pronoun "I" that closes "Thunder Road" with the bombastic dichotomy between one winner and a community of losers becomes a "we." The singular "I" of "Thunder Road" turns into the plural "we" of the album's title track, "Born to Run." The winner/loser dichotomy disappears. It is replaced by a communal search for love that puts the two characters on the same level and erases any trace of individualism as well as of escapism. If, for Frank Sinatra, the big band singer of the small hours, the lady was a tramp, for Springsteen the rocker, who wants to walk in the light of the sun, both he and the girl are tramps in search of real love. Already, halfway through *Born to Run*, and even more so by the end of it, there is a subversion and a displacement of the traditional self-made-man American story that generated the male, originally white, individualistic American identity. In its place there is now a need for a communal search and interdependence. The male character is not a hero; he needs a female companion. Escapism provides neither salvation nor a stable collective identity. The classic American story at the heart of the hegemonic myth of America's identity begins to be subverted through the presence, the position, and the development of the secularized, humanized, and sexualized image of the archetypical Catholic woman. This woman bears a diversified heritage, a set of diverse and differentiated identities and a working-class condition within her that mirrors her author's history. Likewise, she begins to change the man and the author, who wants to change her.

Mary forces the narrator to leave behind his illusion of individual freedom and salvation in place of a town populated by losers. She forces him to face the harsh, physical realities of a threatened community that Springsteen would explore in his next record. Deprived of adolescent dreams, their innocence lost and reacting angrily toward the runaway American Dream, what these characters are now left with are the cynicism and the struggles of a working-class differentiated community of people under attack in *Darkness on the Edge of Town* and falling apart in *The River*. No wonder, then, that a song such as "Mary Lou" that once more proposes the themes and motifs of "Thunder Road," albeit in a lyrical structure determined by garage and punk, was to be left out of *Born to Run*. No wonder, that when these two characters appear once again, five years later in "The River," they find themselves in a different trap than the one represented by the suicidal urban environment of "Born to Run." The trap is now Mary's unwanted pregnancy, her body, and an economic crisis that costs jobs. In this context, the Mary character is once again represented in a subversive way with regard to Catholicism. Once again she illuminates the class condition and relations with a dark light, so to speak. Her pregnancy makes her both sexual and relational. If the economic forces reveal the characters' social conditions, so too does Mary's pregnancy, in order to indicate a causal interconnection between the two.

In "Thunder Road" Mary unfolds the vacuity of male escapism. In "The River" she reveals her identity and that of the narrator, their social origins, and the nature of class conditions in America that the very beginning of the song—a spectacular songwriting achievement that in three short lines encompasses the personal "I," the "referential "they" and the collective "we" that, according to Janet Zandy, characterizes working-class narrative voices (xiv)—exposes. In "Thunder Road" we are told where the narrator wants to go. In "The River" we are told where he is coming from. This is the valley where his future is decided at the very moment of his birth because of his social origins and the culture that comes with them. His class condition and a nuanced cultural upbringing shaped by male hegemony deny him the possibility of overcoming accidental events and his mistake, which is not his alone, buts his and Mary's. Fortunate sons find a way out of their past mistakes and are allowed to become the man at the very top in America. But the narrator of "The River," like that of John Fogerty's well-known song, is no fortunate son. He has been brought up to do the same things his father has done. The class condition is a family affair, a genealogy out of which there seems to be no exit. The future is written at the moment of one's birth. One's birth is one's choices. In "Adam Raised a Cain" the narrator has inherited the flames and sins of a Catholic imagination. In the "The River" he inherits something that is no less big and is way more tangible: he inherits a class condition that, to him, appears to be unchangeable. The chaser of the promised land of *Darkness on the Edge of Town* now wonders if an unfulfilled dream is worse than a lie. He did not leave his town and no longer races in the street. It evokes memories that haunt him like a curse because "on account of the economy" there is little work available. Economy is the force that determines his and Mary's realities. Even the union card he received on his nineteenth birthday is no longer a shelter in a society whose social contract is about to be called into question and fundamentally crushed by the same forces on whose account there is hardly any work—and the jobs that are available do not pay as well as the previous ones. This also explains Mary's silence. In "The River" Mary has no direct voice and seems to be divested of any responsibility in her unwanted pregnancy because economic forces have deprived them of possibilities. The American Dream is no longer runaway. It is gone.

On the other hand, the narrator, too, has no direct voice all the way through to the end of the song. Halfway through it—precisely when he tells us that "on account of the economy" there is not much work—his voice becomes a memory that haunts both him and Mary. The song narrates the nature of class relations among men and women as being relational, dynamic, and situated in the micro-specific history and culture of which the failing economy makes visible. Given the desultory state of the economy, what previously seemed to matter now "vanish[es] right into the air." This is an utterly non-ideological statement that almost plagiarizes Marx's and Engels's utterly ideological statement in *The Communist Manifesto* according to which "all that is solid melts into air," which, in turn, is precisely what makes Springsteen's line utterly ideological.

There are only two options available after the economy fails, and memories have become curses. The first is to drive *together* down to the river, which conserves its symbolic hopefulness regardless of the fact that it is now dry. The other is the ride to take a mother to the unemployment office on Monday mornings as in "Sherry Darling," a song in which Springsteen uses spaces to add race to the interconnections between gender, ethnicity, and class. After the ride to the unemployment office, the narrator tells the girl's mother that if she wants to go home to the ghetto where she lives, she needs to take the subway, where the means of transportation individuates the intricacies of the racial and economic disparity between races in America. The working-class world of Bruce Zirilli is plural even in terms of races. "American Skin (41 Shots)" leaves no doubt about it.

Springsteen's plurality is female. Its representation occurs through women, often women named Mary who become increasingly complex and more and more central in a world that is increasingly threatened by the economic forces that determine it. In "Highway Patrolman" sergeant Joe Roberts lets his criminal brother cross the Canadian border to save him from the electric chair. What determines Roberts's difficult choice is not the fact that family ties matter. Rather it is the fact that they matter because the economic system that determines the forms of society does not reward the hard work upon which the rhetoric of this society—the land of milk and honey—is built. The land and especially the language mirror class condition. Through them Springsteen sets in motion a process whereby memory individuates Joe Roberts's social condition as the result of the mechanism of the market economy. The market economy forced him to take a job as a police officer, in the institution that prevents social turmoil in the same society in which the market economy dictates one's fate, "Them wheat prices kept on droppin' till it was like we were gettin' robbed," remembers Joe Roberts (Springsteen, *Songs* 152). Along with the liminal space, the working-class condition, and memory, returns the Mary character. For the first time since the unrecorded "Mary Lou" of 1978 her name, Maria, clearly individuates an otherness that belongs to a more recent phase of American history. This is the woman who the economically fallen Joe Roberts (whose name reveals an earlier history and a different ethnic group than Maria's) marries. Springsteen uses Mary not only as a symbol of plurality and unity of otherwise separated differences in a fragmented world, but also as a symbol of hope for those who inhabit a working-class world and live in its conditions and within its constraints. As in "Thunder Road," Maria carries origins that reveal an otherness and dances, too. However, whereas in "Thunder Road" the formerly Italian-American Angelina-turned-Mary danced alone, now Maria dances *together* with both Joe Roberts and his brother.

In "Highway Patrolman," as in the song that closes *Nebraska*, "Reason to Believe," Springsteen begins to sing and conceive of unity as a possible, concrete starting point of rebirth for a disintegrated community that it is in urgent need of rebuilding. When this occurs, the Mary character acquires names that indicate both a differentiated plurality and an element of otherness that invests also the musical sources and forms that Springsteen has absorbed. They are more properly ethnic names, such as Maria in "Highway Patrolman" and Mary Lou in "Reason to Believe," another song in which the fable of the work ethic as the path to individual success is chastised in the refrain—that is , in the section which, in a song indebted to the oral and musical tradition of the blues as this one is, reiterates the central message of the lyrics and by doing so underlines the cultural and political value of a black musical form for the lyrical contents and their interdependence.

"Reason to Believe" also begins to signal a more developed representation of the Mary character in the context of a working-class diversified environment. In this song Mary Lou swears to work for her man every day and bring her salary home—another element the song shares with a certain tradition of female blues singers. When Johnny leaves her, her reaction is to simply wait for his return, which is precisely the one fact that puzzles the narrator: how can she find a reason to believe? More important, however, is the fact that work and money, traditionally the stuff of men and husbands, are now provided by Mary Lou. Responsibility is no longer a man's job. It falls on the shoulders of Mary Lou, who is no longer relegated to the home just as she is not in one of Springsteen's most important songs with regard to our context.

In "Car Wash," a trenchant social commentary on the gender and class relations of America plurality, unity and responsibility lie on the shoulders of the women, and so do concrete solidarity and social opposition. Female identities become a plurality of female subjects who voice their opposition to a male-dominated world divided into classes. Mary becomes the helping hand for a mother of two children who works at a car wash. Hers is the place where Catherine, the main character and the narrator of the song picks up her kids after work. Class alienation does not distinguish when it comes to gender; but gender does distinguish, thus complicating and enriching class itself. The result is the unveiling of the brutality of a life that Springsteen describes as one dominated by a hierarchical male hegemony, both in terms of cultural negotiations and economic determinations. Men are absent both physically and in terms of their responsibility as fathers. When they appear, they do so in the semblance of figures who symbolize a gendered social hierarchy. An obviously single mother of two who does not receive any help from her children's father, Catherine works for a dollar and a dime; she hates her boss, and she washes all the European, luxury cars that, on the one hand, reflect the class relations and conditions of her working world, and, on the other, dictate the schedule of her life as a mother. This condition Catherine metaphorically rejects and erases when she sings "And I take 'em one by one / From Mercedes to VWs / I do 'em all and I don't favor none."

As in "Highway Patrolman," here, too, the language individuates social identity, class, and status. As in "Reason to Believe," work is now represented through the performance of a working-class woman. Significantly, at the same time, it is associated with a single mother, the symbol of life reproduction, in opposition to three interconnected elements. The first is male power, which is represented by her boss at the car wash and the handsome man that she pictures handing her a million-dollar recording contract in the final part of the song—which is also a subtle ironic protest against the now-millionaire songwriter, nicknamed "The Boss," who relegates her to such a discomfiting role and, as such, Springsteen's own personal alignment with women, his rejection of a divided and divisive world, and perhaps his statement on a recording industry also dominated by men. The second is the social status embodied by the luxurious European cars that reflect Catherine's subaltern condition and, more important, the lack of possibility of her stepping out of such a condition. The third is another subversion of the symbolic order of Catholicism that traditionally paired work and responsibility with the man, with Joseph.

Along with this comes yet another shift. Now Springsteen links actual solidarity to women who are also mothers, and specifically to a woman by the name of

Mary, in clear opposition to a world controlled by men. The opposition between sexes is even more strongly emphasized by the fact that the symbol of Catherine's condition—the car—is the most powerful symbol of male identity in America. That ultimate and complex symbol traditionally associated with individual male freedom, which in "Thunder Road" had fueled the narrator's dream of the promised land and Mary's refusal to climb in it, is now the symbol not only of the way in which gender effects class relations, but also of Catherine's and Mary's rejection of female alienation. Catherine rejects it. So does Mary in the very act of helping her. And so does their creator, the songwriter who rejects the politics of division, adopting a female voice, representing female solidarity, and subverting the symbolism of his beloved cars to which previously he had attached the hope of reaching the promised land.

At last, Springsteen's women have found a voice—a voice of concrete solidarity which they use to reject any division and claim the right to autonomy and independence regardless of their age and condition. In "Spare Parts" young Janey is abandoned by her boyfriend who got her pregnant when he broke his promise to pull out before ejaculation. He flees west to Texas, another liminal space, while she finds shelter and some comfort at her mother's home. When the baby is born, she takes it to the river, now no longer dry as it was in "The River," in order to kill it. At the last moment she decides to save him, go to the pawn shop and pawn both her engagement ring and her wedding dress for money which Springsteen describes as "cold." As with the chilling economic realities of "Car Wash," this too is an utterly instinctual act—almost a gesture. In the end, it is not unlike the one made by Huck Finn when he tears apart the letter that would return Nigger Jim to slavery. As Huck's act reveals his true nature and exposes a symbolic protest towards the injustice of a slave society, so too Janey's act reveals her nature and that of Springsteen's women.

Springsteen's women are mature, complex, sexual, relational, graceful, and independent women whose plurality the Mary character has come to embody. They continue to grow, struggle, and fight in a world that Springsteen recognizes as increasingly complex and conflict-ridden, where not even the home can provide a secure shelter from its brutality but, rather, becomes a reflection of this world's conflicts. However, the inherent struggle of Springsteen's female characters also becomes a way of rejecting another kind of individualism: self-isolation. There is no illusion whatsoever that the tempests of these marginal spaces can be avoided in the inner, privately owned and supposedly safe space inside the individual. The ties that link wives and husbands and, especially, mothers and sons are also altered and severed. This is a trope that Springsteen has only recently begun to explore. In "Straight Time" Mary watches her husband, another ex-convict, out of the corner of her eye as he plays with their children before he steps out on the porch to ponder the brutal reality of his half-free condition. The place that the narrator of "Thunder Road" invited Mary to leave in order to chase after the promised land is now the site of psychological alienation. The kitchen where she stands unveils the ideology of reality—and the reality of ideology for both men and women. In "The Rising,"

Mary is the concrete memory of hope for the firefighter who climbs the stairs not to reach heaven, but to encounter the hell that will prevent him from returning home to his love, whereas in "Jesus Was an Only Son" she is a mother who cries for that most painful of personal tragedies, the loss of a child, as any mother would do. It is yet another subversion of the symbolic order of institutional Catholicism that the Italian-American songwriter operates through his female character of preference. There is nothing specifically religious about a mother crying over the death of her son, especially when this is the mother of all mothers, so to speak. What matters here is her motherhood and the severed link between a mother and a son. In "Reno," Mary is the wife who the narrator has lost and who mere sexual intercourse cannot replace.

As Springsteen recognizes the complexities and conflicts of an increasingly atomized world, Mary undergoes one last transformation, perhaps the one that encompasses and justifies all her evolutions. She becomes the symbol of Bruce Springsteen's only religion, namely his music—rock and roll. "Mary's Place," a song inspired by Sam Cooke's "Meet Me at Mary's Place," is nothing but an affirmation of the healing and revitalizing power of music and the recognition of the value of black culture for Springsteen. At Mary's place the porch is finally just a space with some furniture in it. It is a place for dancing—which we now recall is the same thing that Mary was doing on the porch that she refused to abandon to chase after the promised land in "Thunder Road." And dancing might very well be the way to start all over again after the loss caused by an unspeakable crime. The only promised land available is the music that Mary embodies. That is why Springsteen keeps returning to this character. Nothing shines like the light of Maria's bed, sings Springsteen in the song by the same title. He lives in the light of Maria's bed he declares in what is, not surprisingly, the most joyous of *Devils & Dust*'s songs as well as the song in which most of the motifs examined here return: the subversion of the symbolic order of Catholicism located now in Maria's bed(!) through the symbol of the roses; the Italian ethnicity of the name that may well recall that of Springsteen's mother who bought him his first guitar—the instrument he learned to make talk, as he relates in "Thunder Road"; and the illusions of liminal spaces traveled by the narrator before returning to Maria's bed, to his music.

It is the music, rock and roll, which allows Springsteen to liberate, revisit, and elaborate the Mary character as the site of articulation of his heritage in dialogue and in contact with a plurality of voices and characters. In turn this allows him to build his vision of a plural and open inclusive community. The attempt to build such an open community, the very act of narrating the people that inhabit it and their realities, is already a subversive act. It is a way of certifying these people's humanity, of testifying to the struggling condition of an autobiographical family's past and a contemporary American present. It serves to link different subjectivities and generations, their stories and their histories. It helps to liberate one's individual memory in order to reach others and deny their oblivion, to erect a shared memory and respect different identities. It is even more subversive because it is a female character, Mary, who embodies such a vision. Mary, in Springsteen's music, ultimately represents a politics of inclusion in place of the usual politics of exclusion. She exposes an egalitarian vision of the world that replaces an individualist vision of it. She incorporates an ethic of mutuality that refuses an ethic of indifference. She stands for an idea of freedom that in conceptual and concrete terms cannot transcend, and indeed is grounded in, the value of work, equality, and interdependence that does away with the idea of freedom as a private, hegemonic male business. In essence, as I have been trying to say all along, hopefully with some clarity, Mary *is* the difference that exists between the politics of "No Child Left Behind" (by whom?) and the politics of "Should I Fall Behind, Wait for Me." Grazie Adele.

Chapter 7

Finding Meaning in Manhood after the War: Gender and the Warrior Myth in Springsteen's Vietnam War Songs

Heather Stur

In a letter to the *Ally*, an anti-war newspaper published during the Vietnam War for GIs in the San Francisco Bay area, veteran James Daniel criticized the military's "manhood game" for its veneration of fighting and sexual promiscuity. He argued that manhood means learning "to truly love—a woman, an idea, a place, a time." Most lonely GIs simply wanted "a meaningful relationship with a member of the opposite sex … and someone to talk to and be with" ("GI Town, Part I"). Bruce Springsteen paints a picture of that desire in "Born in the USA." The song spins the tale of a vulnerable, battle-weary warrior who finds solace in the arms of a Vietnamese woman: "He had a woman he loved in Saigon / I got a picture of him in her arms now." In Vietnam, some soldiers wished to trade the cold companionship of a gun for the friendship of a woman. At home, Vietnam veterans leaned on girlfriends, wives, and mothers to help them survive the transition back to civilian life. Their stories admit fear, uncertainty, and the need to be protected and nurtured, and they contradict the myth that warriors are numb, solitary male fighters blindly dedicated to the service of their nation.

Springsteen's Vietnam songs address the disconnect between the warrior myth and the reality of veterans' experiences during and after the war. The soldier in "Born in the USA," like most Vietnam War veterans, grew up in an era that celebrated the warrior image typified by John Wayne, the loner on the frontier, deft with a gun and determined to beat the bad guys (Baritz 51; Slotkin, *Gunfighter Nation* 519-20). According to the warrior myth, combat is the ultimate rite of passage from boyhood to manhood, and basic training strips the soldier of emotion, civilian identity, and attachment to personal community in order to ensure his loyalty to the military. Fully-fledged warriors then assume the responsibility for protecting women and preserving their nation (Lifton 23-31). But, in Springsteen's reading of the Vietnam War, GIs are not traditional warriors. Rather, they are men who struggle with their emotions, cope with the baggage they have brought home from the war, and turn to women for support as they create their postwar selves.

The image in "Born in the USA" complicates the stereotype of the isolated soldier in two ways. The warrior is in a woman's arms, as though roles have been reversed and she is the protector. He can feel, and he seeks an intimate human connection. By presenting a Vietnamese woman as the guardian of an American male GI, Springsteen suggests that in the lonely and frightening realm of war, human emotions can overpower social categorizations. A crucial moment in Springsteen's ongoing engagement with the Vietnam War, "Born in the USA" provides a space for discussion of how men and women rejected the warrior myth and tried to build community amid the destruction of the Vietnam War. In some of his songs, women are the veterans' protectors. In others, they inspire men's decisions to reject the warrior role and locate their source of manhood in family life.

While they demonstrate an intense awareness of the specific experiences of veterans, Springsteen's Vietnam songs are part of his larger engagement with American identity. His music tells stories of the men who psychiatrist Robert Jay Lifton calls "antiwar warriors," part of an encompassing attempt to redefine the myths employed by US policymakers to enforce existing power structures and justify America's Cold War scramble for global domination. Freedom struggles on the home front called attention to the misogyny that pervaded military thinking, and GIs questioned the purpose of combat. Although some believed in the mission to stop the spread of communism in Southeast Asia, others, particularly soldiers of color, considered the Vietnam War an example of racist American foreign policy.[1] As the war spiraled out of control, a large number of warriors turned against their mission. Army desertions rose from 27,000 in 1967 to 76,634 in 1970. Air Force absent without leave (AWOL) incidents increased by 59 percent in 1971 and 83 percent in 1972 (Baritz 314; Moser 77-81).

After witnessing and participating in the death and devastation of combat, anti-war warriors returned from Vietnam determined to find alternative expressions of their masculinity. They sought a social structure that values both "masculine" and "feminine" characteristics, and honors men and women who fight for peace (Lifton 371-77). This is not to say that disillusioned veterans were immune to gender conflict. Women veterans were not always welcomed into veterans' organizations, and plenty of women's liberationists held all men responsible for a patriarchal culture that devalues females. Whatever their differences, though, groups like Vietnam Veterans Against the War (VVAW) and some women's organizations grappled with problems that had the same source. The warrior myth perpetuates sexism and racism, and alienates men whose military mission had proved anything but heroic. Springsteen's music portrays men and women who work hard to build their lives outside its parameters.

In an interview in *The Advocate* in 1996, Springsteen characterized his work as an exploration of identity formation, and Dave Marsh has noted that he goes about this by giving careful attention to his characters' day-to-day activities (Marsh, *Two*

---

[1]   See various published oral histories, including Mark Baker's. *Nam: The Vietnam War in the Words of the Men and Women Who Fought There*; Bernard Edelman's. *Dear America: Letters Home from Vietnam*; and Wallace Terry's *Bloods: An Oral History of the Vietnam War by Black Veterans*.

Hearts 655; Wieder 211-20). Springsteen's Vietnam stories portray the complexity of veterans' experiences of fundamental issues of American identity. In songs such as "Born in the USA," "Shut Out the Light," "Brothers Under the Bridge," "Highway Patrolman," and "Galveston Bay," his characters wrestle with the terms of the warrior myth in light of shooting wars and culture wars. Their personal interactions are too complex to fit neatly into ideological frameworks. Ever the anthropologist of life at street level, Springsteen shines his spotlight on the most organic of human interactions. He articulates the universality of emotions like love, hurt, uncertainty, desire, and regret, and thus documents compelling stories about themes and events he has not experienced directly.

Although he did not serve in Vietnam, Springsteen's understanding of the human spirit allows him to be a voice for Vietnam veterans and their loved ones. As Kurt Loder said, "Born in the USA" is "one of those rare records—a rousing rock and roll song that also gives voice to the pain of forgotten people" ("Born Again"). A serious motorcycle accident in 1968 left Springsteen with a brain concussion that led to a draft deferment. However, the Vietnam War touched his life when Bart Hanes, the drummer in his first band, was killed there (Marsh, *Two Hearts* 308). After reading Ron Kovic's memoir, *Born on the Fourth of July*, Springsteen set out to help Vietnam veterans, and in 1981 he met Bob Muller, president of Vietnam Veterans of America (VVA). At the time, Muller's struggling organization could not afford to rent an office or print a newsletter, so Springsteen scheduled a series of benefit concerts to help. The shows raised nearly a quarter of a million dollars, and Muller credits Springsteen with VVA's survival (Marsh, *Two Hearts* 310). After the concerts, Springsteen continued his public support of Vietnam vets by writing songs about the war's impact on their private lives.

"Shut Out the Light," "Brothers Under the Bridge," "Highway Patrolman," and "Galveston Bay," in particular, illuminate the experiences of real veterans. The music suggests the centrality of women in veterans' postwar healing, and it explores characters' attempts to identify with social structures not defined by the warrior myth. Frightened husbands turn to their wives for shelter. A soldier tells his child that war is a nightmare, not a glorious manly adventure. In his dreams, a veteran begs "mama" to protect him. Springsteen's music offers an alternative to the story that the military transforms boys into emotionless men who reject the maternalism embodied in mothers, wives, girlfriends, and sisters. "Shut Out the Light" portrays a veteran who returns from the Vietnam War feeling exhausted and scared, not tough and heroic. As he struggles to make the transition from war to peace, he seeks comfort from a woman. In the song's refrain he calls out, "Oh mama mama mama come quick / I've got the shakes and I'm gonna be sick / Throw your arms around me in the cold dark night / Hey now mama don't shut out the light." "Mama" could be his mother, his wife, or a nurse who cared for him in a hospital in Vietnam. Springsteen does not dispute Vietnam veterans' reliance on the support of their fellow soldiers. Rather, he adds the home and relationships between men and women to the list of venues in which to analyze the American social implications of the Vietnam War. In "Shut Out the Light," the veteran lying paralyzed next to his lover experiences a *loss* of manhood through war, and he begs for "mama" to make him well.

Similar themes emerge in countless stories of Vietnam veterans who credit girlfriends or wives for helping them take the first steps toward postwar emotional healing. John Ketwig, a veteran who enlisted in the army in 1966, fell in love with and eventually married a woman—Carolynn—who had been a friend to him when he returned home from Vietnam. Initially, she was simply someone who listened and "had never been ashamed" of Ketwig's status as a Vietnam veteran. She helped him feel comfortable telling his stories at a time when many Americans did not want to face the realities of Vietnam (Ketwig 26). Another veteran attributes his postwar survival to his wife, who took care of him on a practical level as well as an emotional one:

> She knew the kind of trouble I was in emotionally. The way she describes it is that when I came back, I was dead from the neck down. The first crack in all that was when I finally cried. Then for the next two years it was a climbing out, which she had an enormous amount to do with. I was very lucky because Rebecca was on top of the situation and got me where I needed to go quickly. She took care of all the details of my life, let my boss know what was going on. (Baker 276)

Like the veteran in "Shut Out the Light," this veteran relied on a woman to guide him through the healing process, despite the military's insistence that women made them "soft."

All this represents an implicit rejection of the belief that military service is the manly alternative to indulgent mothering—a belief that dates back to the turn of the twentieth century, but asserted itself with particular force in the years leading up to the Vietnam War. Some Americans feared that "overcivilization" at the hands of female teachers and coddling mothers had dulled men's masculine edge. Connecting domestic concerns to foreign affairs, Theodore Roosevelt criticized "the timid man, the lazy man, the over-civilized man" and argued that the United States must assert its might around the world, otherwise "some stronger, manlier power would have to step in and do the work" (Roosevelt). Roosevelt deemed military service the antidote to too much civilization and too much mom (Bederman; also Renda; Hoganson). In the 1950s author Philip Wylie coined the term "momism," blaming dominant and controlling mothers for homosexuality, sons' unfitness for military service, materialism, and consumerism. In Cold War terms, mom weakened the influence the United States could have over newly independent nations in Africa and Asia (Bederman 172).

A decade later, John F. Kennedy and his administration feared that suburban comforts had made American boys "soft" and thus unfit to compete in Cold War competitions. Historian Robert Dean argues that, in order to justify projects like the expansion of the army's Green Berets, Kennedy exploited the fear that a "crisis of masculinity" could weaken American global power (169). The president wrote articles for *Sports Illustrated* and hired Bud Wilkinson, a former University of Oklahoma football coach, to be his physical fitness adviser. Kennedy believed that American men must be "tough" and physically fit to endure "military demands in Europe and the jungles of Asia" (Mrozek 183). According to President Kennedy:

> Physical vigor and health are essential accompaniments to the qualities of intellect and spirit on which our nation is built. It was men who possessed vigor and strength as well as courage and vision who first settled these shores and, over more than three centuries, subdued a continent and wrested civilization from the wilderness. ... In the jungles of Asia and on the borders of Europe, a new group of vigorous young Americans help maintain the peace of our world and our security as a nation. (12)

Kennedy created the President's Council on Youth Fitness, which set standards for physical education at public schools. He stressed the need for sports and organizations such as Outward Bound and the Boy Scouts to instill masculinity in boys who spent their days under their mother's tutelage. The implication here is that, although the ideal post-World War II American family structure featured a breadwinner father and a childrearing mother, mothers could not teach their sons how to be productive, civic-minded men. Jacqueline Lawson contends that military advertisements produced after the Korean War played on the dichotomy of male aggressiveness and female passivity. She maintains that slogans such as "The Marine Corps builds men" assume that a mother cannot teach her son how to be a man (Lawson 15-37; also Rosenberg 59).

Although the military billed itself as a corrective to suburban softness, it relied on an established image of femininity to enforce its definition of masculinity (Adams 193; also Enloe, *Khaki*; Enloe, *Bananas*). When the Pentagon decided to send the Women's Army Corps (WAC) to Vietnam, it requested enlistees who were "extroverts and beautiful" (Morden). The American military did not consider women as fighters or protectors (Christopher 40). In her analysis of American cultural representations of the Vietnam War, Susan Jeffords notes that the warrior myth considers combat an exclusively male realm (xiii). It forbade enlisted women from using or carrying weapons in Vietnam even though they lived and worked in combat zones.

Without weapons, military women often found themselves unprotected in a war zone. Camilla Wagner, a lieutenant with the Women's Air Force, got hit in the leg and back by shrapnel and could not defend herself. Jeanne Bell, who worked in army administrative services in Saigon, remembers her office regularly coming under machine-gun fire. A male commander told Peggy Ready, a first lieutenant in the Women's Army Corps, that if their unit came under attack, all the women should huddle around the flagpole outside of headquarters and wait for the fighting to end (Bunn). Women were not alone in considering the military's treatment of them dangerous, impractical, and bizarre. Male GIs also questioned and rejected the gender ideology that trapped men and women in opposing social positions.

Several of Springsteen's Vietnam songs, most notably "Brothers Under the Bridge," portray the process of trying to move beyond the trap. This song is Springsteen's twist on the image of a father sharing splendid war stories with his son. The song features a soldier who explains to his child the unglamorous death in combat of a fellow GI. The lyrics express battle-weariness at the uncertainties of war and the fear of never knowing whether "[o]ver nothing you [will] end up on the wrong end of someone's knife." The father also admits that the child's mother ultimately became his protector, holding his hand during a Veterans' Day parade as the American flag passes by.

Despite experiencing the kind of bonding that occurs between men in combat, the soldier finds peace in a family, with his wife as his support. Although the warrior myth equates masculinity with a solitary, stoic commitment to a military goal, the song implies that in real life a veteran needs a familial community of men and women to help him grow into manhood. The father in "Brothers Under the Bridge" tells his child that when he returned home from Vietnam, he still was "just a kid." Combat has not made him a "real man" in the warrior mode. Rather, fatherhood—and his wife's support—carried him to adulthood, where love for his child overpowered the immature fear that denouncing war would compromise his masculinity. As a Chicano veteran wrote in *El Barrio*, "You're not much of a man if you let your own people go hungry, live in poverty, and get ripped off by this country" (Oropeza 215).

Veterans' real-life experiences elaborate on the song's implicit rejection of the military's attempts to connect manhood to violence and the degradation of women. For anti-war GIs and veterans, underground newspapers and the coffeehouse movement sometimes provided spaces in which men and women came together to oppose the Vietnam War, and the sexism and racism it symbolized. As combat escalated, GI anti-war newspapers surfaced, providing a forum for soldiers to speak out against the war. In 1967 only three GI newspapers existed, but by March 1972, the US Defense Department had discovered about 245 papers in circulation. Two of the most popular ones, *Fatigue Press*, published near Fort Hood, and *Bragg Briefs*, circulated at Fort Bragg, had readerships of about 5,000 each. GIs and veterans staffed the two papers almost exclusively (Small 98).

The newspapers were often connected to coffeehouses like the Oleo Strut near Fort Hood. Named after shock absorbers on helicopters, the Oleo Strut was one of several GI coffeehouses that opened near military bases in the late 1960s and early 1970s. By 1971 as many as twenty-six coffeehouses existed, some staffed by civilians, others staffed by GIs, all open to the public (Moser 98-99). Clark Smith, a civilian who organized anti-war GIs and veterans in the Oakland area, notes that coffeehouses gave GIs and civilians a forum in which to gather and discuss "the problems we face in society, and how we together can deal with those problems: the war, the army, racism, sexism." Smith believed that veterans gave credibility to the anti-war movement because they had experienced first-hand the horrors of war ("The GI Press").

The coffeehouse movement provided a forum for soldiers to reject the warrior myth that subordinated women and encouraged American muscle-flexing abroad. Like most coffeehouses, the Oleo Strut served coffee and baked goods, and it hosted live music on weekends. But at the tables, GIs discussed their opposition to the Vietnam War and planned anti-war demonstrations. Upstairs, a women's health clinic provided free medical counseling and literature on women's liberation. Volunteers offered legal advice on desertion, obtaining conscientious objector status, and the ramifications of refusing to perform military duties. Coffeehouse organizers helped form the Killeen Women's Group, which occasionally wrote articles about the women's liberation movement for *Fatigue Press*. In one article, writers demanded equal wages and jobs, free birth control, and free abortions, so that women of various income levels could have more control over their health (*Fatigue Press*). GI wives from Fort Hood worked with the Oleo Strut to plan rallies for military families against the war ("Strike Back Campaign").

Collaboration with women allowed male GIs and veterans take a public stand against the sexism of the warrior myth. However, not all anti-war soldiers criticized the military's version of masculinity. In his book on the GI anti-war movement, historian Richard Moser estimates that about 25 percent of GIs participated regularly in anti-war activism (132). They had various reasons for denouncing the war, but anti-war newspapers and coffeehouse activities indicate that some soldiers specifically opposed the masculinity of the warrior myth. Letters GIs wrote to underground newspapers lamented the military's association of masculinity with violence and sexual promiscuity. Base drill sergeants inundated recruits with the belief that the "sign of manhood is the number of women you've made love to":

> When entering the military, a young man is subject to constant propaganda on sex. … Drill sergeants constantly rub in the fact that they "got some last night," tell the married people that "if the army wanted you to have a wife they'd issue you one," and make other cracks such as "who needs a wife when you can get a whore" and "if all wives acted like prostitutes we'd be a lot better off." The army wants to alienate you from your loved ones at home by planting the idea into your head that your wife, girl, or fiancée is cheating on you and that all women are whores. ("GI Town, Part I")

To counteract the military's blatant sexism, *Fatigue Press* encouraged GIs to avoid referring to women as "broads" ("Gooks and Broads").

Some anti-war GIs and veterans—particularly those involved in the coffeehouse movement—considered women as vital allies. Pete Zastrow of VVAW said that women helped anti-war servicemen focus on "vital issues that, while they weren't direct veterans' issues, were issues that veterans damn well ought to be interested in—child care, the rights of women, today it would be homelessness." (Stacewicz 364) VVAW member Mike McCain asserted that "the women taught us boys a whole lot. They were mostly our girlfriends who ended up being some of the most valuable, the most dedicated, the most active, the most disciplined people in the organization" (Ibid. 364). The comments suggest that the veterans sought to create a social alternative to the warrior myth. They found strength in community, they looked to women for guidance, and they honored social activism rather than military valor.

Yet, as Springsteen shows in "Highway Patrolman," not all Vietnam veterans chose kinship over solitude. Acknowledging the difficulty some veterans had transitioning into civilian life after the war, the song recounts the story of Joe and Frankie Roberts, brothers who served in Vietnam, and their complex relationship with a woman named Maria. Joe, a police officer, is his brother's keeper, showing up to bail Frankie out anytime he gets himself in a bind. Maria is a friend of the brothers, and she dances with both of them when they are all together at a local bar. In 1965 Frankie ships off to Vietnam, while Joe settles into civilian life with a farm deferment and marries Maria. By the time Frankie returns home in 1968, the farm has fallen on tough times, and Joe heads off to the war. He makes it home and transitions back into his married life with Maria, but Frankie remains a bachelor and continues to run with trouble. One night, Frankie gets into a serious roadhouse fight, and Joe heads out to investigate the situation. He chases his brother to the Canadian border, but then slows down and lets Frankie go.

Although the lyrics do not describe specifically the relationship between Maria and Frankie, they hint at what might have happened to Frankie if he, not Joe, had married Maria. Perhaps Maria's love could have saved him, helped him heal after Vietnam. Through the character of Maria, Springsteen suggests the importance of women to the Vietnam War narrative. They are warriors in their own ways—the protectors and saviors of veterans. Maria also symbolizes Joe's struggle with his feelings about the warrior myth. Frankie went to war first, so Joe got Maria and accepted his role as a husband. But at the end of the song, Joe's decision to let Frankie disappear into the night suggests a desire to hold on to the warrior myth. Frankie, speeding down a deserted road, represents the lone warrior heading out to the frontier. Despite experiencing the destructiveness of combat, some veterans retained a connection to the John Wayne imagery that defined their understanding of soldiering and masculinity.

In "Highway Patrolman," Springsteen recognizes the difficulty of entering into an intimate relationship after a war experience. Having faced death in a war zone, some veterans avoided intimacy—or "getting too close"—once they returned home. Some feared losing love as they had lost friends in Vietnam. Others believed that they could not spare emotional energy for another person until they healed themselves. In addition, the numbing process of basic training worked on some GIs, and they returned home believing that they had lost their senses of emotion (Lifton 271). Robert Bly, a poet and World War II veteran who counseled Vietnam veterans after the war, blames the military brass for damaging male GIs' perceptions of women. He interviewed a soldier who expressed anger at the military for contradicting what he had learned in his youth about respecting women:

After a month or so in the field suddenly I was shipped for R and R to a whorehouse in Thailand. Something was wrong with that. A lot of us still had feelings toward women. We had feelings about respect for women and what a woman means this way. Something got broken in me, and I'm still angry about that. (Bly 84)

Similarly, many of the veterans interviewed by Robert Jay Lifton testify to the military's corruption of human feelings. As one soldier told him, "Whenever you tried to be human, you got screwed. If you got close, you got burned" (Lifton 268). Therefore, some veterans—like Frankie in "Highway Patrolman"—avoided intimacy. But in Lifton's rap sessions, the veterans usually focused their attention on the man struggling with relationships, as though they knew he needed love to survive (267-79). They tried to help their fellow soldiers discover tenderness and affection as healthy replacements for the warrior myth.

One of the most difficult parts of coming to terms with the war and the warrior myth involved veterans' feelings about their Vietnamese allies, an issue Springsteen confronts in "Galveston Bay." More than one million Vietnamese refugees arrived on American shores after the Vietnam War. Vietnamese who had collaborated with the United States fled their homeland for fear of their lives as communist forces took the nation. Amid the social confusion that accompanied America's first large-scale military defeat, many Vietnamese refugees were greeted with racism. In "Galveston Bay," Le Bing Son and Billy Sutter are Vietnam veterans—Le a soldier for the South Vietnamese Army of the Republic of Vietnam (ARVN) and Billy his American counterpart. However, the American military did not consider its Vietnamese ally its equal in strength or masculinity. Manipulating the gendered nature of the warrior myth, American personnel feminized ARVN, creating a masculine mission for American soldiers to rescue the "passive" and "immature" South Vietnamese GIs (Milliken and Sylvan 321-59).

In "Galveston Bay," when North Vietnamese troops seize Saigon, Le escapes with his family to the United States and settles on the Texas coast. He buys a fishing boat and takes care of his family by harvesting shrimp in Galveston Bay. Billy is also a family man who works the shrimp boats to support his wife and son after returning home from Vietnam. Although Le is a veteran, in the eyes of the Texans who live near Galveston Bay, Le's race negates the masculinity that the warrior myth confers on soldiers. Members of a local Ku Klux Klan chapter try to burn Le's fishing boat in order to force him out of town. Le kills two men in self-defense and is acquitted of the murders, but Billy Sutter sets out to avenge the deaths. At the moment he could have knifed Le, however, Billy lets him live. In that decision, he rejects the role of the detached warrior doing his country's bidding. Le's American neighbors considered him an intruder, and some would have been happy to see him dead. Yet Billy locates his manhood in his responsibility to his wife and son, not in killing, and he returns to them after Le passes by. In the characters of Le Bing Son and Billy Sutter, Springsteen pays tribute to men who refuse to let public beliefs and social constructions destroy them.

"Galveston Bay" makes an important contribution to ongoing studies of the Vietnam War. The song is one of few American depictions of the war that gives a voice to an ARVN soldier. Also, by emphasizing the story of postwar refugees, Springsteen places the Vietnam War and the warrior myth in the context of a legacy of American racism. Although Le Bing Son fought side-by-side with American soldiers in Vietnam, in the United States he was considered not a warrior, but fair game for the Ku Klux Klan. During the war, the American military had little faith in the fighting skills of its ARVN allies. On the home front, some Americans associated their new Vietnamese neighbors with defeat by a weaker race of people.

Race and gender complicated the American military's conventional wisdom that warriors were men fighting to protect their women. America's opponents, the North Vietnamese Army (NVA) and National Liberation Front (NLF—also known as "Viet Cong"), employed female as well as male soldiers.[2] Thus, military slang referred to the Vietnamese collectively as "gooks" or "dinks"—terms based on race, not gender. According to some veterans, the slang was intended to diminish GIs' sense of Vietnamese humanity. If all Vietnamese were considered "subhuman," it would be easier to kill them whether they were men or women (Lifton 202).

However, in addition to asexual slang, American military personnel and policymakers also used specific gendered language when discussing both their allies and their enemies. *Uptight*, a magazine the US Army published for its troops in Vietnam, ran an article about a military training program for ARVN soldiers. American advisers guided Vietnamese officers in preparing the recruits for their intended mission as "Vietnamese fighting men." To ease the loneliness of adjusting to base life, "pretty young Vietnamese women" visited as morale boosters ("The ARVN Recruit" 31-33). Despite US-sponsored training, though, the American military indicated little faith in its ally's fighting potential. Lieutenant Colonel John Paul Vann, who was stationed in Vietnam in the early 1960s, regularly reported that the ARVN was unlikely to win a war (Sheehan 94). He said of ARVN's military abilities: "I consider the performance of the ARVN to be more disgraceful than ever. I can easily establish more enemy contacts on a daily basis myself" (Sheehan 628). In other words, one American man is more effective in combat than an entire army of Vietnamese.

NLF fighters were of the same race as ARVN soldiers, but American personnel viewed the NLF as a masculine competitor. Lyndon Johnson's administration characterized the NLF as "well-motivated," "highly skilled," and a "tough enemy both physically and morally" (Milliken and Sylvan). In Vietnam, the American military engaged in a "contest" of "military power" with the NLF, while many

---

[2]   The North Vietnamese Army, also known as the People's Army of Vietnam, was the official army of the Democratic Republic of Vietnam (North Vietnam). The National Liberation Front was a Communist Party organization based in the Republic of Vietnam (South Vietnam; also called State of Vietnam). Its mission was to organize popular insurgency against ARVN and American. forces. See Anderson.

American GIs considered ARVN men "faggots." On the other hand, they often agreed that "the VC have a lot of balls" (Lifton 196). To fight a feminized enemy would be akin to fighting a girl, an unmanly proposition. But rescuing the feminized ARVN made sense in a context in which "masculine" meant strong and "feminine" meant weak.

Gendered indoctrination began in basic training, the first step toward warriorhood. *Fatigue Press* testified that drill instructors began classes with jokes about Asian women they had known while stationed in Japan or other parts of Asia. The newspaper also reported the story of an Asian-American GI who wanted to marry a Vietnamese woman he met in Vietnam. Various officers in the military chain of command tried to discourage him, telling him that the Vietnamese are "uncivilized," and that he should want to marry a "round-eye." *Fatigue Press* called on its readers to "fight the mentality that keeps Suzy Wong, Madame Butterfly, and gookism alive. The mentality that turns human beings into racist murdering soldiers also keeps Asian Americans from being able to live and feel like human beings here at home" (*Fatigue Press*). Although basic training was designed to desensitize future warriors, disillusioned GIs spoke out against its racism and sexism. Springsteen's characters in "Galveston Bay" do not become anti-military activists, but the song ends on a note of hope that suggests a rejection of combat ideology. In letting Le Bing Son live, Billy Sutter embraces his identity as a husband and father instead of a warrior programmed to kill "gooks."

In his quest to understand and explain the Vietnam War, Bruce Springsteen does not examine war-room decisions or battle tactics. He does what he knows best, peering into human relationships and studying the ways in which the war shaped identities. Some soldiers tried to create an alternative structure that provided space for men *and* women to be caregivers and protectors. Veterans built familial communities with wives and children. They worked with men and women, soldiers and civilians, to oppose the war. Their rejection of the warrior myth in their personal lives amounted to a political statement denouncing America's mission in the world—a mission it needed soldiers to fulfill.

Springsteen's Vietnam music demonstrates his belief in people's ability to challenge and correct their government by questioning the myths it propagates. A soldier sees through the military's gook imagery to find shelter in the arms of a Vietnamese woman. A father refuses to pass the warrior legend down to his child, sharing instead his combat stories about fear and inglorious death. He credits the child's mother, not the military, with helping him become a whole man. An American veteran spares the life of his Vietnamese counterpart, shedding the skin of a desensitized warrior. In Springsteen's Vietnam War stories, the political act of dismissing the warrior fable occurs in the home and within families.

Psychiatrist Robert Jay Lifton's work with Vietnam veterans led him to conceive of a possible future similar to the picture Springsteen paints in "Brothers Under the Bridge." A child might ask, "Daddy, what did you do in the war?" Instead of replying with a glamorous battle story, the father would respond proudly, "I fought in it, rejected it, and then did my best to reveal the truth about it" (Lifton 375).

Telling the truth about the war could involve explaining the effects of the warrior myth on women, men, soldiers, and families, on Vietnamese and Americans. In subtle ways, Springsteen's characters do just that.

PART III
"Lost in the Flood":
Springsteen and Religion

Chapter 8

Bruce Springsteen and the Puritan Ideal of the Promised Land[1]

Spencer L. Allen

In 1641 John Cotton defined the "carnall man" as one who "never served any man but himselfe" ("The Way of Life", 447). For Cotton, the "carnall man" was the inevitable consequence of Adam's fall from grace and banishment from the garden of Eden (Gen. 3) after eating from the forbidden fruit.[2] Of course, this view of the Fall was not original to Cotton. St Paul states:

> Therefore just as one man's trespass led to condemnation for all, so one man's act of righteousness leads to justification and life for all. For just as by the one man's disobedience the many were made sinners, so by the one man's obedience the many will be made righteous. (Rom. 5: 18-19)[3]

For Paul, the redemption offered through the "last Adam" (1 Cor. 15: 45), Christ, is completely dependent on the sin of the first Adam. Similarly, Moses would have had no need to lead the Israelites to the promised land had mankind never been exiled from paradise.[4] For both Paul and Cotton, history unfolded only as a result of Adam's rebellion.

---

[1]   My special thanks to Dr Mark Schantz, Assistant Professor of History at Hendrix College, who playfully suggested this topic in the fall of 1998 and subsequently granted me permission to develop it for Glory Days: A Bruce Springsteen Symposium and this chapter. This subject has also been briefly treated by Jim Cullen (53), who links Springsteen with the Puritans through the concept of the covenant that unites communities.

[2]   The forbidden fruit will forever be associated with the apple due to the popularity of John Milton's 1667 epic poem *Paradise Lost*. Cf. "Pink Cadillac": "They say Eve tempted Adam with an apple."

[3]   All Biblical quotes throughout this chapter are taken from *The Holy Bible: New Revised Standard Version* (Oxford: Oxford UP, 1989). Cf. 1 Cor. 15: 21-22: "For since death came through a human being, the resurrection of the dead has also come through a human being; for as all die in Adam, so all will be made alive in Christ."

[4]   This is not a case of "you can't appreciate the good if you don't have the bad," but is rather a simple reminder that when you are living in paradise, there is no need for a promised land.

There is a significant difference, however, in how these two men conceived of this unfolding history. While both Paul and Cotton relate their religious truths typologically,[5] their applications are very different. Paul presents the man Adam as a type, the one bringing death into the world—for the anti-type of Christ, the one bringing life into the world—in order to better understand the life of Christ as an historical event. Cotton, on the other hand, envisions the Biblical promised land as a type for New England and the Israelites as a type for the New England Puritans.

For the New England Puritans, then, for whom the Fall and its consequences were a daily reality, their experience of America as *the* promised land cannot be simply equated with the geographical attainment of a new Eden and a life of ease. While an Edenic paradise could be restored in the promised land, it, unlike the pre-Fall Eden, had to be continually maintained. Just as Moses warned the Israelites in Deut. 4: 25ff against complacency and the temptations of idolatry (below), which would break their covenant with God and leave them subject to exile, so does Puritan religious ideology demand that the individual continually uphold and strive to fulfill his covenantal duty through vocational hard work on behalf of the common good and morally unimpeachable behavior. Only then might he obtain full reward from his works and yield from the land. Cotton's interpretation is thus a much more intimate and personally relevant use of typology than is Paul's. It is this same self-understanding, rather than mere religious symbolism or abstract metaphor, that Bruce Springsteen employs throughout his work when he discusses the search for the promised land: both the singer and the characters to which he gives voice view themselves as the realization of Biblical narratives in today's world.

While the term "promised land" occurs in no less than nine officially released Springsteen-penned songs,[6] most of these references allude to a dreamy utopian paradise where the grass is greener than in the current oppressive/repressive location. I suggest that this is a complete, if popular, misunderstanding of the Biblical and Puritan promised lands and one which Springsteen himself recognizes, and to an extent corrects, in his later life and work. The promised land is not a utopia and is not a paradise; it is at once a physical place and an abstract concept,

---

[5]   Typology is an interpretational method that emphasizes the relationships between the (proto)type and the anti-type. The type is the historical (or less commonly, literary) person, place, or event that foreshadows the coming of another person, place, or event (that is, the anti-type). The correspondences and differences between the type and anti-type help give meaning to the anti-type for the interpretive community.

[6]   These nine include (listed in order of the first official Springsteen release): "Thunder Road" (1975), "Racing in the Street" (1978), "The Promised Land" (1978), "The Price You Pay" (1980), "Johnny Bye-Bye" (1985), "The Ghost of Tom Joad" (1995), "Galveston Bay" (1995), "Goin' Cali" (1998), and "From Small Things (Big Things One Day Come)" (2003). A tenth song, "Walking in the Street," may also be known to many as "Lovers in the Cold" from the popular *Born to Run*-era bootleg album *War and Roses*, which appears to be an earlier, unfinished version of "Thunder Road."

attainable only by a community-oriented society founded upon interdependence both among its constituents and with God.

By contrasting those characters in Springsteen's corpus who view the promised land as utopia with those who understand it as a renewed commitment to their families and communities, we may observe how the Puritan ethic informs the development of Springsteen's conception of the promised land. On the one hand, the woman in "From Small Things (Big Things One Day Come)" represents Cotton's "carnall man that never served any man but himselfe" (this despite the fact that she worked at a hamburger stand). Her selfish interests consistently pull her away from everyone she has ever known, and her lack of commitment to her family and community is emphatically reflected in her ultimate destination: locked away behind bars and literally, as well as figuratively, exiled from society. On the other hand, both the Mexican immigrants of "Across the Border" and the Vietnamese immigrants and native Texans of "Galveston Bay" work selflessly toward the common good of their communities. Upon entering the land, the immigrants of "Across the Border" will one day "eat the fruit from the vine" supplied by "God's blessed waters" in the promised land, while the latter eventually learn to move beyond revenge and coexist peacefully, all the while harvesting their yield.

The Biblical Concept of the Promised Land

Since both the Puritan and Springsteen promised lands derive from the Biblical narrative of the Israelites leaving slavery in Egypt to conquer Canaan, the land promised to Abraham's descendents—the meaning of the promised land in the Bible—should first be fully explored. In the book of Genesis, God appears to the childless Abram, who has migrated to the land of Canaan, and tells him: "I am the Lord who brought you out from Ur of the Chaldeans to give you this land to possess it" (Gen. 15: 7).[7]

While promising this land to Abram,[8] however, God explains that it will only be the fourth generation of Abram's descendents, returning to Canaan after 400 years of enslavement in a foreign land (Gen. 15: 13-16), who will actually take possession of it. This passage is crucial to our understanding of the promised land for several reasons: first, those who will enter the promised land are identified, and the circumstances and timeline of their entry given; second, the physical boundaries of the land are defined, setting it apart as a cohesive geographical entity; and third, the organization of the land, both political and religious, is determined, with God and Abram entering into a covenant in which God plays the role of the overlord and Abram the vassal (Gen. 15: 18). On this last point, the passage not only uses typical covenant terminology from the current political realm (that is,

---

[7]   All Old Testament translations are my own from the Masoretic Hebrew (*Biblia Hebraica Stuttgartensia*).

[8]   This is not the first time God has promised the land to Abram (cf. Gen. 12: 1-4).

"to cut a covenant"), but also includes a symbolic action, Abram's cutting in two of his animal offering (Gen. 15: 9-10), to symbolize his fate should he break the covenant, which is typical of ancient Near Eastern international treaties. Abram thus accepts the promise of the land on behalf of his descendants and, in return, binds them to God's rule.

Jumping forward some 400 years from Abram to his descendant Moses, we encounter the narrative of the Israelites' march from Egypt to Canaan[9] As virtually everyone knows (if not from the Bible, then from watching Charlton Heston in Cecil B. DeMille's *The Ten Commandments*, 1956), Moses receives the law at Mount Sinai on behalf of the people and they subsequently agree to uphold God's word, stating: "Everything that the Lord spoke, we will faithfully observe" (Exod. 24: 7).[10] Moses then sprinkles them with blood from the sacrifices,[11] proclaiming: "This is the blood of the covenant that the Lord cut with you concerning all these matters" (Exod. 24: 7). Moses and the Israelites, as Abram before them, thus willingly enter into a covenantal relationship with God, accepting his promise of land and protection in exchange for their observance of his laws.

In Deuteronomy, Moses delivers his final address to the Israelites before they cross the Jordan to take possession of the promised land on the other side. Here, at the end of his journey, Moses reminds the Israelites of their forty years wandering in the wilderness (Deut. 1-3); restates the laws they received at Sinai (Deut. 12-26); and renews the covenant between the people and God, including a series of curses and blessings—again typical of ancient Near Eastern treaties—to be applied depending on their behavior (Deut. 27-28). After his speech, Moses ascends Mount Nebo to view the promised land and there dies (Deut. 34: 1-5), never having set foot in Canaan. The explicit reason for his denial into the promised land is never given, leaving both Jewish and Christian traditions to debate the issue from antiquity all the way through to the present day. For Springsteen, this debate is irrelevant; evoking Deuteronomy's treatment of the episode, he recalls it in "The Price You Pay" without explanation or justification:

> Do you remember the story of the promised land
> How he crossed the desert sands
> And could not enter the chosen land

---

[9]   The exodus from Egypt begins in Exodus 14, and the Israelites finally enter the land of Canaan in Joshua 5.

[10]   Cf. Exod. 19: 8, when they accept the covenantal promise that they will become God's chosen people before the actual revelation. Notice, however, that 19: 8 lacks the finality of 24: 7 where they promise to "observe," in addition to "doing" the covenant.

[11]   The sacrifices involved in this ceremony are different from those of Abram in Genesis 15. While Abram's sacrifice was typical of ancient Near Eastern covenantal ceremonies, Moses and the Israelites offer more cultic types of sacrifice: the "holocaust" (which is wholly consumed by the fire on the altar) and the "peace-offerings" (which are returned to the offerer to be eaten as part of a sacred meal. Cf. Exod. 24: 11).

On the banks of the river he stayed
To face the price you pay.[12]

Notably, while Moses' fate is shared by all those who left Egypt (excepting only Joshua and Caleb), the reason why the others cannot enter the promised land is clear: they have demonstrated that they "ain't got the faith to stand [their] ground." ("The Promised Land"). Despite witnessing the miracles performed in Egypt and in the desert, they preferred to return to slavery in Egypt than to trust in God's assistance in claiming Canaan (Num. 13: 32-14: 3), the land he had promised them. Their lack of faith is related in Num. 13-14 when Moses commissions twelve spies to scout Canaan and its inhabitants. While there, they discover the lushness of the land, embodied by a cluster of grapes so impressive that it takes two men to carry it (Num. 13: 23). Returning after their forty-day mission, however, only Caleb and Joshua believe they can possess Canaan; the other ten spies assert:

> We entered the land to which you sent us. It does indeed flow milk and honey, and this is its fruit. However, the people living in the land are strong, and their cities are fortified and large. ... We cannot attack the people because they are stronger than we are. (Num. 13: 27-31)

The Israelites as a group fail to heed Caleb's positive assessment, declaring that they would prefer to die in the wilderness than try to fight for the land God has promised to them (Num. 14: 1-5). Ultimately, they get their wish; God decrees that their corpses will drop in the desert before their children have another chance to enter the promised land (Num. 14: 29-30). Forty years later and immediately prior to his own death, Moses exhorts the next generation of Israelites to heed God's laws, noting that only then will they be able to conquer and retain the land promised to their ancestors: "Now, Israel, keep the statutes and ordinances, which I am teaching you to do, so that you may live and [then] enter and possess the land that the Lord, God of your fathers, is giving to you" (Deut. 4: 1). Moses adds that the world will notice their wisdom and be astonished by their laws, urging the Israelites to keep in mind their unique relationship with God and their consequent role as a model for other nations:

> See, I have taught you statutes and ordinances as the Lord my God commanded that you do so in the land which you are entering to possess it. Faithfully observe them because they are your wisdom and understanding in the eyes of the peoples, who, hearing all these statutes, will say "Indeed, this great nation is a wise and understanding people." (Deut. 4: 5-6)

---

[12]   Indeed, Springsteen's unwillingness or inability to explain why Moses is unable to benefit from his life's work remains a theme throughout the song.

As we shall see, this idea of fulfilling their covenant through upholding God's laws and thus becoming a model society to be emulated by other nations is key to understanding how the New England Puritans viewed their community. Notably, however—and the Puritans understood this well[13]—life in a blessed land flowing with milk and honey, the Biblical symbol of a highly urbanized and organized society, can lead to complacency and sinfulness, and ultimately also to destruction. Moses warns the Israelites against falling victim to this, enjoining them to be ever vigilant in their commitment to the laws: "Just watch yourself conscientiously lest you forget the things that your own eyes saw and lest they depart from your heart [i.e., mind] your entire life. And you shall make [them] known to your children and their children" (Deut. 4: 9). All the while, however, he is aware that what he warns against will one day come to pass: in the time of the Babylonians, the Israelites' rebellion against God's laws and their practice of idolatry[14] will break the terms of their covenant and lead to their exile from the promised land, in much the same manner as Adam and Eve were expelled from Eden:

> When you beget children and grandchildren and grow old in the land, you will act antagonistically, make a sculptured image of any form, and you will act wickedly in a manner displeasing to the Lord your God. ... The Lord will scatter you among the peoples, and just a few of you will remain among the nations thither the Lord will drive you. (Deut. 4: 25-27)

Unlike the expulsion from Eden, however, this one is not permanent.[15] The Lord, as Moses reminds his people, is a compassionate God who will not fail his people.

---

[13]   This is clearly reflected in John Cotton's sermons.

[14]   The prohibition against making any sculptured image or idol is the second of the ten commandments listed in Exodus 20 and Deuteronomy 5 in Jewish and many Christian traditions, including Anabaptists and other Radical Reformers, though not in the Catholic and Lutheran traditions. Both ancient rabbis and modern scholars have viewed the order of the commandments as one of descending importance. The first commandment ("I am the Lord your God" in the traditional Jewish enumeration but "You shall have no other gods besides [or "in addition to"] me" in the traditional Christian enumeration) is the most important of all laws in religions of "the Book." Given that fidelity and exclusivity are synonymous in monotheistic religion, the worship of any deity other than the Lord is incompatible with monotheistic religion (much as extramarital relations are incompatible with a monogamous marriage). The making and worshipping of an idol is wholly antithetical to the worship of the Lord, whether be it by trying to represent him (and breaking the second commandment alone) or by worshipping another god in addition to Him (breaking both the first and second commandments). Thus, in Deuteronomy 4: 25, when Moses warns that the Israelites will one day make an idol, he has singled out the ultimate sin, which will inevitably estrange the Israelites from God and break their covenant with him.

[15]   Upon the expulsion of Adam and Eve, God placed two cherubim with flaming swords east of the garden (Gen. 3: 24), emphasizing the permanence of their exile.

Once those in exile abandon idolatry (Deut. 4: 28)[16] to seek the Lord and abide by his laws, God "will not fail you or allow you to be destroyed. He will not forget the covenant that he swore with your fathers" (Deut. 4: 31).

The Biblical concept of the promised land, then, cannot be equated with an Edenic paradise where an individual can flee for a better life, free from struggle and toil; it is rather a place one enters as part of a community that is bound to God and his laws, and which is meant to serve as a model of good behavior for the rest of the world. Nor is the luxury of the promised land guaranteed forever: once within its borders, constant work and maintenance are required to reap its bounty.[17] Given that even Adam was expected to do upkeep in Eden (Gen. 2: 15), despite God having already planted everything he would need (Gen. 2: 8-9), this is hardly unexpected.

Thus, each individual must continually strive to uphold his part of the community's covenantal relationship with God, not only to draw forth the full bounty of the land but also lest he neglect or forget his obligations and be banished from it. Even for those who are in exile, however, there remains hope: provided they again take up their covenantal duties, they may one day re-enter the promised land.

The Puritan Concept of the Promised Land

During a discussion in "Vision of Kings: Springsteen and the American Dream" in his book, *Born in the USA*, Jim Cullen recognizes the importance of the "covenant" to the New England Puritans and identifies it as the heart of their American dream: for them it is "an implicit pact with God that he would provide for them spiritually if they formed a community to honor him according to his precepts as they understood them" (Cullen 53). While not entirely accurate—the pact was explicit rather than implicit,[18] and God was expected to provide for them

---

[16]   Indeed, this lesson is repeated throughout the books of Judges and Kings by providing examples of the people's failure to exclusively worship the Lord and the misfortunes they endured as a result. Cf. 2 Kings 17 and the destruction of the northern kingdom of Israel by the conquering Assyrian armies.

[17]   Cf. Deut. 30: 9: "And the Lord your God will make you exceedingly prosperous in all your achievements, in your offspring, in your cattle's offspring, and in your land's yield; for the Lord will again delight in prospering you, as he delighted in your fathers."

[18]   Cf. Cotton's *The Way of the Churches of Christ in New England*: "For the joyning of faithfull Christians into the fellowship and estate of a Church, we finde not in Scripture that God hath done it any other way then by entering all of them together (as one man) into an holy Covenant with himselfe, To take the Lord (as the head of the Church) for their God, and to give up themselves to him, to be his Church and people" (Proposition 3, 2). Furthermore, the Puritans, unlike the Israelites, did not envision simply one covenant. They also had the Covenant of Redemption, and the Covenant of Grace, even transforming the concept of marriage from a sacrament to a covenant (Williams 111). Cotton himself

physically rather than spiritually—Cullen's general theme is correct: the Puritans reinforced their self-identification as the New Israel through Biblical terminology. This is supported by an excerpt, also quoted in Cullen's book, from Governor John Winthrop's 1630 lay sermon aboard the *Arabella*:

> [W]ee shall finde that the God of Israell is among us, when tenn of us shall be able to resist a thousand of our enemies, when hee shall make us a prayse and glory, that men shall say of succeeding plantacions: the lord make it like that of New England: for wee must Consider that wee shall be as a Citty upon a Hill, the eies of all people are uppon us. (Winthrop, "Christian Charitie" 93)[19]

Within these two sentences, Winthrop makes several pertinent allusions to both the Old and New Testaments of the Bible. The imagery of a small band of men resisting a much larger opposing force is found in Leviticus 26: 8 and Joshua 23: 10; both these passages recount a renewal of the covenant ceremony between Israel and God[20] with Leviticus 26: 9-10 adding that if the Israelites uphold their obligations, then God will make their crops so abundant that they "will have to send out the old (grain) on account of the new" (Lev. 26: 10). The idea that other nations will praise the glory of New England's harvest further recalls the Biblical imagery in Deuteronomy. 4: 5-6 (above), in which the nations praise the uniqueness of Israel's laws. Finally, Winthrop masterfully weaves a reference to fame, the "Citty upon a Hill," taken from the Gospel of Matthew, into his vision of what New England will become. In the Biblical account, Jesus notifies the crowds gathered before him at the Sermon of the Mount: "You are the light of the world. A city built on a hill cannot be hid. … In the same way, let your light shine before others, so that they may see your good works and give glory to your Father in heaven" (Matt. 5: 14-16). In typical Puritan fashion, Winthrop thus borrows vivid visual imagery from both testaments to remind his fellow pilgrims who they are and what their contribution to the world will be. They, the commissioned New

---

mentioned several of the different covenants and with whom God originally cut them in chapter 1, proposition 3 of his *Way of the Churches of Christ*.

[19]   Cullen's quote, which differs slightly, but not significantly, from this text is found in Winthrop ("Model of Christian Charity" 91).

[20]   Leviticus 26:8 says that five men will chase a hundred and a hundred, ten thousand. Deuteronomy 32, reversing the roles of who gives chase if the Israelites are guilt of vexing the Lord, says one man will route a thousand and two, ten thousand. Joshua 23:10, the only of the three texts placed in the mouth of Joshua, not Moses, says one will chase a thousand. To be fair to Cullen (above), if his statement considering the Puritans' "'covenant' an implicit pact" is based solely upon Winthrop's quoted text, then he is indeed accurate, though short-sighted, since all three Biblical passages are part of larger explicit covenant ceremonies. His statement that God "would provide for them spiritually" remains wholly inaccurate even in the context of Winthrop's sermon, for there Winthrop's mention of the "succeeding plantations" is undeniably a reference to God's physical, not spiritual, provisioning of his people.

England saints, have been charged to build a New Jerusalem in the New World and hasten the apocalypse and redemption. In keeping with this model, the success of the eschaton, or the end times, and the bounty of the harvest[21] are entirely dependent on scrupulous faithfulness to the Biblical model of society. If too many individuals broke faith and betrayed the covenant, the Puritan community would be liable to the same curses that Moses and Joshua had warned the Israelites against: destruction and exile.

That said, the question begs to be asked: "What did the New England Puritans view as behavior reflective of their commitment to God's covenant?" The most immediate and obvious answer, to faithfully keep the law, required a definition of what exactly the proper body of law was. Toward this end, in 1636, the General Court appointed John Cotton, whose views were bound by a rigorous Biblicism, to help frame the laws of New England (Maclear 73); though his work was not ultimately adopted, it would have an indirect influence on the Massachusetts colonial constitution of 1648 (Jordan). Always the typologist, Cotton viewed the local magistrates of Massachusetts as the modern kings of Israel (Emerson 138) and believed that the Puritans were bound by the laws of the ancient Israelites "because God, who was then bound up in covenant with [the Hebrews] to be their God, hath put us in their stead and is become our God as well as theirs, and hence we are much bound to their laws as well as themselves" (Cotton, "Moses" 281). To be sure, Cotton was not suggesting that New Englanders were bound to every ancient Israelite law, distinguishing between the "permanent judicials," or moral (even "natural") laws, to which they *were* subject, and the "temporary judicials," or specific aspects of the ceremonial and cultic laws, to which they were not.[22]

In following the "permanent judicials," the behavior of the Puritans was expected to reflect not only the letter, but also the moral spirit embedded within the laws. Since the Fall of Adam, Winthrop asserted, "every man is borne with this principle in him, to love and seeke himselfe only"; it was thus up to the

---

[21]   In *A Brief Description of New York*, written in 1670, Daniel Denton describes the bounty of the land in ways reminiscent of the spies' description in Numbers 13 (above): 'The Fruit natural to the Island, are *Mulberries, Persimmons, Grapes*, great and small, *Huckelberries, Cramberries, Plums* of several sorts, *Raspberries* and *Strawberries*, of which last is such abundance in June, that the Fields and Woods are died red" (qtd in Parrington 5).

[22]   Not only does Cotton present New England as the modern Israel by basing his "How Far Moses Judicialls Bind Massachusetts" upon Mosaic law, but also he reinforces the comparison by quoting Deuteronomy 4: 6 (above), where Moses reminds the Israelites that their observance of the just laws will serve as a model to the rest of the world (Jordan, "Calvinism"). Indeed, Cotton's division of moral from ceremonial law would not be unexpected from someone interpreting the Old Testament typologically. If we read Cotton's later statement that "the more any law smells of man, the more unprofitable" ("Moses" 284) in connection with his quotation of Deuteronomy 4: 6, then this statement serves not only as a polemic against common law traditions in Europe, but also reinforces just how "just" the Biblical laws, and hence his own proposed laws for the Bay Colony, are.

Puritans, through Christ, to "infuseth another principle love to God and our brother" (Winthrop, "Christian Charitie" 86). Indeed, Winthrop claimed "wee must be willing to abridge our selves of our superfluities, for the supply of others necessities ... always having before our eyes our Commission and Community in the worke, our Community as members of the same body" ("Christian Charitie" 92).[23] Self-interest, consequently, as something that worked against the common good,[24] was considered a sin. To quote Cotton once more:

> So a carnall man, that never served any man but himselfe, call him to distresse in it, and he murmures and cries out at it; but take you a Christian man, that is wonted to serve God in serving of men, when hee hath beene faithfull and usefull in his calling, ... this is the life of faith in the upshot of a mans calling, he layes it downe in confidence of Gods acceptance. ("The Way" 447-48)

For Cotton, and for the Puritans overall, the goal was selflessness, most readily manifested in a solid work ethic. We need only reference Max Weber's *The Protestant Ethic and the Spirit of Capitalism* (1904-1905), which postulates that the Puritan work ethic influenced capitalism through its focus on self-discipline and indefinitely delayed gratification (Williams 114). Much of Weber's thesis regarding the Puritan (more specifically, Calvinist) work ethic is based on the idea that predestination and vocational "calling" intertwine, so that one's good works serve as indirect evidence of being among God's elect. In other words, "God helps those who help themselves."

In addition to maintaining a solid work ethic, the good Puritan was expected to practice acts of charity as he was able.[25] Cotton includes children, the poor, and strangers among those receiving charity from the community. This list of recipients is similar to that found in Deuteronomy where Moses charges the Israelites with the protection of the weak and powerless in their society: "'Cursed is the one who perverts justice due the stranger, the orphan, and the widow.' And all the people shall say, 'Amen'" (Deut 27: 19).[26]

A stranger or foreign resident lacks the protection of the government while a widow or orphan lacks the protection normally afforded by a husband or father.

---

[23] Cf. 1 Cor. 12: 12-27 for Paul's discussion of the body of Christ.

[24] Cotton also references 1 Cor. 10: 24; Phil. 2: 4; and Gal. 5: 6 ("The Way of Life" 439).

[25] Cotton, "The Way of Life" 459: "If a man have the dexterity to manage a great estate, and to overcome it, then the more a man hath, the more good service will he doe to Church and Common-wealth, to children and poore kindred and strangers; and it is faith that thus subdues the world to obedience of the will of God and the service of our brethren; faith carries the world pinioned and shackled that it stirs no further, then that we may doe God and men service with it."

[26] Cf. Exod. 22: 21-22; Deut. 10: 18; 14: 29; 24: 19, 20, 21; 26: 12-13; and the prophetic statement in Isa. 1: 17 and 23.

All three of these categories depend on society for sustenance (cf. Deut. 24:19-21, where the poor collect for themselves food intentionally not harvested, and 26:12-13, where they receive from the Israelites' offerings). Cotton's categories of children, the poor, and strangers thus directly recall those in the Bible. Notably, while many of those in these categories are unable to work at all, it is more likely that what work they do brings in insufficient provisions. It would be morally indefensible not to work if one was able (Govier 131).

To recap, the Puritan ideal of the promised land is best understood when it is placed within the larger context of a covenant with God, comparable to that which the Israelites made immediately before and after they crossed the Jordan River and entered Canaan. Success in the promised land, for both the Israelites and the Puritans, was wholly dependent on their acting in accordance with the terms of the covenant, which included both civil law (though we now consider many of Moses' and Cotton's civil laws to be religious) and moral uprightness, expressed through one's vocational calling and charity performed on behalf of the community, especially toward the poor. Failure to uphold these obligations would bring punishment and the threat of exile. The Puritan promised land was thus never, and should not now, be identified with a utopia. As Nathaniel Hawthorne noted in the *Scarlet Letter* (1850), written some 200 years after Cotton: "The founders of a new colony, whatever Utopia of human virtue and happiness they might originally project, have invariably recognized it among their earliest practical necessities to allot a portion of the virgin soil as a cemetery, and another portion as the site of a prison" (53). This passage embodies the difference between the easy, perfect, and ultimately unattainable world conjured up by the term "utopia," which translates literally and appropriately as "nowhere," and the promised land of the Puritans, which, because of its inhabitants' recognition of their own sinfulness, was not perfect but could still serve as a "Citty upon a Hill" model to the world.

The Springsteen Concept of the Promised Land

Having explored both the Biblical narratives on the promised land, which inform Springsteen's use of related imagery, and the later Puritan concepts of it, which have figured strongly in shaping American self-understanding from the time of the Puritans to the present day, it is now possible to productively examine the representation of the promised land in Bruce Springsteen's corpus of work (see note 6 above). Since the misunderstanding of the promised land as a dreamy utopian paradise occurs early and fairly frequently in Springsteen's writings, it is useful to first examine the song in which this misunderstanding is most starkly apparent: "From Small Things (Big Things One Day Come)." Moving then to a discussion of the two songs most associated with the promised land in the history of rock and roll, "The Promised Land" and "Thunder Road," in which utopian associations remain readily apparent, we end with an analysis of "Galveston Bay" and "Across the Border," which were written during the second half of Springsteen's career and in which the promised land is at last understood in a manner comparable to its Biblical and Puritan presentation.

In "From Small Things," the protagonist is an unnamed teenager constantly in pursuit of more: "At sixteen she quit high school to make her fortune in the promised land / She got a job behind the counter in an all night hamburger stand." When we first meet her, she has already abandoned her mother and education for her dreams of making it big in the promised land. While she takes a job and maintains contact with her mother (if for no other reason than to provide the song's hook), she repeatedly demonstrates a willingness to abandon anything and everything to which she has committed when something that seems better comes along, betraying her immaturity and innate selfishness. In the second verse, she appears to have matured somewhat, staying with the handsome Johnny long enough to buy a house and have a couple of kids;[27] soon, however, her romantic ideals and impulsive, even erratic, behaviors resurface. Her love, like her commitment, "is fleeting," and she leaves the responsibility and stability of her family to run away to Tampa with a "Wyomie County real estate man."[28]

Once again, though she reports home that "[l]ife is just heaven in the sun," the protagonist is unable to commit permanently to the life she has chosen. Florida may well be the utopia she has always mistaken for the promised land—the nowhere for which she has in turn abandoned her mother, her job, and her family—but she ultimately, and inevitably, finds it empty. Her carnal, self-serving instincts, which Cotton would have blamed on Adam and which the Puritans worked assiduously

---

[27]   Significantly, just as she recklessly left her childhood behind for a conventional adolescent fantasy, the man she finds, "lonesome Johnny," is stereotypically "tall and handsome" (perhaps she could not tell if he was "dark" because it was night), suggesting all she ever really wanted was the generic American dream. This interpretation is then reinforced by their purchase of a hillside house and the two (though not 2.5) children. However, there is no mention of a dog.

[28]   Though on *The Essential Bruce Springsteen*, Springsteen sings "Wyomie County," listing it so in the lyrics, Dave Edmunds sings "Wyoming County" in his cover on his album *D.E. 7th* (1982). There are three such counties in the United States: one in western New York, one in northeastern Pennsylvania, and one in southern West Virginia. Bob Crane (*A Place to Stand* 101) believes that any of these is a credible location for the song since each has the rolling waters mentioned in the final verse: the Genesee River, the Susquehanna River, and the Guyandotte River, respectively. Why any of these three places—if the real referent of Springsteen's version—would be considered a "promised land" worthy as a place of escape is unknown. More likely is the possibility that the protagonist left her mother and only made it as far as Wyomie/ing County (which, though unlikely, could even be her home county) before having to give up on her original quest and thence left for Florida, which would more appropriately be labeled a promised land. Against this interpretation, however, is the ironic use of "promised land" in "Racing in the Street." In this song, "all the shut-down strangers and hot-rod angels" are "[r]umbling through this promised land" while the singer and his despondent girlfriend head out to the sea together to find redemption. For a more hopeful interpretation of these lines, see Cullen (121).

to overcome, ultimately lead her into exile from both society and her family, the latter of which was the only thing that might have provided her with the promised land she had been seeking all along. Meanwhile, Johnny, who "prays" rather than waits "for his baby's parole,"[29] dedicates his life to what remains of his family, "[a] blue-eyed daughter and a handsome son," and to the community where his burger order and heart were taken.[30] Broken-hearted, his life is no utopian paradise, but he seems nonetheless to have achieved and maintained his place in the promised land.[31]

In the songs "The Promised Land" and "The Price You Pay," Springsteen sets his narratives in the middle of the desert, using the environment itself to invoke images of the Israelite wanderings in the wilderness. "The Promised Land" begins "On a rattlesnake speedway in the Utah desert," with the singer admitting to "chasing some mirage"; this is a definite change from the girl in "From Small Things," who does not appear to be so self-aware. Here, the singer thinks of himself as committed to his work and to his family ("Working all day in my daddy's garage"), even as he seeks escape from the life he is leading for an easier, and likely more utopian, dream. When he asserts, "I've done my best to live the right way," he appears to be trying to convince himself that he has upheld the Puritan work ethic, which he understands as to "get up every morning and go to

---

[29] This wording implies that she is unlikely to return from exile (or be paroled) anytime soon.

[30] Though not a definitive reading of the lyrics, the songs seem to suggest that Wyomie County is both the location of the burger stand and of the house on the hillside. This may be just an argument from silence, since nothing indicates that they relocated in order to buy the house, but every other relocation the protagonist makes in the song is explicitly marked.

[31] By examining "From Small Things" against the backdrop of Cotton's view of the Fall of Adam and the selfishness of the carnal individual, we get a hint of the theological/ psychological answers to the questions posed by *Nebraska* (1982). In particular, "From Small Things" compares well with the first and last songs on that album: "Nebraska" and "Reason to Believe." In the latter song, lonesome Johnny is not all that different from the groom who is "[w]onderin' where can his baby be" ("Reason to Believe"). Both men desire to be part of a larger community and wait indefinitely for their would-be brides. Also, neither man has any real hope of finding his baby but "Still at the end of every hard-earned day people find some reason to believe." On the other side of the coin, the girl in "From Small Things" is ultimately driven to meaninglessly kill an unsuspecting person, not unlike the Charles Starkweather-based character of "Nebraska." At the end of that song, just moments before his execution, he coldly tells us, "They wanted to know why I did what I did / Well sir I guess there's just a meanness in this world." While Springsteen writes, "There was a stillness on the surface of those pictures [*True Confessions* and Terrence Malick's *Badlands*], while underneath lay a world of moral ambiguity and violence" (*Songs* 136), Cotton reminds us that the morally ambiguous world and its violence are the result of the Fall of Adam: the carnal man has served only himself ever since, which is why "there's just a meanness in this world."

work each day."[32] His dissatisfaction, however, leaves his tension and rage rising until he is ready to snap, "itching for something to start." That he is prepared, and even seems to desire, to "tear this whole town apart" to remove his pain, however, is testimony to his ultimate selfishness: he has no real regard for the well-being of his family or community, and seeks only freedom from and control over his personal oppression. Though aware, deep down, that he is pursuing a mirage, he refuses to give up his chase.

Larry Smith, like many others before him, suggests that the singer's problems will be solved, in the manner of a *deus ex machina*, by the twister forming on the horizon because he, unlike everyone else, has faith:

> This individual is not afraid to test his faith; in fact, he warns that without that faith, the "storm" will be all-consuming. For him, however, the storm may contain cleansing powers that rid life of broken dreams and their consequences. Faith is the key—faith will provide the fuel that ensures that the struggle will yield victory. Faith provides the path to the promised land. (L. Smith 197-98)

This passage fails to define a crucial point: in what exactly does the singer have faith? Finding the mirage he chases—which is by definition an illusion? The opportunity to oppress others, just as he believes he has been oppressed? Proving that he is actually deserving of the title "man?" So considered, these desires (perhaps better considered delusions) are hardly noble or really worthy of faith. Smith's romantic interpretation of the song is as shallow as the singer's commitment to the covenant he shares with his community, and more, with humanity. The storm will not miraculously refocus his life by removing everything that constricts him (L. Smith 218), but it may well lead him to complete despair. The storm may

---

[32] "The working life" appears again in the next song on *Darkness*, "Factory." "Factory" and "The Promised Land" tell the same story, with the father's garage of the latter being the factory of the former. In both songs, the men are devoted to their jobs not because they have been indoctrinated with the Puritan work ethic, but rather because they have no choice but to work in order to survive. This survival, however, is characterized as a slow but implacable path to destruction. In both songs, the singer says the job is slowly killing the workers: after another day's work in the factories, the men have "death in their eyes," while the man leaving his daddy's garage claims to "feel so weak I just want to explode." That someone else will get hurt seems inevitable in "Factory" ("And you just better believe, boy / Somebody's gonna get hurt tonight"). During his discussion of the roles of work versus play in an individual's life, Cullen evaluates the Puritan doctrine of election:

In one sense, it's a fairly straightforward matter: work destroys, play preserves; work pollutes, play purifies. But in this description, grace is not simply conferred to all. Rather, the elect are those who have the strength to play. As in the case of the Puritan religion, however, there is no straightforward equation as to who is saved and who is not; we're not told *which* [Cullen's emphasis] guys start dying, or *why* some come home and wash up, only that some do. For those who do, such salvation—however fleeting or misleading—is a palpable experience. (Cullen 119)

"Blow away the dreams that break your heart / Blow away the lies that leave you nothing but lost and brokenhearted," but there is no indication of what, if anything, will remain.

A better interpretation is provided by Cullen, who notes that "The Promised Land" and related songs from *Darkness on the Edge of Town* "reflect the obsessions of a relatively naïve white boy who is shocked to learn that the world is not his oyster" (64). In this regard, the singer is really no different from the girl in "From Small Things," except, of course, that he has not yet snapped. In "The Price You Pay," the desert is similarly evoked as the setting of the narrative, and the singer himself is a more mature figure; though he recognizes the pain related in "The Promised Land," he has now learned both how to live with it and how to fulfill his responsibility to his community. This is not to say that he is resigned; he defiantly claims: "And girl before the end of the day / I'm gonna tear it down and throw it away." What he plans to tear down in this case is instructive; it is neither himself nor another person but rather the sign "[t]hat counts the men fallen away." Though he has no trouble evoking living narratives of disappointed lives and fallen heroes, reminding the girl and her baby of the denial of Moses' entry into Canaan (above),[33] the singer is unwilling to let stand a monument to this disappointment. This theme is continued in the second and third verses of the song, which describe those who died prior to Moses in the wilderness as a result of their lack of faith (Num. 14, above) as well as they describe modern people. The distinction is clear: while the Biblical references serve as reminders that we are not alone in our struggles, the sign in the song stands only as a monument to futility, a symbol of the inevitability of disappointment. The chorus itself, "Now you can't walk away from the price you pay," the price which man has been paying since the Fall of Adam, emphasizes the necessity of committing oneself to the good of the community, using one's vocational calling despite the personal costs.[34]

---

[33] Springsteen's decision to place the little girl "down on the strand" provides an interesting double-entendre for the song. "Strand," may have been selected primarily because it rhymes with the next four lines (hands, land, sands, land) and is used elsewhere for rhyming purposes (cf. "I Wish I Were Blind"), but the denotations of this word are also telling. *The American Heritage College Dictionary* (1364) defines strand, the noun, as "the land bordering a body of water; a beach," which both recalls the New Jersey shore as well as the place of Moses' final speech to the Israelites and death on Mount Nebo, overlooking the Dead Sea. Moreover, as an intransitive verb, strand recalls stranded, which means "to be brought into or left in a difficult or helpless position." The singer warns the girl that she can run but cannot beat "the price you pay." She and her child, along with the rest of mankind, are stranded and left to make the best of it.

[34] Another song from *The River* seems to answer the complaints of the singer in "The Promised Land." Whereas in "The Promised Land," the isolated singer complains that "your eyes go blind and your blood runs cold," the singer in "Two Hearts"—like the one in "The Price You Pay"—realizes that community removes the sense of isolation and brokenheartedness that plagues the individual in "The Promised Land." The final verse of "Two Hearts" provides the answer and encourages those who are despondent:

The Tunnel of Love Express Tour, along with the subsequent Amnesty International Human Rights Now! Tour, inspired Springsteen to re-examine "Born to Run." On his 1975, *Born to Run* album, "Born to Run" and "Thunder Road" are about adolescents in search of better lives. The more explicit song of the two, "Thunder Road," casts the promised land and heaven as synonymous, representing a utopian paradise: "Heaven's waiting on down the tracks / Oh oh come take my hand / We're riding out tonight to case the promised land."[35] "Born to Run" originally tells a similar story, but with much more exciting visual and musical imagery. In April, 1988, however, Springsteen spoke of the short-sightedness of these adolescent pursuits:

> I guess, when I wrote this song, I thought I was writing about a guy and a girl that wanted to run—and keep on running, and never go back. And that was a nice romantic idea. But I realized that after I put all those people in all those cars, I was going to have to figure out some place for them to go. And I realized that in the end … that individual freedom, when it's not connected to some sort of community, or friends, or their world outside, [that freedom] ends up feeling pretty meaningless. So … that guy and that girl, they were out there looking for connection. And I guess that's what I'm doing here tonight. So this is a song about two people trying to find their way home. (Springsteen, "Born to Run (Acoustic)")

The promised land cannot exist without community and a commitment to its maintenance. The couples in both these songs—like the girl in "From Small Things" and the man in "The Promised Land"—at best achieve a meaningless utopia. Without that connection, which, along with the commitment to a vocation, comprises the real (Biblical and Puritan) promised land, they are left isolated, which "is the most dangerous thing on earth" (Springsteen, 1987, qtd in Duffy 89). This theme is more fully developed in "Galveston Bay," where it is explicitly treated, and in "Across the Border," where it is implicitly so.

> That's if you think your heart is stone
> And that you're rough enough to whip this world alone
> Alone buddy there ain't no peace of mind
> That's why I'll keep searching till I find my special one.

[35] Cf. "From Small Things," wherein "the promised land" and "heaven" are both appellations given to Florida. Additionally, the promised land mentioned in "The Ghost of Tom Joad" may be understood as a reference to the Christian concept of heaven in the afterlife, from which there is no return. However, this could be another ironic use of the phrase, where the preacher's "one-way ticket" brought him to California, only to leave him stranded outside society like so many others on the album (cf. "Sinaloa Cowboys" and "Balboa Park"). Note also that a one-way ticket brought the little boy of "Johnny Bye-Bye" out to the promised land of California, at least when this song is supplemented by Chuck Berry's song of the same title.

"Galveston Bay" relates the story of Le Bin Son and Billy Sutter, two men who, despite their superficially overwhelming differences, actually have a great deal in common. Both men fought to keep South Vietnam free from the communists and both men went "home" to Seabrook, Texas, to make a living. In 1968 Billy returned home and took up the family business. In 1975 Le and his extended family relocated to the promised land along the Gulf Coast and began shrimping. Both men are absolutely dedicated to their families, each kissing his child before heading off to work. Both view themselves as members of a community and are devoted to their vocational callings, which benefit society by providing food. The focus of the story is the point at which the two communities come into direct contact and apparent conflict. Billy, afraid that his livelihood will be usurped by the Vietnamese immigrants, joins up with the Texas Klan in the hopes of scaring them away. His response, classic American xenophobia, seems to have been fueled by the mere presence of Le and his fellow immigrants.[36] That Le killed two Texans in self-defense and then continued to guard his family should not challenge this supposition in any way, as Springsteen himself tells us. Indeed, it reinforces the stability and propriety of Le's devotion to the well-being of his family and to his calling. It is Billy who plays the dynamic character in the song, finally coming to realize that Le and his fellow immigrants have actually become a part of, rather than a threat to, the local community. Cullen says that Billy recognizes their common humanity (72), or brotherhood,[37] but the relationship between the two men may be more accurately defined using the covenantal terminology of the promised land. Both Moses and Cotton would consider these immigrants strangers who, along with the orphans/children and widows/poor, are the proper recipients of charity (above).[38] In this case, Le has left the protection of his homeland with no one to protect his family but himself. He and his cousin fulfill their obligation in working as they are able, reaping the bounty of the land—or in this case the

---

[36]   To twenty-first century pluralists, Le may have perfected the Biblical and Puritan concepts of the promised land because he intends neither to rid the land of its previous inhabitants nor to convert them: his only goal is survival through assimilation.

[37]   Cullen defines brotherhood as "love that transcends boundaries" (138), but Billy's revelation is more one of tolerance and acceptance than love and brotherhood. As usual, Cullen veers toward the more romantic interpretation of the songs.

[38]   Over the years, Springsteen has worked to feed the poor in our own society in many ways, giving direct donations to local food banks in the towns hosting his concerts as well as encouraging concert-goers to donate to local food bank volunteers as they leave the concert venue. On the 2005 Devils and Dust Tour, Springsteen again promoted the local food banks in his introduction to "The Promised Land," reminding his audience that these volunteers "are doing God's work."

sea—so that they are not dependent on handouts,[39] but they remain strangers and are not to be preyed upon.[40]

This brings us at last to "Across the Border." Although the phrase "the promised land," is not explicit here, this is nonetheless the most poetic and romantic of all Springsteen's promised land songs. Ideally, this discussion would end with the song itself, with Springsteen's falsetto and the violin interweaving as they did occasionally during the stadium leg of the Summer Tour 2003. Instead, the following analysis must suffice. On the eve of his crossing the Rio Grande, the singer anticipates the coming voyage with his love, here called his *corazón* (literally, "heart"), into the promised land; there is no sense of urgency here, however, as we saw in "From Small Things," "The Promised Land," "Thunder Road," and "Born to Run." Tonight, the two will sing together, dream together, and rest in knowing that tomorrow's strength is dependent on remaining together.[41] The singer has the same commitment to his family as Le Bin Son and will build a house "[h]igh up on a grassy hill" for it.[42] Of course, his promised land is as much of a dream of something better as is anyone else's, not only that of the girl in "From Small Things" or the man in "The Promised Land," but also that of the ancient Israelites and the New England Puritans. To a degree, this is necessary; if the potential pilgrim's original residence were better than the promised land, there would be no reason to face the dangers of relocation to a strange land. The singer in "Across the Border" imagines that same house on the hillside that came so easily to the girl in "From Small Things" and was abandoned just as easily;[43] the difference here is that this man is willing to selflessly work for the house, to build it with his own hands and to commit to all that comes with it.

Another significant difference between this man and the other seekers in Springsteen's corpus is that he envisions a relationship—perhaps even a covenant—with God in the new land in addition to his covenant with his family and community. Like the Israelites and the Puritans before him, he has faith that the divine will ensure the safety of the journey and the benefit of both the people

---

[39]   In his treatment of "Galveston Bay," Cullen relates that the shrimping industry outside of Houston was highly competitive despite being relatively accessible (70).

[40]   We are given no hint that the relationship between Billy and Le ever develops beyond tolerance. In the end, Billy (and presumably Le as well) gets up, kisses his family, and returns to his vocational calling.

[41]   His bags are already packed in anticipation of the trip to the promised land, as (figuratively) were those of the singer in "The Promised Land" before him.

[42]   That the phrase "high upon a grassy hill" is also evocative of Winthrop's call aboard the *Arabella* for the Puritans to establish their "Citty upon a Hill" further suggests that the singer and his lover understand their responsibility to act as model citizens in their new community, as had the Puritans 300 years earlier.

[43]   That he would have to build his own house stands as an interesting contrast to the Biblical tradition, in which Moses reminds the Israelites that they will occupy whole cities that they did not build and harvest vineyards they did not sow (Deut. 6: 10-11).

and the land. To borrow from "The Promised Land," it is exactly this that serves as the basis for "the faith to stand [his] ground":

> And may the saints' blessing and grace
> Carry me safely into your arms
> There across the border
> For what are we
> Without hope in our hearts
> That someday we'll drink from God's blessed waters

The man seeks the promised land with God's aid, in cooperation with his community, and through his calling to work for the benefit of this same community. Unlike "The Promised Land," where the desert storm violently blows away the hurt incurred from lies and broken dreams, the cleansing achieved in "Across the Border" is tranquil; he will gently "kiss the sorrow from [his lover's] eyes" as they embrace under the open skies. Her healing will be his healing, as well as his blessing and his redemption, and no unsuspecting outsider will be hurt in the process.

It is thus only fitting, as the song ends, that the singer envisions the same bounty in the land that the ancient Israelites saw in southern Canaan (Num. 13, above) and that Daniel Denton found in New York (see note 21, above): "And eat the fruit from the vine / I know love and fortune will be mine / Somewhere across the border." In "Across the Border," the Biblical and Puritan ideals of the promised land are finally realized and fulfilled. To quote Springsteen's intro to "Born to Run" in April, 1988 (Springsteen, "Born to Run (Acoustic)), the violence is stilled and, for a moment, we gain a glimpse of "two people trying to find their way home."[44]

---

[44] A special thanks to Karen Sonik, who edited this article many times over and suggested this concluding sentence.

Chapter 9
From Adam to Jesus: Springsteen's Use of Scripture[1]

Matthew Orel

> Son of man, can these bones live?
>
> Ezek. 37: 3

Introduction

When Bruce Springsteen wrote "Devils & Dust," he presented a situation of what he calls "untenable choices"—choices involving life and death not only for the singer, but for those around him. The singer tells of a dream:

> Well I dreamed of you last night
> In a field of blood and stone
> The blood began to dry
> The smell began to rise

In Ezekiel 37, the prophet has a dream. In a valley of dry bones, he is asked whether the bones can live; upon responding that only God knows, he is commanded to put flesh—and eventually life—into the dry, dead bones. This dream shows Ezekiel an affirmation of God's covenant with Israel and his promise to unify them in a land of peace.

"Devils & Dust" turns Ezekiel's dream on its head: the dream is of dry bones, but the dreamer has no vision of reviving them. What rises from the bones isn't living people, but a smell—a smell of death. Without God's intervention, bones do not come back to life, and people killed in battle stay dead. Biblical visions cannot tell the troops of today that God is, indeed, on *their* side. The vision is frightening. Its adaptation of a familiar Biblical story to tell a modern tale—with a far different ending—gives the song much of its resonance. We *know* this story, but this isn't the spiritually happy ending we've been taught. This story is not simply history or fable, it is *here* and *now,* and the results are in doubt. We don't *know,* in the end, if God is really on our side, but without the evidence, the vision is more apocalyptic than redemptive.

---

[1] I'd like to thank Billy Innes, Dave Marsh, Lauren Onkey, and Beverly Orel for their assistance and suggestions for this chapter.

Priests, Saints, and Floods

Upon seeing the lyrics to "Devils & Dust," my first question was, how did we get to this point? How did Bruce Springsteen, who spent much of his early career taking swipes at the formal religious-based Bible training of his youth, come to use scripture as a component of his narratives? In an interview in 2005 Springsteen said:

> A lot of my entire early schooling was filled with religious imagery and a way of looking at the world through spiritual images. I think some of those things got distorted, but some of those things really stuck and had resonant meaning for me when I went to interpret the world myself through my own work … It's just something I naturally gravitated to. (Interview with Dave Fanning).

In his early career, the distortions were the rule. When Bruce Springsteen auditioned for John Hammond in 1972, Hammond asked him if there were any songs he wouldn't dare record (*John Hammond: From Bessie Smith to Bruce Springsteen*). Springsteen proceeded to play "If I Was the Priest," which included a presentation of the Virgin Mary as a stone junkie whore and the Holy Ghost as running a burlesque show, among other decidedly warped visions.

Springsteen did not include "If I Was the Priest" on any of his subsequent Columbia releases. But the song revealed his willingness to use the imagery that he had been taught—including Biblical imagery—to tell his stories. In those early songs, the Biblical references were typically either vague or superficial, often twisting the roles traditionally attached to well-known characters or events. There's no specific Biblical reference in "If I Was the Priest," but by his alteration of Mary's image Springsteen presented visions of a world gone wrong, and while doing so declared his own rejection of the religious lessons he had been taught.

Springsteen's first Columbia album *Greetings from Asbury Park, NJ* continued the pattern of using Biblical references to assert his disaffection with formal Catholicism. Typically, well-known characters and stories would be introduced in a song or song title, and then used to portray a vision that might be totally contrary to the way in which they are conventionally taught. There are few references to specific Biblical passages; while *images* from the Bible such as saints and the Flood are presented, Springsteen showed little evidence that he was familiar with the underlying text. An example of this would be in "Lost in the Flood," which uses the phrase "immaculate conception" (a phrase not directly from the Bible), even though, in context, the intent appears to be a reference to the Biblical story of the virgin birth.

Even in that first album, Springsteen consistently used Biblical references not to teach Bible or faith, but rather to describe the condition of his world and decidedly human stories. But the Biblical images—and Bruce's often negative reaction to them—often *were* the focus of the story: messed up people were "Lost in the Flood," and the devil appeared as Jesus through the steam in the street. Gypsies substituted for prophets, women were saints, and if you put them together just right you might just find Gypsy Angel Row, for one night anyway. In an interview from 1975, Springsteen said, "I don't go to church. I ain't been to church in eight years. I don't believe in any of that stuff" (Duffy 86). Springsteen's early career reflects this attitude, all the while continuing to use the imagery that he had learned.

Casing the Promised Land

When a person perceives his world as having gone wrong, he might dream of better places. Bruce Springsteen, from his first personal visions through to his most recent views through the eyes of immigrants, outcasts, and discards, has persistently pursued this dream. The general theme of escape to a better place was present in Springsteen's work in many early songs: In "For You," the girl commits suicide to find a better place than the one she was living for; in "Mary Queen of Arkansas" the singer muses about contacts in Mexico; and pretty much the entirety of "Rosalita" is constructed around the idea of getting that girl out of her parents' house in any way possible. These characters all dream of going away and never coming back, even if they don't quite know, really, where they are going. The general theme echoed an Animals song that Springsteen often covered in the mid-1970s: "We Gotta Get Out of this Place."

In the Bible, the story of the promised land is first introduced in the book of Genesis, wherein God promises to Abram the land of Canaan. It is portrayed as a better place, a place of plenty, but also as a place that could not be entered without years of struggle and sacrifice. In short, it was depicted as very nearly exactly the place that Springsteen was seeking, first for himself and then for the song characters he created. While a promise of permanent escape and a better destination has some faint echoes of the Biblical story, Springsteen would become much more explicit about its use through the course of his career. The first explicit reference to the promised land in a Springsteen lyric occurs in "Thunder Road." After the singer says, "we're riding out tonight to case the promised land," he concludes, almost triumphantly, "it's a town full of losers and I'm pulling out of here to win." Although the singer has invited the girl—Mary—to join him, his journey to his proposed land is otherwise solo. "Born to Run" similarly references—though not by name—the promised land as a better place to which just the singer and his companion will go: "Someday girl I don't know when / We're gonna get to that place / Where we really want to go." The mantra "Nobody wins unless everybody wins" was years away; this was no train carrying sinners as well as saints, losers as well as winners. Young Bruce fully intended to leave that old town of losers behind.

In his 1970s-era promised land references, Springsteen's tone is nearly messianic; he will be the one who breaks through where others have failed. And in songs such as "Thunder Road" and "Born to Run," each of which builds to those statements, we can almost—though not quite—believe that those journeys will be made, that the singer's determination will lead him to that special place. "Iceman," an out-take from the *Darkness on the Edge of Town* sessions subsequently recorded on *Tracks*, is more grim, but equally determined:

> We'll take the midnight road right to the devil's door
> And even the white angels of Eden with their flamin' swords
> Won't be able to stop us from hittin' town in the dirty old Ford (*Tracks*)

This is, perhaps, Springsteen's first reference to a specific Biblical passage (Genesis 3: 22-24); at least, it is the first to a non-obvious Biblical passage. The gates of Eden are the devil's door, and Eden itself is the promised land town they're going to hit—presumably to party. In case the intent remains unclear, the singer makes it explicit: "I say better than the glory roads of heaven better off riding / Hell bound in the dirt."

The theme of a promised land recurs on the *Darkness on the Edge of Town* album, most directly in the song "The Promised Land." Seemingly far removed from Springsteen's earlier swipes at his faith and upbringing, the singer declares, "I believe in a promised land," a place that—wherever it may be—is reached only by having the faith to stand one's ground. The singer references "a promised land," rather than the definitive "the promised land"; everyone has one, and somehow he'll find one that's for him. "The Price You Pay" provides the most explicit retelling of the literal Biblical story in Springsteen's work, going back to Moses being denied entry in to the promised land. Here, the singer vows to succeed where others have failed:

> But just across the county line, a stranger passing through put up a sign
> That counts the men fallen away to the price you pay,
> and girl before the end of the day,
> I'm gonna tear it down and throw it away

By this time, the Bible itself had started to become a source for telling his side of things; unlike with "Iceman" just a couple years prior, the story resonates with explicit meaning. While Springsteen would employ more subtlety in his subsequent Biblical references, by the time of "The Price You Pay," his era of using references as mere textual swipes had ended. The theme of the promised land is one to which Springsteen would return repeatedly later in his career as well.

In the Bible Mama

How, though, did Springsteen progress from using the Bible to comment on his own condition and his desire to escape it, to using it as a more general storytelling device? I believe the transition started when Springsteen began using his songs to examine his often stormy relationship with his father. Almost as a matter of course, some of the first images Springsteen turned to, in order to address his family dynamic, came from the Bible. In a 1978 interview for *Creem*, Springsteen was asked about "Adam Raised a Cain." He commented, "I did read the Bible some. I tried to read it for a while about a year ago. It was great. It's fascinating. I got into it quite a ways. Great stories. Actually, what happened was I was thinking of writing that particular song, and I went back trying to get a feeling for it" (Duncan 42).

What was it, in trying to convey his own relationship to his father, in trying to find some universality to it, that caused Springsteen to turn to the Bible for source material? Why the resonance, in particular, in the story of Cain and Abel? Did Springsteen see in it what Steinbeck did, when writing *East of Eden*? Or, did he see the James Dean movie and find his resonance there?

Whatever Springsteen's inspiration for going back to the Bible, what he finally came up with combined two Biblical passages, in a climactic verse screamed out over the full E Street Band:

> In the Bible Cain mama slew Abel
> and East of Eden mama he was cast
> You're born into this life paying
> for the sins of somebody else's past

The first two lines reference Genesis 4: 8-16, in which Adam's first-born son Cain killed his younger brother Abel, and was subsequently exiled. The next two lines invoke the concept of children inheriting the sins of their fathers; in Leviticus 26: 39-42, the people of Israel are told of those who do not uphold the covenant, "because of their fathers' sins they will waste away." Perhaps of greater immediate resonance to Springsteen was the concept of original sin, which originates out of interpretations of Adam's disobeying God's command in Genesis 3.[2] In "Adam Raised a Cain," the sins of the father and son are joined; the son—here the singer—inherits the sins and the flames of the father. What sins of Adam did Cain inherit? And how did that apply to Bruce Springsteen's relationship with his own father?

Unlike some earlier uses of scripture, the passages in "Adam Raised a Cain" did not call into question whether the events depicted in those passages actually occurred, nor did they call in to question the faith of those who believe them as literal truth. But they *did* acknowledge that the issues with which Springsteen wrestled in his own family were as old as mankind itself. And therein was the song's resonance: the very first son of the very first man grew up to become a murderer. *That* is the inheritance in a world gone wrong.

Spare Parts

By the time Springsteen recorded *Tunnel of Love*, his life had undergone a remarkable change: he had grown up, become a superstar, and got married. To

---

[2]   See the section below entitled "The Eleventh Commandment" for Springsteen's onstage comments regarding original sin and choice.

the extent that Springsteen explored using the Bible at all for the suite of songs that became the *Born in the USA* album, the results were typically whimsical and ultimately left unreleased (For example, "Lion's Den") or relegated to use as B-sides (for example, "Pink Cadillac"). For *Tunnel of Love*, Springsteen—perhaps in an effort to make sense of his own marriage—set out to explore adult relationships between men and women. In so doing, he turned back to matters of faith, in particular drawing on the imagery from his youth. All but two of the songs involve at least some invocation of prayer, God, heaven, churches, or angels. Gypsy women appear as prophets once more, both in the album's first single ("Brilliant Disguise") and the corresponding B-side ("Lucky Man"). And, in the album's crucial narrative song, he drew upon the Bible to tell a modern story.

"Spare Parts" tells the story of a young, single mother struggling to find meaning in her life. The lyrics most obviously present a version of a baptism, and of the mother gaining redemption via that act; after holding her son down at the riverside, she finally decides against infanticide, lifts the baby in her arms and carries him home. Authors such as Andrew Greeley and Jim Cullen have examined the baptism aspect of the song in some detail. Greeley, in his 1988 article, "The Catholic Imagination of Bruce Springsteen," wrote, "The story of the young mother, holding her son in the waters of the river under the bright sun, then lifting him up and carrying him home, now sanctified for life, is surely a baptismal image. How could it be anything else?" (Greeley 113). In *Born in the USA: Bruce Springsteen and the American Tradition*, Cullen writes:

> [Janey's] situation stabilizes in the penultimate line ["Waist deep in the water how bright the sun shone"], whose very diction suggests why: her entrance into the water suggests a kind of baptism (her own as well as the child's), while the shining sun could be the face of God (or, perhaps more accurately, Jesus Christ). (188)

While my view is no doubt influenced by my own non-Catholic background, I find Greeley's view to be curiously unimaginative, and Cullen's simply incorrect. The suggestion, as advanced by Cullen, that the song affirms religious ritual or iconography is precisely wrong.

The shining sun may symbolize, in some respect, the deity, and Springsteen has surely used the image of God's light elsewhere (for example, in "Valentine's Day," also on the *Tunnel of Love* album). But "Spare Parts" goes further than simply telling a modern version of sanctification via baptism. Its core message, in my opinion, is not religious. Rather, "Spare Parts" is a breakthrough for Springsteen in using the imagery from Biblical sources to create a secular moral. Janey, having been deceived, impregnated, and ultimately abandoned by her boyfriend, seeks her life back. Her thoughts turn to her son, to sacrificing him, and ultimately herself. Though originating in different circumstances, the ensuing images evoke Old Testament material. The specific image of letting the baby go in the river revisits that of Yochevet and baby Moses; the storyline recalls that of the Akedah—the binding of Isaac, with Janey in the role of Abraham.

Abraham, of perfect faith, was willing—at God's command—to kill his son until the moment God calls to him, upon which Abraham famously answers, "*hineni*, here I am." And God responds, telling Abraham not to lay a hand on the child. Janey is not only of imperfect faith, she's already confessed that sometimes her "whole life feels like one big mistake." When her thoughts turned to killing her son, Janey prays, she cries, essentially screaming out, "*Here I am!*" She's desperate for an answer. And there's *nothing*. God does not—not even when providing the nice, sunny day—command her to save her child. She does that on her own. And in so doing, she saves herself, too.

Why does this usage of the Bible to tell a strictly secular story work so well? Where is the resonance? I suspect that it's because everyone—even those not familiar with Bible stories in general—knows the basic story (or one similar to it) and, in some fashion, everyone has traveled that road. And, because they have been there, the story has resonance, it has meaning, and it can be told as a bit of light in today's ethically convoluted world. Waiting on God's word, as Janey did, wasn't a new idea for Springsteen: he had once written, for "Drive All Night," the lyrics, "I wish God would send me a word, send me something I'm afraid to lose." Janey, having been sent something she was afraid to lose, nearly threw it away anyway. Springsteen's story in "Spare Parts" is not particularly one of faith. Contrary to Cullen's suggestion, Janey didn't literally find Jesus down at the river; she found meaning for herself.

One does not need to know the story of Abraham and Isaac—or, for that matter, the ritual of baptism—to understand Janey's sacrifice or her struggles, and Bruce hardly seems to be preaching the Bible as literal Truth (an idea he explicitly rejected in another song, "Part Man, Part Monkey," that he played on the tour to support the *Tunnel of Love* record, and resurrected in 2005 for the *Devils and Dust* tour). Janey's redemption does not rely on her prayers; ultimately, it relies on her *actions*—her *choices*. Her path will be made—as with the songs throughout the *Devils & Dust* album that follow it—without divine intervention. The use of scripture in "Spare Parts" to tell this story marks a transition point: scripture could now be trusted not just for imagery and personal resonance, but also as story source and for juxtaposition to the real world.

Seven Angels

In the years after the *Tunnel of Love* album, Springsteen's first marriage dissolved, he disbanded the E Street Band, and he temporarily withdrew from recording. When he started writing again, he drew in particular on soul influences for musical inspiration, and repeatedly turned to the Bible as a source for imagery and occasional storytelling. At least half a dozen songs from the ensuing sessions for the *Human Touch* album referenced the Bible in some way. Some of those songs, such as "Seven Angels," included relatively obscure references (Revelations 15:1, "And I saw another sign in heaven, great and marvelous, seven angels having the seven last plagues, for in them is filled up the wrath of God"), while songs such as "Gave It a Name" (Cain and Abel) and "Soul Driver" (the Flood) returned to stories that Springsteen had visited earlier in his career. In the song "Human Touch," Springsteen used together several well-worn Biblical and religious images in service of a single point: tonight it's just the singer and his companion, alone.

> Ain't no mercy on the streets of this town
> Ain't no bread from heavenly skies
> Ain't nobody drawin' wine from this blood
> It's just you and me tonight

The Bible had become, for Springsteen, a source for simple statements and observations.

On the companion album *Lucky Town*, the Bible was used at least twice more, this time in happier songs. In "Leap of Faith," the singer compares the parting of the Red Sea to a more immediate local pleasure.

In "Living Proof," we have possibly the first explicit affirmation in a Springsteen song of God's Biblical attributes (Exodus 34: 6-7). Describing the birth of his first child, he sings, "Searching for a little bit of God's mercy / I found living proof." Springsteen had certainly mentioned God before in songs. "Rosalita" had even mentioned the attribute of God's mercy: "My tires were slashed and I almost crashed but the Lord had mercy." But while those earlier references may have been made in jest, as with "Rosalita," or have been non-specific with regard to affirmation of God's Biblical attributes (for example, "Valentine's Day," which references "God's light"), "Living Proof," both in its song title and its lyrics, is explicit in affirmation. Springsteen, having been transformed by the miracle of seeing his own child, now assumed the role of believer—at least in spirit.

Across the Border

Having found some measure of spiritual peace in his own life, Springsteen still saw, especially from the vantage point of his California home during the early 1990s, parts of a world gone terribly wrong. With *The Ghost of Tom Joad*, he returned to stories of people who were down and out, focusing in particular on tales of the homeless and of people trying to emigrate to the United States from Mexico. In so doing, Springsteen repeatedly turned to the Bible to find resonance, often showing just how far removed 1990s-era California was from the Biblical prophecies. The title track references Matthew 19: 30: "many that are first shall be last; and the last shall be first," and also revisits the story of the promised land:

> Waitin' for when the last shall be first and the first shall be last
> In a cardboard box 'neath the underpass
> Got a one-way ticket to the promised land
> You got a hole in your belly and gun in your hand

The characters here will not become first, they will not be redeemed, and they will find no promised land. God's mercy, which had been invoked in Springsteen songs at least since "Rosalita" rhymed "mercy" with "Jersey," and had been personally affirmed in "Living Proof," is now sought but, as in "The New Timer," is found to be insufficient:

> My Jesus your gracious love and mercy
> Tonight I'm sorry could not fill
> My heart like one good rifle
> And the name of who I ought to kill

With "Across the Border," Springsteen returns again to the story of the promised land. The song does not mention the Bible story explicitly, but just as the Jordan separated the Israelites from their destination, so too does the Bravo separate the would-be immigrant from his destination. The singer intones, as if with perfect faith, of his hopes "[t]hat someday we'll drink from God's blessed waters." But we already know—and we suspect he does, too—that the journey cannot be successful; he will not make it to his promised land.

The promised land story was referenced again in later songs such as the gospel-influenced "Land of Hope and Dreams" (wherein the train carries the losers and the sinners along with the saints and winners to their final destination), but by the time of "Across the Border" we can see the evolution of the theme, from the early boasts ("Thunder Road," "Born to Run"), to the later struggles ("The Price You Pay"), and finally to the impossibilities of reaching the destination intact ("Across the Border" and ultimately "Matamoros Banks," in which the demise of the character from "Across the Border" is confirmed). But even within *The Ghost of Tom Joad* there is one miracle: "Galveston Bay" presents two fishermen, Billy Sutter and Le Bing Son. Billy is presented as a racist who vows revenge on Le, after Le is acquitted on a murder charge. The climactic scene recalls that of "Spare Parts": down at the waterside, Billy is at the moment at which he will fulfill his destiny to take a life, but, like Janey in "Spare Parts," he decides at the last moment to spare the other man's life—and save himself in the process.

"Spare Parts" fairly explicitly uses Biblical and religious imagery to make its point, but "Galveston Bay"—despite its focus on two fishermen (itself a seeming reference to Mark 1: 17: "And Jesus said unto them, Come after me, and I will make you to become fishers of men")—otherwise rejects the imagery (as well as, arguably, the music). No prayers are offered. Not only does God's light not show up at the moment of truth, but it disappears: "Billy stood in the shadows / His K-bar knife in his hand / And the moon slipped behind the clouds." If God made murder difficult for Janey, it would seem that here that He made it easy for Billy: go ahead, do it, I'm not watching, he can't see you. Yet Billy managed to find the same resolution as Janey. Billy's redemption needed no divine intervention, and it is no longer even sought; redemption relies on his actions and choices.

The Rising

Springsteen's most recent material prior to 2001 had consistently focused on the spiritual aspects of his characters: "Land of Hope and Dreams" promises a journey for all to heaven, "American Skin" presents policemen praying over the body of the man they just killed, and "My City of Ruins" is a call both to prayer and to action in the face of local destruction. The Biblical book of Lamentations beseeched God to renew the people as of old; in the midst of utter despair its author declared, "Therefore I have hope ... the Lord will not cast off for ever" (Lamentations 3:31). In "My City of Ruins," strength is sought to do the rebuilding with earthly hands. And with that strength comes the hope, the rebuilding, the rising.

Although "My City of Ruins" was written for *Asbury Park*, its spiritual and literal application to the catastrophic events of 9/11 was almost inescapable. With a minor lyric change, Springsteen performed it on a telethon just days after the attack, and it subsequently became the closing statement of *The Rising*.

The Rising was Springsteen's first album after the national trauma of 9/11, and it dealt in large measure in themes of loss and healing. Intensely spiritual and at times mystical, and occasionally referencing images from other faiths, the album unflinchingly used the Biblical resurrection story as a metaphor for both survivors of calamities and for those less fortunate.

"Empty Sky" explores the notion of choice, while referencing the Bible. The plains of Jordan are first referenced in Genesis 13: 10; Lot, having been given a choice of dwelling place by Abram, chooses the fertile plains of Jordan, rather than the more barren land of Canaan. The choice turns out badly; ultimately, God destroys the cities situated there. The choice isn't obvious; what seemed good might not turn out that way. As related in "Empty Sky," we all have those choices to make: "Of this tree of evil / Of this tree of good." Which tree is which? And how can we know, for sure? These questions, old as the Bible, continue today, to the singer of "Empty Sky," to the singer of "Leah" and "The Hitter" and "Devils & Dust."

Devils and Jesus

Devils & Dust is the second consecutive Springsteen album title invoking Biblically-based events or creatures. If *The Rising* used the resurrection as a metaphor for hope and rebuilding, *Devils & Dust* explored more what happens when hope is lost. Once again, Springsteen draws upon the Bible to tell his stories, focusing on instances where the modern events didn't yield the same results as those in scripture. Previously, I discussed the use of imagery from Ezekiel's dream in *Devils & Dust*. Another song from that album, "Black Cowboys," references Ezekiel's dream more explicitly:

> Come the fall the rain flooded these homes
> Here in Ezekiel's valley of dry bones

It fell hard and dark to the ground
It fell without a sound.

As in *Devils & Dust*, no life is given to the dry bones. Rather, the rain—a consistent metaphor for hard times throughout Springsteen's career—begins a cycle in which a mother fades away to drug use, and her son finally leaves home in search of his own promised land.

"Jesus Was an Only Son" is Springsteen's first use of Jesus in a song title.[3] It is an announcement of sorts: the artist *will* use the Bible to help tell his story. "Jesus Was an Only Song" is respectful and even reverent of its Biblical source:

Well Jesus kissed his mother's hands
Whispered, "Mother, still your tears,
For remember the soul of the universe
Willed a world and it appeared."

Far from reacting against his Catholic school upbringing in a way that informed his earlier use of the Bible, Springsteen here seems finally to have embraced the imagery.

Yet the song, while reverential, is still basically secular and universal in nature: it's about a mother losing her *human* son. As Springsteen described it, "I felt if I approached the song from the secular side that the rest of it would come through." One need not be Catholic or accept Jesus to understand that a child's passing is "a loss that can never be replaced." Finding universal resonance has been key to Springsteen's stories. In describing "Jesus Was an Only Son," Springsteen notes, "Calvary Hill—that's his proving ground, his *Darkness on the Edge of Town*" (Springsteen, *VH1 Storytellers*). What happened to Jesus on a human level, in other words, is what happens to people everywhere.

Making the Biblical human and demystifying the characters have always been key to Springsteen's Biblical usage. When performing "Jesus Was an Only Son," his stage banter eerily recalls some of the characterizations in "If I Was the Priest," while evoking images from the movie *The Last Temptation of Christ*: "You'd have to be thinking, gee, there was that little bar in Galilee, pretty nice little place, weather's good down there, too. I could manage the place, Mary Magdalene could tend bar. We could have kids" (*VH1 Storytellers*). The notion of Jesus simply as deity, or Bible as literal Truth, remains outside the scope of Bruce Springsteen's work. But, in their stories, he has found resonance for the human realities of today.

---

[3]   According to some sources, Springsteen composed a song in the aftermath of Kent State entitled "Where Was Jesus in Ohio"; that song remains unreleased and no recordings are known to be circulating (Leach).

The Eleventh Commandment

While Springsteen's song lyrics have shown increasing reverence for scripture over the course of his career, his onstage use of Biblical imagery for storytelling has retained healthy doses of both humor and irreverence. One of Springsteen's most famous onstage stories was for the song "Growin' Up." In that story, as presented in the late 1970s, he would tell the tale of what his parents wanted for him, inevitably leading to him deciding—against his parents' wishes—to follow his dream to become a rock star. Some versions of the story might have gypsy ladies (in the role of prophets); others might have spacemen, Santa Claus, or even lawyers. Indeed, a version of the story featuring an attorney was included on the *Live 1975-85* album.

But Bruce had another version, too. In that version, Bruce is eventually sent to God to talk about his vocation. And, in perhaps his most irreverent twisting of Bible stories, he would say, approximately:

> God looks at me. He says, "I know. I know. See, what they don't understand is, Moses screwed up. There was supposed to be an Eleventh Commandment. Actually, Moses was so scared after ten—it was a great show, the burning bush, the thunder, lightning, you shoulda seen it—he went back down the mountain. You see, what these guys don't understand is that there was *supposed* to be an Eleventh Commandment. And all it said was: *LET IT ROCK!*" (Marsh, *Two Hearts* 206)

Another song that lent itself easily to a stage story was "Pink Cadillac." This is one of the few Springsteen songs in which irreverence made its way into the song lyrics: "They say Eve tempted Adam with an apple / But man I ain't going for that / I know it was her Pink Cadillac." The stage story during the later stages of the Born in the USA tour, complete with stage props such as a huge map, expanded on this conflict between spiritual purity and earthly desires:

> Now where did this conflict begin? Well, it began in the beginning—in a place called the Garden of Eden. Now the Garden of Eden was originally believed to have been located in Mesopotamia. But the latest theological studies have found out that its actual location was ten miles south of Jersey City, off the New Jersey Turnpike. That's why they call it *the Garden State*! ... In the Garden of Eden, there was no sin, there was no sex. Man lived in a state of innocence ... Now, when it comes to no sex, I prefer the state of guilt that I live in. (Marsh, *Two Hearts* 511-12)

Springsteen's onstage irreverence with Biblical stories continues, to an extent, today. In addition to the story for "Jesus Was an Only Son," he has resurrected a version of the Garden of Eden story, combined with a twist on resurrection. As Springsteen remarked during a show in August 2005, in Grand Rapids, Michigan:

We carry with us the seeds of all the things that we build and create, and that's real ... and we also carry with us the seeds of our destruction. That's real, too. And I guess in theory that was God's ...

I suppose it was meant as a punishment. That was the whole story of East of Eden, you know?

I'm not sure that it is. Life would have been pretty boring. How many walks around the garden can you take, I mean, you know? THEN WHAT? You keep coming back to that apple tree. It ain't going anywhere. [laughs] Neither is that urge. [laughs]

So my whole theory is the whole thing was planned like that in the first place. That the whole idea that there was a choice there was ... I don't think so. [laughs]

There's a great line in *Wise Blood*, Flannery O'Connor wrote, was it, a guy starts a Church for Jesus Christ, Dead, Buried and Remaining That Way. [laughs]

It's an idea ... This is "The Hitter." [laughs] (Springsteen, "Introduction")

The pairing of a seemingly light take on a Biblical story with such a heavy song may seem incongruous on the surface, but Springsteen's take on the notion of *choice*, as evidenced in his otherwise light story, gives the song its resonance and power. One can sense the word "plan" coming after "God's," and then a diversion in the narrative—a diversion to "punishment." That the mere notion of having been given a choice was, itself, *punishment*! And, *that* was the plan, since *that* choice was no choice at all. It summarizes where Springsteen has most recently landed with the Bible—finding resonance in its stories and yet still rejecting religious formalities.

Appendix: A Compendium of Biblical References in Springsteen Songs

The following Springsteen songs either explicitly reference scripture, or, by my interpretation of them, use the Bible in some way. Although the list is certainly not complete, it provides a sense of the extent to which—and the manner in which—Springsteen has used Biblical references over the course of his career. The listing for "Year" marks, as best I can determine, when Springsteen wrote the song lyrics.

Song Title	Year	Key Lines / Passages	Notable Biblical References
"Resurrection"	1969	\<song title\>	Resurrection
"Where Was Jesus in Ohio"	1970	\<song title\>	Biblical character: Jesus.
"If I Was the Priest"	1972	"Virgin Mary / She runs the Holy Grail saloon …"	Biblical characters: Virgin Mary, Jesus, Holy Ghost …
"It's Hard to Be a Saint in the City"	1972	"The devil appeared like Jesus through the steam in the street"	Biblical characters: Jesus, the devil.
"Lost in the Flood"	1972	"nuns run bald through Vatican halls pregnant, pleadin' immaculate conception"	The Flood; the virgin birth.
"Wild Billy's Circus Story"	1973	"Jesus send some good women to save all your clowns"	Jesus; the promised land.
"Rosalita (Come Out Tonight)"	1973	"My tires were slashed and I almost crashed but the Lord had mercy"	God's mercy (Exodus 34: 6-7, etc.); the promised land.
"So Young and In Love"	1975	"There's flying angels on your fire escape / They lie to your mama for you, try to keep you safe"	Revelation 8: 13: "And I beheld, and heard an angel flying through the midst of heaven, saying with a loud voice, Woe, woe, woe, to the inhabiters of the earth by reason of the other voices of the trumpet of the three angels, which are yet to sound!"
"Thunder Road"	1975	"Riding out tonight to case the promised land …"	The promised land.
"Born to Run"	1975	"Someday girl I don't know when / we're gonna get to that place / Where we really want to go / and we'll walk in the sun"	The promised land.
"Fire"	1977	" … Samson and Delilah …"	Biblical characters: Samson and Delilah.
"Iceman"	1977	"We'll take the midnight road right to the devil's door / And even the white angels of Eden with their flamin' swords / Won't be able to stop us from hittin' town in the dirty old Ford"	Genesis 3: 24: "So He drove out the man; and He placed at the East of the garden of Eden angels, and a flaming sword which turned every way, to keep the way of the tree of life."

Song Title	Year	Key Lines / Passages	Notable Biblical References
"Adam Raised a Cain"	1977	"In the Bible Cain slew Abel / and East of Eden he was cast / You're born into this life paying / for the sins of somebody else's past"	Genesis 4: 8: "Cain rose up against Abel his brother, and slew him." Original sin (Genesis 2-3) Leviticus 26: 39: "Those of you who are left will waste away in the lands of their enemies because of their sins; also because of their fathers' sins they will waste away."
"The Promised Land"	1978	"I believe in a promised land"	The promised land.
"The Price You Pay"	1979	"Do you remember the story of the promised land / How he crossed the desert sands / And could not enter the chosen land / On the banks of the river he stayed / To face the price you pay"	Moses' punishment— Numbers 20: 12: "Because you did not believe in Me, to sanctify Me in the eyes of the children of Israel, therefore you shall not bring this assembly into the land which I have given them."
"Drive All Night"	1979	"I wish God would send me a word / send me something I'm afraid to lose	The binding of Isaac; Jonah's gourd (Jonah 4: 6-10).
"From Small Things (Big Things One Day Come)"	1979	"At sixteen, she quit high school / to make a fortune in the promised land"	The promised land.
"Dedication"	1981	"Well, way back in the Bible time / A cat named Noah built an ocean liner / Everybody laughed when he told him why / But when the rain came Noah was high and dry"	The Flood (Genesis 6-8).
"Atlantic City"	1982	"Maybe everything that dies, someday comes back"	Resurrection.
"Lion's Den"	1982	"I'm Daniel waitin' in the lion's den"	Daniel 6: 16: "The king gave the command, and Daniel was brought and thrown into the den of lions."
"Wages of Sin"	1982	"Wages of sin, we keep paying / Wages of sin for the wrongs that we've done / Wages of sin, we keep paying / Wages of sin, that's how we have our fun"	Romans 6: 23: "For the wages of sin is death."

Song Title	Year	Key Lines / Passages	Notable Biblical References
"Pink Cadillac"	1982	"They say Eve tempted Adam with an apple / But man I ain't going for that / I know it was her pink Cadillac"	Genesis 3: 6: "And when the woman saw that the tree was good for food, and that it was pleasant to the eyes, and a tree to be desired to make one wise, she took of the fruit thereof, and did eat, and gave also unto her husband with her; and he did eat."
"Darlington County"	1984	"My eyes seen the glory of the coming of the Lord"	The Messiah—(Battle Hymn of the Republic).
"Spare Parts"	1987	<the entire final stanza>	The binding of Isaac (Genesis), the baby Moses (Exodus), baptism.
"Part Man, Part Monkey"	1988	"Well did God make man in a breath of holy fire / Or did he crawl on up out of the muck and mire / Well the man on the street believes what the bible tells him so / Well you can ask me, mister, because I know"	Genesis 2: 7: "Then the Lord God formed man of the dust of the ground, and breathed into his nostrils the breath of life; and man became a living soul."
"Seven Angels"	1990	<song title>	Revelations 15: 1: "I saw another great and marvelous sign in the sky: seven angels having the seven last plagues, for in them God's wrath is finished."
"Gave It a Name"	1990	"In the fields of the lord / Stood Abel and Cain / Cain slew Abel 'neath the black rain"	Genesis 4:8.
"Soul Driver"	1990	"Rode through forty nights of the gospels' rain / Black sky pourin' snakes, frogs / And love in vain"	Genesis 7: 12: "And the rain was upon the earth forty days and forty nights." Exodus 7: 10: "Aaron cast down his rod before Pharaoh and before his servants, and it became a serpent." Exodus 8: 2: "And Aaron stretched out his hand over the waters of Egypt; and the frogs came up, and covered the land of Egypt."
"Happy"	1992	"A promise of a better world to come"	"World to come (*olam haBa*)"—Biblical interpretation

Song Title	Year	Key Lines / Passages	Notable Biblical References
"Human Touch"	1992	"Ain't no bread from heavenly skies"	Exodus 16 (manna); also, Matthew 26 (sacraments).
"Man's Job"	1992	"… my feet / They're made of clay"	Daniel 2: 33: "… its legs of iron, its feet part of iron and part of clay."
"Leap of Faith"	1992	"Now you were the Red Sea I was Moses / I kissed you and slipped into a bed of roses / The waters parted and love rushed inside / I was Jesus' son sanctified"	The promised land, the parting of the Red Sea (Exodus 14: 21)
"Living Proof"	1992	"Searching for a little bit of God's mercy / I found living proof"	Exodus 34: 6-7: "The Lord, the Lord, God, merciful and gracious, long-suffering, and abundant in goodness and truth; keeping mercy unto the thousandth generation, forgiving iniquity and transgression and sin."
"The Ghost of Tom Joad"	1995	"Waitin' for when the last shall be first and the first shall be last / In a cardboard box 'neath the underpass / Got a one-way ticket to the promised land"	Matthew 19: 30: "Many that are first shall be last; and the last shall be first"; the promised land."
"The New Timer"	1995	"My Jesus your gracious love and mercy / Tonight I'm sorry could not fill my heart"	God's mercy.
"Youngstown"	1995	"When I die I don't want no part of heaven / I would not do heaven's work well / I pray the devil comes and takes me / To stand in the fiery furnaces of hell"	Heaven and hell; the devil.
"Across the Border"	1995	\<entire song\>	The promised land.
"Galveston Bay"	1995	\<story of two fishermen\>	Mark 1: 17: "And Jesus said unto them, Come after me, and I will make you to become fishers of men."
"Idiot's Delight"	1998	"I met up with St. Peter/He was working at the pearly gates …"	Biblical character: St Peter.

Song Title	Year	Key Lines / Passages	Notable Biblical References
"Land of Hope and Dreams"	1999	"You don't know where you're goin' / But you know you won't be back"	The promised land/*Olam HaBa.*
"My City of Ruins"	2000	"… rise up …"	Resurrection.
"The Rising"	2002	"Come on up for the rising …"	Resurrection.
"Empty Sky"	2002	"On the plains of Jordan / I cut my bow from the wood / Of this tree of evil / Of this tree of good"	Genesis 13: 10: "And Lot lifted up his eyes, and beheld all the plain of the Jordan, that it was well watered every where, before the LORD destroyed Sodom and Gomorrah, like the garden of the LORD, like the land of Egypt."
"Devils & Dust"	2003	"Well I dreamed of you last night / In a field of mud and bone …"	Ezekiel 37: 1: "The hand of the LORD was upon me, and the LORD carried me out in a spirit, and set me down in the midst of the valley, and it was full of bones … "
"Black Cowboys"	1997	"Come the fall the rain flooded these homes / Here in Ezekiel's valley of dry bones"	The Flood (Genesis 7); Ezekiel's dream (Ezekiel 37).
"Maria's Bed"	1997	"Been on a barbed wire highway 40 days and nights"	Matthew 4: 1-2: "Then Jesus was led by the Spirit into the desert to be tempted by the devil. He fasted for forty days and forty nights, and afterwards he was hungry."
"Jesus Was an Only Son"	2005	<entire song>	Biblical characters, writings and locations.

Chapter 10
Life Right Now: Springsteen and Spirituality

Scott Wagar

On every date of his 1999-2000 tour with the E Street Band, Bruce Springsteen would adopt a faux-preacher mode and bellow, during his performance of "Light of Day": "Unlike my competitors, I shall not, I will not promise you life everlasting. But I can promise you life … RIGHT NOW!" Yet it was hardly the first instance in which Springsteen had evoked spirituality and religion in his work. From the pregnant nuns "pleading immaculate conception" in "Lost in the Flood" on his first album, to Mary in "Thunder Road" "praying … for a savior," to the Exodus references in "The Price You Pay" and other songs, to the soon-to-be-lost child in "Jesus Was an Only Son" from *Devils & Dust*, Springsteen's music has consistently displayed the influence of his Catholic upbringing and attendant exposure to Judeo-Christian images and narratives. But while there is no question that spirituality and religion are themes to which Springsteen has returned throughout his career, varying interpretations of his attitude toward these subjects have been advanced by scholarly critics. Kate McCarthy has suggested that "Thunder Road," for example, tells a story in which one of Springsteen's recurring images, the automobile, "becomes a metaphor for the rejection of otherworldly religious promises [offered by mainstream Christianity] and the affirmation of the possibility of an alternative, this-worldly redemption" (29). Similarly, she claims that *Nebraska*'s "Open All Night" "rejects the Christian faith the culture offers, identifying it with an irrelevant, and often oppressive, otherworldly spirituality …" (31).

Jim Cullen, as part of his book-length study of Springsteen's place in what Cullen terms "the American Tradition," argues that Springsteen's lyrics, music and in-concert stories have tended to display a "specifically Christian" (181) and even more specifically Catholic perspective on spiritual issues—a perspective that sometimes even uses "the language of faith" (195) to ostensibly deny a belief in mainstream religion. Cornel Bonca, meanwhile, notes that, despite Springsteen's apparent rejection of at least some aspects of Christianity, the spiritual impulse in his songs and performances seems only to have strengthened:

> In [Springsteen's] early work, which is filled with fallen Catholic school boy images—nuns, saints, crosses, church bells, etc.—there's no attempt to give the religious any weight, but since the late 80s, his lyrics have been filigreed with unironized religious images: "Cautious Man" (from *Tunnel of Love*) notes how the moonlight on the protagonist's wife's face fills "their room in the

beauty of God's fallen light"; the tormented ex-lover in "I Wish I Were Blind" (from *Human Touch*) sees that "the world is filled / with the grace and beauty of God's hand"; the new father in "Living Proof" (from *Lucky Town*) calls his newborn son "a little piece of the Lord's undying light." The ritual, the rules, the submission of Christianity have dropped away, but the awe of the religious has remained and intensified, as has the sense of moral responsibility—and for Springsteen it's rock and roll's job to help keep that awe, that responsibility and reverence toward life, alive.

Springsteen's most recent songs and in-concert comments suggest a further move in the direction noticed by Bonca. The lyrics of "Devils & Dust" feature Biblical allusions and repeatedly use the word "God," but Springsteen's delivery of the phrase "God-filled soul"—especially in the song's last line—simultaneously hints at both reverence and scorn, as if to suggest that while the belief in a "God-filled soul" may be worthwhile, the conventional religious understanding of what a truly God-filled soul would contain is insufficient.

In 2005's *VH1 Storytellers*, Springsteen acknowledges the debt that "Jesus Was an Only Son" owes to the songwriter's Catholic heritage by proclaiming that "once you're a Catholic, there's no getting out," but then goes on to suggest that his primary motivation in writing the song was to understand and portray Jesus simply as a human being and an earthly son. Introducing the same song at another concert several weeks after the *Storytellers* appearance, Springsteen compared the Catholic Church to a sports team of which he is longer a fan but in which he retains a certain detached interest. His ruminations on the song from *Storytellers* end with the comment that "I think whatever divinity we can lay claim to is hidden in the core of our humanity." Whether Springsteen is including Jesus in this "we" is, in the context of Springsteen's unorthodox comments, decidedly unclear. But it is perhaps also worth pointing out here that "Jesus Was an Only Son" ends with a reference to "the soul of the universe" in a place we might expect the word "God." It seems that Springsteen ultimately presents in this song as a believer in a higher power, but one that is named—and perhaps understood—more in the writer's own terms.

Even a brief examination, then, demonstrates the complex role of religious and spiritual issues in Springsteen's work. But while some critics, and even the artist himself, have distanced Springsteen from mainstream religion while simultaneously acknowledging the importance of a spiritual impulse in his work, it appears that a connection has not yet been made between Springsteen and the group of Americans who profess an interest in spirituality on their own terms: those who identify as "spiritual, but not religious." Scholar Robert C. Fuller, in his study of the history of "unchurched America," *Spiritual, But Not Religious*, argues that there exists in the United States a "spiritual, but not religious" tradition falling outside of mainstream religious boundaries but that it is no less real, influential, or spiritually mature for that. I want to suggest that this notion provides one avenue toward a richer understanding of spirituality in Springsteen's work—an understanding that acknowledges, but is not necessarily limited to, a Judeo-Christian framework.

Springsteen as Spiritual, But Not Religious

Fuller suggests that about 20 percent of Americans fall into the "spiritual, but not religious" category (5). He notes that in recent times "spiritual" and "religious," which are in fact synonyms, have come to be differentiated, with the former "associated with the private realm of thought and experience" and the latter "connected with the public realm of membership in religious institutions, participation in formal rituals, and adherence to official denominational doctrines" (5). Attempting to define one of his key terms, Fuller asserts that:

> ... spirituality exists wherever we struggle with the issue of how our lives fit into the greater cosmic scheme of things. This is true even when our questions never give way to specific answers or give rise to specific practices such as prayer or meditation. We encounter spiritual issues every time we wonder where the universe comes from, why we are here, or what happens when we die. We also become spiritual when we become moved by values such as beauty, love, or creativity that seem to reveal a meaning or power beyond our visible world. An idea or practice is 'spiritual' when it reveals our personal desire to establish a felt-relationship with the deepest meanings or powers governing life. (8)

Those who label themselves as spiritual, but not religious are, says Fuller, interested in spirituality to a greater or lesser degree but "reject traditional organized religion as the sole—or even the most valuable—means of furthering their spiritual growth"; many of these people, he suggests, "have had negative experiences with churches or church leaders" (6). Such seekers, Fuller claims, rather "[embrace] an individualized spirituality that includes picking and choosing from a wide range of alternative religious philosophies" (6). He further suggests that the spiritual interests of these Americans are exerting increasing influence on the spiritual understanding and practices of those who do consider themselves churchgoers (9). In addition to those in the spiritual, but not religious category, Fuller identifies a set of "unchurched" Americans who, for any of a number of reasons, maintain a relationship of some sort with organized religion while still keeping too much distance to be considered full members (3).

It is not entirely clear where Springsteen and his work would fit into this paradigm, but the possible connections are intriguing. In a 2005 *New York Times* interview, Springsteen, discussing the apparently Christian aspects of *Devils and Dust*, flatly declares, "I'm not a churchgoer,"[1] but notes that he has grown to accept the influence on his songwriting of what he calls the "none-too-subtle form of brainwashing" employed during his Catholic education (Pareles, "Bruce Almighty" 1). Notably, he says, he has come to believe that "I've inherited this

---

[1]   While my intent here is to examine the message more than the biographical life of the artist, it makes sense to look at the evidence of Springsteen's comments about his personal beliefs.

particular landscape [of Christian imagery] and *I can build it into something of my own*" (emphasis added). This final comment is especially interesting in the context of the present discussion because it suggests a move toward the individualized spirituality identified by Fuller as one of the hallmarks of the spiritual, but not religious. But Springsteen also observes in the same interview that "I've been back to the church on many occasions." One such occasion, according to a 2002 *Rolling Stone* interview which notes that Springsteen ordinarily "rarely attends" church, was immediately after 9/11, when he brought his family in "with the rest of the wannabes" (Binelli).

Springsteen's comments may seem to project the image of a conflicted seeker, a self-declared non-churchgoer who openly criticizes his religious upbringing but nevertheless occasionally returns to church and—perhaps with a twinge of residual Catholic guilt—describes himself as a "wannabe" when that church attendance is based primarily on acute personal need. His songs—as we have already seen with "Devils & Dust" and "Jesus Was an Only Son" and will continue to observe—also display this "mixed" spirituality. Springsteen appears to have "reject[ed] traditional organized religion as the sole—or even the most valuable—means of furthering ... spiritual growth" and to have embraced the importance of an individualized path while still feeling, and to some degree possibly even embracing, a connection to his religious roots. The influence of a "spiritual, but not religious" outlook seems apparent, but the pull of organized religion has not entirely abated.

Springsteen, however, is surely not alone in this; his uncertain place in Fuller's model is probably shared by a large number of Americans, and his forthrightness about the confusion inherent in such deeply personal matters is, I would suggest, very possibly an important reason for the ongoing strength of the bond between Springsteen and his audience. Fuller himself acknowledges the complexity of the situation when he uses, as an introductory example, a thirty-eight-year-old woman, brought up as a Catholic, who attends Mass only a handful of times annually but thinks of herself as "deeply spiritual." She meditates at least an hour a day before a home altar on which she has placed "eighteen candles, an amulet attached to a photo of her grandmother, amethyst crystals used in healing meditations, oriental incense, a Tibetan prayer bell, a representation of the Virgin of Guadalupe, and some other traditional Catholic items" (2). This example is interestingly reminiscent of the introduction to Springsteen's "Mary's Place" from *The Rising*, in which the narrator, presumably a bereaved spouse wishing for the other's return in the wake of 9/11, informs us that "I got seven pictures of Buddha / The prophet's on my tongue / Eleven angels of mercy [are] / Sighin' over that black hole in the sun." Later in the song, the narrator claims, "I got a picture of you in my locket" as well as "seven candles / In my window lighting your way." The story here seems to be that of a desperate lover drawing upon multiple religious and spiritual options—"pullin' all the faith I can see," as the lyrics tell us—when one option alone no longer seems enough to get the (impossible) job done. A connection between Springsteen's narrator and Fuller's example of the nominally Catholic woman is not hard to make. Given the show-stopper position granted to "Mary's Place" in Springsteen's concerts since 2002 and the song's musical similarity to his semi-autobiographical classic "Rosalita," we can also easily imagine that Springsteen feels a close kinship with his narrator, who, the evidence suggests, may well be among the spiritual, but not religious.

"Faith Will Be Rewarded"

That the narrator of "Mary's Place" is "pullin' all the faith I can see" is worth noticing, however, not only because it directly points toward a break with religious orthodoxy. Springsteen's very use of the word "faith" here continues a tradition of sorts within his work, and the word makes an interesting point of examination if we want to move toward further exploration of Springsteen's spiritual, but not religious leanings. "Faith" is often used in songs throughout Springsteen's career, making notable appearances in older favorites "The Promised Land" and especially "Thunder Road," whose lyric, "Show a little faith, there's magic in the night," became not only a standard spot in concert for Springsteen to temporarily turn vocal duties over the to the crowd, but also the source of a fans' phrase often used to encourage belief that they would be able to get tickets to sold-out Springsteen shows. But Springsteen appears to have rejuvenated the word for his audience—and perhaps for himself—when he used it in the new song "Land of Hope and Dreams," which closed most shows on his 1999-2000 tour. Many fans who attended multiple concerts on the tour adopted Springsteen's gesture of raising an open hand in the air (still clutching a guitar pick between two fingers) while singing the word "faith" during "Land of Hope and Dreams"—"Faith will be rewarded"—and the line became a new catchphrase for loyal members of Springsteen's audience. Springsteen's next new album, *The Rising*, mentioned "faith" in fully a third of its songs.

We might well ask, then, how "faith" functions in Springsteen's songs, particularly since 1999 and "Land of Hope and Dreams." In this song—which has, perhaps not coincidentally, been officially released only in a live version recorded in front of more than 15,000 fans—the place to which the singer promises to take his addressed audience is one in which everyone, "whores and gamblers," "losers and winners" included, is welcome. "Dreams," we are told, "will not be thwarted," and "faith will be rewarded." It is never clear exactly where this utopia can be found, but, notably for our purposes, there is no overt indication that it is a Christian heaven. Bonca suggests that the song is in fact about America: "[N] ot the real one, of course, but the dream America … the mythic America." This is a plausible argument, because "Land of Hope and Dreams" differs notably from two of its lyrical antecedents, Woody Guthrie's "This Train is Bound for Glory" and The Impressions' "People Get Ready," in that it eschews openly religious language. Guthrie's train explicitly leaves behind all "but the righteous an' the holy," and "People Get Ready" predicts the coming of a locomotive that requires belief in God as a condition of transit. But the faith to be rewarded in Springsteen's song seems more along the lines of what Bonca has in mind: a faith in what America could be, or, more generally, in how people might treat each other in an ideal world. Of course, many expressions of Christianity put forth a more fully inclusive vision of salvation consistent with that expressed in "Land of Hope and Dreams," but, especially in the context of the song's antecedents, Springsteen's call for faith in this song is striking in that it seems to ask for *worldly* faith— faith not in a faraway God, but in humanity itself. McCarthy's insight about the imagined possibility of "an alternative, this-worldly redemption" (29) in the much earlier "Thunder Road" (also, we may remember, the source of "Show a little faith …") appears to hold here, too.

The Rising, written largely after the 1999-2000 tour and in the context of post-9/11 America, uses "faith" in ways similar to that in "Land of Hope and Dreams." In many respects, the album finds Springsteen grappling with the same question he had addressed in 1982's "Reason to Believe": "How at the end of every hard day / people find some reason to believe." But whereas the narrator in "Reason to Believe" can only tell us that humanity's apparently inexplicable belief seems "kinda funny" to him, *The Rising* takes faith seriously. "Into the Fire," inspired by the firefighters who climbed into the doomed World Trade Center towers, calls, like "Land of Hope and Dreams," on existing musical and lyrical structures associated with religion, but subverts expectations by keeping the song's theme closer to earth. Springsteen openly acknowledged in interviews that he sought a gospel feel for the song's chorus, which, as Mark Binelli points out, also "doubles as a prayer," with its wish, "May your strength give us strength / May your faith give us faith / May your hope give us hope / May your love give us love." However, the "prayer" here is addressed to fellow humans, not to any divine being, and the wish expressed appears to be that the fallen heroes' faith in the importance of *their* duties will increase our faith in our own. *The Rising*'s final song, "My City of Ruins," includes a prayer for faith that *is* explicitly directed to a "Lord"; importantly, though, this faith is needed not for praise, but to help the singer believe in his own ability to rebuild—"with these hands"—his shattered *earthly* world, which includes a run-down city and a lost relationship. Two other *Rising* songs that mention faith—"Worlds Apart" and "Countin' on a Miracle"— also place it in an earthly and even physical context. The narrator of "Worlds Apart" tells a lover, "I seek faith in your kiss and comfort in your heart." "Countin' on a Miracle," meanwhile, features (like "Mary's Place") a bereaved narrator who, addressing his lost lover, insists that "If I'm gonna believe / I'll put my faith / Darlin' in you," and later, that "Your heaven's here in my heart." Springsteen himself addressed the issue in a *New York Times* interview from the time of *The Rising*'s release:

> You have to come to grips with the real horrors that are out there . . . [a]nd then all people have is hope. That's what brings the next day and whatever that day may bring. You can't be uncritical, but just [have] a hope grounded in the real world of living, friendship, work, family, Saturday night. And that's where it

resides. That's where I always found faith and spirit. I found them down in those things, not some place intangible or some place abstract. And I've really tried to write about that basic idea my whole life. (Pareles, "Kind of Heroes")

On *Devils & Dust*, Springsteen is suddenly rather silent about faith. What he does tell us comes in the words of the title track's narrator who claims that "… every woman and every man [wants to] find the love that God wills / And the faith that He commands," but then asserts that "… tonight, faith just ain't enough." We should notice that in this rare example of doubt in the power of faith, the "faith" at issue is rather clearly an orthodox belief in a higher power, which is in contrast to the faith found in "Land of Hope and Dreams" and on *The Rising*.

So "faith," for Springsteen, seems to be a powerful notion—and indeed a reality—that, even as he flirts with its use in a religious sense, is most directly tied to the earthly plane, to "life right now." If "faith" in Springsteen's sense is so central to his work, though, we may ask whether this work truly explores spirituality or instead primarily emphasizes a kind of humanism. While this is a reasonable question, a look at Springsteen's songbook quickly reminds us that inquiries into ultimate meaning are plentiful: in the examples given by Bonca about "the awe of the religious," in the reference to "the soul of the universe" in "Jesus Was an Only Son," in the way *Lucky Town*'s album-length tale of hard-won happiness ends on an existential note with "My Beautiful Reward," and in the amazement of the abandoned groom in "Reason to Believe" at how the "river [rushes] on so effortlessly," just to name a few.

And, crucially, it is hardly as if "life right now" has nothing to do with spirituality. Indeed, in Eastern and especially Buddhist thought as it is popularly understood in America, awakening to the present moment is a spiritual ideal. But can we reasonably see a connection between the work of Springsteen, a New Jersey boy who, by his own admission, has never fully shaken off the influence of the Catholic Church, and an ancient Eastern tradition? Here, it makes sense to turn once again to Fuller.

"Seven Pictures of Buddha": Springsteen and Buddhism?

One prominent line of "unchurched" American spiritual thought traced in *Spiritual, But Not Religious* is that influenced by "the Mystic East" (Fuller 77), and Fuller dedicates ten pages of his compact (178-page) text to the influence of Eastern traditions on American spirituality. He gives special attention to the influence of Zen Buddhism on the 1960s and 1970s counter-culture (83), and, pointing out signs of more recent American interest in Buddhism, notes that over 200 books in print use the word "Zen" in the title and that about 800,000 European-Americans are "convert" Buddhists (86-87). Indeed, he says, "the past two generations of Americans have been exposed to non-Biblical religious ideas to an extent unprecedented in Western cultural history" and, as a result of the growing public acceptability of Eastern notions in particular, more and more Americans "feel encouraged to adopt an eclectic approach to religious belief" (86). In the course of examining some of the peculiarities of "American Buddhism," Fuller cites scholar Peter Gregory's claim that "Americans justify their interest [in Buddhism] 'in terms of values that are thought of as 'American'—such as self-realization, freedom, transforming relationships, getting in touch with one's experience, [and] living more fully in the moment or the world ...'" (Gregory qtd in Fuller 87).

"[S]elf-realization, freedom, transforming relationships, getting in touch with one's experience, living more fully in the moment or the world": I would argue that Gregory's list of "values" drawing Americans to Buddhism is quite similar to a list we might create enumerating ideals expressed in Springsteen's work. In fact, given the relative spiritual adventurousness of Springsteen's generation, America's continually growing interest in Buddhism, and the evidence of his songs and public rhetoric, it seems something of a wonder that it took Springsteen until 2002 to include as prominent a reference to Buddha as the opening line of "Mary's Place" ("I got seven pictures of Buddha"). As Fuller points out, the message of twentieth-century Zen popularizer D.T. Suzuki was that "the goal of Zen was not to help us experience a different reality, but rather to make us suddenly awaken to the sacred character of this reality" (83). We will remember that Springsteen, in a 2002 interview, claimed that the "real world" rather than "some place intangible or some place abstract" was where he "always found faith and spirit," and that he claims to have "tried to write about that basic idea [his] whole life." Springsteen's view of his own core message, then, can be seen as remarkably close to that of one the main strands of popular Buddhist thought in America.

If we look again at Springsteen's idea of faith in this context, we see some further intersections with American Buddhism. Fuller introduces the chapter containing his examination of Eastern spirituality by identifying a series of general trends in the thought of "spiritual, but not religious" Americans. The first of these, which Fuller also claims is the "most important," is that "[s]piritual seekers are concerned with the individual's right, even duty, to establish his or her own criteria for belief. Religious beliefs ... must be tested by experience. [Spiritual seekers] do not want to be required to accept religious doctrines on faith" (75-76). Buddhist monk and author Thich Nhat Hanh, cited by Fuller as a popular source of Buddhist knowledge among Americans (84), addresses the issue of faith similarly in *Going Home: Jesus and Buddha as Brothers*, another work in the vein of his bestselling *Living Buddha, Living Christ*:

> True faith comes from how the path you are taking can bring you life and love and happiness everyday. You continue to learn so that your happiness and your peace, and the happiness and peace of the people around you, can grow. You don't have to follow a religious path in order to have faith. But if you are committed only to a set of ideas and dogmas that may be called faith, that is not true faith ... We have to distinguish between true faith and blind faith. (Nhat Hanh, *Going Home* 71-72)

According to Nhat Hanh, this "true faith" comes from our own experience in living and cannot be based on ideas alone: "There is something more important than notions and perceptions, and that is our direct experience of suffering and of happiness. If our faith is made of this direct experience and insight, then it is true faith and it will never make us suffer" (*Going Home* 77). Springsteen's expressed ideas about faith appear to fit into Fuller's model, and to agree with Nhat Hanh: whether formal religion is involved or not, faith that matters is faith grounded in our daily lives and experiences and the people around us.

The importance of direct experience is also a key component of the second prevailing theme in "unchurched spirituality" identified by Fuller:

> Personal spirituality has to do with cultivating a mystical feel for God's presence in the natural world. What makes a religious idea "true" is whether it helps individuals become inwardly receptive to what Emerson described as the "divinity that flows through all things." (76).

As evidenced by Fuller's use of the term "Mystic East," mystical experience—what a teacher such as Nhat Hanh might refer to more simply as insight—is popularly understood as a key component of Buddhism. We have little evidence outside of Springsteen's songs to suggest that he has an interest in mysticism, but some of these songs certainly hint at a perception of a higher power present in daily life. For instance, the examples cited by Bonca (whose essay on Springsteen, incidentally, is found in an online journal of non-religious spirituality called *Killing the Buddha*) all refer to the presence of the divine in the world:

> "Cautious Man" ... notes how the moonlight on the protagonist's wife's face fills "their room in the beauty of God's fallen light"; the tormented ex-lover in "I Wish I Were Blind" ... sees that "the world is filled / with the grace and beauty of God's hand"; the new father in "Living Proof" ... calls his newborn son "a little piece of the Lord's undying light."

Cullen, meanwhile, points to the "frankly mystical" (191) dimension of *Lucky Town*'s "My Beautiful Reward," whose last verse finds the song's existentially confused narrator transformed into—or perhaps at one with—a bird soaring above a river.

This final image in "My Beautiful Reward" suggests an additional link between Springsteen's work and a spiritual, but not religious perspective in general and popular American Buddhism in particular. If we are interested in searching for signs of a perceived "divinity that flows through all things" in Springsteen's songs, we cannot ignore his frequent use of the (flowing, of course) river as an image and setting. For our purposes, one of the most notable examples of a river in Springsteen's work may be found in *Nebraska*'s "Reason to Believe." Like "My Beautiful Reward," "Reason to Believe" presents us with a narrator searching for meaning, but the singer in "Reason to Believe" appears even more desperate. The

song, a litany of death and heartbreak, features a river in the final two of its four verses. In the first of these, a baby baptized in the river suddenly becomes "an old man [who] passes away" and is prayed over in a cemetery. There is surely some indictment of organized religion in this verse ("Lord, won't you tell us/ tell us what does it mean"), but the narrator's demand for meaning is ultimately deeper, addressed to God himself.

What seems to connect this song to a Buddhist perspective, however, is its last verse, in which an expectant groom's bride fails to appear at a riverside altar. We do not know if the bride intentionally abandoned her husband-to-be or was hurt or killed on the way to the wedding. But in some ways that information makes no difference, because, in any case, the groom is left to "[watch] the river rush on so effortlessly." If we understand the river to be mocking the groom, it is easy to add this final indignity to the others cataloged in the song and view "Reason to Believe" as the most despairing of Springsteen compositions. But we can imagine an alternative reading in which the effortless river is instead a teacher of sorts, reminding the groom that nature's very lack of effort and worry makes it worth emulating, and it is reasonable to imagine a Buddhist viewing the situation in this way. Zen Buddhism in particular is popularly known for its focus on nature; Steve Hagen's bestselling *Buddhism Plain and Simple*, for instance, cites falling leaves, with their utter lack of "goal-oriented" (85) activity, as exemplars of the Buddhist notion of "right action." While a Buddhist would not deny the suffering of the groom or the narrator in "Reason to Believe," he or she might find in the song's final verse the only kind of lesson that could possibly assuage the narrator's hopelessness. Considering that spiritual insight is known for manifesting itself in times of utter despair, we can even go so far here as to imagine that the groom could emerge from the experience transformed—and thus see a hint of a happy ending in a song that may otherwise seem to resist such a reading.

Aside from their potential role as examples of nature at work, flowing waters have some specific uses in Buddhist teachings. Of special note here is an analogy cited by Hagen in which humans make the mistake of "see[ing] ourselves as we would a cork in a stream. What we do not realize is that there is only stream. What we fancy as particular is, from the first, only movement, change and flow" (87). Hagen's example calls into play the important Buddhist ideas of impermanence and no-self, which Nhat Hanh discusses without metaphor: "[S]ince, according to Buddhism, nothing is permanent and what we normally call a self is made entirely of non-self elements, there is really no such entity as a self" ("First Flash" 205).

At first glance, these teachings might seem rather removed from a discussion about Springsteen, but they stem from one other Buddhist idea—the notion of interconnectedness—which can clearly be linked to values held dear in Springsteen's work. "Nobody wins unless everybody wins" has become one of Springsteen's best-known public statements, and the same spirit is at work in "Land of Hope and Dreams," in the observation of "American Skin (41 Shots)" that "We're baptized ... in each other's blood," in "Matamoras Banks" giving

voice to a man who dies (in a river) attempting to cross from Mexico to the United States. And this spirit also informs Springsteen's 1985 remark that:

> I never look out at my crowd and see a bunch of faces … It's never happened. Any night I've ever been onstage, I see people … That's why, before the show, we go out and check the sound in every section of the room. Because there's some guy sittin' back here, and he's got a girl with him, and … it's like, this is their seat. And what you hope for is that the same thing goes the other way—that when they look up at you, they don't just see some person with a guitar. (Loder, "Bruce!" 169)

To Springsteen's statement we can compare Thich Nhat Hanh's reflection on his experience with translating sponsorship applications for Vietnamese orphans:

> Before I begin to [work with the applications], I look into the eyes of the child in the photograph … I feel a deep link between myself and each child, which allows me to enter into a special communion with them … I no longer see an "I" who translates the sheets to help each child, I no longer see a child who received love and help. The child and I are one: no one pities, no one asks for help, no one helps. … These are moments of non-discrimination mind. (*Miracle* 157)

Popular Buddhist author Jack Kornfield says that, "When the Buddha confronted the question of identity on the night of his enlightenment, he came to the radical discovery that we do not exist as separate beings" (282). In the same vein, though perhaps not intentionally, scholar Bryan K. Garman notes that during a 1996 concert performance of Woody Guthrie's "Tom Joad," Springsteen included Guthrie's speculation that "[E]verybody might be just One Big Soul" (192). After the "Tom Joad" performance, Springsteen suggested that "salvation isn't individual … [that] maybe we don't rise and fall on our own" (*A Race of Singers* 192).

Ultimately, it is the expression of these kinds of idea that most strongly suggests some "interconnectedness" between Springsteen's work and Buddhist thought. Springsteen is almost certainly not a closet Buddhist per se, but he is part of a generation and an age for which, as Fuller notes, exploration of Eastern ideas is increasingly common and has to some degree become an ingrained part of American culture. And as we have seen, Springsteen's work and public rhetoric suggest that he is a spiritual seeker with an open mind and a sensibility that reaches for—and perhaps, if Buddhist views hold any truth, intuits—connection rather than division: "What separates people," he told Kurt Loder, "are the things that are in their heart … I know that before I started playing [music], I was alone. And one of the reasons I picked up the guitar was that I wanted to be part of something" ("Bruce!" 169).

Conclusion

It has long been clear that, although his relationship with Christianity is complex and marked by ambivalence, Springsteen's interest in religious and spiritual issues is strong. I have suggested that Fuller's discussion of the apparently growing "spiritual, but not religious" segment of the American population may provide a valuable framework for further exploration and appreciation of the role of these issues in Springsteen's career. I have also suggested that it may be interesting and worthwhile to consider Springsteen in the light of a particular faith tradition outside Christianity: in this case, Buddhism, a tradition which, at least in its popularized form, is no longer alien to many Americans.

We can ultimately see spirituality in Springsteen's work as multifaceted and expansive, but also grounded: it seems clear that one of Springsteen's key spiritual ideals is a focus on "the real world"—a world that includes guitars, rock and roll, work, family, "Saturday night," "whores and gamblers," "saints and sinners"— in short, "life right now," whatever it may hold. Fuller similarly opines that "a part of the problem of American culture is that we haven't been helped to see the spiritual importance of everyday activities" and suggests that America's spiritual, but not religious tradition may be a part of the solution (173). If we consider Springsteen's work in this broader spiritual context, we can better understand not only his music itself, but perhaps also how that music serves as a touchstone for listeners following spiritual and religious paths of all types.

PART IV
"It's Hard to be a Saint in the City": Springsteen, Ethics, and Social Justice

Chapter 11

"The Country We Carry in Our Hearts Is Waiting": Bruce Springsteen and the Art of Social Change

Edward U. Murphy

Dr. King once said that the arc of the moral universe is long but it bends towards justice. It bends towards justice, but here is the thing: it does not bend on its own. It bends because each of us in our own ways put our hand on that arc and we bend it in the direction of justice.

Barack Obama (April 4, 2008)

Introduction

All I'm trying to do now is get music to my audience that is relevant to the times we're living in and to the times in their lives.

Bruce Springsteen (Interview with Mark Hagen)

On January 18, 2009, a few days before Barack Obama became the forty-fourth American president, Bruce Springsteen had the distinct honor of opening the "We are One" concert on the steps of the Lincoln Memorial. Before the president-elect and vice-president-elect, their families, half a million or more people, and a global television audience, he sang "The Rising" with a gospel choir. Later, he joined Pete Seeger for a massive sing-along of Woody Guthrie's classic "This Land is Your Land," including the two often-forgotten "radical" final verses. At that moment, America's honorable tradition of musical dissent merged with the nation's hopes that its young, black president would succeed in overcoming the disasters left over from the Bush-Cheney years. Springsteen must have felt an electric charge linking the past, present, and future of the long struggle for social justice in the United States.

In fall 2004 Springsteen had been the headliner of the Vote for Change tour, an unprecedented, if unsuccessful, effort by popular musicians to defeat an incumbent president and change the direction of the country. For many years he had written and performed socially conscious songs, raised money and publicity for various causes, and made comments both on stage and in interviews that unmistakably revealed his humanitarian values and liberal politics. In 2004 his fear and loathing of the Bush administration resulted in an entirely new level of political involvement: his role as a principal organizer of the Vote for Change concerts, his endorsement of the Kerry-

Edwards ticket in an op-ed in the *New York Times*, and his personal campaigning with John Kerry in the closing days before the election. His song "No Surrender" became the campaign's semi-official song. Springsteen's short and concise speeches introducing the candidate at campaign rallies were arguably more effective than those by Kerry himself. He concluded both the op-ed and his onstage commentary with these resonant words: "The country we carry in our hearts is waiting."

By the mid-2000s, in response to the misadventures of the Bush administration and the tragedy of the Iraq War, rock and roll seemed to recover its political voice. Neil Young released his blistering anti-Bush album *Living with War* in 2006. That summer, Crosby, Stills, Nash and Young reunited for a highly political concert tour that made provocative connections between Vietnam and Iraq, Nixon and Bush, the imperative to protest and government attempts to suppress freedom of speech. In 2005 the generally apolitical Rolling Stones released the song "Sweet Neo Con," a scathing attack on Bush that opened with the lines "You call yourself a Christian / I think you're a hypocrite." Green Day's bestselling 2004 album *American Idiot* is essentially an anti-Bush rock opera. Many other artists, young and old—including Pearl Jam, Steve Earle, Pink, Conor Oberst, Randy Newman, Jackson Browne, and Burt Bacharach—also released music explicitly critical of the Bush administration.

After the great disappointment of the 2004 election, the first indication that all this activity would not be in vain was the Democratic sweep of Congress in 2006. Two years later Barack Obama's election to the presidency was the occasion for great rejoicing by all opponents of the Bush-Cheney administration. Springsteen's endorsement of Obama in April 2008 was widely publicized and considered to be a significant coup for the campaign. Although no Vote for Change tour occurred, he made several appearances for Obama in fall 2008, singing his songs and making an eloquent case for the Democratic nominee. On the Sunday before the election, Springsteen and Obama appeared together in Cleveland and brought out their wives and children on stage. It turned out that candidate himself (like Kerry before him) was a big fan of the man and his music, and "The Rising" became an unofficial theme song of the presidential campaign.

Questions arise. Does any of this musical activism make a difference? More generally, can artists working in various media, such as music, literature, or film, actually contribute to the making of social change? If so, how would this happen? One kind of contribution musicians can offer is to help out in the campaigns of progressive candidates, as Springsteen and many other musicians did by making appearances on the stump for Kerry and Obama. Today, videos can have a huge impact. Will.i.am's "Yes We Can" video mixed celebrities, music, and parts of Obama's speeches. A huge hit on YouTube, it was a very effective vehicle for the candidate's inspirational message. A different kind of approach to social change avoids direct electoral politics; rather, let the music itself help to create a climate for social change—specifically, progress towards a more just, more equal society. Bob Dylan, John Lennon, Bob Marley, and Bono are four artists whose work can plausibly be said to have had fostered progressive social change. Dylan's

"Masters of War" and "Chimes of Freedom," Lennon's "Give Peace a Chance" and "Imagine," and Marley's "Redemption Song" and "One Love" are classic protest songs that raise political awareness and inspire listeners. As lead singer of U2, Bono has written such galvanizing songs as "Pride in the Name of Love" and "Sunday Bloody Sunday." Of course, one would be hard-pressed to identify a cause-and-effect relationship between protest songs and subsequent social change, but it is also clear that the popular music influences public opinion, especially among youth. During the 1960s Dylan's early political songs, such as "The Times They are a-Changin'," "Blowin' in the Wind," and "Chimes of Freedom," became anthems of the civil rights and anti-war movements. Dylan, The Beatles, The Rolling Stones, The Who, and other bands became hugely popular symbols of youth rebellion, affecting contemporary political developments more indirectly than directly. They did so by changing the cultural terrain on which politics is played.

Springsteen and Social Commentary

> My songs, they're all about the American identity and your own identity and the masks behind the masks behind the masks, both for the country and for yourself. And trying to hold onto what's worthwhile, what makes it a place that's special, because I still believe that it is.
>
> Bruce Springsteen (qtd in Levy, "Bruce Springsteen")

Springsteen clearly aspires to the kind of impact that rockers had in the 1960s, but times are different. Although the youth rebellion of the 1960s was long ago, by 2006 his and his fellow rockers' revulsion against the Bush administration turned out to be shared by the vast majority of the American people. Springsteen himself became one of the most prominent Bush critics in the artistic community. Over the course of his long career, the kid from Freehold, New Jersey, has evolved from an avatar of restless youth to a tribune of the white working-class to a troubadour for the poor and marginalized to an American musical icon and a widely respected liberal voice. How has he deployed that voice? In this chapter I would like to concentrate on Springsteen's songwriting and discuss the ways in which he has communicated his social and political views. Songs such as "The Promised Land," "The River," "Born in the USA," and "The Rising," each a commentary on American life, have become touchstones to millions of fans around the world. The songs on *Darkness on the Edge of Town* (1978) articulate a deep longing for a better life and a country that lives up to its promise. Those on *Nebraska* (1982) suggest a crisis of faith in the American dream. To be sure, not all of Springsteen's songs address sociopolitical themes, but a sizeable number do— besides the aforementioned, such songs as "Lost in the Flood," "Factory," "Point Blank," "Johnny 99," "This Hard Land," "Streets of Philadelphia," "The Ghost of Tom Joad," "Sinola Cowboys," "My City of Ruins," "Devils and Dust," and "Long Walk Home," to name just a few. None of these is didactic or an explicitly political protest song. The few exceptions include "Held Up Without a Gun" (which protested against high gasoline prices circa 1980) and the anti-war "Last to Die" on the *Magic* album.

Far from directly telling the listener how to think or feel, most of Springsteen's social commentary songs tell stories. They are typically first-person confessionals in which the narrator, usually male, offers an account of his life or how he ended up in his current situation. In these songs Springsteen seeks to engage the listener in the experience of walking in the shoes of characters such as undocumented immigrants, unemployed workers, homeless veterans, criminals, and the like. Examples include "Born in the USA," "The River," "Darlington County," "Highway Patrolman," "The Line," and "Streets of Philadelphia." Few other songwriters write so frequently in character to address sociopolitical themes, although Bob Dylan, Neil Young, Steve Earle, Mark Knopfler, and Randy Newman are among those who have skillfully done so. In this chapter I want to focus on this aspect of Springsteen's songwriting because it highlights a particular kind of relationship between art and social change.

Albums such as *Darkness on the Edge of Town, The River, Nebraska, Born in the USA, The Ghost of Tom Joad, Devils & Dust,* and *Magic* can all be seen as Springsteen's commentary on what he sees as the erosion of the American Dream. During an appearance for Barack Obama during the 2008 campaign, Springsteen remarked, "I've spent most of my creative life measuring the distance between that American promise and American reality" (qtd in Valania). At the outset of the Vote for Change tour, he elaborated on his role as an artist in a *New York Times* op-ed:

> A nation's artists and musicians have a particular place in its social and political life. Over the years I've tried to think long and hard about what it means to be American: about the distinctive identity and position we have in the world, and how that position is best carried. I've tried to write songs that speak to our pride and criticize our failures. . . . Through my work, I've always tried to ask hard questions. Why is it that the wealthiest nation in the world finds it so hard to keep its promise and faith with its weakest citizens? Why do we continue to find it so difficult to see beyond the veil of race? How do we conduct ourselves during difficult times without killing the things we hold dear? Why does the fulfillment of our promise as a people always seem to be just within grasp yet forever out of reach? (Springsteen, "Chords for Change")

Art and Social Justice

> Imagination is the chief instrument of the good ... art is more moral than moralities. For the latter either are, or tend to become, consecrations of the status quo. ... The moral prophets of humanity have always been the poets even though they spoke in free verse or by parable.
>
> John Dewey (348)

What, in fact, is the role of the artist in achieving a better society? According to John Dewey, socially engaged art, whether music, visual art, fiction, poetry, or other forms has the capacity to shake people out a passive acceptance of social injustice. Philosophers Martha Nussbaum (*Upheavals of Thought*) and Richard Rorty argue that novels, such as Richard Wright's *Native Son* or Charles Dickens's *Oliver Twist*, can fire the moral imagination of readers and inspire compassion for, and solidarity with, those in different life circumstances. Harriet Beecher Stowe's 1852 novel *Uncle Tom's Cabin*, in dramatically depicting the pain and injustice visited upon fugitive slaves, had an enormous impact on public opinion in the American North prior to the Civil War. The documentary photography of Lewis Hine, Jacob Riis, Dorothea Lange, Walker Evans, Robert Frank, and Sebastião Salgado has certainly affected public discourse in bringing the actual lives of the dispossessed into greater focus. Spike Lee's 2006 documentary film on the tragic effects of Hurricane Katrina, *When the Levee Breaks*, is a model of how this is done. As Dewey said, "art is more moral than moralities" in stitching together a wider moral community.

One of Springsteen's great gifts as an artist is his ability to establish a sense of shared fate between his audience and the often-dispossessed subjects of his songs. As a "moral prophet of humanity" in Dewey's sense, he uses his imaginative powers to create flawed or struggling or even dying characters who earn an empathetic response among those who might otherwise not be able to picture themselves in those circumstances. In asking hard questions, he offers not answers per se, but human stories that reveal the contradictions between American ideals and American reality. Springsteen can be seen as an inheritor of a robust American tradition of liberal and radical dissent, comprising prophets and rebels. This tradition links Thomas Paine to Martin Luther King, Elizabeth Cady Stanton to Betty Friedan, and Henry David Thoreau to Rachel Carson. In similar fashion, a visible thread of populist politics, prose, and poetry runs from Walt Whitman to John Steinbeck to Woody Guthrie to Pete Seeger to Bob Dylan to Bruce Springsteen—and to the likes of John Mellencamp, Steve Earle, and England's Billy Bragg.

At their best, Springsteen's story songs foster compassion for those who are less fortunate or, in his own words, whose "souls are at risk." His narratives are of a piece with writers like Steinbeck or photographers like Jacob Riis in challenging audiences to question received truths and to break out of an unthinking complacency. They address a classic problem faced by liberals and all those advocating a higher level of national and international social solidarity. As Robert Morris asks, why care for the stranger? There are both intellectual reasons and affective reasons to give our time and resources to the less fortunate. In following Kant's dictum to act according to universal law or Christ's commandment to help the poor and weak, we may do so out of principled belief. We also might act out of ideological conviction or a strong sense of social responsibility. However, many people do not have such strong beliefs, do not act upon them at least in political terms, or are selective about which groups they view as deserving of generous government assistance. It is here that the artists' role in expanding the moral imagination of their audience can become very important.

Progress toward social justice is typically a political process that requires changes in laws, norms, and institutions. For reform to occur, influential citizens or the voting public must either be pressing for change or at least become sympathetic to it. The War on Poverty in the 1960s, for example, was partly a response to the success of the civil rights movement. With the enactment of the 1964 Civil Rights Act and the 1965 Voting Rights Act, the logical next step for the movement and its allies was to address the poverty and economic inequality that disproportionately afflicted black Americans. During the Great Depression, the Farm Security Administration sent out photographers to document the condition of the rural poor. These photographs of destitute families shocked the conscience of those who saw them, rallying public support for New Deal programs to assist poor farmers and landless migrants. In 1939 John Steinbeck chronicled the suffering of the Joad family in *The Grapes of Wrath*, which was the basis for the equally influential John Ford movie.

In order to "set the table" for policy change in favor of the poor and dispossessed, the public—or its influential or politically active segments—must not only become aware of the issue or group in question, but also feel sympathy for those who are suffering, judge that their situation is (to some degree) unjust and wrong, and be willing to support action to change it. Two challenges must be surmounted. The first is to reframe the old-fashioned prejudice against historically stigmatized groups typically viewed as lazy or immoral. The second challenge is to address the decline in national solidarity, of a sense of "all for one, and one for all" (Putnam, *Bowling Alone*). American society seems to be increasingly fragmenting into multiple groups separated by class, education, political affiliation, region, sexual orientation, religion, and race-ethnicity. The feeling of shared fate has eroded. In particular, economic inequality has become notably worse during recent decades, and the gap between the rich and those of moderate and low incomes has not been so wide since the 1920s (Massey, *Categorically Unequal*). An unfortunate feature of American life is the extent to which the culture of American individualism justifies and rationalizes great inequalities.

Springsteen's Story Songs

> It's the old job of putting yourself in somebody else's shoes, while you've got a foot in your own shoe.
>
> Bruce Springsteen (Interview with Mark Hagen)

> The verses are the blues, the chorus is the gospel.
>
> —Bruce Springsteen (qtd in Pareles, "His Kind")

In the face of widening social division, however, art can bind us closer together. It can help us understand what's important, expand our empathetic imagination, inspire greater concern for others, and remap the moral community. Let's start by taking Springsteen's "Streets of Philadelphia" as a brief example. The first two verses are quite vivid:

> I was bruised and battered and I couldn't tell what I felt
> I was unrecognizable to myself
> Saw my reflection in a window
> I didn't know my own face
> Oh brother are you gonna leave me wasting away
> On the streets of Philadelphia
> I walked the avenue till my legs felt like stone
> I heard the voices of friends vanished and gone
> At night I could hear the blood in my veins
> Just as black and whispering as the rain
> On the streets of Philadelphia.

This song is a narrative by a lonely and gravely ill man, written and widely heard at a time when AIDS was a probable death sentence in the United States. He has been abandoned by his friends. As he wanders around the city, wasting away, he finds that he is, in Springsteen's unforgettable phrase, "unrecognizable to myself." Such finely drawn portraits of lives on the edge, such as "Streets of Philadelphia," can contribute to social change, albeit modestly, by developing feelings of compassion in the hearts of listeners who may previously unaware of, or unable to empathize with, "the other"—those members of marginalized groups who are different from the mainstream of white, affluent, straight America. The point, of course, is that we are not so different: our dreams, our aspirations, our desire not to suffer needlessly and alone are all part of our common humanity.

I will now examine in their entirety the lyrics of two other Springsteen songs: "Matamoros Banks" from *Devils & Dust* (2005) and "Brothers under the Bridge" from *Tracks* (1998) and *18 Tracks* (1999). In the former, Springsteen renders an unforgettable portrait of the life and death of a Mexican migrant worker:

> For two days the river keeps you down
> Then you rise to the light without a sound
> Past the playgrounds and empty switching yards
> The turtles eat the skin from your eyes, so they lay open to the stars
> Your clothes give way to the current and river stone
> 'Till every trace of who you ever were is gone
> And the things of the earth they make their claim
> That the things of heaven may do the same

The song commences with horrifying images: a waterlogged dead body, eventually floating to the water's surface, lidless eyes "open to the stars," stripped of clothes and any identifying information. These striking pictures seem likely to become etched in the mind of the listener. The dead body had a life, an intimate relationship with a loved one whom he expected to meet again. We can identify with these feelings, and feel what they both have lost:

> Over rivers of stone and ancient ocean beds
> I walk on sandals of twine and tire tread
> My pockets full of dust, my mouth filled with cool stone
> The pale moon opens the earth to its bones
> I long, my darling, for your kiss, for your sweet love I give God thanks
> The touch of your loving fingertips
> Meet me on the Matamoros
> Meet me on the Matamoros
> Meet me on the Matamoros banks.

Here the story has its chronological beginning. The migrant's moonlit, almost Biblical journey to the promised land is arduous and lonely, yet he seems resolute. He offers thanks to God and shares a sweet and tactile memory of his lover. Springsteen's purpose here, skillfully rendered with just a few brushstrokes, is to paint a compelling portrait of this man in order to assist his audience in identifying with his struggle for a better life:

> Your sweet memory comes on the evenin' wind
> I sleep and dream of holding you in my arms again
> The lights of Brownsville, across the river shine
> A shout rings out and into the silty red river I dive.

In this verse the narrator describes his hopes and the beginning of his end. Then Springsteen sets the scene that led to the poor man's demise: after a signal, in the light of Brownsville, Texas, the migrant jumps into the "silty red river" where we know he will drown. His last thoughts are his hopes and dreams of sharing the new country with his loved one.

"Matamoras Banks is deeply evocative and moving. The economy of language, the shockingly vivid details of the aftermath of drowning, the warmth and intimacy of the first-person portrait of the doomed migrant—all these elements constitute a powerful and unforgettable story that might actually change one's feelings about undocumented people who die trying to share in the American Dream.

"Brothers under the Bridge," although little known, is another masterpiece of social observation. It was written around the time of *The Ghost of Tom Joad* album and performed frequently during that tour in 1995-1997. The song is a first-person narrative by a homeless Vietnam veteran.

Saigon, it was all gone
The same Coke machines
As the streets I grew on
Down in a mesquite canyon
We come walking along the ridge
Me and the brothers under the bridge.

With these initial verses, we learn that our narrator is a Vietnam veteran living with other homeless men under a bridge in a California canyon.

Come the Santa Ana's, man, that dry brush'll light
Billy Devon got burned up in his own campfire one winter night
We buried his body in the white stone high up along the ridge
Me and the brothers under the bridge.
Had enough of town and the street life
Over nothing you end up on the wrong end of someone's knife
Now I don't want no trouble
And I ain't got none to give
Me and the brothers under the bridge.

Although the men have escaped the city and created their own community, the canyon life is still dangerous. The narrator expresses his vulnerability and resignation:

I come home in '72
You were just a beautiful light
In your mama's dark eyes of blue
I stood down on the tarmac, I was just a kid
Me and the brothers under the bridge.
Come Veterans' Day I sat in the stands in my dress blues
I held your mother's hand
When they passed with the red, white, and blue
One minute you're right there … and something slips …

Here we discover the intensely moving fact that he is telling this story to his grown child, who is maybe about the same age as he was when he returned from the war. Since he is homeless, we can surmise that this damaged soul may have had only intermittent contact with his child—with all the loss and guilt on his part that would entail. The final heartbreaking verse contrasts our narrator's tenuous grasp of reality against the strong, patriotic images of a Veterans' Day parade that he attends.

"Streets of Philadelphia," "Matamoros Banks," and "Brothers under the Bridge" certainly evoke strong feelings of empathy for the narrator/protagonists. Springsteen's writing focuses on two levels, giving us details of the protagonist's inner life as well as sketching a larger social canvas. What David McCullough has written about Dickens could easily be said of Springsteen's best writing: "I love the way he sets a scene. He said, in his great admonition to writers, 'Make me see.' I try to make you see what's happening and smell it and hear it. I want to know what they had for dinner. I want to know how long it took to walk from where to where" (qtd in Fisher 2). The vivid detail serves another purpose: what ethnographers sometimes call *Verstehen*, or understanding. It is significant that these dark tales are each told in the first person, which more effectively conveys the narrator's inner life than a more external, third-person point of view. By bringing us so intimately into these men's lives, into their personal world-view, Springsteen's narratives in these songs should generate an empathetic response on the part of most listeners.

In this light, how do the heart-wrenching stories in "Streets of Philadelphia," "Matamoros Banks," and "The Brothers under the Bridge" fit with Nussbaum's criteria for the evocation of compassion? The seriousness test is clearly met, as one man is presumably dying, another is dead, and the other is just hanging on to his humble way of life. With respect to responsibility, each man has taken a path that turned out badly. The first is a gay man infected with a deadly disease, the second is an illegal immigrant floating lifelessly in a river, and the third is a Vietnam veteran who is homeless. In each case, the price they paid is disproportionately high. Springsteen does not spell it out, but the listener knows that the men's fates were shaped by larger economic and political forces. In these songs, Springsteen carefully paints heartbreaking portraits that could easily induce a listener to identify with each man's struggle and to feel that "there but for the grace of God go I." Springsteen's audience may initially believe that it has little in common with an AIDS victim, a dead migrant from south of the border or a mentally ill Vietnam veteran living in a canyon, but his writing powerfully evokes a sense of place and inner life, where the listener can imagine facing the protagonist's choices and observe his story with cinematic detail in the mind's eye.

The Rising album was, of course, Springsteen's response to the 9/11 attacks. Every song on that 2002 album referred in some way to the pain, loss, resilience, and renewal stemming from those terrible events. Coming five years before *Magic*— before the nation had, in his view, lost its way—it was a work of consolation rather than anger. The title song has become a kind of modern classic. It depicts a firefighter entering the World Trade Center on 9/11 with "a sixty pound stone" on his back and "a half mile line" on his shoulder He meets death:

> Spirits above and behind me
> Faces gone, black eyes burnin' bright
> May their precious blood forever bind me
> Lord as I stand before your fiery light.
> Li, li, li, li, li, li, li, li, li
> I see you Mary in the garden
> In the garden of a thousand sighs
> There's holy pictures of our children

Dancin' in a sky filled with light
May I feel your arms around me
May I feel your blood mix with mine
A dream of life comes to me
Like a catfish dancin' on the end of the line.
Sky of blackness and sorrow (a dream of life)
Sky of love, sky of tears (a dream of life)
Sky of glory and sadness (a dream of life)
Sky of mercy, sky of fear (a dream of life)
Sky of memory and shadow (a dream of life)
Your burnin' wind fills my arms tonight
Sky of longing and emptiness (a dream of life)
Sky of fullness, sky of blessed life (a dream of life).
Come on up for the rising
Come on up, lay your hands in mine
Come on up for the rising
Come on up for the rising tonight.

These lyrics are brilliantly evocative. As the narrator faces death, he sees "black eyes burnin' bright" and then he seems to enter a liminal stage and sees Mary, mother of Jesus—or Mary, possibly his wife—and "holy pictures of our children." His life passes before him. A "dream of life" comes to his mind, and he sees a succession of visions that seem to encompass different perspectives on life and death: first, a "sky of blackness and sorrow" and finally a "sky of fullness, sky of blessed life." The song ends with a Christian-inspired refrain to "lay your hands in mine / Come on up for the rising." What is the rising? It could be, literally or figuratively, the ascent to heaven.

However, on *The Rising* album, the gospel chorus of "My City of Ruins" implores the residents of a beaten-down city to "rise up": "I pray Lord / With these hands / For the strength, Lord / With these hands / For the faith lord / With these hands / Come on rise up / Come on rise up / Rise up, rise up." Both songs employ strikingly Christian imagery. In "My City of Ruins," the narrator tries to inspire the city—and by extension, everyone who lacks hope or faith—to rise up from the ashes. He extends a helpful hand—not an individual hand, but a communal hand. In "The Rising," the narrator invites the dying man to come to the rising, as if it's a religious ritual of rebirth. Or it could simply mean: let us together rise up above this tragedy and go on with both sadness and strength.

A Political Turn

We've had an enormous moral, spiritual, economic collapse. People go to storytellers when times are like that, and our band was built from the beginning for hard times.
Bruce Springsteen (*The Daily Show* with Jon Stewart, 2009)

In the aftermath of his deep involvement with the Kerry campaign in 2004 and his great frustration with its failure, Springsteen became more openly political in his music. It is clear that the war in Iraq, which he opposed from the start, caused him to speak out forcefully. Springsteen's 2005 *Devils & Dust* album presented story-songs covering such politically salient topics as an American soldier's anguish in Iraq ("Devils & Dust"), the perils of ghetto life ("Black Cowboys), and death on the US-Mexican border ("Matamoras Banks"). On tour his remarks about President Bush, Vice President Cheney, and Iraq were far more pointed and direct than during The Rising tour of 2002-2003. With the 2006 *Seeger Sessions* CD, Springsteen revived and reinterpreted folk-music classics associated with the legendary activist Pete Seeger, including civil rights and anti-war anthems. On tour, these and additional songs such as "Bring 'em Home" and "How Can a Poor Man Stand Such Times and Live" became part of a larger populist narrative condemning the Bush administration for its failed imperial dreams in Iraq and its bungled effort in the Gulf Coast after Hurricane Katrina. In 2007 Springsteen released *Magic*, the most political album of his career. With the full power of the E Street Band, he presented a cohesive set of songs that amounted to a sustained attack on the Bush presidency. Although many of the songs could be interpreted either politically and personally, his intent was clear. The title song, ostensibly about an illusionist or magician, was a thinly veiled attack on the Bush-Cheney administration's ability to manipulate the public while engaging in nefarious activities. On tour, in case anyone missed his point, he told audiences that the song was not about a magician but about the current administration's penchant for trickery and deceit. He also regularly introduced "Living in the Future" by with a statement decrying the Bush-Cheney administration's policies on detention without trial, illegal wiretapping, the prison at Guantanamo, extraordinary rendition, and torture. Substantial segments of Springsteen's audience were offended by his aggressively liberal politics. At a concert I attended in August 2008 at Gillette stadium in Massachusetts, a group of young men started to chant "USA, USA" loudly as Springsteen denounced the Bush administration's policies on civil liberties.

Magic was not only political; it was angry. With cold fury, Springsteen railed against the Bush administration in songs that ranged from the didactic ("Last to Die") to the deeply tragic ("Gypsy Biker," Devil's Arcade") to the elegiac ("Long Walk Home"). Several songs conclude with words of despair. In "Livin' in the Future," Springsteen lamented: "My ship Liberty sailed away on a bloody red horizon / The groundskeeper opened the gates and let the wild dogs run." In "Your Own Worst Enemy," the final lines are: "Your own worst enemy has come / Everything is falling down / Your own worst enemy has come to town ... / Your flag it flew so high / It drifted into the sky." So, Ship Liberty has sailed away, the wild dogs are running, and our flag is drifting off into space. There's more. The title song, "Magic," concludes with striking images of violence: "On the road the sun is sinkin' low / There's bodies hangin' in the trees / This is what will be / This is what will be." This last shocking image, of bodies in trees, could be a reference to Goya's *Disasters of War* series of paintings, which Springsteen may have viewed at the Prado in Madrid during his frequent concert tours of Spain. He's clearly implying that that bodies hanging in trees are the consequence of the lies and disastrous policies of the Bush-Cheney administration. What isn't entirely clear is whether the bodies are the innocent victims of those policies, or the leaders themselves.

In the song "Last to Die," an anguished Springsteen sings, "Who'll be the last to die for a mistake?" This is a paraphrase of then anti-war activist John Kerry's famous comment in 1971 to the Senate Foreign Relations Committee. It's a bitter sentiment and an awkward question in the context of the Iraq War. However, he goes further, concluding the song with this striking thought: "Darlin' will tyrants and kings fall to the same fate / Strung up at your city gates?" In suggesting here that Bush and Cheney *et al.* might deserve the kind of ignominious end meted out by frenzied mobs during the French Revolution, Springsteen indicates just how furious he is. It is a widely shared fury. Two songs on *Magic* are first-person narratives by survivors of those dead or damaged by the Iraq War. "Gypsy Biker" appears to be told by a buddy of a dead veteran. One of the most striking verses is the ritual sacrifice of his motorcycle by his friends:

> We rode her into the foothills
> Bobby brought the gasoline
> We stood 'round her in a circle
> As she lit up the ravine
> The spring high desert wind
> Rushed down on us all the way back home.

Springsteen describes a town divided between war supporter and opponents, but none of this matters to the dead. He bitterly concludes: "To them that threw you away / You ain't nothin' but gone / Our Gypsy biker is comin' home."

"Devil's Arcade" has a similar theme, but here the mood is simply sad. The narrator seems to be a woman, presumably a girlfriend or wife, recounting her relationship with a grievously wounded veteran.

> You said heroes are needed, so heroes get made
> Somebody made a bet, somebody paid
> The cool desert morning, then nothin' to save
> Just metal and plastic where your body caved

There are memories of sex, of togetherness, and hopes for the future, of a normal life: "A house on a quiet street," "The glorious kingdom of sun on your face," "A bed draped in sunshine, a body that waits / For the touch of your fingers." In both "Gypsy Biker" and "Devil's Arcade," Springsteen paints detailed portraits of survivors' pain. In the last verse of the former song, the dead soldier's buddy has lost faith altogether and is doing lines of coke. At the end of the latter song, the woman simply repeats "the beat of your heart" over and over with aching intensity while the music quietens down to reflect the sound of a heartbeat. These songs vividly demonstrate that the cost of war is visited not only on the soldiers themselves, but also on all those who knew and loved them.

"Long Walk Home," in contrast, is nostalgic in tone. It is thematic centerpiece of *Magic*, a meditation on where America found itself in 2007. The narrator of this song revisits his hometown and finds that people and places he knew are long gone. The key verse is this:

> My father said "Son, we're lucky in this town
> It's a beautiful place to be born
> It just wraps its arms around you
> Nobody crowds you, nobody goes it alone.
> That you know flag flying over the courthouse
> Means certain things are set in stone
> Who we are, what we'll do and what we won't."

Springsteen is describing life in an idyllic town, where citizens support one another and observe bedrock values. But it has vanished. The town, of course, is a metaphor for the America that has been lost under Bush. The flag over the courthouse tells us "who were are, what we'll do and what we won't." Springsteen has made it very clear in comments on stage and in interviews how horrified he is at the Bush administration's violation of civil liberties, use of torture, and ignoring of the Geneva conventions. The song ends with the repeated refrain "It's gonna be a long walk home." We have a long way to go repair the damage done to the soul of the country and to recover our values. "Long Walk Home", I believe, is a brilliant and poignant summation of Springsteen's hope that America can find its moral compass again. In interviews since the election of Barack Obama to the presidency, he has shared his joy that the big-hearted and inclusive country that he has always believed in and written about has turned out to be real.

Can a Song Change the World?

> I think that the time when music could change the world is past. I think it would be
> very naive to think that in this day and age … I think the world today is a different
> place, and that it's time for science and physics and spirituality to make a difference
> in this world and to try to save the planet.
>
>   Neil Young (qtd in Moulson)

So what? Does "The Rising," "Long Walk Home," "Streets of Philadelphia" or any other music, no matter how resonant, really have an impact on the world? A skeptical view has been recently taken by Neil Young, who surprised many people in early 2008 when he proclaimed that music cannot change the world. Ever the contrarian, Young even wrote a song about it called "Just Singing a Song

Won't Change the World" released on his 2009 CD *Fork in the Road*. This is the same man who wrote an entire album attacking President Bush and the Iraq War, and played anti-war concerts with Crosby, Stills, and Nash before hundreds of thousands of people during the summer of 2006. In fact, it's hard to believe that that Young's efforts, along with those of thousands of other activists around the country, did not have a positive effect on the political climate of a nation that, only a few months later, threw the Republicans out of Congress on exactly these issues—President Bush's incompetence or worse, and the chaotic situation in Iraq at that time. However, in the same interview at Sundance, he went on to elaborate his goals for the CSNY "Living with War" concerts and the resulting film that he directed.

> This is all I'm going to do, I won't be doing anything else and I don't want to sing any. pretty songs; we can only sing about war and politics and the human condition ... The goal was to stimulate debate among people, and I hope that to some degree the film succeeds in doing that. (Moulson)

Perhaps Neil Young is right. If music and film can't change the world, they can at least stimulate debate. It is obvious that political organizing, campaigns, and laws are more directly related to achieving social justice, but public debate is part of that process. Young also argues that science and technology and spirituality may be more important than song in saving the planet. By 2009, in fact, he was spending enormous amounts of his time and money in working with engineers to develop a high-mileage electric car, which turns out to be the subject of his *Fork in the Road* album. Art may have relatively little to do directly with science and technology, but it surely is related to spirituality in that it can create a sense of transcendence and connectedness with something larger than ourselves. Protest songs can present situations that outrage us, raise us to cause, and forge a communal sense of purpose. Spiritual songs may resonate with our deepest, perhaps hidden, selves. Novels, films, and songs offer us a way to gain emotional insights into the lives of others and expand our moral horizons. In an interview with *The Progressive*, singer-songwriter Eliza Gilkyson held forth with her own thoughts about art and social change:

> It's a little vain to think that art has some super power to change things, but art can make people feel safe to feel. ... It can create a safe environment that lets people experience things, whether it's the shadow or the beauty ... I think art can help us learn to think for ourselves, to de-anesthetize ourselves. It gives us opportunities to choose between healing and destruction. It makes us aware of the choices ... For me, it's empathy. ... We struggle with ourselves, which means we should be able to connect with other people's struggles. You need the facts, the analysis to figure out what to do, but empathy is the first ingredient. For me, music and politics are both about trying to find that place to connect. (Qtd in Jensen 2)

Gilkyson makes several valuable points. First, art can awaken people's deadened sensibilities and help them experience latent or uncomfortable feelings, positive and negative. Second, art and music, in fostering empathy, provides a valuable connection between a person's own struggles and those of others. In this way, it serves to create an imagined community of previously solitary souls.

How can art establish communal bonds across a social landscape fragmented by race, ethnicity, class, religion and other divisions. Nussbaum outlines three elements that can be expected to evoke a compassionate response in an observer (listener, reader, viewer) of an unfortunate event bringing harm to an individual or group. First, the suffering must have sufficient gravity or severity. Second, the sufferer must be perceived either as not being responsible for his pain, as being less than fully responsible, or as not deserving the amount of suffering his actions have wrought. Third, the person who is suffering must evoke some sense of common identity with the observer (Nussbaum, *Upheavals of Thought*). An underlying challenge, however, is "the difficulty of imagining other people," as Elaine Scarry puts it. It is not so easy to enter into the experience of another, to truly share the joys or sorrows of someone else. This difficulty is only magnified with respect to people beyond our immediate circle or community. It is even more difficult to imagine the lives and feelings of members of groups whose experience seems far outside our own. An example might be the challenge faced by a middle-class white American to understand the experience of destitute men who cannot break the cycle of homelessness. Or consider the difficulty of a young American college student trying to imagine the world-view of Pakistani widows.

How can the problem of distant others become more real to us—less abstract, more concrete? The best way is surely to meet and talk with people whose backgrounds are very different from us. Of course, practical considerations of time, money, language, and geography prevent us from getting to know well more than a small segment of the diverse peoples of this world. Art, music, literature, ethnography, journalism, photography, film, and video offer us a far more accessible and efficient means of seeing the world outside of our immediate experience. What Springsteen does so well is to write and perform songs that say: you have more in common with this very different person than you imagine. This amounts to expanding the boundaries of the moral community, and enlarging the definition of who is "us" as opposed to "them."

However, even if we grant that art can foster such feelings of compassion and empathy in its audience, two questions arise. First, is the affected audience large enough to reach a critical mass and to influence public opinion or political elites? Second, is there a necessary relation between feelings of compassion, whether generalized or specific, and actual social change? In other words, does greater empathy among the public for the vulnerable "other" lead to greater social justice? To answer the second question first, it is surely true that greater public sympathy for, say, migrant workers or the homeless could contribute to the creation of a political climate where new laws or regulations might be enacted to help them. With respect to the first question, the impact of any single work of art is at best modest. The only way to think about the effect of socially engaged art is that the cumulative effect of many kinds of contributions can collectively influence the moral and political climate of society. Art can, as Gilkyson argues, awaken something within us—sensitizing us to the struggles of others. Images from the mass media, whether from a popular song or a TV news show, can lead both to greater public awareness of individual or group suffering and to the establishment of a visceral, emotional bond between the viewer/listener and the people in trouble. In turn, these factors can motivate members of the public to donate money or time to specific charitable causes and foster legislative and policy changes in support of such groups as southern blacks in the civil rights era, Vietnam veterans, tsunami victims, or AIDS sufferers.

Springsteen and Social Change

> I'm interested in the kind of country that we live in and leave to our kids. I'm interested in trying to define what that country is. I've got the chutzpah or whatever you want to say to believe that if I write a really good song about it, it's going to make a difference.
>
> Bruce Springsteen (Interview with Mark Hagen)

Let's try to be specific about the extent to which Springsteen and his work have helped to foster social change, if at all. During the period 2005-2008, Springsteen released three albums of increasingly pointed political commentary: *Devils & Dust*, *The Seeger Sessions*, and *Magic*. As he toured behind each album, his concerts became highly politicized events in which he took a prophetic stance from the stage against greed, inequality, exploitation, political manipulation, the abrogation of civil liberties, and the Iraq War. As noted above, Springsteen's musical activism was part of a broad revolt against the Bush administration. The close relation between his anti-Bush beliefs and the content of his musical output is underlined by the fact that, only days after Bush was out and Obama was sworn in as president, Springsteen released the resolutely non-political, rather upbeat album *Working on a Dream*.

How shall we assess the impact of Springsteen's work? Let's take "The Rising." This song is one whose meaning has changed as the political and social context has changed between its release in 2002 and 2008. Songs exist in the public domain and often live lives of their own. The public receives, uses, and understands art in ways that might be different from the artist's intentions. Originally a deeply spiritual requiem for those who died in 9/11, "The Rising" went on to become a key theme song of the Obama campaign. It was played at virtually every campaign stop immediately before or after the candidate appeared on stage. When President-elect Obama concluded his victory speech in Grant Park on November 4, 2008, the first music out of the loudspeakers was the "The Rising." For the insurgent Obama campaign, the metaphor of "rising" was resonant musically, visually, and politically. The widely seen campaign logo featured a rising sun over an American flag. Obama and his supporters framed the campaign as a kind of uprising to take back America. So it was no accident that "The Rising" was the opening musical performance of the pre-inaugural concert on the Mall in Washington.

Another well-known Springsteen song is 1993's "Streets of Philadelphia." Along with the Jonathan Demme movie *Philadelphia* for which it was written, the song has a place as among many significant pop culture messages in the 1990s that contributed to changing broader public attitudes towards people with HIV-AIDS. The song was and still is widely played on the radio. Although not everyone who recognizes the song may even know what the song is about, a large number of people do know and appreciate its message. By the 1990s gays and lesbians, who had been viewed with suspicion, disgust, and incomprehension, came to be perceived as more like "us." Those suffering from the HIV-AIDS found greater political support. As gays and lesbians become more visible in the media and in society more generally, they become normalized in the eyes of the majority of their fellow citizens.

What of "Brothers under the Bridge"? It is a remarkably poignant song. In contrast with "The Rising" and "Streets of Philadelphia," it has been heard by relatively few people. The song was buried on the *Tracks* compilation and played occasionally during the Tom Joad tour of the mid-1990s, which concentrated on smaller arenas. Those who love the song were deeply moved, as it conjures what it's like and what it feels like to be a homeless Vietnam veteran. No song, unfortunately, is going to have much of a social impact unless a wide audience hears and responds to it. In contrast, Springsteen's "Born in the USA" song in the mid-1980s reached a vast audience. The *Born in the USA* album was a blockbuster, and its title song was widely played on the radio. As most people know now, it is the bitter lament of an unemployed Vietnam veteran. Although "Born in the USA" was famously misunderstood by many as a patriotic anthem, its message of compassion for Vietnam veterans was also clear. Springsteen's anger at the injustice of the way in which the nation was treating veterans was perhaps less well understood. Nevertheless, it is reasonable to conclude that the song, given its huge exposure, helped generate greater public awareness of the plight of Vietnam veterans—too many of whom were struggling at a time of public apathy about homelessness, substance abuse, and physical and mental health issues.

Springsteen's contribution to the veterans went beyond his songs. In 1981 he and the E Street Band held a benefit concert in Los Angeles for the fledgling Vietnam Veterans of America organization. At the September 2005 Springsteen conference at Monmouth University, founder Bobby Muller flatly stated that the VVA would not exist without Springsteen's public and financial support during the 1980s. Of course, it is the activists who do the actual nitty-gritty work of organizing and advocacy—and who deserve the primary credit for success— but artists like Springsteen can provide needed publicity and funds to boost organizational effectiveness. And songs like "Born in the USA" have the capacity to make a particular cause better known, perhaps even fashionable.

Can "Matamoros Banks" have a similar effect for undocumented immigrants crossing the southwestern border of the United States? It is doubtful: unlike "Born in the USA" or "Streets of Philadelphia," this austere song was not heard by millions of people on the radio. The *Devils & Dust* CD was not a commercial juggernaut like *Born in the USA* twenty years earlier. Like the Ghost of Tom Joad tour in the mid-1990s, the solo acoustic Devils and Dust tour of 2005 was a small-scale affair. Nevertheless, with scores of shows in Europe and America, the total audience must have numbered several hundred thousand. That's a lot of people who were probably moved not only by Springsteen's performance of the song itself, but also by his pointed commentary. For example, at his October 25, 2005 concert in Worcester, Massachusetts, Springsteen offered this compelling introduction to "Matamoros Banks":

> Every year there's hundreds of people that die trying to get across our southern border. This was a very, very hot summer, and they die of dehydration in the desert or drown in the rivers. And, if you eat strawberries and tomatoes, or eggplant, or lettuce, these are all crops that can't be machine-harvested. Machines can't get those things—there are people out there picking those. And if you eat any of those things and enjoy any of those things . . . their hands, they're at your table. (Springsteen, "Comments from the Stage")

At a concert I attended in Bridgeport, Connecticut on July 20, 2005 Springsteen's introduction to "Matamoros Banks" included an observation that the *New York Times* had run an article just that day about a humanitarian group that was dropping food and water from the air for migrants along the border. Springsteen urged his audience to read the article and support the group, which opposes the self-appointed vigilantes currently preying on helpless immigrants. It was a small gesture, perhaps, but something positive. Multiplied thousands of times by artists and activists and journalists, these small actions cumulate into social change.

Tea and sympathy alone for migrant workers, of course, are not enough. Solidarity with the oppressed does not itself make social change. As Neil Young now argues, songs can't change the world. Charity is not enough. Individual acts of generosity are always needed, and private charities—whether community agencies, faith-based groups, or large foundations—are essential. However, social change ultimately involves utilizing the political process to enact collective, institutional change by means of government and law. The goal is social justice. Take the question of undocumented immigrants. Although its actions are invaluable in saving lives, the group that assists impoverished migrants on the southwestern border does not make social change, as such. As Springsteen says, what is needed is a "humane immigration policy." To achieve that, a social movement, an organized campaign, funds, staff, volunteers, posters, email lists, media, lobbying, protests, and ultimately legislation are necessary. But an absolutely essential first step towards that goal is to put human faces upon the faceless, to give voices to the voiceless, to highlight injustices in a way that moves the public, and to offer assistance where useful. Songs like "Matamoras Banks" and those on *The Ghost of Tom Joad* do that very well, even though the audience potentially affected by the song numbers in the thousands, not millions.

Conclusion

> Is it possible that the experience of empathy is really nothing more, and nothing less, than the breakthrough of an awareness that we humans share an intrinsic unity? Are we indulging in what Ralph Waldo Emerson called a "larger imbibing of the common heart?"
>
> Sue Monk Kidd

Scientist Daniel Levitin contends that there are six types of songs: those of joy, friendship, love, religion, knowledge, and comfort. However, many songs fall into more than one category. For example, "We Shall Overcome," seems to be one of friendship. An anthem of the civil rights movement, it produces a sense of solidarity, especially among those singing it. Derived from the Negro spiritual tradition, it can also be understood as a song of religion in promising a better day to come. "The Rising" can be interpreted as song of religion and one of comfort. "Matamoras Banks," in contrast, is a knowledge song. Listeners learn and hopefully feel emotion about the tragic life and death of a nameless migrant. The fact that the protagonist, heading for a new beginning in the United States, loses his life is likely to seem unfair to most listeners. When art can sensitize us to instances of injustice, it just might galvanize us to seek to right certain wrongs and fight the powerful who protect the status quo.

In the late 1700s Thomas Clarkson initiated what may have been the world's first successful social movement, the British anti-slavery campaign. After more than fifty years of struggle and advocacy, parliament finally abolished slavery within the British Empire in 1838. *Bury the Chains*, Adam Hochschild's great study of this monumental achievement, describes how Clarkson and his fellow activists gathered witnesses and collected documentation that would show to the public and lawmakers exactly and concretely just how brutal life was on slave plantations:

> They believed that because human beings had the capacity to care about the suffering of others, exposing the truth would move people to action ... the way to stir men and women to action is not by Biblical argument, but through the vivid, unforgettable description of acts of great injustice done to their fellow human beings. The abolitionists placed their hope not in sacred texts, but in human empathy. (366)

Hochschild argues, in short, that the anti-slavery campaign was successful because it was able to engender not only compassion for the slaves, but also a sense among the public that the chattel status and inhumane treatment of slaves was morally wrong. It enlarged the moral community. To win this battle required a kind of cultural shift in the way the public perceived both black slaves as human beings and slavery as an institution. And it took a highly coordinated campaign sustained over decades to make it happen.

The Make Poverty History and One campaigns are current cases in point. Their goal is to achieve a similar sort of moral awakening among today's public as that achieved in the past by the anti-slavery and civil rights movements. Their strategy is to foster the belief that extreme poverty (living on less than a dollar a day) in the developing world is morally wrong, cannot be accepted, and must be addressed aggressively until it is eliminated. The campaign works in collaboration with the United Nations Millennium Project which, with the (insufficient) financial support of the rich countries, has set specific poverty reduction targets for the coming decades. Bono and Bob Geldof are prime movers of this campaign, and they have repeatedly lobbied both the US Congress and world leaders to pledge enough funds to make their goal a reality. The main purpose of the Live-8 megaconcerts of August 2005 was to expand awareness and to convince the public, particularly the young, that it is possible to eliminate extreme poverty. In attacking complacency and fatalism as enemies of social change, artists and activists can play a key role in altering public consciousness.

In short, appeals to compassion and our common humanity by activists are essential but, in order to change the world, they must be part of a larger, organized movement. Artists, however, have a key role to play beyond raising money and publicity for a worthy cause. In Harper Lee's *Too Kill a Mockingbird*, Atticus Finch advises his daughter Scout: "You never really understand a person until you consider things from his point of view—until you climb into his skin and walk around in it" (Lee 30). Of course, the novel and film themselves broaden our moral perspective by painting a vivid portrait of small-town bigotry in the American South and, in the country lawyer played in the film by Gregory Peck, inspiring individual heroism. Similarly, the heart-wrenching narratives of Springsteen songs such as "Born in the USA," "The Rising," "Matamoros Banks," "Brothers under the Bridge," and "Streets of Philadelphia" create pictures in the listener's mind, touch our common heart (in Emerson's phrase), and offer not only consolation, but also hope. These kinds of songs and stories inevitably raise questions about how to respond.

In fact, the work of political activists and socially conscious artists can be seen as complementary. Together or independently, they can present and publicize compelling narratives of how specific marginalized peoples' suffering constitutes an unacceptable violation of widely held norms of decency. Activists and engaged artists can highlight the concrete situations of those who lack the opportunity for a good life; utilize the emotional force of empathy and the common moral intuition that social injustices, if uncovered, should be rectified; challenge the authority of those who justify the existing order; try to convince a large enough portion of the public that change is not only possible but desirable; and gather together and mobilize supporters in a hopefully successful campaign in pursuit of social justice.

Springsteen's success as a socially engaged musician relies on his unparalleled ability to communicate. First, as a performer, he is second to none. Like the younger Bob Dylan, his songs wouldn't mean as much to audiences if they weren't sung and played with complete conviction and awesome power. Onstage, he generates a utopian sense of community between himself, the great E Street Band, and the audience. Long an inspiring figure to fans, including President Obama, his concerts are both cathartic and celebratory, and often described as quasi-religious communal experiences. Second, over the past thirty-five years, Springsteen has not only built a large and loyal following, but has also earned a wider reputation as a popular artist of rare integrity and thoughtfulness. His iconic standing in the United States and around the world accords his political interventions far more attention and influence than those of almost all other celebrities from the arts and entertainment worlds. Third, he employs narrative form—storytelling—as a primary method of communicating ideas musically. In *The Political Brain*, George Lakoff argues that the human brain is most comfortable receiving and processing information in terms of pictures, stories, and metaphors. Rather than telling his audience what to think about issues of concern to him, Springsteen invites his listeners to use their imagination to walk in the shoes of his characters. Fourth, in speaking or writing on political issues, he tries to articulate his views in inclusive and patriotic terms. He consistently frames his criticism of social and political conditions as egregious violations of widely held American ideals. A progressive patriotism insists that the promise of the American Dream should be available to everyone, and that the federal government is key to making this enduring ideal a reality (Beinart). In his songs and statements, Springsteen speaks persuasively of the need for the American nation to recover its fundamental values. He often employs religious, as well as patriotic, language. Springsteen's 2004 *New York Times* op-ed ended with these words:

> It is through the truthful exercising of the best of human qualities—respect for others, honesty about ourselves, faith in our ideals—that we come to life in God's eyes. It is how our soul, as a nation and as individuals, is revealed. Our American government has strayed too far from American values. It is time to move forward. The country we carry in our hearts is waiting. ("Chords for Change")

Springsteen's work in dramatizing both the injustices and possibilities in our society is part of a venerable American tradition that extends back to Whitman and Thoreau, Guthrie and Steinbeck, Seeger and Dylan, and continues into the future. These "moral prophets of humanity" awaken our common heart and offer a beautiful vision of a more compassionate and just world.

Chapter 12

Springsteen's Search for Individuality and Community in Post-1960s America[1]

Jason P. Stonerook

The work of Bruce Springsteen challenges us to rethink our concept of "politics." I am not sure if one can describe my own understanding of politics as "classical" or "republican," but it is certainly rooted in the thinking of people working in that tradition, such as Aristotle, Machiavelli, the Founding Fathers, and, most importantly, Hannah Arendt. In her book *The Human Condition*, Arendt defines politics as people "acting and speaking together" (198). This entails more than congregating socially with one another; it involves the interaction of people in a public space where individuals actively make their unique identities known to one another out in the open where they can truly discover freedom in its active form. This pluralistic interaction drives the engine of politics and is ultimately the end of politics; great politicians are great not because they can order an action to occur, but because they can bring people together to interact with one another. This purely political experience—discovered by the Greeks and the colonial Americans and articulated well by Arendt—emphasizes both individuality and community. It is the individual's duty to maintain his or her freedom of thought and action in order to add his or her voice to the *polis*; those who make the greatest contributions to the polis through bold individual action and coalition building are said to demonstrate *arête*, *virtu*, or what Tom Wolfe has more recently labeled "the Right Stuff." At the same time, the individual cannot act alone but must act in public before the eyes of others, where words and actions take on meaning. They must work for the public (as opposed to private) good, which in the end means promoting politics, pluralism, and the public space, and they must interact with others. Politics ends when this community of interaction ceases to exist.

Springsteen seems to stick up for this brand of politics, which I think accounts for a fairly large portion of his popularity. I think it explains why conservatives are willing to put up with Springsteen's liberal positions, just as Springsteen has

[1] I thank Buz Bogage, Paul DeGooyer, Monica Fennell, Ben Gellman, Hannah Gellman, Stephen Gellman, Robert Hershberger, Jonathan Miller, David Paul, David Quigley, Sheila Willer, and the organizers of the "Glory Days" symposium for sharing the road; my first-year seminar and winter-term students at DePauw University for indulging my interest in Springsteen and Ford; and Dean Neal Abraham for providing conference travel funds.

recently said in an interview that he enjoys the work of John Wayne although he does not support Wayne's conservative views (Wenner 73). This Arendtian view of politics is pre-ideological—Arendt in fact despises ideologies because they tend to homogenize the political space and remove the potential for spontaneous action from public life—and seems to appeal to people as a pure brand of politics untainted by a partisan agenda or personal ambition. It sounds fair in the way it makes all individuals equal in the public space yet allows for individuals to excel on the basis of skill. It reflects the ideal of American politics, and because Springsteen embraces this view of politics, he is viewed as a "mythical" American character in the company of figures such as Huckleberry Finn, Rick Blaine, Walt Whitman, Louis Armstrong, Joe DiMaggio, and Benjamin Franklin.

Yet with the exception of the young "Gilded Age" Huckleberry Finn, Springsteen stands apart from these individuals because he appears to us during a "depoliticized" period of American history. Springsteen grabbed the nation's attention in 1975, just as America entered the post-1960s, post-civil rights, post-Vietnam, post-Watergate era. Government and politics did not have a good name during this time. Americans backed away from the highly charged political debates of the 1960s and retreated into the private realm. At the same time, as the influence of the mass media became apparent, politicians decided they needed to play by its rules, effectively turning the public into bitterly divided ideological camps and narrowly-focused factions. The result of all this was a depoliticized, privatized, and massified America. When looking back over the past ten years of American history alone, evidence of privatization and depoliticization abound: politicians' and citizens' general disdain for "big government"; President Clinton's narrow appeal to "soccer moms," using household issues such as the V-chip and school uniforms; the increasing dependence on private institutions to manage public problems such as law enforcement and education; an impeachment battle that hinged more on sex than crime; the pocketbook appeal of tax-cut politics; the utter lack of debate over a looming war in Iraq; and the lackluster, uninspiring performance of the parties' presidential nominees in the 2004 election. This era of privatized politics may have reached its peak in the aftermath of Hurricane Katrina, which revealed both President Bush's weakness as a spontaneous public actor and the government's long-term failure to prepare for and address a looming public problem.

The depoliticization and privatization of America is also chronicled in the works of Robert Bellah *et al.* and Robert Putnam. Their respective books, *Habits of the Heart* and *Bowling Alone*, provide compelling evidence that the American people themselves have retreated from the public space into the private realm.

For their 1985 book *Habits of the Heart*, the team of Robert Bellah, Richard Madsen, William Sullivan, Ann Swidler, and Steven Tipton interviewed a number of Americans to survey their views on individualism and community. In their updated introduction published in 1996, Bellah *et al.* argued that America was undergoing a "crisis of civic membership" where "temptations and pressures to disengage from the larger society" abound "at every level of American life and in every significant group" (xi). As a result, American communities found it increasingly difficult to deal with public problems while individuals grew more and more isolated from communities that would normally boost their public sense of self and identity. Bellah *et al.* found evidence of this in many sectors of society: gated suburban communities with privatized personal services; abandoned urban centers; a growing emphasis on "family values" and volunteerism that failed to address structural social problems that needed to be addressed by concerted public action; and governmental policies that disproportionately benefited the wealthiest, widened the income gap, and reduced support for the most vulnerable citizens.

In their introduction, Bellah *et al.* also mention the work of Robert Putnam, whose 1990 work *Bowling Alone* is now considered a classic in political science. In his famous example, Putnam observed a decline in league bowling since the 1960s, yet noted that the number of bowlers had risen in that same timeframe. (Hence, the notion of "bowling alone," although that is a somewhat misleading phrase; the key point is that fewer people are making a regular commitment to recreational league bowling, not that people are wandering aimlessly into bowling alleys to truly "bowl alone.") This is symbolic of a decline in what Putnam identifies as "social capital," or the benefits for society that accrue from social interaction. Putnam notes that over the past fifty years participation in associations—one of the key factors that Tocqueville held responsible for America's vibrant democracy—had declined in all areas of American society, including political party membership, voting, campaign activities, the PTA, community clubs, church attendance, union membership, dinner parties, family dinners, card parties, neighborhood activities, and so on. The result is that the informal ties that bind America together are not as strong as they once were, meaning that Americans are perhaps less likely to look out for one another, or are now less inclined to participate in a community activity for the sake of community involvement. The benefits for society that come from social interaction—most notably the feeling that an individual has a responsibility to care for the well-being of his or her community and neighbors—are reduced. Individuals find themselves more alone in times of need. Social networks built up through associations that members of a community could potentially call upon to solve a public issue deteriorate. Social problems that require greater resources than an individual can muster alone go unsolved.

Although Bellah *et al.* and Putnam wrote their works in the 1980s and 1990s respectively, social commentators had been observing the shift from public to private as early as the 1970s. Tom Wolfe observed "the greatest age of individualism in American history!" in an essay from 1976 titled "The Me Decade and the Third Great Awakening." Wolfe portrayed a self-centered nation obsessed with "*Me ... Me ... Me ... Me ....*" in the areas of New Age religion, the therapeutic industry, and the sexual revolution. Rock and roll performers growing out of the 1960s folk-rock tradition chronicled the privatization of American culture. Crosby, Stills, Nash and Young identified the tipping point in 1970 on the album *Déjà Vu* as they found themselves torn between the public ambitions of the 1960s on songs like "Woodstock" and "Almost Cut My Hair" and the peaceful domesticity of songs such as "Our House" and "Country Girl." Joni Mitchell and Jackson Browne probed the isolation they now found in romantic relationships, most notably on Mitchell's *Blue* album and on Browne's *Late for the Sky* LP and in the song "The Pretender." On *Hotel California*, particularly on the title track and the song "Life in the Fast Lane," the Eagles descended into the era of self-indulgence to find the hippie ideals of sunny California replaced with the privatized decadence of sex, drugs, and the pursuit of wealth.

Springsteen fits into this story as well. My main essay examines Springsteen's attitudes toward individualism and community (although often not explicitly in the context of Arendtian politics), the phenomena of depoliticization and privatization, and the work of Bellah and Putnam. I will leave it up to the reader now to bring these points of view to bear on my chapter, although I will offer a rough guide over the next few paragraphs.

At first glance, Springsteen's attitudes toward government suggest that he is also part of the process of depoliticization. His comments throughout the 1980s regarding the national government reveal a distrust of politics, but while this is likely part of his upbringing, it may also indicate a belief that the federal government had already depoliticized itself to a point where it was no longer worth his energy to interact with it. Instead, Springsteen created his own public political space through his concerts and his emphasis on local charitable work. (This philosophy still motivates Springsteen; in justifying his participation in the 2004 Vote For Change tour, Springsteen often said he hoped to create through his concerts a space where people could congregate and confront a number of difficult ideas together.)

Historically, Springsteen's outlook toward individuality is found primarily on *Born to Run*, particularly on the title track and "Thunder Road." Using the car as a metaphor, Springsteen understands that ambitious individual public action involves risk and daring, and that such actions often end in wrecks. It is only through this risk that true freedom—the freedom of action in the public space—can be found. He celebrates those who succeed as heroes while paying respect to those who dared to act yet failed. Springsteen models this brand of political *arête* or *virtu* on stage in his concerts which seem to exist for their own sake, as if the risky act of rock and roll would perish if he did not act to keep its spirit alive. The necessity of action is symbolized on stage by Steven Van Zandt, the bandana-ed outcast and host of a garage rock radio show, the "keeper of all that is righteous on E Street," who reminds us that, despite Springsteen's superstar status, he is still at heart a three-chord garage rocker living in the shadows of New Jersey and striving for glory in the public's eye.

Springsteen's key criticism of American society is that it no longer values or supports bold public action. Instead, contemporary American society now celebrates private virtues accessible only to those who can afford to buy them. These wealthy individuals have basically dropped out of society and no longer acknowledge a responsibility to the larger community; just as the ancient Greeks regarded a leader who cut himself off from interaction with his fellow citizens as an unpolitical tyrant, Springsteen regards these modern loners, holed up in their mansions on a hill, as non-political as well. Those who do act in the public space learn that the social networks which used to support public action are now gone. When these individuals fail, not only is no one there to help them back to their feet, but no one is even there to witness their action in the first place. Unseen and outside of what Arendt would call "the space of appearance," Springsteen's lost heroes are often literally in the "dark," whether they are dancing there or hiding out on the edge of town. It is Springsteen's ambition to reconnect individual action to communities, to rebuild social capital and its network of support, and to once again value political action and the pursuit of the public good.

Springsteen's liberal political beliefs and emphasis on economic justice complicates this interpretation of his work. Springsteen often views distributive justice as the end of politics (and may even argue that it precedes it). Arendt would argue that the true end of politics is the perpetuation of the political space. Springsteen certainly holds up this end of Arendt's philosophy, but he would probably diverge from Arendt when it comes to what Arendt labels "the social question." Still, much of Springsteen's work represents an attempt to reclaim a public space for public action and "repoliticize" the "depoliticized."

Bruce Springsteen: Individuality and Community in Post-1960s America

Although an argument could be made for Elvis Presley, no rock and roll musician is more attached to the spirit of America than Bruce Springsteen. Fans find the classic touchstones of the American Dream in his music: rugged individualism, working-class perseverance, small town camaraderie, unbridled optimism, and a sheer sense of joy updated for the modern day through the sound of raucous rock and roll. Americans from all backgrounds claim Springsteen as their own: liberals and conservatives, Democrats and Republicans, blue collar and white collar, the vast middle class.

Yet few rock and roll musicians are more misunderstood than Bruce Springsteen. Many of his songs, while holding out for hope, are gripped with despair, desperation, and human tragedy. The characters in his songs are the victims not only of their own professed mistakes, but also of a society that has turned its back on them. If the possibilities of the open road run through all of Springsteen's albums, car wrecks litter the landscape, symbolizing more than the glorious dangers that come from taking risks in America but also decay, abandonment, and death. This part of Springsteen's music is lost on most of his listeners.

The message of Bruce Springsteen's music cannot be reduced to simple slogans. His work is much more complex and subtle. Springsteen is a post-1960s rock musician who shifted the focus of rock music away from teenaged dramas and expansive social/political movements to the daily struggles of adults and the communities in which they lived. In this setting, Springsteen embraced the individual drive to take control of one's own destiny and improve his or her standing in life, but he also emphasized the obligations that individuals and communities shared with one another to keep both strong. Springsteen's music criticized America in the 1970s and 1980s for emphasizing the individual at the expense of the community and denying individuals a real chance at social mobility––a mindset which, Springsteen argued, served to isolate individuals and weaken communities. Yet by the end of the 1980s Springsteen became disillusioned with his audience, who, in attaching their own individualistic outlook to Springsteen's work, overlooked the equal emphasis Springsteen placed on community.

Glory Days: Springsteen and Post-1960s America

While baby boomers are typically associated with rock and roll's coming of age in the 1960s, it is often forgotten that baby boomers were primarily the *audience* for rock and roll and not actually performing the music on the national scene during the decade. Not until the 1970s did the baby boom generation, represented by acts such as the Eagles, Jackson Browne, and Billy Joel, begin recording music for a wide audience. This group of artists, while heavily influenced by the events and music of the 1960s, essentially tried to make sense of a post-60s, post-Vietnam, post-civil rights, post-Watergate America.

Bruce Springsteen falls into this category. Springsteen was a post-1960s rock and roll musician in three respects: first, his work retreated from the exhausting, highly charged political conflicts that characterized the 1960s and was not overtly political; second, his music described an America where baby boomers were now adults facing adult responsibilities such as work, marriage, and raising families; and third, Springsteen turned away from mass movements and mass political action to focus on local initiatives that could address social problems.

Unlike other musicians such as Bob Dylan, John Lennon, or Marvin Gaye who, through their music, were defining the culture of the 1960s, Springsteen was a product of the decade. Born in 1949, Springsteen's experiences as a teenager in a blue-collar family from Freehold, New Jersey, balanced out the counter-cultural ideals he heard in Dylan or The Beatles. The social issues of the time rarely intruded on the day-to-day affairs of his hometown. Springsteen said in 1984 that "[t]here wasn't any kind of political consciousness down in Freehold in the late Sixties. It was a small town, and the war just seemed very distant" (Loder, "Born Again"). As Jefferson Morley writes, Springsteen, although a social outcast, found himself on neither side of the social debate that raged throughout the 1960s:

> Springsteen emerged from the heart of the post-60s generation, from "Middle America," with the emphasis on the middle. He didn't belong to the relatively small counterculture that dominated elite college campuses and mass media coverage—though he was influenced by it. He was into cars, not acid or the Viet Cong. Yet in 1967, when he graduated from high school, he had long hair and didn't want to go to Vietnam. Nor did he belong to the "Silent Majority,"

that substantial but usually exaggerated part of the American public that wasn't young or black, that wasn't protesting, that wasn't rejecting traditional values, and that resented the "anything goes" attitude of many who were. Springsteen was, as he sings in one of his songs, "caught in a crossfire I don't understand." (Morley, "Darkness On the Edge of the Shining City")

The politics of the 1960s took place on the periphery of Springsteen's social consciousness, yet he could not entirely avoid the turmoil of the times, as he occasionally indicated in his music. For example, Springsteen's characters on *Born in the USA* are often unwillingly sucked into the politics of the decade. The main character on the album's title track is sent off to Vietnam after a scrape with the law. In "My Hometown," racial tensions engulf the main character's high school, but "there was nothing you could do." By the end of the song, the forces of a postindustrial economy leave the character stranded and helpless in a downsized community. In Springsteen's view, people could not shape national politics; instead, national politics *happened* to them in ways outside of their control.

By the time Springsteen began recording his first albums, the social movements of the 1960s had fragmented and people were seeking ways to distance their personal lives from the intense politics of the preceding years. Springsteen reflected this mood in his music. Although he began to address some social concerns in 1978 with the release of *Darkness on the Edge of Town*, Springsteen's music was not overtly political, especially when compared with the previous decade's socially conscious songwriters. In the dreary "Factory," instead of sloganeering about working conditions, Springsteen simply bears witness to industrial workers who push through their work and leave their jobs everyday broken and exhausted:

> Through the mansions of fear, through the mansions of pain
> I see my daddy walking through them factory gates in the rain
> Factory takes his hearing, factory gives him life
> The working, the working, just the working life.

As in "Factory," "Downbound Train," describes the tough economic times blue-collar workers faced in the postindustrial era of the 1970s and 1980s. Again, Springsteen avoids overt political statements and chooses instead to report directly on the struggles of working-class Americans:

> I had a job, I had a girl
> I had something going mister in this world
> I got laid off down at the lumber yard
> Our love went bad, times got hard
> Now I work down at the carwash
> Where all it ever does is rain
> Don't you feel like you're a rider on a downbound train.

Instead of following the traditional rock and roll practice of casting teenagers as social outcasts in songs, Springsteen placed working-class adults in the role. While many of the 1950s and 1960s teenage dramas about broken hearts and boring lives seemed of enormous importance to adolescents, they were ultimately trivial concerns. That could not be said about Springsteen's protagonists, who seemed trapped in the setting of their youth and, as he sings in "Thunder Road," "scared … that maybe we ain't that young anymore." The song "Tunnel of Love" is set on a carnival ride—an amusement typically enjoyed by adolescents—that serves as a metaphor for facing the pressures of growing into a serious adult relationship: "Then the lights go out and it's just the three of us / You me and all that stuff we're so scared of / Gotta ride down baby into this tunnel of love."

The fact that Springsteen's outcasts were grown men and women rather than teenagers made the problems they faced more pressing, gave their actions greater consequence, and easily turned failure into tragedy. If Springsteen did write a song about a typically teenage concern, he often set it against an adult responsibility. Parties no longer offered an escape from the doldrums of school but served to alleviate the demands of work, as in the song "Out in the Street":

> I work five days a week girl
> Loading crates down on the dock
> I take my hard earned money
> And meet my girl down on the block
> And Monday when the foreman calls time
> I've already got Friday on my mind.

Characters needed cars not just for cruising but for getting to a job, or, as in the humorous song "Sherry Darling," to drive an annoying mother-in-law to the unemployment agency. ("You can tell her there's a hot sun beatin' on the black top / She keeps talkin' she'll be walkin' that last block / She can take a subway back to the ghetto tonight.") Romantic relationships also did not come without the price of growing up. In Springsteen's adult world, falling in love could mean marriage, and break-ups sometimes meant divorce. Sex was no longer a frivolous topic buried beneath innuendo, but often led to the responsibilities of parenthood, as in "The River":

> Then I got Mary pregnant
> And man that was all she wrote
> And for my nineteenth birthday I got a union card and a wedding coat
> We went down to the courthouse
> And the judge put it all to rest
> No wedding day smiles no walk down the aisle
> No flowers no wedding dress.

While the man and woman in "The River" watched their youth come to an end together, the responsibilities of adulthood drove the couple in "Spare Parts" away from each other:

> Bobby said he'd pull out Bobby stayed in
> Janey had a baby it wasn't any sin
> They were set to marry on a summer day
> Bobby got scared and he ran away

Janey survives as an adult at the end of the song by pawning her wedding dress and engagement ring for some "good cold cash."

Springsteen's characters struggle with more than just the realization that they have grown up, but also with gaining the respect that adults deserve, a yearning that leads the main character in "The Promised Land" to defiantly proclaim, "Mister, I ain't a boy, no I'm a man." No song in Springsteen's catalog captures the longing to break free from a youthful past better than "Glory Days," a song populated by characters who never moved on to greater moments than those they experienced in high school. Singing as the main character, Springsteen hopes for something better:

> And I hope when I get old I don't sit around thinking about it
> But I probably will
> Yeah, just sitting back trying to recapture
> A little of the glory of, well time slips away
> And leaves you with nothing mister but
> Boring stories of glory days.

While Springsteen recognizes the characters in "Glory Days" could aspire to more, he also fears the options available to them—particularly decent work, which, as alluded to in the other songs on *Born in the USA*—ultimately "leaves [them] with nothing," stranding them in adult lives with only the memories of their youth.

Springsteen did not place great faith in modern politics' ability to solve the social problems facing the adult characters on his albums. Although he describes characters who lead desperate lives, he never resorts to demanding political solutions to their problems. Politics simply does not hold a central place in Springsteen's life. Apart from describing the results of the 1980 election as "frightening" at a concert in Arizona the day after election day (Gilmore, "The Voice of the Eighties") and offering a teasing retort to President Reagan's suggestion in 1984 that *Born in the USA* embodied everything that was good in America, Springsteen generally shied away from making his political preferences known to the public. When interviewed by *Rolling Stone* two weeks before the 1984 election between Ronald Reagan and Walter Mondale, Springsteen admitted that he was registered to vote yet "not registered as one party or another." He continued, "I don't generally think along those lines. I find it very difficult to relate to the whole electoral system as it stands. ... I suppose if there was somebody who [I] felt strong enough about at some point, some day, you know. ..." When asked later if he had ever voted, he replied, "I think I voted for McGovern in 1972," a full twelve years earlier (Loder, "Born Again"). Eight years later, in another interview with *Rolling Stone* conducted in Los Angeles during the 1992 riots, Springsteen continued to express frustration with a political system that "has really broken down" and was likely, in his estimation, to return President George H.W. Bush to the White House. Although he cited liberal politicians such as Jerry Brown and former candidate Jesse Jackson as people who appealed to him, he lamented the fact that "there hasn't really been anyone who can bring ...ideas to life, who can make people believe that there's some other way" (Henke). In Springsteen's view, a wide gulf existed between what politics could realistically accomplish and what needed to be done in society.

Instead, Springsteen replaced rock's emphasis on broad social movements with a focus on local communities. Although his songs could be about Anyplace, USA, works such as "My Hometown," "The Promised Land," and "Jungleland" were small-scale dramas typically set within the universe of a town. (Even the songs from *The Rising*, Springsteen's album about 9/11, are domestic in scope and never comment on the national and international politics surrounding the event.) Rather than offering (or criticizing) political solutions to problems, Springsteen urged fans to get involved in their communities as a way of addressing social concerns. Springsteen believed that he could best create social change by modeling good local community action through his band instead of promoting social causes in his lyrics. After expressing frustration with the choices facing American voters in 1984, he suggested a turn to local initiatives: "I want to try to adjust to work more directly with people; try to find some way that my band can tie into the communities that we come into. I guess that's a political action, a way to just bypass that whole electoral thing. Human politics. I think that people on their own can do a lot" (Loder, "Born Again"). In 1981 he raised $100,000 at a concert for the Vietnam Veterans' Association and continued to support charity events throughout the decade (Cocks, "Round the World"). His Born in the USA tour marked the full emergence of his model of community activism. At concert after concert he urged his audience to contribute to local food banks and then gave money to those groups himself (Barol, "He's On Fire" 50). Instead of waiting for government to address broad social issues, Springsteen turned to the goodwill of local citizens to solve problems in their own neighborhoods.

Springsteen believed that individuals working together could solve the problems of the 1970s and 1980s. This outlook emphasized the importance of living life both as an individual and as a member of a community. The next two sections will examine Springsteen's understanding of the individual and the community.

Born to Run: Springsteen and Individual Freedom

In a 1985 *Rolling Stone* interview, Springsteen highlights the intrinsic individual drive ("drive" is a key word here) to take control of one's own life and turn it into something worthwhile: "I first started to play [rock and roll] because ... I wanted to be proud about myself, to feel good about myself. And I found the guitar, and that gave it to me; it gave me my sense of purpose and a sense of pride in myself ...It was my lifeboat, my lifeline" (Loder, "Artist of the Year"). Springsteen's guitar—a symbol of not just rock and roll, but also the ability to *create* music—liberated Springsteen. It gave him a sense of pride, an internal sense of dignity, which helped him face the world on his own. With a guitar in his hands, Springsteen could save himself by creating his own world to live in. The guitar also gave him a purpose by unleashing a pent-up longing to use the freedom he inherently possessed to escape the blue-collar life of the New Jersey shores. It gave him a means to use his freedom, which gave him a sense of self-worth, which increased his personal freedom yet again, and so on. This was Bruce Springsteen's version of the American Dream as set in the late twentieth century.

The individual holds a central place in Springsteen's music. His rise to fame in the 1970s and 1980s and his focus on individual action links Springsteen to the "Me Generation" mentality that manifested itself during those decades, although such an analysis is ultimately incomplete without a conception of community that juxtaposes Springsteen with the "Me Generation" mindset. Nothing is more glorified in Springsteen's work than an individual who takes the chance to burst out of the confines of his or her existence. The characters who populate Springsteen's songs—especially on *Born to Run*—are individuals with dreams of making a better life for themselves, despite the risks that accompany such actions.

Springsteen's characters are motivated by a search for individual freedom. At its most fundamental level, Springsteen's sense of freedom is a form of liberation, a "freedom from" something such as work, one's hometown, or the past. Ideally, Springsteen's characters find this "freedom from" on their own; they will not need to be emancipated, because they will be able to emancipate themselves. Consequently, at a deeper level, Springsteen's characters are also searching for a "freedom to," or a means to empower themselves and escape their confines. Reflecting on his music in 1978, Springsteen said, "All the characters [on the LPs] and everything is about the attempt to gain control of your life" (Marsh, "Raises Cain")—an attempt to use freedom to get freedom. Yet Springsteen's characters, as Jefferson Morley specifies, are not "seeking the freedom of 'anything goes'" ("Darkness On the Edge of the Shining City"). They are not seeking freedom to use it recklessly or irresponsibly but rather to make a place for themselves where they can live meaningful adult lives. For example, although Springsteen's characters are often seen celebrating, parties are always a way of liberating oneself from work, not to blow off the responsibilities of work. (Work, after all, is a community of people, and, as will be discussed in the next section, the individual always has a responsibility to the community regardless of the amount of freedom they have gained.)

The individual quest is an intrinsic drive for Springsteen. As the title of his breakthrough album proclaims, the characters in Springsteen's songs are "born to run"; they do not rest in their current position, satisfied with what they have, but rather enter the world with aspirations and try throughout life to fulfill them. Social mobility, the ability to improve one's standing in life, is therefore central to Springsteen's thinking if people are to realistically increase their freedom. In a 1978 interview, Springsteen said, "My songs are all *action* songs. ... All my songs are about people at that moment when they've got to do *something*, just do *something*, do *anything*" (Nelson). Springsteen's characters are not lazy or satisfied with their standing in life but act to create a better world for themselves. Those denied social mobility end up trapped in their existence. Springsteen's music implies that social mobility is necessary for freedom to be a reality.

Social mobility also means taking risks. Springsteen's music does not promise anything other than the *chance* to take control of your life, as he indicated in this quote from 1981: "All you can do is say there's possibilities, some are gonna stand, some are gonna fall, and then try to say that the search and the struggle is a life-affirming action" (Schruers, "Secret of the World"). Failure occurs frequently in Springsteen's music, but characters are honored for losing because they were acting on their freedom to gain more freedom. At the climax of "Jungleland," an operatic number set in the alleys and shadows off the New Jersey Turnpike, street hoods leading dangerous lives are immortalized, despite a harsh existence:

> In the quick of a knife
> They reach for their moment
> And try to make an honest stand
> But they wind up wounded
> Not even dead

Even though risk is dangerous, it is life-affirming. Regardless of all the risk, the struggle alone is worth it. In "Prove It All Night," Springsteen shows that his characters understand both the reward and the risk: "Everybody's got a hunger, a hunger they can't resist / There's so much that you want, you deserve much more than this ... / Girl you want it, you take it, you pay the price." The commitment to the search for a better life is a kind of dogma in Springsteen's vision. In a 1984 interview, Springsteen emphasized the kind of religious devotion that fuels his characters: "I guess in *Born to Run*, there's that searchin' thing; that record to me is like religiously based, in a funny kind of way. Not like orthodox religion, but it's about basic things, you know? That searchin', and faith, and the idea of hope" (Loder, "Born Again"). Getting the reward is a different kind of satisfaction because there is always a reward simply in the process of striving to live a better life. Greil Marcus identified this theme in his 1975 review of *Born to Run* in *Rolling Stone*, writing that the songs on the album are "tales of kids born to run who lose anyway. … And yet the music is exhilarating. … As a ride through terror, it resolves itself finally as a ride into delight."

For Springsteen, the freedom and risk that comes with social mobility is symbolized by the car, which appears frequently in his music. (The "street" is also a similar symbol.) The car enables the characters in Springsteen's songs to take action while also providing a link thematically between songs. Springsteen commented in a 1978 interview that, "[the car imagery] is just a general thing that forms the action in a particular way. The action is not the imagery, you know. The heart of the action is beneath that stuff" (Nelson). The car is essentially the vessel that carries the dreams of individual characters.

The car is also a crucial image in Springsteen's two foremost statements of individual action, "Born to Run" and "Thunder Road." Following a rumbling instrumental introduction that mimics the sound of a car engine, the opening lines of "Born to Run" glamorize the car as a means for ambitious but down-on-their-luck kids to escape from a stultifying town, but also indicate the risk (and potential death) that comes with taking that chance:

> In the day we sweat it out in the streets of a runaway American dream
> At night we ride through mansions of glory in suicide machines
> Sprung from cages out on Highway 9,
> Chrome wheeled, fuel injected
> And steppin' out over the line
> Baby this town rips the bones from your back
> It's a death trap, it's a suicide rap
> We gotta get out while we're young
> 'Cause tramps like us, baby we were born to run.

While "Born to Run" begins with the sound of a car revving up, "Thunder Road" starts with only a harmonica and a quaint piano accompaniment before building into an instrumental rock coda of epic scope. The story of a rock and roll boy trying to persuade a girl named Mary to ride off with him into a better future of their own making, the escalation from the harmonica intro (an instrument often heard in folk music) to the sweeping guitar and saxophone conclusion helps turn the small town story of two individuals about to risk it all into a mythic American drama. When Springsteen first mentions a car—the means of liberation—"Thunder Road" turns instrumentally from a gently rolling ballad to a passionate rock number. In the song, the road promises to lead the couple to freedom; all they have to do is drive it if they dare:

> With a chance to make it good somehow
> Hey what else can we do now
> Except roll down the window
> And let the wind blow back your hair
> Well the night's busting open

> These two lanes will take us anywhere
> We got one last chance to make it real
> To trade in these wings on some wheels
> Climb in back
> Heaven's waiting on down the tracks

Yet, as in "Born to Run," the characters in "Thunder Road" understand that the car is not an easy way out—a lesson the boys turned down by Mary in the past found out the hard way:

> There were ghosts in the eyes
> Of all the boys you sent away
> They haunt this dusty beach road
> In the skeleton frames of burned-out Chevrolets.

In "The Promised Land," the road and car are again important images, but Springsteen has started developing a less optimistic view toward the promise the open road holds:

> On a rattlesnake speedway in the Utah desert
> I pick up my money and head back into town
> Driving cross the Waynesboro county line
> I got the radio on and I'm just killing time
> Working all day in my daddy's garage
> Driving all night chasing some mirage
> Pretty soon little girl I'm gonna take charge.

While the road still holds the danger of a "rattlesnake," it is not clear now that the road leads to the future. The road only appears to lead to another "mirage," but the driver is holding out the hope that he will soon be able to take control of his destiny. Still, the options seem more limited. Instead of leaving town, he is returning; instead of setting out on his own, he earns his pay by fixing cars for others to escape with; even when he is driving, he is "just killing time." The song is ultimately a hopeful song (the chorus proclaims, "I believe in the promised land"), but there is a creeping sense that the odds have increased against Springsteen's characters.

This changing mood can also be seen in the album art for *The River*, directed and designed by Jimmy Wachtel. The album's lyric sheet features a prominent picture of "Cadillac Ranch," a public art installation in Texas featuring a row of cars buried hood-first in the ground. The sculpture portrays the automobile as a monument, yet the sheer number of upended cars also creates a tragic effect in the context of Springsteen's songs. Springsteen finds glory in cars and even in a car crash, but the picture and lyrics force the listener to wonder if we should be standing in awe as we observe so many wrecked opportunities to rebuild our shared sense of community.

The Ties That Bind: Springsteen and Community

After *Born to Run*, Bruce Springsteen increasingly grew to believe that individual success could only occur within the framework of a community. In order to balance the individual with the community, Springsteen emphasized the values of reciprocity and social obligation. While the individual should be able to strike out on their own, the community should also be there to support their endeavor and respect their attempt, especially if he or she faltered. On the other hand, the individual needed to look out for other individuals as well as the community that supported their own initiatives. Springsteen modeled the responsibility he felt individuals had to the larger community through his relationship with his fans and in his contributions to the cities his tour passed through. He also offered those who felt cut off from their communities a place of belonging through his music and live performances. Finally, Springsteen underscored the importance of community through the nature of his concerts and in the composition of his band, the E Street Band.

Springsteen attempted to model his understanding of reciprocity and obligation primarily in the realm of live performance. Although his albums remain the most enduring expression of his ideas, a complete understanding of his work must include his concerts. Springsteen gained his initial cult status as a tireless club performer who put on shows lasting into the early hours of the morning. By the Born in the USA tour he would play to sold-out arena crowds for over four hours. Springsteen concerts were major events and, especially early in his career, dwarfed his album releases in importance. When asked why the band put so much effort into their concerts, Springsteen replied that, "It all ties in with the records and the values, the morality of the records" (Marsh, "Raises Cain"). That "morality" centered on Springsteen's understanding of community and the place of the individual within it.

Springsteen approached concerts as not only entertainment, but also as a way of building community. Rock and roll was a bond shared between himself, the band, and every member of the audience. Unlike other tours in the 1970s that relied on spectacle to dazzle the audience (as exemplified by the rock band Kiss), Springsteen's live shows became quasi-religious experiences that brought a congregation of fans together in a kind of rock and roll church service. Paul Nelson observed this religious aspect of Springsteen's concerts in 1978 when he wrote:

> After "Born to Run," when the crowd offers him a tremendous ovation, he subverts the applause by holding up his guitar as if it were some communal instrument of magic, something which he alone does not own. All of a sudden, I

realize that we are making this glorious not for the pride of one man but for the
power of rock and roll.

If his concerts had a kind of religious quality to them, however, it was not intended
to be a spiritual effect but rather a communal effect; rock and roll was meant to bring
people together, not bind them to a belief system. In a 1992 interview, Springsteen
explained his views on religion. His perspective on the topic emphasized the act of
congregation over the act of worship:, "I don't buy into all the dogmatic aspects,
but I like the idea of people coming together for some sort of spiritual enrichment
or even just to say hi once a week" (Henke). Church, like his concerts, was a place
where people came together to find strength in one another.

The physicality of Springsteen's concerts also suggested community. He
developed a reputation as a tireless performer. As Dave Marsh observed in 1975,
"Springsteen races back and forth like an unleashed puppy" ("A Rock Star"),
offering the audience a release of energy through himself. Earlier in his career,
when he still regularly played small venues, he would physically enter the audience
not simply by walking out into it, but by dancing on tabletops and climbing into
the balcony before leaping back down to the piano. Most significantly, during his
1978 tour, he would leap into the audience, leading Marsh to write, "one is always
worried that his consummate trust in his fans is going to let him down. But night
after night he gets away with it" ("Raises Cain"). While the leap is important as
a risky individual act, the catch by the audience is even more significant. The
catch represents community and the faith that individuals can take chances yet
find support in those around them. Placed together, the leap and catch capture the
relationship between individual and community in Springsteen's music.

Springsteen expanded his idea of community beyond his concert audiences.
As mentioned earlier, Springsteen tried to involve himself and the E Street Band
in local community projects during stops along the Born in the USA tour. He said,
during that tour:

> I guess that's what I'm trying to figure out now: Where do the aesthetic issues
> that you write about intersect with some sort of concrete action, some direct
> involvement, in the communities that your audience comes from? It seems to be
> an inevitable progression of what our band has been doin', of the idea that we
> got into this for. We wanted to play because we wanted to meet girls, we wanted
> to make a ton of dough, and we wanted to change the world a little bit, you
> know? (Loder, "Born Again")

Although Springsteen began his career with the personal goal of hitting it big, he
progressively developed a greater focus on contributing back to the community.

Springsteen rarely sang directly about building community, choosing instead
to sing about people cut off from social relationships. Through his music and
concerts, he hoped to create a community for people who felt disconnected from
society. Robert Palmer described Springsteen's shows as "offer[ing] a collective

catharsis" for his listeners, where those who lived the struggles that Springsteen wrote about in his lyrics could come together and find relief in his music and the company of others who shared similar experiences (C13).

Springsteen approached rock and roll in much the same way as musicians earlier in the century approached the blues: as a way of alleviating the day-to-day pain that burdened his audience and himself. As the quote that ended the section on individuality demonstrated, rock and roll offered Springsteen a "lifeline" back to a personal feeling of pride and purpose that he had lost as a blue-collar teenaged outcast. Empathizing with others who also felt displaced and alone in society, Springsteen sought to infuse his music with the message that he understood their problems; in turn, he hoped that people would find his music a source of strength in tough times. In this sense, his music was a kind of postindustrial blues through which a scattering of displaced workers could create a community with others who shared their struggles.

Musically, Springsteen created this community through big, sing-along choruses on buoyant songs like "Hungry Heart," "Born in the USA," and "Glory Days." The arrangements of many songs also emphasized community by showcasing the ensemble of individuals who made up the E Street Band. This aspect of Springsteen's music is especially emphasized on the first half of *The River* on songs such as "Sherry Darling," "Out in the Street," and "Crush on You." On these songs, the E Street Band joins in on ragged, unrehearsed harmonies that single out the voices of distinct members on sing-along choruses, all but urging listeners to join in with them. "Sherry Darling" and "Crush on You" also have noisy backgrounds full of hooting, hollering, and handclaps, replicating the atmosphere of a live communal show.

Springsteen turned the E Street Band into a model of community. The band, with a mix of session men like Max Weinberg and homegrown talent like Danny Federici, brought the "white-collar" world of corporate music together with the "blue-collar" garage rock scene. Steve Van Zandt appeared on stage as Springsteen's longtime friend; Van Zandt was also the band's hipster outcast, his inclusion suggesting that there was always room for old friends and social misfits. When Van Zandt left for a solo career prior to the Born in the USA tour, he was replaced by Nils Lofgren; when Van Zandt returned in 1995, Lofgren stayed on, signifying that once a member of the group you always remained a member (that is, as long as you were a member by the time *Born to Run* was released in 1975). Clarence Clemons, who almost always appeared as Springsteen's sideman and brother-in-arms, and Patti Scialfa, who joined in 1984, made the E Street Band a multiracial and multigendered outfit. Music served as the link between the members. As Springsteen said in 1978, "You can tell by looking at 'em that this isn't a bunch of guys who have a whole lot in common. But somehow the music cuts right through all that" (Marsh, "Raises Cain").

Some commentators have suggested that Springsteen's rhetoric on community is the talk of a wise businessman trying to sell his product to the buying public. The professionalism Springsteen demonstrated in his approach to concerts suggests that he was more sincere than that. Bruce Jackson, Springsteen's sound mixer, explained that:

> At every date, [Springsteen] goes out and sits in every section of the hall to listen to the sound. And if it isn't right, even in the last row, I hear about it and we make changes. I mean every date, too—he doesn't let it slip in Davenport, Iowa, or something. (Marsh, "Raises Cain")

Springsteen felt an obligation to his fans, saying, "Some guy bought a ticket, and there's a promise made between the musician and the audience. When they support each other, that's a special thing" (Schruers, "Boss is Back"). On tour in 1978, Springsteen became upset after learning only 250 seats at a Los Angeles club concert had been made available to the public, denying many of the people who had waited in line to get into the show the opportunity to get a ticket. Even after being told that another 120 tickets would be distributed through radio show giveaways, Springsteen remained furious. At the show he apologized and took responsibility, explaining that he did not play "private parties anymore." As Dave Marsh, who had been covering Springsteen in Los Angeles, explained, Springsteen believed that "[t]his was *his* show, and it should have been done properly" ("Raises Cain").

Springsteen also maintained a reciprocal relationship with his audience by keeping his album and concert prices low. Although he became wealthy following the release of *The River*, he never jacked up his prices to bring in more revenue at his audience's expense. Tickets for the Born in the USA tour sold for $17.50, a reasonable price in 1985 given the fact that a year earlier Michael Jackson's "Victory" stadium tour with his brothers had pushed ticket prices up to a substantial $30.00 (Barol, "He's On Fire" 53). His three-record live set, *Bruce Springsteen and the E Street Band Live/1975-85*, sold wholesale for only $19 (Cocks, "Bruce Springsteen"), a bargain in the mid-1980s when Prince priced his single-record albums between $10 and $15.

Springsteen intended to create a public space where the individual and community could coexist and flourish together. Individuals needed to act, but they would only succeed with the support of the community. In addition, communities could only survive if individuals looked out for more than themselves by helping their neighbors and respecting the dignity of everyone in the community. Yet by 1978 Springsteen was beginning to see that this vision of America was a distant reality.

Born in the USA: Springsteen's Critique of American Society

Bruce Springsteen's critique of the American system was that society, while claiming to support conceptions of the individual and the community similar to his own, had turned those notions into hollow sentiments. Springsteen argued through his music that American society, despite glorifying the individual's search for personal freedom, did not reward personal endeavor but instead shut down avenues of social mobility that the individual could use to improve his or her position in life. In addition, not only was taking a risk in the 1970s and 1980s ever more likely to end in failure, but simply getting by on a day-to-day basis became terribly daunting for many, particularly working-class, Americans. People became grew isolated from each other and were left to fend for themselves. Consequently, Springsteen found that individual failure was no longer tied to individual risk, but to a failure of community. The community offered no support, whether at a large collective level (such as in government or business) or at the level of a personal relationship (such as marriage.) People quit looking out for each other and left their sense of reciprocity and obligation behind as they grew increasingly self-centered. Left alone with their struggles, people lost their sense of self-worth. Only individuals with no connection to one another remained, resulting in millions of individual tragedies that inevitably weakened communities, too.

Springsteen increasingly came to view the risks that people took to achieve freedom as unfulfilling. Social mobility—the means to a better life and personal independence—was no longer a reality. Springsteen again symbolized social mobility with the car, but the options his drivers faced grew bleaker as he passed from the 1970s to the 1980s. Roads led nowhere or wandered aimlessly into the desert. Car wrecks, as portrayed in songs such as "Born to Run" or "Thunder Road" as memorials to the horror and exhilaration of individual risk, became the remnants of tragedies. "Badlands," the song that opens *Darkness on the Edge of Town*, begins with a car crash:

> Lights out tonight
> Trouble in the heartland
> Got a head-on collision
> Smashing in my guts, man.

By the end of the first verse, the main character's hopes have become a nightmare in which social mobility is not a reality:

> Talk about a dream
> Try to make it real
> You wake up in the night
> With a fear so real
> Spend your life waiting
> For a moment that just don't come.

Springsteen's outlook became more pessimistic by 1980 with the release of *The River*. "The Price You Pay," a journey by car through a wasteland where "a stranger … put up a sign / That counts the men fallen away," surveys the toll exacted from individuals by false hope:

You make up your mind, you choose the chance you take
You ride to where the highway ends and the desert breaks

....

Now they'd come so far and they'd waited so long
Just to end up caught in a dream where everything goes wrong

The road to the "Mansion on the Hill" from *Nebraska* is blocked by "gates of hardened steel," denying the citizens of a decaying industrial city access to a path that could improve their lives. "Working On the Highway" from *Born in the USA* turns the car into an insult:

I work for the county out on 95
All day I hold a red flag and watch the traffic pass me by
In my head I keep a picture of a pretty little miss
Someday mister I'm gonna lead a better life than this.

In this song, the main character, who is incarcerated, can only stand by and watch as others use their means of social mobility.

The cover art on two of Springsteen's albums also suggest an end to social mobility. The cover of *Born in the USA* by Annie Leibovitz (Figure 12.1) is one of rock and roll's most recognizable images (chosen, as Springsteen claims, because his rear end looked better than his face), yet the photo is just as misunderstood as the music on the album. The blue-collar outfit and flag in the background is more than working-class patriotism, especially when compared with another more dynamic photograph taken by Leibovitz. That picture was used as the cover art for the "Born in the USA" single and appeared on the cover of the November 15, 1990, issue of *Rolling Stone*. Featuring a picture of Springsteen leaping in the air as he strikes his guitar in front of a broader flag background, this image suggests motion and action. The photograph used on *Born in the USA* however—which, as the LP's cover art, would be the image forever immortalized with the music— is stationary. Springsteen's face is not in the picture, obscuring his identity. The American flag, with its broad horizontal stripes, acts as a barrier or a wall preventing forward progress. The cramped arrangement of the shot suggests that he has limited mobility, a key theme of *Born in the USA*.[2]

---

[2]   My interpretation of the *Born in the USA* cover is based on another writer's interpretation of that photograph. Unfortunately I cannot locate the source that interpretation came from—I must have read it in passing in a library or bookstore. All I can say is that my interpretation is not my own and that someone else's thoughts—thoughts I regard as very insightful and that have left a lasting impression on the way I think about Springsteen— should be credited in this space.

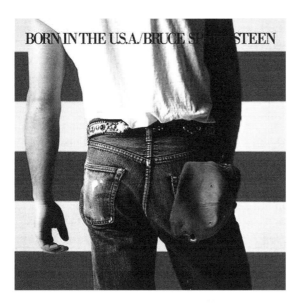

Figure 12.1   *Born in the USA* album cover

Figure 12.2   *Nebraska* album cover

The image on the front of *Nebraska* (Figure 12.2.) also matches that album's stark tone. Shot by David Kennedy in dreary black and white from the interior of a car, the photograph surveys an empty, flat countryside and a narrow gray highway apparently stretching to the edge of the earth. The sky is filled with threatening, low-hanging clouds. The only sign of civilization outside the car and the road is a faintly visible fence. There is essentially nothing in the photo and no sign of the driver's destination. Adding insult to the image is the bold red lettering, which, besides identifying the artist and album title, screams "STOP" like a blood-red traffic light. As though a journey to nowhere was not harrowing enough, a demand to halt is even more dejecting.

In addition, Springsteen saw tremendous risk for individuals simply living a working-class lifestyle in America. Danger was no longer confined to risky endeavors, but to daily existence as well. In "Wreck On the Highway," from the album *The River*, the main character is returning home from work when he comes across a car crash and a dying victim pleading for help. He watches as an ambulance gives the dead man his final ride down the road. The memory haunts the main character in nightmares, leading him to cling closer to his wife as they sleep. The wreck in "Wreck On the Highway" is distinctly different from the "burned-out Chevrolets" of "Thunder Road," where the cars stand as a testament to failed attempts at glory. In "Wreck On the Highway," the wreck is something the character came upon during a routine drive home from his job, an accident he could easily have been a part of. There is no glory in this crash.

Those who find themselves abandoned by their community often end up isolated, alone, and hopeless in Springsteen's songs. The main character in "Jackson Cage" drifts into anonymity:

> Driving home she grabs something to eat
> Turns a corner and drives down her street
> Into a row of houses she just melts away
> Like the scenery in another man's play
> Into a house where the blinds are closed
> To keep from seeing things she don't wanna know
> She pulls the blinds and looks out on the street
> The cool of the night takes the edge off the heat.

Those who lose their place in their communities often remain out of the sight of others. This happens to the main character in "Darkness on the Edge of Town," who loses his wife, his money, and his drive to succeed. He simply tells people, if anyone wants to talk to him, that he will be waiting in the "darkness on the edge of town," or on the edge of community, out of sight but nearby if anybody cares enough to help him.

On *Nebraska*, Springsteen surveys a world in which individuals are cut off from one another and lose track of the ties that bind them to society. The characters on *Nebraska* are lonely individuals who appear deluded and misled by their dreams. The title track to *Nebraska* retells the story of the Starkweather murder spree from the 1950s, suggesting that isolation and the need to take some kind of personal action pushed the killer over the edge:

I can't say that I'm sorry for the things that we done
At least for a little while sir me and her we had us some fun
…
They wanted to know why I did what I did
Well sir I guess there's just a meanness in this world.

In "Johnny 99," another story about a murderer, the killer takes personal responsibility for his actions but also cites an unconcerned community for helping push him over the edge:

Now judge I got debts no honest man could pay
The bank was holdin' my mortgage and they was takin' my house away
Now I ain't sayin' that makes me an innocent man
But it was more 'n all this that put that gun in my hand,

In a 1984 interview, Springsteen explained that *Nebraska* detailed the stories of desperate people searching for meaning in their lives but who found themselves abandoned by their community. The selfishness of their community seeped into their horrendous actions as they tried to add some purpose to their lives:

That's one of the most dangerous things, I think—isolation. *Nebraska* was about that American isolation: what happens to people when they're alienated from their friends and their community and their government and their job. Because those are the things that keep you sane, that give meaning to life in some fashion. And if they slip away, and you start to exist in some void where the basic constraints of society are a joke, then life becomes kind of a joke. And anything can happen. (Loder, "Born Again")

In Springsteen's view, the community failed to live up to its promise when people failed to realize they were members of a larger group who needed to look out for each other. Individuals quit being members of their community and served their personal ends only, leaving each person to fend for themselves.

Springsteen believed that the community failed at many levels. The government abdicated its responsibility to community and focused on individual risk without ensuring decent opportunities for success. Springsteen did not have much faith in government to begin with, but the actions of the Reagan administration only left him more cynical. In a 1984 *Rolling Stone* interview, he declared Reagan out of touch with the concerns of working-class Americans: "You see the Reagan reelection ads on TV—you know: 'It's morning in America.' And you say, well, it's not morning in Pittsburgh. It's not morning about 125th Street in New York. It's midnight, and, like, there's a bad moon risin'" (Loder, "Born Again"). In addition, the corporate sector served only the selfish needs of individuals in management at the expense of the individual worker and the communities they served. "Factory" and "My Hometown" survey desolate industrial wastelands where work did not lift people up but, rather, degraded their dreams.

"Born in the USA" is Springsteen's foremost critique of the larger community's failure to live up to its responsibilities. Horrendously misinterpreted by the masses as a patriotic anthem, the song is instead a scathing condemnation of an America that has left some citizens behind and alone. (It is interesting to note that Springsteen originally wrote "Born in the USA," as an acoustic track for *Nebraska*.) Describing a man who has had few options in life since birth, Springsteen shouts the opening lines of the song behind dissonant synthesizers and a clanging percussion part that re-creates the sound of a factory:

> Born down in a dead man's town
> The first kick I took was when I hit the ground
> You end up like a dog that's been beat too much
> Till you spend half your life just covering up.

The listener soon learns that the main character is a Vietnam veteran who returns to the United States and finds there are no jobs or veteran's benefits available to him. Although he gave his time to his country and lost a brother in the war, he is still trying to get back on his feet a decade after his tour of duty ended. The chorus, a defiant recitation of the song's title, asserts his citizenship while denouncing the promise of the American Dream. The song ends with a refutation of Springsteen's trademark song, "Born to Run" and its embrace of social mobility: "I'm ten years burning down the road / Nowhere to run ain't got nowhere to go."

Springsteen also observed the failure of personal relationships. Personal relationships and marriages failed as couples thought more about their individual needs and less about the bonds of their union. In "The Ties That Bind," Springsteen criticizes a partner who fears the autonomy she would lose by making room for him in her life:

> Cheap romance, it's all just a crutch
> You don't want nothin' that anybody can touch
> You're so afraid of being somebody's fool
> Not walkin' tough baby, not walkin' cool
> You walk cool, but darlin', can you walk the line
> And face the ties that bind

Just as a degree of selflessness is necessary to keep the ties that bind strong in a community, a degree of selflessness is also necessary in romantic relationships. Springsteen's songs urge his listeners to emphasize with the couple as a unit rather than as two separate individuals.

The hard working-class life also pushed couples apart, as in songs like "I'm Goin' Down" and "Dancing In the Dark," where a night shift turns a couple into strangers. The muffled synthesizers driving the song accentuate its dreary theme and the monotonous lifestyle of its characters:

> I get up in the evening
> And I ain't got nothing to say
> I come home in the morning
> I go to bed, feeling the same way
> ....
> I need a love reaction
> Come on now baby gimme just one look
> You can't start a fire sitting 'round crying over a broken heart

Shifting away from social concerns, Springsteen devoted *Tunnel of Love* almost exclusively to doubts about married life by presenting listeners with characters uneasy with devotion and commitment. As Steve Pond writes in his review of the album:

> Since [*Darkness on the Edge of Town*, Springsteen] has written about the promises our country makes to its people and the way it reneges on those promises, about the dreams our land inspires and the things that stifle those dreams. ... On *Tunnel of Love*, Springsteen is writing about the promises people make to each other and the way they renege on those promises. ("Review")

On "One Step Up," the main character finds that he and his wife keep making the same mistakes in their troubled marriage and are growing further apart:

> Woke up this morning my house was cold
> Checked out the furnace she wasn't burnin'
> Went out and hopped in my old Ford
> Hit the engine but she ain't turnin'
> We've given each other some hard lessons lately
> But we ain't learnin'
> We're the same sad story that's a fact
> One step up and two steps back.

The song ends in an affair and with the main character admitting that he was only pretending to be committed to his wife.

Although there is hope at the end of *Tunnel of Love* on "Valentine's Day," *New York Times* reviewer Jon Pareles writes that the album ultimately "extends Mr. Springsteen's fatalism even further, dousing the last glimmer of unexamined hope and blocking the last escapist fantasies" ("Review" 29). Not only have communities comprising businesses and neighbors failed, but communities of two—marriages—are also crumbling in selfishness and suspicion, symptoms

of the times. On "Brilliant Disguise," Springsteen takes this perspective a step
further, singing:

> I'm just a lonely pilgrim
> I walk this world in wealth
> I wanna know if it's you I don't trust
> 'Cause I damn sure don't trust myself.

Alone and unwilling to reach out emotionally to another person, the main character
in "Brilliant Disguise" ends up doubting himself. Cut off from his community and
others, he loses his own identity.

Springsteen suggests that society's failure to look out for others not only dooms
individuals, but also ultimately destroys communities. If no one is concerned with
the well-being of the individuals around them, the community those individuals
are charged with maintaining will decay. "My Hometown" surveys the damage
that self-centered business practices wreak on small towns:

> Now Main Street's whitewashed windows and vacant stores
> Seems like there ain't nobody wants to come down here no more
> They're closing down the textile mill across the railroad tracks
> Foreman says these jobs are going boys and they ain't coming back to your hometown

The song ends with the main character and his wife talking about moving south
to personally pursue a better life, but the consequence would be abandoning his
community. It would also mean abandoning the life he's made for himself and
his children, breaking his bond to his hometown that his father passed on to him.
Springsteen sings as the song ends, "I'm thirty-five, we got a boy of our own now
/ Last night I sat him up, behind the wheel and said son take a good look around /
This is your hometown." The empty plains of *Nebraska* have been replaced with
an industrial ghost town.

While critiquing the hollow promise of the American Dream in the 1970s
and 1980s through his music's lyrics, Springsteen attempted to restore a sense
of community to American life with his energetic music and concerts. He hoped
that he could show people their connections to others while at the same time
offering those who had been left behind by their communities a lifeline back
in. The individualistic message of the times, however, dominated his audience's
interpretation of his music, and Springsteen's message of community fell on deaf
ears. By the mid-1980s Springsteen had lost faith in the possibility that people
might take the message in his music to heart as many incorrectly interpreted his
work as an affirmation of the status quo.

Brilliant Disguise: Springsteen and Disillusionment

In his review of *Tunnel of Love*, Jon Pareles writes in the first sentence that "Bruce Springsteen doesn't trust myths" ("Review" 1). This was a very accurate description of Springsteen's world-view in 1987. By that year, many in Springsteen's audience were listening to Springsteen's music and following his career with a kind of mythical admiration that distorted the message he intended to convey to his audience.

Springsteen grew disillusioned with the nation's interpretation of *Born In the USA* following its release. By attempting to reveal the myth behind the American Dream, Springsteen instead found his audience turning his music and his public personality into a myth. While his intention with *Born in the USA* was to expose the American Dream as a shallow promise and to criticize the disconnect between the individual and the community, his audience turned it into a patriotic affirmation of the status quo. At the same time, Springsteen attempted to back away from his newfound status as a rock icon, which had reduced him in the eyes of the public to a one-dimensional all-American rock superstar.

Although some rock critics understood the meaning of *Born in the USA*, Springsteen's audience did not grasp the album's critique of late-twentieth century America. Many seemed to base their understanding of the album on a quick glance at the cover; for many, the flag, blue jeans and T-shirt, baseball cap, and title turned the record into a patriotic statement during an era of resurging national pride.

Born in the USA was also swept into election-year politics. President Reagan, whom voters would re-elect in a landslide victory in 1984, cited Springsteen's music in a campaign stop in New Jersey in September of that year. Reagan said:

> America's future rests in a thousand dreams inside our hearts. It rests in the message of hope so many young people admire: New Jersey's own Bruce Springsteen. And helping you make those dreams come true is what this job of mine is all about. (Qtd in Cullen 2).

Springsteen wanted nothing to do with party politics and especially not those of Ronald Reagan, whose policies, Springsteen believed, promoted selfishness at the expense of the less fortunate in communities, but the president's comments linked Springsteen's music to the kind of rugged individualism that Springsteen had attempted to expose as a problem in America.

Less than a week earlier, conservative commentator George Will attended a Springsteen concert and wrote about the experience in a column for the *Washington Post*. Will, like others, did not grasp the depth of Springsteen's message:

> I have not got a clue about Springsteen's politics, if any, but flags get waved at his concerts while he sings songs about hard times. He is no whiner, and the recitation of closed factories and other problems always seems punctuated by a grand, cheerful affirmation: "Born in the USA!"

His songs, and the engaging homilies with which he introduces them, tell listeners to "downsize" their expectations—his phrase, borrowed from the auto industry, naturally.

It is music for saying goody-bye to Peter Pan: Life is real, life is earnest, life is a lot of work, but ....

"Friday night's pay night, guys fresh out of work / Talking about the weekend, scrubbing off the dirt ... / In my head I keep a picture of a pretty little miss / Someday mister I'm gonna lead a better life than this."

An evening with Springsteen ... is vivid proof that the work ethic is alive and well. (A14)

While both men observe the resilience of working-class Americans, Will mistakenly sees Springsteen's music as a cheery, patriotic affirmation of Reagan's America. Will did not hear the social commentary in Springsteen's music or the desperate hopes of his characters, and certainly did not understand Springsteen's intentions as a live performer, which was to create a community to help people cope with their economic circumstances and shed light on others in that community who needed help.

Springsteen attempted to clarify the public's misunderstanding of *Born in the USA* in 1987. In an interview with *Newsweek* that year, Springsteen shot down the "myth" that "Born in the USA" was an endorsement of national pride and an affirmation of a version of the American Dream that focused on individuals while estranging people from their communities and others:

The guy in ["Born in the USA"], he wants to destroy that [America-first] myth. It's not helpful. It's not useful. It brings people down in guilt and shame, if they feel they're not living up to it in some fashion. ... Myths don't bind us together. They keep us strangers from each other. Strangers from our communities, from our country, from our friends and our children and our wives. And ultimately from ourselves. (Barol, "Myths" 77)

Eventually, Springsteen began to distance himself from the record. In a 1992 interview with *Rolling Stone*, he "shrugged off [*Born in the USA*] as a rock record," saying that people made the album "more thematic than it probably was" (Henke). He remained critical of the album in 2002, declaring in another interview with *Rolling Stone* that "I was always unsatisfied with that album. That was one I really struggled with and never felt like I got the whole thing right. But your own wrestling in that department doesn't really have anything to do with the way something is received, or the way your fans hear it" (Binelli).

Springsteen also tried to distance himself from his public image. His fan base, which had grown significantly larger following the release of *Born in the USA*, revered him as a full-blooded patriot, a working-class superstar who worked hard over the years and was now finally rewarded for his perseverance. Springsteen did not want to be admired as a rugged individual or as the heroic American blue-collar worker, however; his success was an aberration in a nation which he believed did not value risk or the dedication of its workers. Springsteen was simply trying to reach out to struggling working-class Americans and welcome them back into a community in which neighbors looked out for them. "BRUCE SPRINGSTEEN, ROCK STAR," overshadowed that message and turned his music and his life into a myth as hollow as the American Dream in the mid-1980s. Springsteen found the substance of his message lost on people caught up in his celebrity:

> I really enjoyed the success of *Born in the USA*, but by the end of that whole thing, I just kind of felt "Bruced" out. I was like "Whoa, enough of that." You end up creating this sort of icon, and eventually it oppresses you. … So when I wrote *Tunnel of Love*, I thought I had to reintroduce myself as a songwriter, in a very non-iconic role. … You can get enslaved by your own myth. (Henke)

Springsteen hoped to call his myth into question. In interviews after the *Born in the USA* hysteria, he increasingly advised readers to "Trust the art, not the artist" (Corn and Morley). He responded to the hype generated by *Born in the USA* with *Tunnel of Love*, a subdued meditation on marriage and romance haunted by characters filled with self-doubt. Springsteen hoped that the somber, introspective mood of *Tunnel of Love* would lead his audience to question his status as a heroic and flawless cultural icon. In "Ain't Got You," Springsteen admits that he is ridiculously wealthy and that "[w]hen [he] walk[s] down the street people stop and stare," yet, despite his money and fame, he still has trouble forming a basic, meaningful romantic relationship. In "Brilliant Disguise," a song about a marriage between two people who do not really know each other, Springsteen tells his lover (who could just as easily represent his audience):

> So when you look at me
> You better look hard and look twice
> Is that me baby
> Or just a brilliant disguise.

Jay Cocks writes in his review of *Tunnel of Love* that "[t]here is, in fact, much lyrical speculation on manhood in this record, as if Springsteen, disgusted with the rock-Rambo hype that surrounded him during the *Born in the USA* concert tour, decided to right the balance" ("Review"). With the audience's knowledge that he had recently married,[3] the songs about marital relationships made people wonder about the state of his marriage and, sung in the first person, made Springsteen

---

[3]   For clarity's sake, Springsteen married Julianne Phillips in 1985. He married E Street Band member Patti Scialfa in 1991.

fallible and less mythic. At the same time, it drew people's attention to his private life.

Springsteen sought to defy the public's expectations of himself with *Tunnel of Love* and its subsequent tour. For the tour, Springsteen changed the blocking onstage to signal that his shows were no longer what people were accustomed to. When asked why he made the change, Springsteen said, "You can get to a place where you start to replay the ritual, and nostalgia creeps in. And I decided to mix it up. … And I wanted to get to a spot where if people came to the show, there'd be a feeling of like, well, it's not going to be this, it's going to be something else" (Henke). He also reinterpreted two of his most recognizable songs. His concerts in 1987 and 1988 featured a harsh electric rendition of "Born in the USA" that, according to Steve Pond, sounded like a "brutal modern-day blues" that "lack[ed] any of the patriotism that some people insisted on reading into it on the last tour" ("Tunnel Vision"). Springsteen also performed "Born to Run" as an acoustic number, explaining to the audience beforehand that the song was now less about running, or the search for fulfillment, and more about finding peace at home. John Rockwell described the song as a "ruminative lament, slow and serious, each word enunciated with solemn precision," which allowed his audience a better opportunity to uncover the meaning behind the lyrics (S2).

The audience did not respond to *Tunnel of Love* with the same enthusiasm with which they greeted *Born in the USA*. The public at large seemed more interested in his marriage than his message, which largely fell on deaf ears. Springsteen grew disillusioned with his work as he watched people read the wrong meaning into his music. The community he had intended to create with his music—one in which people could take risks to improve themselves and find either real reward if they succeeded or shelter if they failed—never materialized. Instead, he found a self-centered audience that took an interest in him as a patriot and as a celebrity. Reflecting on the 1980s from 1992, Springsteen said, "I guess you get to a place where your old answers and your old dreams don't really work anymore" (Henke). In addition, he felt that his connection with much of his audience was superficial, and that he really did not fit in with the mindset of the decade: "[I]n the eighties, I was writing and singing about what I felt was happening to the people I was seeing around me or what direction I saw the country going in. And that really wasn't in step with the times, either" (Henke). Bruce Springsteen's perspective on the role of the individual and community in the lives of Americans in the 1970s and 1980s ultimately put him at odds with the predominant attitudes of his era.

Chapter 13

"American Skin (41 Shots)," "Galveston Bay," and the Social Psychology of Prejudice

Steven Fein

"Forty-one Shots"

In the middle of a sold-out concert in Atlanta, Georgia in the summer of 2000, Bruce Springsteen debuted a new song. The song began with Springsteen plaintively chanting the words, "41 shots." From those words alone, much of the audience instantly understood what the song was about. Just hours later, word of this unreleased song had spread to New York City, setting off a firestorm of controversy. Heads of two police unions called for a boycott of Springsteen's upcoming concerts in New York. One called him "a dirtbag" and "a floating fag" for singing a song about this issue. Fans and activists called the song "brilliant" and "compassionate." What was so incendiary about the words "41 shots"? As the concert-goers in Atlanta, the police in New York, and many people around the world quickly inferred, this was an allusion to the tragic death a year earlier of a West African immigrant in New York City, who was killed in a hail of forty-one bullets in the vestibule of his apartment building.

On February 4, 1999, just after midnight, a street vendor named Amadou Diallo entered his apartment building. He was spotted by members of the Street Crime Unit, an elite unit of officers who patrolled that and other crime-ridden areas of the city. The unit had been extraordinarily successful in reducing crime, but its methods were often criticized for being too aggressive. In particular, it was clear that African-American and Hispanic men were singled out by the unit. Thousands of African-American and Hispanic men were stopped, frisked, and searched. That winter night in 1999, Amadou Diallo would have been one more of them. Four white police officers from the unit thought that Diallo fitted the description of a serial rapist they had been looking for, and that he seemed suspicious as he appeared to duck into his building to avoid them. As they approached and told him to raise his hands, he reached into his pocket and began to pull out a black object. Thinking that the object was a gun, the police opened fire. Forty-one shots. Nineteen of them hit Diallo, and he lay dead in the vestibule. The police removed the black object from his hand. It was a wallet. Diallo did not have a weapon.

Protesters held rallies in the days that followed, chanting "forty-one shots" and holding up wallets. The controversial use of "racial profiling," in which the police use race as a factor in determining whom to stop and search for possible criminal activities, came under renewed attack. The Street Crime Unit was disbanded. Many politicians, columnists, and citizens defended the police, noting how difficult it is to make life-or-death decisions in the blink of an eye. In March, 2000, the four police officers were found not guilty of any criminal charges.

Springsteen's song was fair and balanced, neither condemning nor condoning the police's actions, but instead highlighting the tragic consequences of living in such a violent, dangerous society. But it did raise the critical question of whether the officers' perception of a gun rather than a wallet came from their "eyes" or their "heart." The implied question was whether stereotypes associated with the color of Diallo's skin made the officers more likely to misperceive the wallet as a gun. Although none of us can ever know whether this was the case in the Diallo tragedy, the research discussed in this chapter explains why and how such an implication is quite plausible. Moreover, the research presented here can shed light on other social psychological processes through which stereotyping and prejudice influence people's thoughts, feelings, and actions. In general, the purpose of this chapter is to illustrate how social psychological research can contribute to our understanding of the subtle but profoundly important causes and consequences of stereotyping and prejudice, and to connect these processes not only to Springsteen's controversial song, "American Skin," but also to "Galveston Bay"—a song that reflects a very different, but equally relevant, set of processes underlying stereotyping and prejudice. In so doing, this chapter attempts to highlight the relevance of Springsteen's work to understanding important, and complex, societal issues, and, in turn, to illustrate how a deeper understanding of these societal issues can make one appreciate Springsteen's work all the more.

"It Ain't No Secret"

In addition to chanting "41 shots" at the beginning of "American Skin," Springsteen later repeats the phrase, "It ain't no secret," eventually completing the point, and concluding the song, with the final repeated lines: "You can get killed just for living / In your American skin." To many, this is far from a secret. But to many more, it is not so well known and much less understood. While discussing the tragedy in the American Gulf Coast in the wake of Hurricane Katrina during his keynote address at the Glory Days symposium, Dave Marsh relayed the words of author Daniel Wolff, saying that although "the river"—a key metaphor in Springsteen's work—can sometimes wash away one's sins, at other times it can reveal them. The Diallo shooting and its aftermath may have revealed some of our collective sins to those who were willing and able to look, but there was also a concerted effort to make us all look away—to close the wounds by denying their existence.

It was this intense desire of the New York City police and its defenders to have the world move on from the incident and look away that provided the fuel that ignited the Springsteen controversy. Even after those people who were upset by Springsteen's song could eventually read the lyrics and have the opportunity to see that the words and message were not as inflammatory as assumed, and once they could see that Springsteen was not "exploiting" the tragedy by publicizing or even selling the song during the controversy, the mere act of calling attention to the incident was, many argued, Springsteen's indefensible and destructive action. Indeed, more than three years later, members of the New York City police *still* could not tolerate Springsteen playing this song. After Springsteen played the song at the first of his three shows at New York's Shea Stadium, which concluded another world tour in October 2003, a high-ranking police official ordered that there would be no police escort out of the stadium for Springsteen and his band after the next show.

There is an episode of the popular 1990s TV sitcom *Seinfeld* in which one of the characters is dating a man whose race she cannot discern. Although she insists that his race would not make any difference to her, she "just really want[s] to know." As the four (white) principal characters sit around a coffee shop, discussing this predicament, they feel nervous and guilty even talking about the issue. Indeed, when an African-American waitress comes to their table and hands them their check, their guilt is evident as they all heap money on the table in an effort to tip her more than generously, trying to assuage their sins of discussing the taboo topic of race. This scene humorously illustrates how difficult it is for many Americans to even discuss issues of race. Adding the intensity and seriousness of a tragedy such as Diallo's to the mix makes it all the more difficult and disturbing.

That is not to say that no one discussed the incident. Far from it. In the days and weeks following the Diallo shooting, and then again around the time of the trials of the police officers, the media featured the typical floods of officials, spokespeople, politicians, and others. As with most issues played out in the popular media, however, these were rarely constructive, reasoned discussions. Rather, these were opportunities to yell, moralize, preach, and sound supremely confident in the veracity of one's own point. Virtually everyone voiced outrage at one or the other side of the debate. The debate in question, of course, was whether the police fired forty-one shots at an unarmed man because he was black, or whether racism had nothing to do with the incident and was only being raised to smear the motives and reputation of police officers who were simply trying to protect themselves from an uncooperative and potentially deadly suspect, independent of his race.

A key question, though, was rarely if ever raised: how can this debate be judged? On what evidence are points made? The arguments in such dialogue tend to be made with passion and conviction, but typically they are based in whole, or large part, on speculation. People—especially those who dominate public discourse—tend to be confident in their powers of observation and intuition, but decades of research in social psychology have made it clear that people's ability to infer the causes of others' or even their own behavior is remarkably unreliable.

Much research has demonstrated that our thoughts and memories of what we do is far more subject to error and bias than we realize, but our insight into *why* we do the things we do is even more suspect. When critics of the police blasted the racism that helped pull the triggers, or when defenders blasted the critics for suggesting such bias, the arguments rested on the ephemera of speculation. The speculation may have been based on years of relevant experience and may have been bolstered by data concerning crime rates or incidence of erroneous shootings by race, but these speculations by themselves could never resolve the debate.

How can anyone know what caused the police officers to misperceive a wallet for a gun and open fire on Diallo? The simple but important truth revealed by research is that we cannot know. Even the officers who shot Diallo cannot know. How can they or others know if they would have been as quick to shoot at a white man in an identical situation? What social psychological research can teach us, however, is whether and how race can influence the kind of split-second decisions faced by the police that night, and whether race can have such influence independently of racist motives or beliefs. Moreover, this research stands in contrast to the much more subjective analyses that dominate public discourse about these issues, and offers an alternative approach that is needed to contribute to our understanding of these complex problems.

We're Baptized in these Waters

For the past decade and a half, a great deal of research in social psychology has demonstrated how stereotyping works at both automatic and controlled levels, and that these levels sometimes work at odds with one another. Part of the power of stereotypes, however, is that they can bias individuals' perceptions and responses *even if they do not personally agree with these beliefs*. Baptized in the waters of a common culture, members of a society learn at an early age what values and associations are prevalent. Frequent or significant exposure to these values and associations can have enduring effects, even if individuals eventually reject these ideas and try to distance themselves from them.

This growing body of research indicates that individuals may automatically activate stereotypes when they are exposed to members of groups for which popular stereotypes exist. Thus, just as many of us are automatically primed to think "eggs" after hearing "bacon and," we also are primed to think of concepts relevant to a stereotype when we think of a stereotyped group. The key point is that these associations can be strong even among people who do not endorse the stereotype, just as the notion of "eggs" can be activated after hearing "bacon and," even among people who never eat bacon and eggs. To be sure, people can control the potential effects of these associations in various situations. We do not have to eat bacon and eggs just because the association is primed, just as we do not have to discriminate against an African-American job candidate despite the readily accessible negative stereotypes. However, there can be dissociation between our conscious beliefs and controlled behaviors on the one hand, and our automatic processes on the other. For one thing, we often are not aware that a particular stereotype has been activated in our minds or how it can subtly but significantly influence our perceptions and behaviors. In addition, we often are in situations where we do not have the time or cognitive resources available for deliberative thinking and behavior. The perception and reaction may be as immediate as an involuntary reflex, or they may be made in the midst of myriad other demands on our thoughts and energy.

In one important demonstration of these ideas, Devine exposed white college students to subliminal presentations on a computer monitor. For one group, these presentations consisted of words relevant to stereotypes about black people, such as "Africa," "ghetto," "welfare," and "basketball." Subliminally presented information is presented so quickly that perceivers do not even realize that they have been exposed to it. Thus, these students were not consciously aware that they had seen these words. Being subliminally primed with a lot of these words caused the participants to activate the African-American stereotype more generally, which subsequently biased their interpretations of another person's behavior. The activation of the African-American stereotype made these participants more likely to perceive the ambiguous actions of another individual as hostile. Most noteworthy in this study, however, was the finding that these effects occurred even among participants who did not consciously endorse the stereotypes in question. Even if one does not have racist attitudes, awareness of negative stereotypes can operate automatically and outside of conscious awareness, biasing perception and action, despite one's more egalitarian cognitions and intentions.

More recently, research has demonstrated that perceivers are more likely to exhibit negative stereotype activation and evaluations in response to African-American faces if the faces are more racially prototypic (Blair, Judd and Fallman; Maddox). This is not a bias that most people are aware of, or, therefore, concerned about. Its effects, however, can be profound, as suggested by research by Eberhardt, Davies, Purdie-Vaughns, and Johnson, which examined predictors of whether a criminal defendant was likely to be sentenced to death. Examining more than 600 death-penalty-eligible cases tried in Philadelphia, Pennsylvania, between 1979 and 1999, these researchers found that in cases involving a white victim, the more the defendant's physical appearance was stereotypically black, the more likely he would be sentenced to death.

Is it a Gun? Is it a Knife? Is it a Wallet? This is Your Life

Can such automatic activation cause people to be more likely to misperceive an object as a gun rather than as a wallet, or to lower the threshold to decide to shoot rather than wait, if the target of their perception is a black man than a white man? Do racist beliefs or feelings underlie such biases? Research inspired directly by the Diallo incident has addressed these very questions. In the first published research based on the shooting, Payne had undergraduate students at a large university engage in a task that required them to make the kind of decision the police had to make: very quickly identify an object as a weapon or as not a weapon (such as a tool). Pictures of these objects were presented on a computer screen, but immediately preceding them was a quick presentation of a black or white male face. The pictures were presented for fractions of a second. Payne found that the participants were significantly more likely to mistake a harmless object for a weapon if it was preceded by a black face rather than a white face. This difference was less likely to emerge if the participants were given more time to make this judgment. In sum, when decisions had to be made very quickly, as they are in a "this is your life" situation faced by the police, white participants were more likely to falsely identify a hand tool for a hand gun.

Correll, Park, Judd, and Wittenbrink also investigated this issue, but they constructed a situation even more like the one faced by the police. Rather than first present the race of a person and then present an object, these researchers designed a video game to present them simultaneously, and the participants had to decide whether to shoot or not shoot the person who appeared on their screen. Some of the targets were white men, and others were black men. Some of them held guns, and others held harmless objects (such as a cell phone or wallet). If the target held a gun, the participants were supposed to hit a "shoot" button as quickly as possible. If he held a harmless object, they were to hit a "don't shoot" button as quickly as they could.

As in the Payne study, participants showed a bias consistent with racial stereotypes. If the target held a gun, they were significantly quicker to press the "shoot" button if he was black than if he was white. If the target held a harmless object, they took significantly longer to press the "don't shoot" button if he was black than if he was white. In addition, participants were more likely to mistakenly "shoot" an unarmed target if he was black than if he was white.

These studies, as well as several others that were conducted after this initial wave of experiments, used somewhat different methods and were conducted in different locations, but they provide converging evidence that when the decision must be made very quickly, a black man in the United States is more likely to be mistakenly perceived as holding a gun than is a white man. It is important to note, though, that the participants in these studies were not police officers—they were undergraduate students or people from the community. Police officers receive extensive training in these kinds of tasks. But as Anthony Greenwald, one of the researchers cited above, observed, "Police receive training to make them more sensitive to weapons, but they don't get training to undo unconscious race stereotypes or biases" (qtd. in Kassin 184).

Are police officers vulnerable to such biases, and can they be trained to undo them? Plant and Peruche found evidence suggesting "yes" as the answer to both questions. They were able to use police officers as participants in their computer simulation study, and, consistent with the results of the research already discussed here, the officers were more likely to mistakenly "shoot" an unarmed black than an unarmed white target. After undergoing an extensive training program designed to break the association between black targets and weapons, this racial bias in weapon identification was eliminated.

Is it in Your Heart? Is it in Your Eyes?

Although this recent and growing body of research suggests that an individual's answer to the potentially life-threatening questions "Is it a gun? Is it a knife? Is it a wallet?" can depend on whether the person holding the object is black or white, another question is whether or not this bias is driven by racist attitudes or beliefs. This may be what Springsteen is asking when he changes the chorus, late in the song, to add the words, "Is it in your heart? Is it in your eyes?" Did the participants in the research discussed above exhibit this "shooter bias" because they believed in their hearts that the threshold for shooting a black suspect should be somewhat lower than shooting a white suspect? Several pieces of evidence point to the same kind of dissociation discussed earlier in this chapter between individuals' attitudes, on the one hand, and their rapid judgments and actions on the other. That is, even if one does not have negative feelings or endorse negative stereotypes about African-Americans, one may show strong evidence of a racial bias in misperceiving a wallet as a gun. For example, Correll *et al.* found that the magnitude of the "shooter bias" was *not* related to the participants' levels of racial prejudice. In addition, African-American participants in the Correll *et al.* study showed the same bias against black targets as did white participants, again suggesting that racial prejudice is not necessarily reflected in this bias. Rather, *awareness* of the stereotype was a necessary factor, but endorsing it was not.

This is not to suggest that holding very racist beliefs and sentiments would not have any effect. Of course it would. But a key point is that acknowledging that race likely played a role in the killing of Amadou Diallo is not necessarily a condemnation of the individual police officers' attitudes and beliefs. Living in our culture may be a sufficient trigger for this kind of violent reaction. And in its promotion of that more subtle but powerful point lies much of the power, and intelligence, of Bruce Springsteen's song.

More research is being conducted to address these issues further. One line of research that some colleagues and I are conducting is designed to assess whether this bias is, as "American Skin" asks, "in your eyes." That is, to what extent do people literally *see* a gun rather than a wallet, as opposed to having different thresholds for responding as if the person were holding a gun or a wallet. Is it a perceptual or a response bias? This is a subtle but potentially important distinction that can promote a more complete understanding of the psychological processes involved. Whatever the ultimate answers, it is quite clear that these questions raised by Springsteen in "American Skin" are justifiable questions to ask, and they can be addressed in a relatively objective, reasoned way to help expand our knowledge about these complex issues. That you can get killed for living in your

American skin is no secret to some, but there remains tremendous room for better understanding the how and the why, as well as the question of what can be done to attenuate or eliminate these biases.

Harvesting Galveston Bay

There is a great distance between the settings of "American Skin" and "Galveston Bay"—from the streets of New York City to the delta country of the Texas coast. In style and content, too, the songs are markedly different. And whereas the debut of "American Skin" launched floods of controversy, the song "Galveston Bay" made nary a ripple. But in its own way, "Galveston Bay" raises a related set of questions as "American Skin" does, and through it Springsteen again shines a light into the dark recesses that too many of us would rather keep out of sight.

"Galveston Bay" tells the story of two men who come from completely different worlds and yet live remarkably parallel lives. First is the story of Le Bing Son, who "fought side by side with the Americans" in Vietnam and at the end of the war "brought his family to the promised land." The delta country along Texas's Gulf coast reminded him of home, and he bought a shrimp boat with a cousin and harvested Galveston Bay. Next is Billy Sutter's story. Sutter, for whom this land had always been home, also fought in Vietnam. He inherited his fishing boat from his father and also harvested Galveston Bay. In trading verses between these two characters, Springsteen reveals the humanity common to these two very different men. They each rise early in the morning, kiss their sleeping children, and try to make a living by casting their nets into the water.

Through a few details deftly sprinkled in the song, Springsteen suggests the suffering and feelings of threat that Billy and many of his friends endured. Being injured in Vietnam and then watching the refugees compete with him for the finite resources in Galveston Bay, seemed to threaten Billy's sense of his place in the world, his self-image and his feelings of security. As social psychological research has demonstrated, these feelings of being under threat can translate into prejudice toward others. In my own research (for example, Fein, Hoshino-Brown, Davies, and Spencer), I have found that when their self-image is threatened in some way, people become more likely to use negative stereotypes, or exhibit negative feelings or behaviors, toward members of other groups. For example, in one study (Fein and Spencer), participants received either positive or negative feedback about their performance on a test of social and verbal skills—feedback that temporarily boosted or threatened their self-esteem. They next took part in what was supposed to be a second experiment in which they evaluated a job applicant. All participants received a photograph of a young woman, her résumé, and a videotape of a job interview. In half the cases, information suggested that the woman was Jewish, and in the other half information suggested that she was not. (On the campus where the study was held, a negative stereotype of the "Jewish American Princess" was evoked by upper-middle-class Jewish women from New York.)

There were two important results (see Figures 13.1a and 13.1b). First, among participants whose self-esteem had been threatened by negative feedback, the apparently Jewish woman was rated significantly more negatively than the apparently non-Jewish woman—even though their videotaped interview and their credentials were identical. This bias did not emerge, however, among participants whose self-esteem had not been threatened—they rated the women the same whether or not she seemed to be Jewish. Second, among the participants who had received the self-esteem threat, the more they derogated the Jewish woman, the more their self-esteem improved. Taken together, the results suggest that a blow to one's self-image evokes prejudice—and the expression of prejudice helps to repair that self-image.

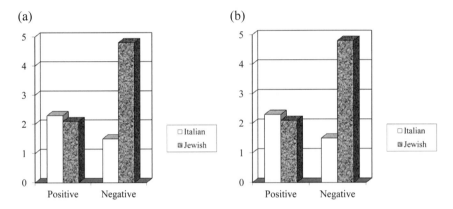

Figure 13.1   Average rating of the woman (a) or increase in participants' self-esteem (b) as a function of whether participants had received positive or negative feedback about their performance on a test, and whether the woman they were judging apparently was Jewish or not (control condition). The higher the bars, the more positively they evaluated the woman (a) or exhibited a post-experiment increase in their own self-esteem (b)

Source: Adapted from Fein and Spencer.

Characters in Springsteen's songs often face such blows to how they see themselves and their ability to make their way in the world. Sometimes, as in "Badlands," they feel "caught in a cross fire" that they "don't understand." Or, as in "The Promised Land," they "feel so weak" in the face of all these forces that they "just want to explode." Their means of dealing with these forces vary from song to song; sometimes they are heroic against them, sometimes they fail tragically. Part of the power of "Galveston Bay" is the subtlety with which this psychological cross-fire is suggested. There is none of the bombast and defiance of "Badlands" or the romance of "Meeting Across the River." Instead, it is the quiet revelation of a key cause of intergroup hostility and discrimination.

Just as the participants in Fein's and Spencer's study seemed to take out their frustrations by using the easily accessible hammer of a popular negative stereotype to knock down the member of an out-group, Billy Sutter and his friends in "Galveston Bay" take out their own frustrations on an easily recognizable out-group, the Vietnamese. An out-group that stands out physically and socially from one's own group provides a much easier target of one's frustrations and fears than do the more abstract threats of a difficult economy or of dreams unfulfilled. And so, "Soon in the bars around the harbor was talk / Of America for Americans / Someone said, 'You want 'em out, you got to burn 'em out.'" More animosity builds until the final showdown in the shadows one late summer night, as Billy takes out his K-bar knife to kill Le Bin Song. As the drama peaks, Billy sticks his knife back into his pocket, takes a breath, and lets Le pass. It is a powerful moment, and the non-violent ending is a bit surprising, given the socio-psychological forces that seem to be compelling Billy to take desperate action. The final verse then brings Billy back to his shared humanity with Le, as he rises early in the morning, kisses his sleeping wife, and casts his net back into the water. Somewhere not far away, Le presumably is doing the same.

As in "American Skin," Springsteen deftly illustrates in "Galveston Bay" the day-to-day realities of living in a complex social world—a world in which people share so many similarities while at the same time stand worlds apart. We often do not recognize how our thoughts, feelings, and actions toward others may be motivated by factors having nothing to do with these others. Indeed, in my own research, most participants feel worse, not better, if they are led to realize that they have derogated others as a function of their membership in a stereotyped group. Indeed, one of the best ways to attenuate the negative effects of self-image threat on stereotyping and prejudice is to make these processes clear. Removed from the shadow of automatic, implicit reactions, these processes are less inevitable and more controllable. Perhaps that is why Billy chose not to kill Le. Ultimately, Billy had to confront what he was doing. Killing Le in this fashion would not have been an automatic, reflexive move. It would have been cold and calculating, and its naked reality may have been too revealing.

In Your American Skin

In 1981 Bruce Springsteen played a benefit concert for veterans of the Vietnam War. When he came on stage, Springsteen talked about the difficulties many Americans had in acknowledging the horrors of the war or the plight of the war veterans. He said that:

[It's] like you're walking down a dark street at night, and out of the corner of your eye, you see somebody getting hurt or somebody getting hit in a dark alley but you keep walking on because you think it don't have nothing to do with you. You just want to get home. Well Vietnam turned this whole country into that dark street and unless we're able to walk down those dark alleys and look into the eyes of the men and the women that are down there and the things that happened, we're never going to be able to get home ... (qtd. in Marsh, *Bruce Springsteen on Tour* 140)

A very similar metaphor can apply to contemporary issues of racism and other forms of prejudice and discrimination. Although, in many ways, it is very clear that racial prejudice and discrimination have been lessening in the United States over the last several decades, it is also clear that prejudice and discrimination can be much more subtle, lurking beneath surfaces and behind corners. We may see its shadow and not be sure whether it is real or an apparition. Subtle, undercover forms of racism can be just as hurtful as more blatant forms, in part because their subtlety allows them to slip through people's defenses. People who truly want to be fair-minded don't realize the extent to which their reactions and behaviors are influenced by racial stereotypes and prejudices. And often it seems impossible to know whether and to what extent racism exists in a particular situation.

The outcry of the police and others in reaction to Springsteen's "American Skin" was a defense mechanism designed to prevent society from looking down that dark alley and testing to see whether that shadow reflects something real or illusory. Without looking—deeply, carefully, rationally, bravely—we as a society cannot "get home," at least not to the home most of us want for ourselves. Methodologically rigorous research can shed much needed light into this darkness. Bruce Springsteen has been shining his own bright light into the darkness on the edge of towns, and into the recesses of the human psyche, throughout his career. Sometimes looking into the light is where the fun is, as Springsteen sang in "Blinded by the Light." But sometimes looking into the darkness is frightening and dangerous, and yet it is essential to do this because it is where important truths are revealed.

To some, "[i]t ain't no secret / You can get killed just for living / In your American skin." But it should also not be a secret why and how this happens, and what the factors are that can make this less likely to happen. In "American Skin" Lena gives her son a deadly serious lesson in how to minimize the danger of a hypothetical encounter with a police officer. This hard-earned wisdom is critically important to communicate. At a broader level, it is critically important for all of us to learn and communicate the lessons that research can teach us. Only through education, research, and the kind of commitment to not walking past the problem—a commitment that Springsteen has modeled increasingly in his own work and life—can a more comprehensive understanding of these issues be realized. Sometimes revealing sins is the difficult, but necessary, first step in washing them away.

Chapter 14

Shaking the City's Walls: Teaching Politics with the Boss

John Massaro

Individual freedom when it's not connected to some sort of community or friend or
the world outside ends up feeling pretty meaningless.
> Bruce Springsteen, Los Angeles Sports Arena, 1988, introducing "Born to Run
> (Acoustic)" *Bruce Springsteen: The Complete Video Anthology/1978-2000*

I never realized until this course how much of a fan Bruce is of fans.
> SUNY Potsdam College Student, January 2001

I teach a course entitled "Walk Tall: Beauty, Meaning and Politics in the Lyrics
of Bruce Springsteen" at SUNY Potsdam. Some people, including at least one of
New York's elected officials, have questioned whether there can be any worthwhile
connections linking Springsteen's lyrics and politics that are appropriate to a
college classroom (Lucadamo 30). In response to those raising such concerns, I
like to point out, only semi-facetiously, that one well-respected Greek philosopher,
a fellow named Plato, saw very real connections linking music, politics, and
scholarship. He once observed that "when the modes of music change, the
fundamental laws of the state always change with them" (Plato 113). In the current
vernacular, Plato might simply have noted that "when the music changes, the walls
of the city shake." More than 2,000 years later, another scholar of music, Jerry
Lee Lewis, looked around the rock scene and concluded there was a "whole lot of
shaken' going on." Taken in combination, Plato and Jerry Lee suggest—at least
to me but, I suspect, to many others as well—that music does have the capacity to
significantly affect the political system.

Beyond my desire to make my students more aware of the politically relevant
messages present in some rock lyrics, my reasons for offering the course range
from the self-indulgent to the scholarly. I am a professor of politics and a
Springsteen fan. Springsteen and I stand on some common ground. We were born
and raised in New Jersey, share an Italian heritage (Bruce's mother's maiden name
was Zirilli, my mother's was Cirelli), our fathers once worked as bus drivers,
we both had severe and tortuous cases of acne as teenagers, and we spent many
years "down" the shore "chasin' the factory girls under the boardwalk." I suspect
Bruce was a great deal more successful in that latter endeavor than I. In addition,
it appears that both Springsteen and I have had past battles with depression and
the need of therapy (Alterman, *Ain't No Sin* 201-209) and have now found some

peace in the uplifting love of a spouse and children. Self-indulgence aside, my major justification for the course is that Springsteen's lyrics powerfully express how one's political consciousness develops—or, at least, can and should ideally develop.

In this essay, I present an overview of my Springsteen course as well as introduce the overarching theme of the course, "Springsteen's Lyrics and Personal Political Development." Discussion of both of these topics will, I believe, support the view that Bruce Springsteen and his lyrics can be and, indeed, often are political.

"Politics" and Political Themes in Springsteen's Lyrics

At the outset, I should make clear what I mean by the term "politics." Robert Dahl has described "politics" as existing wherever one can discern "any persistent pattern of human relationships that involves, to a significant extent, control, influence, power, or authority" (Dahl 4). Dahl's definition of the political is an admittedly broad one that includes not only matters involving governmental institutions and behavior (which I refer to as "traditional politics"), but also matters involving power, influence, authority, and control in connection with any and all non-governmental institutions (which I refer to as "non-traditional politics.")

The fact that politics broadly involves both governmental and non-governmental institutions and behavior is evident in Dahl's reference to both the "ubiquity of politics" and to his warning that "many associations that people do not regard as 'political' possess political systems: private clubs, business firms, labor unions, religious organizations, civic groups, primitive tribes, clans, perhaps even families" (4). One might appropriately add to Dahl's list, the term "musical associations" and even, perhaps, the lyrics of a particular rock performer. The beauty and the challenge of Dahl's definition lies in the fact that as long as one can make a solid case for the presence of patterns of power, influence, control or authority in any phenomenon, even in the phenomenon of Springsteen's lyrics, one has arrived at the political.

While this chapter will only focus on the theme of "Springsteen's Lyrics and Personal Political Development," it might be helpful at this point to at least briefly note other political themes that are highlighted in the course. These include the following:

- Populism, Democracy and the American Dream
- The Work and Play Ethics and Politics
- Community
- Patriotism
- Manhood, Womanhood and the Politics of Love
- The Underclass
- Racism
- Politics and Our Better Angels

I feel compelled to note that I have found Jim Cullen's insightfully thematic *Born in the USA: Bruce Springsteen and the American Tradition*, Eric Alterman's engagingly biographical but also thematic *It Ain't No Sin to Be Glad You're Alive: The Promise of Bruce Springsteen*, and Dave Marsh's indispensable *Bruce Springsteen: Two Hearts: The Definitive Biography, 1972-2003* to be particularly helpful in my development of these themes.

I should also note that in employing Dahl's definition of politics to examine political themes in Springsteen's lyrics, I am essentially interested in doing just that. I am only marginally interested in Springsteen's direct forays into traditional politics, such as his campaign efforts in behalf of John Kerry, and am much more focused on the political themes and messages lying either directly or, more often, indirectly in his lyrics. Put simply, I am decidedly more interested in the politics in Springsteen's work than I am in the work of Springsteen in politics.

Listening without Hearing: The Politics of Lyrics?

One often unrecognized way in which Bruce Springsteen's music and all popular music can be political stems from a common failing in the way most of us listen to musical lyrics or in fact don't listen to such lyrics. Most people, more than 60 percent, according to one estimate, listen to rock and roll without paying any attention at all to the lyrics (Gracyk 65). This suggests, of course, that many listeners of popular music and/or of Springsteen might not ever become cognizant of the political nature of the lyrics or, for that matter, of any message reflected in the lyrics. To say that many people are oblivious to the themes and messages in music, Springsteen's included, is not to say, however, that these themes and messages do not exist. More careful listening—perhaps a listening associated with treating these lyrics as a primary and fundamental text for a college class in which the instructor can offer helpful insights and direction—can bring these themes and messages to the surface. Parenthetically, it should be noted that in my class I require each student to have in front of them a lyric sheet which they can consult as we listen to an extensive array of Springsteen's albums.

This same general ignoring of the lyrics in popular music on the part of many also enables any potential message manipulators to more easily interpret the lyrics of rock to support or otherwise reinforce their agenda and this, of course, can also be political. Manipulating messages, of course, forms a significant part of contemporary political life, with its attention to propaganda, "spin," and sound bites.

As most Springsteen fans know, Ronald Reagan, whether intentionally or not, was one of these people. He once said, of course, that the Springsteen song, "Born in the USA," conveyed a "message of hope" (qtd in Alterman, *Ain't No Sin* 159). And while there is at least a spark of hope in this song, as there are in most Springsteen treatments, one must note that if Reagan had ever really listened to and, indeed, heard the lyrics of "Born in the USA," he would have realized that Springsteen is hardly focused on hope. To the contrary, Springsteen, through the voice of a disillusioned Vietnam veteran, is seemingly indicting the United States for its alleged racist and ill-conceived war against the Vietnamese and for its deplorable treatment of returning Vietnam veterans.

Note the following words that start the song: "Born down in a dead man's town / The first kick I took was when I hit the ground / You end up like a dog that's been beat too much / Till you spend half your life just covering up." This is hardly the upbeat vision of hope and pride Reagan sought to embody. Springsteen tellingly and politically notes that the young Americans who fought and died in this war were not generally the children of the wealthy elite, but rather the sons and daughters of the working class and the poor. The United States' criminal justice system often cut a deal with these unfortunate souls by offering them a position in the military in lieu of a prison sentence. Springsteen conveys this by noting that the veteran in "Born in the USA," "[g]ot into a little hometown jam / So they put a rifle in my hand / Sent me off to a foreign land / To go and kill the yellow man." Also note that the returning veteran can find neither personally nor financially rewarding work in the American system even a decade after returning from the Vietnam War. Springsteen tells us in words which Reagan, and many others, never heard that the veteran, who served his country well, now has "[n]owhere to run, ain't got nowhere to go."

Springsteen has since testified to his belated realization that at times the message of his lyrics can get distorted or lost in the beat and rhythm of his music. After the tremendous success of Springsteen's release of "Born in the USA," several youngsters decked out as "The Boss," likely in denim jackets, jeans, and cool bandanas, did some Halloween "trick or treating" at the Springsteens' residence. Springsteen has reported that when he answered the door, these ersatz E Streeters would greet him with triumphantly raised fists and a resounding refrain of "I was born in the USA." The real "Boss" could not resist teasingly but affectionately challenging them to sing the next line of the song. Not unexpectedly, few if any of the miniature Bruce-look-a-likes knew any lyrics of the song beyond "I was born in the USA" (Springsteen, *Songs* 164). No doubt, this and similar events and, of course, the notorious Reagan misinterpretation have taught Springsteen something about the reception of his music and the clarity of his message, political or otherwise. He understands now that the message of his lyrics, however straightforward, can be significantly influenced by the way in which the song is presented above and beyond the lyrics. As a wiser Springsteen, post-"Born in the USA," put it, "A songwriter writes to be understood. Is the way you choose to present your music its politics? Is the sound and form your song takes its content? … I learned a lesson about how pop and pop image is received" (*Songs* 164).

The "Walk Tall" course highlights three significant sub-themes associated with the overarching theme of personal political development. These sub-themes are alienation, individualism, and love. Springsteen's writing about the theme of personal political development can help in the crucial quest for self-understanding and political effectiveness. Political scientists have long associated both the extent and success of one's involvement in politics with one's so-called sense of political efficacy—the degree to which one feels that one can influence the political setting (Edwards *et al.* 277). And because the "Walk Tall" course is offered primarily to young college students who are likely confronting critical identity concerns at one of life's often perplexing crossroads, Springsteen's message can be especially meaningful and beneficial.

The three noted sub-themes roughly correspond to the feelings and experiences people often confront in critical stages in human development (Erikson 55-82, Nussbaum, *Cultivating Humanity* 60, Primeaux 1-15 *passim*). In the adolescent stage, humans are generally self-absorbed in attempting to discover just who they are and, in that daunting self-discovery process, often experience alienation and confusion as well as indifference to concerns beyond themselves. Alienation can best be described as a feeling of being detached or withdrawn from one's society. After this stage, adolescents can advance to a young adulthood stage where, as individuals, they attempt to make their own impact on the external world in many diverse ways, including, of course, through personal achievement. In the adult stage, well-adjusted individuals can, at least ideally, become capable of establishing genuinely loving and healthy relationships with an ever-widening circle of people. Despite the seemingly lock-step nature of these stages, people do not inevitably or easily pass through them like turnstiles at a subway station. Life is not so neat and tidy. Concerns about alienation, individuality, and love endure. And so, even while Springsteen's lyrics can be seen to reflect his own passage through these stages in the traditional chronological order—and, for example, the lyrics of *Tunnel of Love* can easily be seen to express a more mature view of life and love than *Born to Run*—it should not be surprising to find these sub-themes present in the earliest, as well as the latest, of Springsteen's work.

Adolescence: Alienation, Loneliness, Fear, and Confusion

Springsteen's lyrics often reflect the alienation, loneliness, fear, and confusion prominent in adolescence. The alienated teenager of "Growin' Up" not only strolls "all alone through a fallout zone" but, when asked to "sit down," he must "stand up." The autobiographical "Bad Scooter" (Bruce Springsteen) of "Tenth Avenue Freeze-Out" finds that while the "whole world's walking pretty," he's still "searching for his groove." Springsteen's young and lost people, insecure in their own identity, can be without a clue in trying to comprehend significant political forces shaping their environment and, like the struggling souls of "Badlands," can get "caught in a cross fire that [they] don't understand."

Two of Springsteen's earlier and most famous songs, "Thunder Road" and "Born to Run," reflect the seemingly universal frustrating moods associated with adolescence. The young and confused lover of "Thunder Road" pleads with his girlfriend, Mary, not to "turn [him] home again" because he "just can't face [himself] alone again"—a clear cry of alienation and loneliness. He also confesses his own fear about going out on the mysterious and unknown highway of life, Thunder Road, seeing it as "[l]ying out there like a killer in the sun" not unlike a rattlesnake in the afternoon heat waiting to strike, in a deadly instant, youthful and inexperienced prey such as Bruce and Mary.

In class, I particularly stress the gender equality in the lyrics of "Thunder Road." In this context, these lyrics help suggest that the themes of alienation, loneliness, fear, and confusion are universal human concerns shared by both genders in their adolescent years, if not throughout their lives. For example, Springsteen notes that Mary is not a striking, drop-dead gorgeous Angelina Jolie-type. She is just a regular everyday young woman who, as Springsteen tells us, "ain't a beauty," but she's "alright." But Springsteen notes that just as Mary is nothing special, neither is he, describing himself as "not a hero" and as one who can only offer Mary the redemption that lies "beneath this dirty hood." Equality of the sexes is also keenly seen in Springsteen's pledge that he will not be Mary's knight in shining armor nor will he will put her on a pedestal like some fragile doll. Their relationship is one approaching equality. He tells her: "[m] car's out back / If you're ready to take that long walk / From your front porch to my front seat / The door's open but the ride it ain't free." I also highlight the classic final line of "Thunder Road" in which Springsteen signals the way in which many alienated young people feel about the confines and restrictions of the hometown in which they were raised. Although many of us come to love our hometown as we age, as adolescents, we are bound to see it as the main character of "Thunder Road" does: "It's a town full of losers / And I'm pullin' out of here to win."

"Born to Run," another Springsteen anthem, is a yawping call to all lost, confused, and scared young people. Springsteen is keenly aware that troubled adolescents might often feel that fleeing from their responsibilities and embracing the escape promised by a car and the open road remain their only hope of deliverance and salvation. Note the lyrics of a typical but fitting teenage drama and exaggeration in "Born to Run":

> Baby this town rips the bones from your back
> It's a death trap, it's a suicide rap
> We gotta get out while we're young
> 'Cause tramps like us, baby, we were born to run.

Notice also that these runners just want to run. They really have no idea where they are going. There is no mature plan beyond flight in "Born to Run," a realization Springsteen has sagely brought to the attention of audiences in his later years. See, for example, his introduction to an acoustic version of "Born to Run" ("Born to Run" (Acoustic)).

Because the students often perceive their very own feelings about adolescence articulated in Springsteen's lyrics, a common bond soon seems to connect them.[1] One student attributed this connection to her finding that Springsteen's lyrics can "often parallel meanings in each of our lives." Assessing the lyrics of Springsteen's "Wild Billy's Circus Story," another student took some comfort in the fact that "like the individuals of the circus, Springsteen often felt like an outsider, mainly when he was younger." Another seemingly, if, hopefully only momentarily, alienated class participant confided, "I want to be Mary and jump in his [Bruce's] car and ride off down Thunder Road. Who knows what lies ahead but it can't get much worse or disappointing." Another student, obviously acquainted with the struggles of adolescence, succinctly noted the fear and confusion she was confronting at this stage in her life: "I am at the point where I have to choose where to drive; so "Thunder Road" is a relevant song. There is a large level of uncertainty when you are in your early twenties, and this is accompanied by fear."

Young Adulthood: Individualism and Fighting Back

In a second stage of psychological/political development, adolescents begin to advance to a young adulthood level where, as developing individuals, they begin to find themselves and make their own impact on the external world. Springsteen's lyrics emphasize this theme of individuality, especially in the form of self-assertion and fighting back. The troubled, out-of-step young man of "Growin Up" glimpses at least a ray of hope in his ability to find "the key to the universe in the engine of an old parked car." In "New York City Serenade," Springsteen advises that those who can "walk tall" will best traverse the mean streets of life. In this context, to "walk tall" signifies the self-assertion of either truly being proud and unafraid or, at least, trying to appear that way and pulling it off. Asserting individuality through achievement is clearly evident in "Thunder Road" as the young man expresses personal pride in learning "how to make it [his guitar] talk." The empowerment associated with finding one's individuality is also reflected in "Tenth Avenue Freeze-Out"'s once alienated Bad Scooter now confidently empowered to "bust this city in half." Developing one's individualism, one's unique talents and abilities, is politically significant because such development strengthens a person's own sense of political efficacy and can both enable and embolden him or her to fight to shape the world to reflect his or her own hopes and dreams. This phenomenon in vividly portrayed in Springsteen's "Badlands," "Racing in the Street," and "Darkness on the Edge of Town."

In "Badlands," the escapist running away of "Thunder Road" and "Born to Run" seemingly end, and Springsteen's maturing protagonist no longer meekly and passively succumbs to, or flees from, life's troubles. Now, he stands and fights

---

[1]   Please note that all references to students' responses to Springsteen's lyrics are taken from course journals or essays. The writers have not been identified for reasons of privacy.

back more maturely against perceived evils. Rather than fleeing these troubles, he now wants to defiantly "spit in the face of these badlands." And he will no longer run but stand and confront the evils of the world. As Springsteen states, "Badlands you gotta live it everyday / Let the broken hearts stand / For the price you've gotta pay / We'll keep pushin' till it's understood / And these Badlands start treating us good." I also stress the fact that in "Badlands," Springsteen begins to convey a more generalized, if oversimplified, version of the nature of traditional politics in the United States: "Poor man wanna be rich / Rich man wanna be king / And a king ain't satisfied / Till he rules everything."

In "Racing in the Street," Springsteen tells us that people who never learn to follow their own individualistic spirit will likely be beaten down by life. These souls, no matter what their age, will, according to Springsteen, "start dying little by little, piece by piece." On the other hand, those maturing individuals with a well-developing sense of self will more likely be able to withstand even the backbreaking and dispiriting work they might be forced to endure in the often unforgiving American political/economic system. Their individualistic passion, in Springsteen's metaphoric words, will often liberate them by enabling them to "come home from work and wash up / And go racin' in the street." And he offers a universal call to youth to not immaturely run away or passively accept their plight in life, but to fight back against system-imposed limitations. There clearly is political meaning, if not an outright rebellious and defiant warning, in the final stanza: "Tonight, tonight, the highway's bright / Out of our way, Mister, you best keep / 'Cause summer's here and the time is right / For racin' in the street."

And finally, the determination to fight back is clearly seen in the protagonist of "Darkness on the Edge of Town." Springsteen suggests that even for those who try to run away from life, from their roots, from themselves, there will always be a reckoning with the pain and sorrow of life. He metaphorically describes this reckoning as the "darkness on the edge of town." And what does one do when one confronts that inevitable darkness? Immature, insufficiently politically developed people try to escape from assuming personal responsibility for the quality of their lives by resorting to flight and avoidance and even death, but such an approach is not for mature, politically conscious individuals. They bravely go out to confront the danger directly, taking personal responsibility for those aspects of their lives subject to their control. As Springsteen notes:

> Tonight I'll be on that hill 'cause I can't stop
> I'll be on that hill with everything I got
> Lives on the line where dreams are found and lost.
> I'll be there on time and I'll pay the cost
> For wanting things that can only be found
> In the darkness on the edge of town.

Students in the class clearly see their own quest for individualism and self-actualization reflected in Springsteen's lyrics. One astutely noted in her journal:

"You have to make yourself happy. You have to love yourself and fight for yourself. Your work or partner can add happiness but in the end it's just you and so you better like who you are." Similarly, another student, employing Springsteen's favorite metaphors, wrote: "This is the point where I am supposed to figure out how to make my guitar talk. There are many roads I can take. I think the point is I at least have to try one road, rather than stay stagnant."

Adulthood: Expanding Circles of Love

In a third stage of mature or adult political/psychological development, well-adjusted individuals become capable of looking and loving beyond themselves. They can begin to establish genuinely loving relationships with an ever-widening circle of people and communities. Beyond the most important love of self, the sub-theme of mature love appears in Springsteen's lyrics in at least four related forms. These involve love of a partner, friends, children, and community. The first of these, romantic love, is a common and prevalent theme in popular music, and Springsteen has written his share of these romantic songs. One of my favorites in this genre is Springsteen's "If I Should Fall Behind," which I present to the class. In this song, Springsteen openly pledges his mature commitment to stay by his partner's, his soul-mate's, side throughout their life together, no matter what troubles befall them. His pledge is simple but profound: "I'll wait for you / And should I fall behind / Wait for me." The song represents the beauty reflected in the intimate and unqualified love between a couple. And yet, this song becomes even more poignant and powerful when, in performance, Springsteen and the E Street Band, including Bruce's spouse, Patti Scialfa, turn it into a celebration not simply of the love between a man and a woman, but of the love that can also exist among good friends.

Springsteen's lyrics of love, romance, and friendship reflect his belief that in a genuine loving relationship, all lovers gain a strength that is so much greater than the sum of their parts. This is Springsteen's way of suggesting that it is the inherent power of love of a partner and/or friends that enable lovers and friends together to conquer forces that would more easily defeat them as separate individuals. Such empowerment is, of course, interpersonal and political. A few years ago Springsteen made a generally unnoticed gesture that reflected his mature growth as a male. This gesture, in my view, wonderfully testifies to his unending respect of, and sensitivity toward, two people he has loved: Julianne Phillips and Patti Scialfa. Knowing how seriously Springsteen approaches his lyrics and how rarely he alters them once they have been recorded, it is a significant event, at least for Springsteen junkies like me, when he does make a lyric change. At a May 19, 2005, Devils and Dust concert in New Jersey there definitely was a change of lyrics in Springsteen's rendition of "The Wish," a song dedicated to his mother. The original lyrics read in part: "Well, I found a girl of my own now, ma, I popped the question on your birthday" (*Tracks*). However, on that May night in New

Jersey, Springsteen sang the following, altered lyrics: "I have a girl of my own, Mom / Time just slips away."

There are probably many explanations for this change in lyrics. My own interpretation is that out of mature and sensitive consideration for the feelings of both Julianne Phillips, his first wife and the one to whom he "popped the question" on his mother's birthday, and for Patti Scialfa, his present wife and mother of his children, he changed these lyrics. Given the February 22, 1987, date of the original recording of "The Wish," for *Tracks*, a date several years *before* his 1991 marriage to Scialfa, the reference to "popping the question" can only be to Phillips. Still, and likely because that reference might painfully call to mind the unsuccessful Phillips and Springsteen marriage, the lyrics "popped the question on your birthday" were changed that night to "Time just slips away." I find that gesture to be not only very meaningful and touching, but also indicative of his commendable personal growth in becoming more and more cognizant of the feelings and presence of others—in this instance, both Phillips and Scialfa.

In "American Skin (41 Shots)," Springsteen draws upon the New York City's police's controversial and allegedly racially-tinged slaying of Amadou Diallo. He conveys, among other political concerns, a pragmatic warning to young minorities that they should "always be polite" to police authorities or run the risk of being "killed just for living in your American skin." Springsteen's apparent love of an ever-expanding community, a most mature political act, is reflected in "Land of Hope and Dreams." In this song, the unending struggle for equality for all people is epitomized in a simple train heading to a destination of sunshine and freedom and taking on all people. Fittingly, in an expansive view of community, Springsteen's train not only carries saints, winners, and kings, but also the more numerous and often more forgotten of us— sinners, losers, whores, gamblers, fools, and the broken-hearted.

Springsteen's album *The Rising* speaks even more directly to the politics of his expanding vision of community, and this vision is further reflected in his bold, fan-base-threatening involvement in the Kerry campaign and his speaking out more forcefully on matters associated with traditional politics. Please note that this conclusion does not necessarily rest on my agreement with the substance and direction of Springsteen's political involvement, but rather with the mature sense of responsibility he evinces in contributing thoughtfully to national and international political discourse. *The Rising*'s political dimensions are especially interesting for many reasons not the least of which is that many reviewers have not always grasped its political aspects. And, as explained below, this occurred, at least in part, because of a failure to truly understand the nature of politics. Too often, we only perceive politics as a mechanism for maintaining some civility in a world of fatally flawed, if not outright hostile, humans. Still, politics in its patterns of power, control, and authority of influence can also appeal to the higher and more noble attributes of human beings.

A major review in *Time* by Josh Tyrangiel concluded: "What's missing on *The Rising* is politics." To the contrary, *The Rising* is not only a respectful, rocking, and fitting testimony to the events of September 11, 2001, and its aftermath; it is also distinctly political. Yet, although the conclusion that *The Rising* lacks a political perspective is erroneous, it is, nonetheless, understandable. A common but critical mistake is to conclude that it is the sole or even primary nature of politics for some to employ power, influence, control or authority to achieve selfish or malevolent ends or to force others manipulatively, aggressively and, perhaps, duplicitously to do what they would not ordinarily choose to do. Power and its related terms can, however, also be used to attain benevolent ends as well as in assisting others to achieve goals in accordance with their hopes and dreams. People can be moved to action by appealing not only to their demons, but also to their better angels.

Springsteen's *The Rising* deftly avoids the politics of fear and hate, the politics of threatening to harm or otherwise bully or manipulate others. In the album, he refuses to pander to the reactionary Right's post-9/11 jingoistic and macho version of the politics of vengeance and retaliation, calling for the humiliation and extinction of Osama bin Laden, Al Qaeda, and perhaps Islam itself. On the other hand, he does not embrace the radical Left's dogmatic version of politics, tracing the events of September 11 to the greed, arrogance, and insensitivity of American imperialism and unilateralism. Springsteen eschews the political differences emphasized by each of these camps in order to emphasize our human similarities. In timely fashion, he offered the balm of the politics of love and understanding, the politics of human compassion and tolerance, the politics of the better angels that he trusts lie within the hearts of all of us. Even though Springsteen does not present a specific political blueprint on how to achieve the peaceful and just world community he envisions, he challenges listeners to never lose sight of this worthy goal.

The Rising features several notable illustrations of such themes as the politics of love and community, and a caring and compassionate humanity. There is Springsteen's caution against pursuing a knee-jerk, vengeful reaction to return hate for hate, violence for violence, terror for terror. In "Lonesome Day," he notes:

> Better ask questions before you start to shoot
> Deceit and betrayal's bitter fruit
> It's hard to swallow, come time to pay
> That taste on your tongue doesn't easily slip away.

Springsteen also asks us to forget past grudges, past hatreds, past killings employed by some to promote vengeful deeds that will cause still more pain, hatred and death. He urges us to seek peaceful solutions by consistently reminding us of the commonality of the human spirit. Interestingly, Springsteen's appeal, while often invoking a deity, is not made to a God or even gods in heaven, but rather to people on earth. In the fittingly titled "Worlds Apart," he notes:

> Sometimes the truth just ain't enough
> Or is it too much in times like this
> Let's throw the truth away, we'll find it in this kiss
> In your skin upon my skin, in the beating of our hearts
> May the living let us in before the dead tear us apart.

And in the bouncy "Let's Be Friends (Skin to Skin)," he endorses the politics of togetherness, cooperation, and community, forsaking the traditional politics of divisiveness, conflict, and hatred.

> The time has come to let the past be history
> Yeah, if we could just start talkin'
> …
> There's a lot of walls need tearing down
> Together we could take them down one by one.

The humanistic nature of the politics extolled in *The Rising* is evident in the album's most compelling, most significant song, "Paradise." Springsteen presents two people, one a Moslem, the other a Christian. Both have been victimized by the politics of hate. While the lyrics are, perhaps, intentionally ambiguous, it appears that the Moslem is a parent, spouse, or friend, left behind to mourn the death of a beloved female suicide bomber who has taken her own life and, likely, the lives of others. In the next verse, Springsteen introduces the widow of a Pentagon employee killed in the September 11 attack. While the Moslem and the Christian are separated by many miles and by different cultures and religions, Springsteen connects them through the commonality of human suffering and longing. Neither survivor can find solace in ethereal thoughts that his or her deceased loved one is now in some version of paradise. And even when they do gain a mystical glimpse of their departed, they see their eyes not reflecting peace but as being "as empty as paradise."

Springsteen seems to be suggesting that the power to bring about a loving global community in which such senseless deaths do not occur rests not with appeals to dogma or even to the Divine, but within the hearts and minds of humanity. However well-intentioned, appeals for a peaceful, loving, benevolent world community, made beyond our own sense of humanity, are likely doomed to fail. Springsteen suggests that unless we are willing to work toward that goal together and whether a divine force hears our prayers or not, the responsibility for a loving society rests with us. While never denying God's love and power, Springsteen calls upon us to accept primary human responsibility for making the world a safer, saner, and just place. Notably, the final verse of "Paradise" depicts an anguished survivor who is tempted to escape this responsibility and join a mourned loved one by drowning him or herself. He or she realizes the futility of this gesture and re-embraces life and the human condition of trying to make the best of an imperfect world.

I break above the waves
I feel the sun upon my face.

Springsteen is calling upon all of us to embrace life, our common humanity and each other. And that is distinctly and importantly political. I am confident, moreover, that the telling connection between themes in Springsteen's lyrics and personal political development and, especially, the thoughtful, provocative and politically sophisticated responses of the students on my course convey a hopeful promise that Springsteen will continue to make connections with today's and future generations. In so doing, their lives and communities, political or otherwise, will be enriched. Springsteen's lyrics can help inform attentive listeners that they are not alone in this world, that they possess precious and unique talents and abilities, that they can and should open their hearts to more and more love, and, perhaps most importantly, that they can be a political force in shaping their own lives and those of many others. Springsteen's lyrics can, indeed, teach what it means to be political in the best sense of that word.

Works Cited

Books and Articles

Adams, Nina S. "The Women Who Left Them Behind." *Give Peace a Chance: Exploring the Vietnam Antiwar Movement.* Ed. Melvin Small. Syracuse: Syracuse U P, 1992. 182-99.

Alterman, Eric. *It Ain't No Sin to be Glad You're Alive: The Promise of Bruce Springsteen.* Boston: Little, Brown and Company, 1999.

The American Heritage College Dictionary (AHD, Fourth Edition. Boston: Houghton Mifflin Company, 2002)

Anderson, David L. *The Columbia Guide to the Vietnam War.* New York: Columbia UP, 2002.

Appy, Christian G. *Working-Class War: American Combat Soldiers and Vietnam.* Chapel Hill: U of North Carolina P, 1993.

Arendt, Hannah. *The Human Condition.* Chicago: U of Chicago Press, 1958.

"The ARVN Recruit." *Uptight.* United States Army, Vietnam. Summer 1971.

Baker, Mark. *Nam: The Vietnam War in the Words of the Men and Women Who Fought There.* New York: Berkley, 1981.

Bakopoulos, Dean. *Please Don't Come Back from the Moon.* New York: Harcourt, 2005.

Baraka, Amiri. "The Meaning of Bruce." *Spin Magazine* Nov. 1985: 51, 80.

Baritz, Loren. *Backfire: A History of How American Culture Led Us Into Vietnam and Made Us Fight the Way We Did.* New York: Morrow, 1985.

Barol, Bill. "He's On Fire." *Newsweek* 5 Aug. 1985: 48-54.

———. "'Myths Keep Us Strangers': Springsteen On Love, Fear, and Rock and Roll." *Newsweek* 2 Nov. 1987: 76-78.

Bederman, Gail. *Manliness and Civilization: A Cultural History of Gender and Race in the United States, 1880-1917.* Chicago: U of Chicago P, 1995.

Beinart, Peter. "The War over Patriotism." *Time* 26 June, 2008. 18 Mar., 2009. <www.time.com/time/magazine/article/0,9171,1818195,00.html>.

Belafonte, Harry. *Very Best of Harry Belafonte.* RCA, 2001.

Bellah, Robert N., Richard Madsen, William M. Sullivan, and Ann Swidler. *Habits of the Heart.* Berkeley: U of California P, 1996.

Biblia Hebraica Stuttgartensia. ed. K. Kelliger and W. Rudolph. Stuttgart: Deutsche Bibelgesellschaft, 1977.

Binelli, Mark. "Bruce Springsteen's American Gospel." *Rolling Stone* 22 Aug. 2002: 62-68.

Binelli, Mark. "Bruce Springsteen's American Gospel." *Rolling Stone*. 22 Aug. 2002. RollingStone.com. 24 Mar. 2003. <www.rollingstone.com>.

Bissell, William Cunningham. "Engaging Colonial Nostalgia." *Cultural Anthropology* 20.2 (2005): 215-48.

Blair, I.V., C.M. Judd, and J.L. Fallman. "The Automaticity of Race and Afrocentric Facial Features in Social Judgments." *Journal of Personality and Social Psychology* 87 (2004): 763-78.

Bluestone, Barry. "Deindustrialization and Unemployment." *Deindustrialization and Plant Closure*. Ed. Paul D. Staudohar and Holly E. Brown. Lexington: Heath, 1987. 3-15.

Bly, Robert. "The Vietnam War and the Erosion of Male Confidence." *The Vietnam Reader*. Ed. Walter Capps. New York: Routledge, 1991. 82-86.

Bodnar, John. *Remaking America: Public Memory, Commemoration, and Patriotism in the Twentieth Century*. Princeton: Princeton UP, 1992.

Bonca, Cornel. "Save Me Somebody: Bruce Springsteen's Rock 'n' Roll Covenant." *Killing the Buddha* 29 July 2001. <killingthebuddha.com/mag/witness/save-me-somebody-bruce-springsteens-rock-n-roll-covenant>.

Bonetti, Kay. "An Interview with Richard Ford." In Guagliardo, *Conversations with Richard Ford* 21-38.

"Born in the USA." *The Vietnam Experience: A Concise Encyclopedia of American Literature, Songs, and Films*. Ed. Kevin Hillstrom and Laurie Collier Hillstrom. Westport: Greenwood, 1998. 43-50.

Boym, Svetlana. *The Future of Nostalgia*. New York: Basic Books, 2001.

Bunn, Austin. "Unarmed and Under Fire: An Oral History of Female Vietnam Vets." *Salon Magazine* 11 Nov. 1999. <www.salon.com/mwt/feature/1999/11/11/women/>.

Butsch, Richard. "Ralph, Fred, Archie, and Homer: Why Television Keeps Re-creating the White, Male Working-Class Buffoon." *Gender, Race, and Class in Media*. Ed. G. Dines and J. M. Humez. Thousand Oaks: Sage Publications, 2003. 575-85.

Caldwell, Gail. "The Sound of Success: Richard Ford Puts Each Sentence to the Test." In Guagliardo, *Conversations with Richard Ford* 44-48.

Cavicchi, Daniel. *Tramps Like Us: Music and Meaning among Springsteen Fans*. Oxford: Oxford UP, 1998.

Christgau, Robert. "Yes, There is a Rock-Critic Establishment (But is That Bad for Rock?)." *Village Voice* 26 Jan. 1976. <www.robertchristgau.com/xg/rock/critics-76.php>.

Christopher, Renny. "I Never Really Became a Woman Veteran Until I Saw the Wall." *Vietnam Generation* 1.3-4 (1989): 33-45.

Clark, Candace. *Misery and Company: Sympathy in Everyday Life*. Chicago: U of Chicago P, 1997.

Cobble, Dorothy Sue. *The Other Women's Movement: Workplace Justice and Social Rights in Modern America*. Princeton: Princeton UP, 2004.

Cocks, Jay. "Bruce Springsteen and the E Street Band Live—1975-1985." *Time* 10 Nov. 1986: 113.

———. Review of *Tunnel of Love*, by Bruce Springsteen. *Time* 12 Oct. 1987. <www.time.com/time/magazine/article/0,,965729,00.html>.

———. "Round the World, a Boss Boom: Springsteen Is Rock's Spirit In the Night." *Time* 26 Aug. 1985: 69-71.

Cohen, Lizabeth. *Making a New Deal: Industrial Workers in Chicago, 1919-1939*. Cambridge: Cambridge UP, 1990.

Coles, Robert. *Bruce Springsteen's America: The People Listening, A Poet Singing*. New York: Random House, 2003.

Cone, James H. "The Blues: A Secular Spiritual." *Write Me a Few of Your Lines: A Blues Reader*. Ed. Steven C. Tracy. Amherst: U of Massachusetts P, 1999. 231-51.

Coontz, Stephanie. *The Way We Never Were*. New York: Basic Books, 1992.

Corn, David, and Jefferson Morley. "Beltway Bandits: Springsteen's Freeze-Out." *The Nation* 23 Apr. 1988: 559.

Correll, J., B. Park, C. M. Judd, and B. Wittenbrink. "The Police Officers' Dilemma: Using Ethnicity to Disambiguate Potentially Threatening Individuals." *Journal of Personality and Social Psychology* 83 (2002): 1314-29.

Cotton, John "How Far Moses Judicialls Bind Massachusetts." In '*Moses his Judicials': Transactions of the Massachusetts Historical Society*. Second Series, XVI. Ed. Worthington C. Ford.

———. *The Way of the Churches of Christ in New England, Measured by the Golden Reed of the Sanctuary*, London: Matthew Simmons, 1645.

Cotton, John "The Way of Life." *The Way of Faith*. New York: AMS Press, Inc., 1983.

Cowie, Jefferson. "Nixon's Class Struggle: Romancing the New Right Worker," *Labor History* 43 (2002): 257-83.

———. "'A One-Sided Class War': Rethinking Doug Fraser's 1978 Resignation from the Labor-Management Group." *Labor History* 44.3 (2003): 307-14.

———. "'Vigorously Left, Right, and Center': The Crosscurrents of Working-Class America in the 1970s." *America in the Seventies*. Ed. Beth Bailey and David Farber. Lawrence: UP of Kansas, 2004. 75-106.

Cowie, Jefferson, and Joseph Heathcott, eds. *Beyond the Ruins: The Meanings of Deindustrialization*. Ithaca: Cornell UP, 2003.

Crane, Bob. "A Place to Stand: A Guide to Bruce Springsteen's Sense of Place." In Sawyers, *Racing in the Street* 337-446.

———. *A Place to Stand: A Guide to Bruce Springsteen's Sense of Place*. Baltimore: Palace Books, 2002.

Cullen, Jim. *Born in the USA: Bruce Springsteen and the American Tradition*. New York: HarperCollins, 1997.

Dahl, Robert. *Modern Political Analysis*. 5th ed. New Jersey: Prentice Hall, 1991.

The Daily Show with Jon Stewart, MSNBC. 19 Mar. 2009. <www.comedycentral. com/>.

Davis, David Brion. *Inhuman Bondage: The Rise and Fall of Slavery in the New World*. Oxford: Oxford UP, 2006.

Davis, Fred. *Yearning for Yesterday: A Sociology of Nostalgia*. New York: Free Press, 1979.

Dawidoff, Nicholas. "The Pop Populist." In Sawyers, *Racing in the Street* 246-65.

De Capite, Michael. *Maria*. New York: John Day, 1943.

Dean, Robert D. *Imperial Brotherhood: Gender and the Making of Cold War Foreign Policy*. Amherst: U of Massachusetts P, 2001.

Denton, Daniel. *A Brief Description of New York, formerly called New Netherlands*. London 1670.

Devine, P.G. "Stereotypes and Prejudice: Their Automatic and Controlled Components." *Journal of Personality and Social Psychology* 56 (1989): 5-18.

Dewey, John. *Art as Experience*. New York: Capricorn, 1958.

Di Donato, Pietro. *Christ in Concrete*. Ed. Fred Gardaphé. New York: Signet Classic, 1993.

"Discography: Bruce Springsteen [Artist page]." *Rolling Stone Magazine*, n.d. Web. 10 Oct. 2010. <www.rollingstone.com/music/artists/bruce-springsteen>.

Duffy, John, ed. *Bruce Springsteen: In His Own Words*. London: Omnibus, 1993.

Dunbar, Paul Laurence. *The Life and Works of Paul Laurence Dunbar*. New York, Kraus, 1971.

Duncan, Glynda. "Author Returns to Native State." In Guagliardo, *Conversations with Richard Ford* 3-6.

Duncan, Robert. "Lawdamercy! Springsteen Saves! Testimony from the Howling Dog Choir." *Creem* Oct. 1978: 38-43.

Eberhardt, J.L., P.G. Davies, V.J. Purdie-Vaughns, and S.L. Johnson. "Perceived Stereotypicality of Black Defendants Predicts Capital-Sentencing Outcomes." *Psychological Science* 17 (2006): 383-86.

Edelman, Bernard. *Dear America: Letters Home from Vietnam*. New York: Norton, 1985.

Edsall, Thomas Byrne, and Mary D. *Chain Reaction: The Impact of Race, Rights, and Taxes on American Politics*. New York: Norton, 1991.

Edwards III, George C., Martin P. Wattenberg, Robert L. Lineberry. *Government in America: People, Politics, and Policy*. Study and brief seventh ed. New York: Pearson Longman, 2004.

Edwards, Thomas R. "After You've Gone." *The New York Review of Books* 18 Jul. 2002: 53-54.

Emerson, Ralph Waldo. *Self-Reliance and Other Essays*. New York: Dover, 1993.

Enloe, Cynthia. *Bananas, Beaches, and Bases: Making Feminist Sense of International Politics*. Berkeley: U of California P, 2000.

———. *Does Khaki Become You? The Militarization of Women's Lives*. London: Pandora Press, 1988.

Erikson, Erik H. *The Life Cycle Completed: A Review*. New York: Norton, 1982.

Faulkner, William. *Sanctuary*. New York: Vintage International, 1993.

Feather, Leonard. *Jazz*. Los Angeles: Trend Press, 1959.

Fein, S., and S.J. Spencer. "Prejudice as Self-Image Maintenance: Affirming the Self through Derogating Others." *Journal of Personality and Social Psychology* 73 (1997): 31-44.

Fein, S., E. Hoshino-Brown, P.G. Davies, and S.J. Spencer. "Self-Image Maintenance Goals and Sociocultural Norms in Motivated Social Perception." *Motivated Social Perception: The Ontario Symposium.* Ed. S.J. Spencer, S. Fein, M.P. Zanna, and J.M. Olson. Mahwah, NJ: Erlbaum, 2003. 21-44.

Fisher, David Hackett. "Resurrecting the Revolution." *Boston Globe* 22 May 2005. 1-5   <articles.boston.com/2005-05-22/ae/29212049_1_david-mccullough-simon-schuster-george-iii/2>.

Fitzgerald, Francis Scott. *The Great Gatsby.* New York: Simon and Schuster, 1996.

Flippo, Chet. "Bruce Springsteen: A Rock and Roll Evangelist for Our Times." *Musician* 73 (1984): 54-55.

Folks, Jeffrey J. "Richard Ford's Postmodern Cowboys." In Guagliardo, *Conversations with Richard Ford* 141-56.

Ford, Richard. "The Boss Observed." *Esquire* Dec. 1985: 326-29.

———. *Independence Day.* New York: Contemporaries, 1996.

———. *A Multitude of Sins.* New York: Knopf, 2002.

———. *Rock Springs.* New York: Vintage, 1988.

———. *Wildlife.* New York: Atlantic Monthly, 1990.

Frank, Thomas. *What's the Matter with Kansas?* New York: Metropolitan, 2004.

Fraser, Steve. "The Labor Question." *The Rise and Fall of the New Deal Order: 1930-1980.* Ed. Steve Fraser and Gary Gerstle. Princeton: Princeton UP, 1989. 55-85.

Frisch, Michael H. "Prismatics, Multivalence, and Other Riffs on the Millennial Moment." *American Quarterly* 53.2 (2001): 193-231.

Frith, Simon. "The Real Thing—Bruce Springsteen." In Sawyers, *Racing in the Street* 130-39.

Frow, John. *Time and Commodity Culture: Essays in Cultural Theory and Postmodernity.* Oxford: Oxford UP, 1997.

Fuller, Robert C. *Spiritual, But Not Religious: Understanding Unchurched America.* Oxford: Oxford UP, 2001.

Garman, Bryan K. "The Ghost of History: Bruce Springsteen, Woody Guthrie, and the Hurt Song." *Popular Music and Society* 20 (1996): 69-120.

———. *A Race of Singers: Whitman's Working-Class Hero from Guthrie to Springsteen.* Chapel Hill: U of North Carolina P, 2000.

"The GI Press." Publication details unknown.

"GI Town Part I." *Fatigue Press*, August 1971.

Gilmore, Mikal. *Nightbeat: A Shadow History of Rock and Roll.* New York: Doubleday, 1998.

———. "The Voice of the Eighties." *Rolling Stone* 15 Nov. 1990. <www.rollingstone.com>.

Goodman, Fred. *Mansion on the Hill: Dylan, Young, Geffen, Springsteen and the Head-On Collision of Rock and Commerce.* New York: Random House, 1997.

"Gooks and Broads." *Fatigue Press*, Issue 11 (date missing).

Gorz, André. *Farewell to the Working Class: An Essay on Post-Industrial Socialism*. London: Pluto, 1982.

Govier, Trudy "The Right to Eat and the Duty to Work." *Philosophy of the Social Sciences* 5 (1975): 125-43.

Gracyk, Theodore. *Rhythm and Noise: Aesthetics of Rock*. Durham: Duke UP, 1996.

Greeley, Andrew M. "The Catholic Imagination of Bruce Springsteen." *America* 6 Feb. 1988: 110-15.

Grondahl, Paul. "'Poet of Everyday Life' Has a Romantic Side." Guagliardo, *Conversations with Richard Ford* 66-70.

Guagliardo, Huey, ed. *Conversations with Richard Ford*. Jackson: UP of Mississippi, 2001.

———. "Introduction." In Guagliardo, *Conversations with Richard Ford*. xi-xvii.

———. "The Marginal People in the Novels of Richard Ford." In Guagliardo, *Conversations with Richard Ford*. 3-32.

Gunderson, Edna. "Devils in the Details." *The Asbury Park Press* 15 May 2005. <www.app.com/apps/pbcs.c11/article?date=20050515+category+ENT+ART No5051>. [Website no longer available.]

Guthrie, Woody. *Pastures of Plenty—A Self-Portrait: The Unpublished Writings of An American Folk Hero*. Ed. Harold Leventhal and Dave Marsh. New York: HarperCollins, 1990.

———. "This Train Is Bound for Glory." Lyrics. *www.able2know.com*. 18 Nov. 2002. <www.able2know.com/-forums/about1143-0-asc-10.html>.

Hagen, Mark. "Meet the New Boss." *The Guardian* 17 Jan. 2009. <www.guardian.co.uk/music/2009/jan/18/bruce-springsteen-interview>.

Hagen, Steve. *Buddhism Plain and Simple*. New York: Broadway, 1997.

Halle, David. *America's Working Man: Work, Home and Politics among Blue Collar Property Owners*. Chicago: U of Chicago P, 1984.

Hamington, Maurice. *Hail Mary? The Struggle for Ultimate Womanhood in Catholicism*. New York: Routledge, 1995.

Harper, Ralph. *Nostalgia*. Cleveland: Case Western Reserve UP, 1966.

Hawthorne, Nathaniel. *The Scarlet Letter: Complete, Authoritative Text with Biographical Background and Critical History plus Essays from Five Contemporary Critical Perspectives with Introductions and Bibliographies*. Ed. Ross C. Murfin. Boston: Bedford Books of St Martin's Press, 1991.

Henke, James. "Human Touch—Bruce Springsteen: The Rolling Stone Interview." *Rolling Stone* 6 Aug. 1992. <www.rollingstone.com>.

Herr, Michael. *Dispatches*. London: Pan, 1978.

Hobsbawm, Eric. "Inventing Traditions." *The Invention of Tradition*. Ed. E. Hobsbawm and T. Ranger. Cambridge: Cambridge UP, 1983. 1-15.

Hobson, Fred. "*The Sportswriter*. Post-Faulkner, Post-Southern?" In Guagliardo, *Conversations with Richard Ford* 83-96.

Hochschild, Adam. *Bury the Chains: Prophets and Rebels in the Fight to Free an Empire's Slaves*. Boston: Houghton Mifflin, 2005.

Hochschild, Arlie. "Let Them Eat War." *Mother Jones* 8 Oct. 2003. <www. higherintellect.info/texts/politics/Hochschild%20Arlie%20-%20Let%20 Them%20Eat%20War.pdf>.

Hoganson, Kristin. *Fighting for American Manhood: How Gender Politics Provoked the Spanish-American and Philippine-American Wars*. New Haven: Yale UP, 1998.

Huyssen, Andreas. "Present Pasts: Media, Politics, Amnesia." *Public Culture* 12.1 (2000): 21-38.

The Impressions, "People Get Ready." Lyrics. 30 Aug. 2005. <www.lyricsxp.com/ lyrics/p/people_get_ready_the_-impressions.html>.

Jeffords, Susan. *The Remasculinization of America: Gender and the Vietnam War.* Bloomington: Indiana UP, 1989.

Jensen, Robert. "Empathy is the First Ingredient." *The Progressive* Oct. 1 2005. 1-2. <www.alternet.org/media-culture/26190/>.

Jonas, Gerald. *Dancing*. New York: Harry N. Abrams, Inc, 1992.

Jordan, James. "Calvinism and 'The Judicial Law of Moses': An Historical Survey." *Journal of Christian Reconstruction* 5 (1978). <www.reformed.org/ ethics/Jordan_judicial_laws_Moses.html#fnB53>.

Kassin, Saul, Steven Fein, and Hazel Rose Markus. *Social Psychology*. 8th ed. Belmont, CA: Wadsworth, 2010.

Kennedy, John F. "The Vigor We Need." *Sports Illustrated* 16 Jul. 1962: 12-15.

Ketwig, John. "… and a Hard Rain Fell." *Unwinding the Vietnam War: From War into Peace*. Ed. Reese Williams. Seattle: Real Comet, 1987. 10-37.

Kidd, Sue Monk. "A Common Heart." *The Washington Post* 4 Dec. 2005. <www. washingtonpost.com/wp-dyn/content/article/2005/12/01/AR2005120100929. html>.

Klein, Joe. *Woody Guthrie: A Life*. New York: Knopf, 1980.

Kobre, Michael. "'On Blessing Avenue': Faith, Language and the Search for Meaning in the Works of Bruce Springsteen and Walker Percy." *Reading the Boss: Interdisciplinary Approaches to the Works of Bruce Springsteen*. Ed. Roxanne Harde and Irwin Streight. Lanham: Lexington Books, 2010. 41-52.

Kornfield, Jack. "No Self or True Self?" In Smith, *Radiant Mind* 281-86.

Korstad, Robert, and Nelson Lichtenstein. "Opportunities Found and Lost." *Journal of American History* 75 (1988): 786-811.

Koscielski, Frank. *Divided Loyalties: American Unions and the Vietnam War.* New York: Garland, 1999.

Kovic, Ron. *Born on the Fourth of July*. New York: McGraw-Hill, 1976.

Lakoff, George. *Moral Politics*. Chicago: U of Chicago P, 1996.

———. *The Political Brain*. Penguin. 2008.

Lawson, Jacqueline. "'She's a Pretty Woman ... for a Gook': The Misogyny of the Vietnam War." *Fourteen Landing Zones: Approaches to Vietnam War Literature.* Ed. Philip K. Jason. Iowa City: U of Iowa P, 1991. 15-37.

Leach, John. "Bruce Springsteen—On the Tracks." *Brucebase* 10 Mar. 2005. <www.brucebase.shet-land.co.uk/1.htm>. [Website no longer available.]

Leder, Priscilla. "Men with Women: Gender Relations in Richard Ford's *Rock Springs.*" In Guagliardo, *Conversations with Richard Ford* 97-120.

Lee, Harper. *To Kill a Mockingbird.* New York: Warner. 1960.

Leeming, David and Jake Page. *Goddess: Myths of the Female Divine.* New York: Oxford UP, 1994.

Levitin, Daniel J. *The World in Six Songs.* New York: Dutton. 2008.

Levy, Joe. "Bruce Springsteen: The *Rolling Stone* Interview." *Rolling Stone* 1038 (1 Nov. 2007): 50-52, 53-54, 56

Levy, Peter B. The New Left and Labor in the 1960s. Urbana: U of Illinois P, 1994, 46-63.

Lichtenstein, Nelson. *State of the Union.* Princeton: Princeton UP, 2002.

Lifton, Robert Jay. *Home from the War: Learning from Vietnam Veterans.* Boston: Beacon Press, 1992.

Lipsitz, George. *Rainbow at Midnight: Labor and Culture in the 1940s.* Urbana: U of Illinois P, 1994.

———. "Dilemmas of Beset Nationhood." *Bonds of Affection: Americans Define Their Patriotism.* Ed. John Bodnar. Princeton: Princeton UP, 1996. 251-73.

Loder, Kurt. "Artist of the Year: Bruce!" *Rolling Stone* 28 Feb. 1984. <www.rollingstone.com>.

———. "Born Again—Bruce Springsteen: The Rolling Stone Interview." *Rolling Stone* 6 Dec. 1984. <www.rollingstone.com>.

———. "Bruce!" *Bruce Springsteen: The Rolling Stone Files.* New York: Hyperion, 1996. 167-69.

Lucadamo, Kathleen. "Prof Offers Bruce 101." *New York Daily News* 6 Mar. 2005: 30.

Maclear, James "New England and the Fifth Monarchy: The Quest for the Millennium in Early American Puritanism." *Puritan New England: Essays on Religion, Society, and Culture.* Ed. A. T. Vaughan and F. J. Bermer. New York: St Martin's Press, 1977.

Maddox, K.B. "Perspectives on Racial Phenotypicality Bias." *Personality and Social Psychology Review* 8 (2004): 383-401.

Maharidge, Dale, and Michael Williamson. *Homeland.* New York: Seven Stories, 2004.

Mangione, Jerre. *Mount Allegro. A Memoir of Italian American Life.* Syracuse: Syracuse UP, 1998.

Marcus, Greil. *Invisible Republic.* New York: Henry Holt, 1997.

———. Rev. of *Born to Run*, by Bruce Springsteen. *Rolling Stone* 9 Oct. 1975. <www.rolling-stone.com>.

Marino, Gigi. "Angelina." *The Dream Book: An Anthology of Writings by Italian American Women*. Ed. Helen Barolini. New York: Shocken, 1985. 101-105.

Marsh, Dave. *Born to Run: The Bruce Springsteen Story*. New York: Dell, 1981.

———. *Bruce Springsteen on Tour, 1968-2005*. New York: Bloomsbury, 2006.

———. "Bruce Springsteen Raises Cain." *Rolling Stone* 24 Aug. 1978. <www.rollingstone.com>.

———. *Bruce Springsteen: Two Hearts: The Definitive Biography*. New York: Routledge, 2004.

———. *Glory Days: Bruce Springsteen in the 1980s*. New York: Pantheon, 1987.

———. "A Rock Star Is Born." *Rolling Stone* 25 Sept. 1975. <www.rollingstone.com>.

Marx, Karl, and Engels Friedrich. *The Marx-Engels Reader*. Ed. Robert C. Tucker. New York: Norton, 1978.

Mason, Bobbie Ann. *In Country*. New York: Harper and Row, 1985.

Massey, Douglas S. *Categorically Unequal*. New York: Russell Sage, 2007.

Mazziotti Gillan, Maria. "Angelina." *From the Margins: Writings in Italian Americana*. Ed. Anthony Tamburri, Fred Gardaphé, and Paolo Giordano. West Lafayette: Purdue UP, 1991. 86-88.

McCarthy, Kate. "Deliver Me from Nowhere: Bruce Springsteen and the Myth of the American Promised Land." *God in Details: American Religion in Popular Culture*. Ed. Eric Michael Mazur and Kate McCarthy. New York: Routledge, 2001. 23-45.

Milliken, Jennifer, and David Sylvan. "Soft Bodies, Hard Targets, and Chic Theories: U.S. Bombing Policy in Indochina." *Journal of International Studies* 25.2 (1996): 321-59.

Mills, C. Wright. "Letter to the New Left." *New Left Review* Sept./Oct. 1960: 22.

Morden, Bettie J. *The Women's Army Corps, 1945-1978*. Washington, DC: Government Printing Office, 2000. <www.army.mil/cmhpg/books/wac>.

Morley, Jefferson. "Darkness On the Edge of the Shining City: Bruce Springsteen and the End of Reaganism." *The New Republic* 23 Mar. 1987. <www.tnr.com/article/books-and-arts/75367/darkness-the-edge-the-shining-city>.

———. "The Phenomenon." *Rolling Stone* 10 Oct. 1985: 74-75.

Morris, Richard. *Rethinking Social Welfare: Why Care for the Stranger?* New York: Longman, 1986.

Moser, Richard R. *The New Winter Soldiers: GI and Veteran Dissent During the Vietnam Era*. New Brunswick: Rutgers UP, 1996.

Moulson, Geir. "Neil Young: Music Can't Change the World." *The Huffington Post*, 8 Feb. 2008. 19 Mar. 2009. <www.huffingtonpost.com/2008/02/08/neil-young-music-cant-c_n_85747.html>.

Mrozek, Donald. "The Cult and Ritual of Toughness in Cold War America." *Rituals and Ceremonies in Popular Culture*. Ed. Ray B. Browne. Bowling Green: Bowling Green University Popular Press, 1980. 178-92.

Nelson, Paul. "Springsteen Fever: Rocker Comes Out of the 'Darkness.'" *Rolling Stone* 13 Jul. 1978. <www.rollingstone.com>.

New Jersey Municipal Data Book (2005). Palo Alto: Information Publications, 2005.

Nhat Hanh, Thich. "The First Flash of Lightning." In Smith, *Radiant Mind* 200-206.

———. *Going Home: Jesus and Buddha as Brothers*. New York: Riverhead, 1999.

———. *The Miracle of Mindfulness*. Boston: Beacon Press, 1975.

Noble, David W. *Death of a Nation: American Culture and the End of Exceptionalism*. Minneapolis: U of Minnesota P, 2002.

Nussbaum, Martha C. *Cultivating Humanity: A Classical Defense of Reform in Liberal Education*. Cambridge: Harvard UP, 1997.

———. *Upheavals of Thought: The Intelligence of Emotions*. Cambridge: Cambridge UP, 2001.

O'Brien, Tim. *The Things They Carried*. New York: Broadway, 1990.

O'Rourke, Meghan. "Interview with Richard Ford." In Guagliardo, *Conversations with Richard Ford* 185-203.

Oropeza, Lorena. "Antiwar Aztlán: The Chicano Movement Opposes U.S. Intervention in Vietnam." *Window on Freedom: Race, Civil Rights, and Foreign Affairs, 1945-1988*. Ed. Brenda Gayle Plummer. Chapel Hill: U of North Carolina P, 2005. 201-21.

Palmer, Robert. "Springsteen's Music Hits Chord of America." *New York Times* 6 Aug. 1985: C13.

Pareles, Jon. "Bruce Almighty." *New York Times* 24 Apr. 2005: 1.

———. "His Kind of Heroes, His Kind of Songs." *New York Times* 14 Jul. 2002: sec 2, 1+.

———. Review of *Tunnel of Love*, by Bruce Springsteen. *New York Times* 4 Oct. 1987: sec. 2, 1.

Parrington, Jr, Vernon Louis. *American Dreams: A Study of American Utopias*. New York: Russell and Russell, 1964.

Percy, Will. "Rock and Read: Will Percy Interviews Bruce Springsteen." In Sawyers, *Racing in the Street* 305-20.

Petrusich, Amanda. "Bruce Springsteen—*Devils & Dust*." Review of *Devils & Dust*, by Bruce Springsteen. Pastemagazine.com. Issue 16. 22 Oct. 2010. <www. pastemagazine.com/action/article/1731/review/music/bruce_springsteen _devils_dust>.

Pfeil, Fred. *White Guys: Studies in Postmodern Domination and Difference*. New York: Verso, 1995.

Phillips, Amy. "Adult Imagery: The Boss, My Lord, in a Flatbed Ford, Slowing Down to Preach at us and Pornographize." Review of *Devils & Dust*, by Bruce Springsteen. *The Village Voice*. 19 April 2005. Web. 16 Oct. 2010. <www. villagevoice.com/2005-04-19/music/adult-imagery>.

Philips, Kevin P. *The Emerging Republican Majority*. New York: Doubleday/ Anchor, 1970.

Pirttijärvi, Johanna. "21.04.05 Asbury Park, NJ, Intro to 'Black Cowboys." [Online Transcript of Bruce Springsteen rehearsal show, 21 April 2005.]

Storyteller. Brucebase.org. 15 June 2008. 15 Sept. 2010. <www.brucebase.org. uk/stories/280405.htm>.

———. "21.04.05 Asbury Park, NJ, Intro to 'Jesus Was An Only Son'." [Online Transcript of Bruce Springsteen rehearsal show, 21 April 2005.] *Storyteller.* Brucebase.org. 15 June 2008. 15 Sept. 2010. <www.brucebase.org.uk/ stories/280405.htm>.

———. "21.04.05 Asbury Park, NJ, Intro to "Leah." [Online Transcript of Bruce Springsteen rehearsal show, 21 April 2005.] *Storyteller.* Brucebase.org. 15 June 2008. 15 Sept. 2010. <www.brucebase.org.uk/stories/280405.htm>.

———. "21.04.05 Asbury Park, NJ, Intro to "Long Time Comin'." [Online Transcript of Bruce Springsteen rehearsal show, 21 April 2005.] *Storyteller.* Brucebase.org. 15 June 2008. 15 Sept. 2010. <www.brucebase.org.uk/ stories/280405.htm>.

———. "21.04.05 Asbury Park, NJ, Intro to 'Silver Palomino'." [Online Transcript of Bruce Springsteen rehearsal show, 21 April 2005.] *Storyteller.* Brucebase. org. 15 June 2008. 15 Sept. 2010. <www.brucebase.org.uk/stories/280405. htm>.

———. "21.04.05 Asbury Park, NJ, Intro to 'The Hitter'." [Online Transcript of Bruce Springsteen rehearsal show, 21 April 2005.] *Storyteller.* Brucebase.org, 15 June 2008. Web. 15 Sept. 2010. <www.brucebase.org.uk/stories/280405. htm>.

———. "28.04.05 Dallas, TX, Intro to 'Reno'." [Online Transcript of Audience tape, 28 April 2005, released on 2-CD set "Devils & Dallas."] *Storyteller.* Brucebase.org. 15 June 2008. 15 Sept. 2010. <www.brucebase.org.uk/ stories/280405.htm>.

Plant, E.A., and B.M. Peruche. "The Consequences of Race for Police Officers' Responses to Criminal Suspects." *Psychological Science* 16 (2005): 180-83.

Plato. *The Republic. The Dialogues of Plato.* Vol. III. Trans. B. Jowett. 3rd ed. New York: Macmillan, 1892.

Pond, Steve. "Bruce Springsteen's Tunnel Vision." *Rolling Stone* 5 May 1988. <www.rollingstone.com>.

———. Rev. of *Tunnel of Love*, by Bruce Springsteen. *Rolling Stone* 3 Oct. 1987. <www.rolling-stone.com>.

Primeaux, Pat. *The Moral Passion of Bruce Springsteen.* San Francisco: International Scholars, 1996.

Puterbaugh, Parke. Rev. of *Greatest Hits*, by Bruce Springsteen. *Rolling Stone* 705. 6 April 1995. <www.rollingstone.com/music/albumreviews/greatest-hits-19950406?print=true>.

Putnam, Robert D. *Bowling Alone: The Collapse and Revival of American Community.* New York: Simon and Schuster, 1990.

Reagan, Ronald. "Address to the United Brotherhood of Carpenters and Joiners of America, 34th General Convention." *Proceedings of the General Convention of the United Brotherhood of Carpenters and Joiners.* Chicago: 31 Aug.- 4 Sept. 1981.

————. *A Time for Choosing: The Speeches of Ronald Reagan, 1961-1982*. Ed. Alfred A. Balitzer and Gerald M. Bonetto. Chicago: Regnery Gateway, 1983.

Reed, Adolph. "Reinventing the Working Class: A Study in Elite Image Manipulation." *New Labor Forum* Fall 2004: 26.

Renda, Mary. *Taking Haiti: Military Occupation and the Culture of U.S. Imperialism, 1915-1940*. Chapel Hill: U of North Carolina P, 2001.

Robertson, Roland. "After Nostalgia? Willful Nostalgia and the Phases of Globalization." *Theories of Modernity and Postmodernity*. Ed. B. S. Turner. London: Sage, 1990. 45-61.

Rockwell, John. "Bruce Springsteen Has a Grown Up Way With a Song." *New York Times* 12 June 1988: S2.

Roediger, David R. "What If Labor Were Not White and Male?" *Colored White: Transcending the Racial Past*. Berkeley: U of California P, 2002.

Roosevelt, Theodore. "The Strenuous Life." Speech. Chicago, 10 April 1899. <voicesofdemocracy.umd.edu/roosevelt-strenuous-life-1899-speech-text>.

Rorty, Richard. *Achieving our Country: Leftist Thought in Twentieth-Century America*. Cambridge: Harvard UP, 1998.

Rosenberg, Emily. "Foreign Affairs after World War II: Connecting Sexual and International Politics." *Diplomatic History* (1994): 59-70.

Sanders, Seth, and Mike O'Flaherty. "44,000,000 Ronald Reagan Fans Can't Be Wrong!: Rock and the Backlash." *The Baffler* 15 (2002): 81.

Sawyers, June Skinner, ed. *Racing in the Street: The Bruce Springsteen Reader*. New York: Penguin, 2004.

Scammon, Richard, and Benjamin J. Wattenberg. *The Real Majority*. New York: Coward McCann, 1970.

Scarry, Elaine. "The Difficulty Imagining Other People." *For Love of Country: Debating the Limits of Patriotism*. Ed. Joshua Cohen. Boston: Beacon, 1996. 98-110.

Schruers, Fred. "The Boss is Back." *Rolling Stone* 27 Nov. 1980. <www.rollingstone.com>.

————. "Bruce Springsteen and the Secret of the World." *Rolling Stone* 5 Feb. 1981. <www.rollingstone.com>.

Scott, A.O. "The Boss Bibliography." *New York Times* 3 Jul. 2005: 10-11.

September 11, 2001 Victims. 2005. <www.september11victims.com>.

Sheehan, Neil. *A Bright Shining Lie: John Paul Vann and America in Vietnam*. New York: Vintage, 1988.

Sheehy, Colleen. "Springsteen: Troubadour of the Highway." In Sawyers, *Racing in the Street* 352-57.

Singer, Peter. "Outsiders: Our Obligations to Those Outside our Borders." *The Ethics of Assistance: Morality and the Distant Needy*. Ed. Deen K. Chatterjee. Cambridge: Cambridge UP, 2004. 11-33.

Slotkin, Richard. *The Fatal Environment: The Myth of the Frontier in the Age of Industrialization, 1800-1890*. Middletown: Wesleyan UP, 1985.

————. *Gunfighter Nation: The Myth of the Frontier in Twentieth-Century America*. Norman: U of Oklahoma P, 1998.

Small, Christopher. *Musicking: The Meanings of Performing and Listening*. Hanover: UP of New England, 1998.

Smith, Adam. *The Theory of Moral Sentiments*. Amherst: Prometheus, 2000[1759].

Smith, Jean, ed. *Radiant Mind: Essential Buddhist Teachings and Texts*. New York: Riverhead, 1999.

Smith, Larry. *Bob Dylan, Bruce Springsteen, and American Song*. Westport: Praeger, 2002.

Springsteen, Bruce. "Bruce Springsteen on His Mother." Excerpt from Interview by Per Sinding-Larsen, originally aired on SVT (Swedish Television). *YouTube*. 27 Aug. 2009. 11 Oct. 2010. <www.youtube.com/watch?v=LUH980m1H28>.

Springsteen, Bruce. "Chords for Change." *New York Times* 5 Aug. 2004. <select. nytimes.com/search/restricted/article?res=F20A12FB3E580C768CDDA1089 4DC404482>.

————. "Comments from the Stage on Farmworkers," 25 Oct. 2005. *Backstreets*: #85 Spring/Summer 2006.

————. Interview with Dave Fanning. *The Dave Fanning Show*. RTÉ 2FM. Dublin, Ireland. 4 Jul. 2005.

————. "Introduction to 'The Hitter.'" Unpublished performance. 3 Aug. 2005.

————. "It Happened in Jersey." *Esquire* Aug. 2005: 92-99.

————. *Songs*. New York: Avon, 1998.

Stacewicz, Richard. *Winter Soldiers: An Oral History of the Vietnam Veterans Against the War*. New York: Twayne, 1997.

Steinbeck, John. *The Grapes of Wrath*. New York: Penguin, 1987[1939].

Stewart, Susan. *On Longing: Narratives of the Miniature, the Gigantic, the Souvenir, the Collection*. Baltimore: Johns Hopkins UP, 1984.

Streight, Irwin. "Flannery O'Connor of American Rock." *Reading the Boss: Interdisciplinary Approaches to the Works of Bruce Springsteen*. Ed. Roxanne Harde and Irwin Streight. Lanham: Lexington Books, 2010. 53-75.

"Strike Back Campaign." *Fatigue Press*, Issue 25 (date missing).

Sugrue, Thomas. *Origins of the Urban Crisis: Race and Inequality in Post-War Detroit*. Princeton: Princeton UP, 1996.

Tavers, Len. *Celebrating the Fourth: Independence Day and the Rites of Nationalism in the Early American Republic*. Amherst: U of Massachusetts P, 1997.

Teixiera, Ruy A., and Joel Rodgers. *America's Forgotten Majority: Why The White Working Class Still Matters*. New York: Basic Books, 2000.

Templeton, Sir John. *Agape Love: A Tradition Found in Eight World Religions*. Philadelphia: Templeton World, 1999.

Terry, Wallace. *Bloods: An Oral History of the Vietnam War by Black Veterans*. New York: Random House, 1984.

Turner, Bryan S. *Orientalism, Postmodernism, and Globalism*. London: Routledge, 1994.

Turner, Frederick Jackson. "The Significance of the Frontier in American History." *The Early Writings of Frederick Jackson Turner*. Madison: U of Wisconsin P, 1938. 185-229.

Tyrangiel, Josh. Review of *The Rising*, by Bruce Springsteen. *Time* 27 July 2002. <candysroom.freeservers.com/bruceweb78.html>.

Valania, Jonathan. "Bruce Springsteen Inspires Voters With Passionate Acoustic Set at Philadelphia Rally." *Rolling Stone* 6 Oct. 2008. <www.rollingstone.com/music/news/bruce-springsteen-inspires-voters-with-passionate-acoustic-set-at-philadelphia-rally-20081006#ixzz1erWlSnDU>.

Weber, Max. *The Protestant Ethic and the Spirit of Capitalism*. Ed. Talcott Parsons. New York: Charles Scribner's Sons. 1930[1904-1905].

Walker, Elinor Ann. "An Interview with Richard Ford." In Guagliardo, *Conversations with Richard Ford* 131-46.

———. "Redeeming Loneliness in Richard Ford's 'Great Falls' and *Wildlife*." In Guagliardo, *Conversations with Richard Ford* 121-40.

———. *Richard Ford*. New York: Twayne, 2000.

Wallis, Jim. *God's Politics: Why the Right Gets It Wrong and the Left Doesn't Get It*. San Francisco: HarperSanFrancisco, 2005.

Wenner, Jann. "We've Been Misled." Interview of Bruce Springsteen. *Rolling Stone* 14 Oct. 2004: 73-76.

Wieder, Judy. "Bruce Springsteen: The *Advocate* Interview." In Sawyers, *Racing in the Street* 211-21.

Will, George F. "Bruce Springsteen's USA." *Washington Post* 13 Sept. 1984: A14.

Williams, Peter. *America's Religions: From their Origins to the Twenty-First Century*. Chicago: U of Illinois P, 2002.

Wills, Garry. *Inventing America: Jefferson's Declaration of Independence*. Garden City: Mariner, 1978.

Winthrop, John. "A Model of Christian Charity," *The Puritans in America: A Narrative Anthology*. Ed. A. Heimert and A. Delbanco. Cambridge: Harvard UP, 1985.

Winthrop, John. "Christian Charitie; a Modell Hereof." *Puritan Political Ideas: 1558-1794*. Ed. E.S. Morgan. Indianapolis: The Bobbs-Merrill Company, Inc., 1965.

Wolf, Daniel. *4th of July, Asbury Park. A History of the Promised Land*. New York: Bloomsbury, 2005.

Wolfe, Tom. "The Me Decade and the Third Great Awakening." *Mauve Gloves and Madmen, Clutter and Vine*. New York: Bantam, 1976. 117-54.

Zandy, Janet. "Introduction." *What We Hold in Common: An Introduction to Working-Class Studies*. Ed. Janet Zandy. New York: Feminist Press of CUNY, 2001.

Zweig, Michael. *The Working Class Majority: America's Best-Kept Secret*. Ithaca: Cornell UP, 2000.

Albums, Videos, DVDs and Movies

Alterman, Eric. *Bruce Springsteen: The Complete Video Anthology: 1978-2000.* New York: Columbia Music Video, 2001.

A Vision Shared: A Tribute to Woody Guthrie and Leadbelly. Dir. Jim Brown. Columbia Music Video, 1998.

Collins, Judy. *Tribute to Woody Guthrie.* Warner Bros, 1976.

Dylan, Bob. *The Bootleg Series, Vols. 1-3.* Columbia, 1991.

Guthrie, Woody. *Bound for Glory.* 1943. New York: Plume, 1983.

———. *Dustbowl Ballads.* 1940. Rounder Records, 1988.

———. *Library of Congress Recordings.* 1940. Rounder Records, 1988.

John Hammond: From Bessie Smith to Bruce Springsteen. Dir. Hart Perry. CBS Records, 1990.

Kazan, Elia, ed. *On the Waterfront.* Columbia Pictures, 1954.

Mellencamp, John. *Uh-Huh.* Mercury/Universal, 1983.

Prima, Lou. *Angelina.* Prima Magnagroove, 1973.

Springsteen, Bruce. *Born in the USA.* Columbia Records, 1984.

———. *Born to Run.* Columbia Records, 1975.

———. "Born to Run (Acoustic)," DVD, *The Complete Video Anthology/1978-2000*, CMV, 2001.

———. *Bruce Springsteen and the E Street Band Live/1975-1985.* Columbia, 1986.

———. *Darkness on the Edge of Town.* Columbia Records, 1978.

———. *Devils & Dust.* Columbia Records, 2005.

———. *Devils & Dust.* Dir. D. Clinch. Prod. Bruce Springsteen. 2005. DVD – DualDisk Columbia Music Video, 2005.

———. *The Ghost of Tom Joad.* Columbia Records, 1995.

———. *Greetings From Asbury Park, NJ.* Columbia Records, 1973.

———. *Human Touch.* Columbia Records, 1992.

———. *Live in New York City.* DVD. Columbia Music Video, 2001.

———. *Lucky Town.* Columbia Records, 1992.

———. *Nebraska.* Columbia Records, 1982.

———. *The Rising.* Columbia Records, 2002.

———. *The River.* Columbia Records, 1980.

———. *Tracks.* Columbia Records, 1998.

———. *Tunnel of Love.* Columbia Records, 1987.

———. *VH1 Storytellers.* DVD. Columbia Music Video, 2005.

———. *The Wild, the Innocent and the E Street Shuffle.* Columbia Records, 1973.

The Grapes of Wrath. Dir. John Ford. 1940. Fox Home Entertainment, 2004.

Index